Everybody Eats Well in Belgium Cookbook

Everybody Eats Well in Belgium Cookbook

RUTH VAN WAEREBEEK
WITH MARIA ROBBINS

Illustrations by MELISSA SWEET

WORKMAN PUBLISHING • NEW YORK

Extract on page 13, from *The Man Who Wasn't Maigret: A Portrait of George
Simenon* by Patrick Marnham. ©1993 by Patrick Marnham. Reprinted by permission of Farrar, Straus &
Giroux, Inc. All rights reserved.

Library of Congress Cataloging-in-Publication Data
Van Waerebeek, Ruth.
Everybody eats well in Belgium cookbook / by Ruth Van Waerebeek with Maria Robbins:
illustrations by Melissa Sweet.
p.   cm.
Includes index.
ISBN 1-56305-41-6 (pbk.). — ISBN 0-7611-0106-3 (hc)
1. Cookery, Belgian. I. Title
TX723.5.B4V36 1995
641.59493—dc20
95-32828 CIP

Cover design by Paul Gamarello
Book design by Paul Gamarello and Gwen Petruska
Cover and book illustrations by Melissa Sweet

Workman books are available at special discount when purchased in bulk
for special premiums and sales promotions as well as fundraising or educational use.
Special book editions or excerpts can also be created to specification.
For details, contact the Special Sales Director at the address below.

Workman Publishing Company, Inc.
708 Broadway
New York, NY 10003-9555
Manufactured in the United States of America

First printing January 1996
10 9 8 7 6 5 4 3 2 1

This book is dedicated to three wonderful women—
Marie, Jeanne, and Anny—
my inspiration in life and for this book.

···

Likewise, I owe a great thank-you
to Maria Robbins, my co-writer,
Jane Dystel, my agent, and Suzanne Rafer, my editor,
for believing in me
and making a dream come true.

Contents

✹

A cool herring salad at a summer picnic, a slice of deeply flavored pork liver pâté with prunes on a winter's eve, creamy country cheese packed with garden-fresh herbs anytime—these are just a few of the dishes that serve as starters for a lingering evening meal or snacks for a lazy Sunday afternoon.

Today, as they have for centuries, hearty broths simmer through the night over wood-burning stoves in deep rural Belgium. Come morning, they'll find their way into soups resplendent with the season's bounty: tangy potato buttermilk soup, heady with freshly grated nutmeg, bold tomato soup laden with tiny delicately spiced meatballs, and deep green spinach soup laced with sorrel.

No matter where you are in Belgium, the sea is never far. And in this fish-lover's paradise, seafood is celebrated—from the national dish, steamed tender mussels served with crispy Belgian fries to juicy eels basking in a luxurious lemony cream sauce to firm fresh herring baked *en papillote* with herbed butter.

Poultry and Game

109

In days gone by, a humble stewed hen was the centerpiece of the frugal Belgian farmer's Sunday meal, while extravagant city dwellers dined lavishly on crisp roast chickens. At either table, it was a feast. Some other notable bird preparations: partridge and red cabbage simmered in rich, dark ale and poached chicken blanketed in a lemon *velouté* sauce.

Meat

145

Long a mainstay of the national cuisine, meat is still king of the Belgian kitchen. In a manner befitting royalty, robust, succulent cuts of beef, pork, lamb, and venison are stewed in hearty red wine, roasted with pungent mustard, and sautéed with piquant gin and juniper berries.

Cooking with Beer

173

Belgian beer has all the nuances and nobility of its Gallic counterpart, wine. When paired with luscious honey-toned fruits or intense caramelized onions, beer lends a bittersweet quality to soul-warming dishes: comforting tender meatballs braised with endives in blond beer, rabbit sautéed with cherry beer and tart dried cherries, beef stewed in red currant jelly and dark beer.

Vegetable and Fruit Side Dishes

197

Honest, homey techniques celebrate fresh fruits and vegetables—with pleasingly complex results: Sweet young Brussels sprouts are bathed in a simple brown butter. The noble Belgian endive is braised with lemon and sugar. And crisp autumn apples are simmered into the ultimate comfort food: applesauce.

Potatoes

Whether they're fried, baked, boiled, puréed, stuffed, or gratinéed, potatoes are a staple of any Belgian meal, be it casual or formal. Here are crisp Belgian fries—the national snack—and golden potato croquettes. Also, the Belgian variation on the universal favorites—mashed potatoes and stuffed baked potatoes.

Waffles, Pancakes, and Breads

In Belgium, any celebration calls for crunchy, freshly baked, feather-light waffles—dusted with plenty of powdered sugar. And during the coldest stretches of winter, pancake festivals soothe with the promise of the coming sun. Here are waffles filled with sour-cherry compote, buckwheat pancakes topped with bubbling Gruyère, and yeasty bread with a crunchy sugar topping for afternoon tea.

Desserts

Light, lacy butter cookies from Brugge, dense, nutty, spiced beer cake, a tart overflowing with summer's ripest fruits—and, of course, chocolate in all its splendor. Rooted in medieval times, these traditional Belgian desserts—perhaps the most beloved aspect of Belgian cuisine—indulge the national sweet tooth.

Basics

Fresh Tomato Sauce, Béchamel Sauce, Homemade Mayonnaise, Spiced Vinegar, and more.

Conversion Chart and Index

Europe's Best-Kept Secret

When shopping for dinner, a Belgian will happily go 20 minutes out of her way if it means her family will enjoy a better loaf of bread or a more tender bunch of asparagus. Food is an extremely important part of Belgian life. Not only do Belgians spend considerably more money on food than the average American, but they also devote a great deal more time and energy to discussing it, shopping for it, preparing it, and consuming it. The Belgian approach to food is perhaps best summed up in the following motto: We eat three times a day, so we'd better try to make a feast of it every time.

But what is Belgian food? When faced with this question, most Americans might answer, after a puzzled pause, "French?" "German?" or, perhaps, "Dutch?" Even other Europeans find Belgian cuisine enigmatic. To a great extent, that sad fact is our own fault, since Belgians tend to keep a low, even self-effacing international profile. But it is all the more confounding when you consider that Belgian food is truly some of the finest Europe has to offer and that Belgium has more three-star restaurants per capita than France.

Although present-day Belgium can aptly be described as a nation tied to its traditions, its very culture sprang from a pastiche of foreign influences. Over the centuries, Belgium has been invaded by almost every other European people—including the Romans, Vikings, Spanish, French, Germans, and Dutch—effectively becoming a meeting point for the Germanic cultures of northern Europe and the Latin cultures of the south. Favorite cooking techniques, ingredients, and styles of the invaders were picked up by the natives, who by the Middle Ages, had developed a cuisine they could call their own. Now we Belgians are fond of saying that our food is cooked with French finesse—and served in portions of German generosity.

At some point, the urge to forge and preserve this hard-won and slow-cooked identity eventually became a sort of national mania, reflected in a native suspicion of strangers and a hard-shelled, highly conservative resistance to any further exotic influence. Our customs, traditions, folklore, and festivals were frozen in time, along with our cuisine, which has remained doggedly faithful to its origins.

A MEDIEVAL BIRTH

Belgian cuisine is still deeply rooted in medieval cookery. The influence of the Middle Ages, a time when Flemish culture was very highly developed, can be seen today in the way we use condiments, mustards, vinegars, and dried fruits to obtain delicate balances of sweet-and-sour or sweet-and-salty in the same dish; in our use of fresh and dried fruits and nuts, particularly almonds, to enhance flavor and presentation. The spices we use so abundantly to season everything from meats to vegetables, desserts, and wine—nutmeg, cinnamon, peppercorns, saffron, ginger, and bay leaves—can be traced back to the spice trade of the Middle Ages. We love fresh herbs, particularly chervil, tarragon, thyme, sage, parsley, and chives. These are the same ones that grew in the herb gardens of the medieval monsteries, and we use them lavishly. We drink more beer than wine and produce more than 300 varieties, many of them crafted by small artisanal brewers whose family recipes and techniques go back hundreds of years. The exuberant and subtle beer cuisine of Belgium is just now beginning to have an influence outside of our borders.

Belgians love potatoes in nearly every guise; fried potatoes are practically the Belgian national dish. Mussels, another passion, are eaten regularly in great quantities, always accompanied by Belgian fries. Belgians are definitely a nation of meat lovers, consuming large quantities of pork, beef, veal, chicken, and rabbit. We also eat a large amount of game, everything from rabbit to wild boar, and wild birds of every sort—duck, grouse, quail, partridge, and dove. We often make a meal of our excellent charcuterie accompanied by a selection of breads and a glass of beer.

We are famous for our fresh vegetables (who has not heard of Belgian endive or Brussels sprouts?) as well as for waffles, and of course, chocolate. Belgians have a very well-developed sweet tooth; I think it is fair to say that we have unparalleled cravings for chocolate. Not only do we produce some of the finest chocolate in the world, but the average Belgian consumes nearly seven pounds more per year than his American counterpart. In short, everybody eats well in Belgium.

Given this bounty of wonderful food, it may surprise you to learn that there are few cookbooks devoted to Belgian cooking published in Belgium. The reason is simple: In Belgium, the secrets of cooking are still transmitted orally. Recipes, techniques, traditions, tastes, and passions are passed along from generation to generation in a country where "family values" is not merely a political catchphrase but a living reality. Our cuisine, like our nation, is at heart bourgeois—home cooking at its best.

For that reason, I want to introduce you to Belgian cooking through three generations of Belgian mothers and daughters: my great grandmother Marie, her daughter Jeanne, and her granddaughter (my mother) Anny. I am now a professional

X

chef, and a cooking teacher at Peter Kump's Cooking School in New York City, and I learned about cooking in their busy kitchens in the medieval city of Ghent, where I grew up. These women are truly remarkable cooks, and each is thoroughly Belgian in her approach to cooking. Yet from each of them I have learned a distinct and recognizable style.

MARIE

My great grandmother Marie was a simple country woman, a farm wife whose plain, hearty cuisine represents the more or less unchanging aspects of Belgian peasant family fare as it has existed for centuries. The farm provided all of her ingredients, and tradition framed her menus. She was eighty-six years old when she died in 1972 and had been a part of my life for thirteen years. We were very close. A visit to my great grandmother meant stepping into a world of living history. Marie, in her farmhouse near the tiny village of Oostrozebeke, lived her life much the same at the end of her days as she did fully sixty or seventy years before.

Alas, most of the details of her small red-brick country house are vague now in my memory, but I remember her kitchen so clearly—the large round table surrounded by wicker chairs, the crucifix on the wall flanked by gleaming silver candelabras, and the huge grandfather clock with its satisfyingly loud tick-tock.

But most powerfully I remember the *leuvense stoof,* the large potbellied stove that dominated the entire room and was really the heart of the whole house. The stove demanded, and received, constant attention—there was wood to fetch, coals to rake, ashes to remove, then, more wood, more coals, more ashes, over and over. No wonder Marie had never traveled far beyond the confines of her village, had not even visited the shore of the North Sea, a mere 20 kilometers away, until she was well over forty years old. Besides her family—her husband, four children, and mother-in-law—she had cows, chickens, and her garden, plus that stove to keep alive. She was tied down by necessity. If, rising early in the still-dark morning and going first to the kitchen to heat water for coffee, for washing up, and for cooking, she found the stove cold, its last embers dead, it meant hours to build a new fire from scratch. Those were hours spent shivering in the cold, deprived of the most basic comforts. But in the end, of course, the stove would respond to her attentions and pay her back in full. Marie knew every inch of it—which spot on the surface was the hottest, which one just warm enough to keep a pot of coffee going through the morning, where in its capacious oven to bake the crustiest bread. No bread I have ever tasted could compare in flavor or texture to hers.

And in the cold northern European winter, the family would huddle around the stove in the evening, and by the light of a candles, tell stories to pass the long, dark hours. And huddled we were, because underneath the bulging potbelly of that stove there was a recess for our feet. And so we sat, like so many spokes on a wheel, our legs stretched luxuriously to catch every bit of warmth the stove could offer. No warmth I have ever felt has been as cozy.

For me, the enduring memories of my great grandmother live on primarily in my senses of smell and taste. The scent that I associate most strongly with her is that of fresh air and sunshine, like clean linen that's been hung outside to dry. And the foods she prepared to feed her family I still prepare today—hearty, satisfying dishes like soup with potatoes and buttermilk, and the robust stew of potato, cabbage, and carrots called *stoemp*. Interestingly, the foods she prepared conform almost exactly to the dietary guidelines that have been pronounced healthy for today—very little meat and an emphasis on complex carbohydrates and fresh fruits and vegetables.

JEANNE

My grandmother Jeanne is an artist, an independent and somewhat gentrified woman, who often used to cook for a large circle of friends. Her home was in a rural area, but her social milieu was bohemian and worldly. She has led a gregarious life full of friends and entertaining, all on an extremely tight budget. Buying or bartering what she needed from her neighbors, she adapted traditional recipes to her taste, and brought her own creative flair to the process.

She was a middle child of Marie, but while Marie was the consummate countrywoman, Jeanne was utterly convinced, from her earliest years, that she was never meant for the country life, and did everything in her power to set herself apart from the other village girls. Creative in every aspect of her life (particularly at getting her sisters to do her share of the farm chores), she somehow always managed to turn herself out in smart frocks, with her hair fashionably coiffed, more often than not set off by a hat of her own design. But like so many young people who rebel against their circumstances in life, she made plenty of mistakes before she got where she wanted to go.

Jeanne was nineteen when she married a local boy, probably thinking of it as a first step toward independence. But she had three children before she realized that she was more trapped in her small village than ever before. Divorce was the only way out. But in the 1930s, divorce was shocking and rare even among cosmopolites. In a small, rural, tradition-bound Catholic village, it was an unpardonable offense, and she found herself almost completely ostracized. Her children were taken away from her to be raised by her husband's family. The effect of this treatment, though, was far from chastening; indeed, it was positively liberating, for it removed the social ties that had always constrained her.

She left the village and went out on her own as a *modiste*—designing hats for wealthy, fashionable women. Against all odds, she became a success. And she was not completely alone. Her daughter Anny (my mother), who was as independent-minded as Jeanne, went to live with her.

Eventually, in her early thirties, Jeanne settled in St. Martens Latem, a lovely Flemish village nestled cozily on the banks of the Leie river on the outskirts of Ghent. The area had always been famous for the beauty of its pastoral landscape. Ironically, it was not so different from the very village she had fled, but—and this was very important—at the time that Jeanne moved there, it was already quite famous as an artists' colony. Most of the artists were neither famous nor rich (although some of them would become so later on), but they lived a wonderful, spirited life filled with shared interests and camaraderie in surround-

ings of great physical beauty. It was a style that Jeanne found much to her liking, and it was here at last that she found friends for a lifetime.

Jeanne had always been interested in painting and not long after she moved to St. Martens Latem, she met and began studying with Leon Desmet. Desmet, a master printer and painter's painter, had a considerable reputation among the cognoscenti, but he had never been discovered by the world at large, and far from famous, he was also far from financially secure. Yet by all accounts, he was a truly charismatic man of enormous *joie de vivre,* endless optimism, and tremendous generosity to his large circle of friends and admirers. Jeanne and Leon Desmet became great friends. She often modeled for his paintings and they frequently entertained their many friends together. On his deathbed he appointed her the guardian of his work and asked her to see that it was preserved. To this end she turned his house and studio into a museum to preserve and show his work.

Jeanne has a real gift for hospitality, and in those days, her house was always full of hungry artists, friends, and visitors from town. She was proud of her culinary abilities and loved to emerge from the kitchen with something wonderful, which looked as good as it tasted. But she was never the kind of woman to spend all day in the kitchen. Her specialties were simple dishes, quickly prepared, and soups and stews that could be made ahead and reheated when necessary. For Jeanne, a meal was and remains an occasion for great conversation among friends and colleagues— a stimulant for the wonderful flow of words and ideas that to her are as nourishing and necessary as the food itself.

Lavish hospitality and generosity were the very heart and soul of her attitude toward cooking. Her particular genius was for living like a lord on a beggar's purse—a feat made possible by the bounty of the countryside, which provided her with rabbit, deer, and pheasant from the fields and vast quantities of eel and other freshwater fish from the river. But whatever she cooked, the portions were always big and hearty, and there was always enough for a few last-minute guests.

As a little girl I was enchanted by my glamorous grandmother. When I read about Cinderella, the fairy godmother had my grandmother's face. She has always been a woman of great elegance and style, and today, in her eighties, she is as chic as ever. She is an exquisitely cultivated woman who pays the most critical and discerning attention to every detail.

To me she has always been an inspiration—a woman who could do anything and everything and always had a good time doing it. There were no chores in her life. Cooking was not a job but a source of pleasure and enjoyment, a necessary part of life. Her gardening was filled with joy and beauty. Her painting was a natural part of her life, and she set up her easel in any room she happened to be occupying, so that her kitchen always smelled of simmering soups and stews, herbs, spices, flowers, and paints. She taught me that hospitality should be a natural part of everyday life, and it is a lesson that has gained many lifelong friends all over the world.

ANNY

My mother, Anny, is very much an urban woman: She has lived her entire adult life in the medieval city of Ghent and is married to an urbane and cultivated man. My father, a serious gourmet and wine connoisseur, is a lawyer and judge by profession. She has entertained his clients and visitors from all over the world and is without a doubt a sophisticate in many ways. Yet, as is often the case, certain undeniable traits that skipped the second generation have reasserted themselves in the third. Despite the urban trappings and her free-spirited style, Anny's life more closely resembles that of her grandmother, Marie, than that of her mother. Her life revolves around her family and is devoted entirely to their well-being.

Quite apart from her children (my sister, my brother, and me), my mother took care of a veritable menagerie of animals. All through my childhood, our house was home to an amazing collection of pets. There were dogs and cats, of course, but Mother also collected stray wild animals with the passion of a Dr. Doolittle. There were endless convalescent birds with broken wings, dozens of wee cowering motherless baby mice, several foul-mouthed parrots; a succession of rabbits (all named Prutske), and a boisterous and uninhibited monkey named King Louis, who terrorized and ruled our household for four years.

Instead of a farm, my mother manages an immense, old twenty-room town house dating back to the early 1800s. But my mother's true talent lies in the preparation of the day's meals. Daily she launches a shopping expedition that takes her into the social heart of the town—the marketplace. While gathering news, trading jokes, and indulging in small gossip, she searches out and buys the freshest and best ingredients available from the Belgian countryside.

In a nation whose shoppers almost universally pride themselves on being demanding and particular, my mother's reputation among farmers and shopkeepers is preeminent. She is a striking sight as she sets out on foot each day accompanied by her two large dogs and often, in days past, with King Louis the monkey, astride one of the dogs. With a huge rucksack on her back, she makes her way to the center of Ghent and the old market square. She flits from one to another choosing her vegetables as carefully as the diamond merchants in Antwerp choose their stones. Having selected her produce, she heads for the shops—this bakery has the best bread, that butcher has the best meat, and the best mustard is found in that shop. (Yes, there is a shop devoted exclusively to mustard, and it has been there since 1700).

My father was and still is a very hardworking man, yet to my knowledge he never once missed a family dinner, even if it meant going back to his office afterward. Dinner might last for one and a half hours or even two, but it was a time for everyone to share their day's experiences. When the family gathered at the table, whether it was for breakfast, lunch, dinner, or afternoon coffee, worldly concerns and everyday worries were left behind. It was a time for the restoration of body and soul, and that is what my mother's meals provided, and what they continue to provide.

My mother's cooking is distinguished by her passion for vegetables and for natural, clean flavors, and by her generous hand with fresh herbs. She has a delicate touch with fish and chicken, and in general, her cuisine is leaner and lighter than Jeanne's or Marie's. The exception to this is her wicked ability to create fabulous desserts. My father has an incurable sweet tooth, and for him a meal is not complete without dessert, so every lunch and dinner has a sweet finale.

RUTH

These are the influences that have made me the cook I am today. I have inherited a sense of adventure and independence from my grandmother that has taken me on travels around the world. At the same time I have a love of home life that helps me turn wherever in the world I happen to be into a cozy and hospitable retreat. The cooking skills I learned at the hands of my three great teachers have helped me become a professional chef, with a strong desire to pass on my own knowledge to those who want to learn it. And the conservative, traditional Belgian in me has prompted me to write this book, to preserve the recipes that live on in my family and to draw a little portrait of my country, showing how it is that everyone eats well in Belgium.

Appetizers, Salads, and Small Plates

Something to Whet the Appetite

We have a saying in Belgium that one should stretch all good things in life so that one can enjoy them as long as possible. This is certainly applied to our cuisine on a daily basis and is one of the reasons we take our meals so seriously. Even in the most humble homes there is nothing casual about lunch, a break in the day's routine that typically lasts an hour to an hour and a half, or dinner, a family affair over which we linger for a very minimum of an hour. A table is set and people sit down to eat a meal that always consists of at least two courses and more often three. There is always something to start with—a soup in the winter, a fish salad in the summer, a slice of pâté or a composed salad—before the main course is served.

The appetizer course is meant to pique the diner's appetite and interest in the rest of the meal. It provides variety and encourages the diner to eat a little bit of everything, a much more attractive approach than eating a lot of just one thing. On a practical level, appetizers allow the cook to recycle leftovers and to make other more expensive ingredients go further. Certainly this opening course is a showcase for the cook's creativity and tal-ent—whether you transform some leftover seafood with a tangy vinaigrette into a salad or turn a piece of cheese into a croquette or a quiche. Nor do appetizers need to be expensive. Just look at the wonderful salads that can be prepared with raw winter vegetables such as cabbages, beets, and celery root.

Many of the recipes in this section can do double duty. Served in small quantities, they make admirable appetizers. A more generous portion of the same dish, accompanied by good bread, easily can serve as a light lunch or supper. In short, the possibilities for creativity and imagination are many, and you should use these recipes as they best fit your lifestyle.

2

Asparagus, Flemish Style

ASPERGES OP VLAAMSE WIJZE
•
ASPERGES A LA FLAMANDE

In Belgium, this dish is prepared with white asparagus, a special variety planted in deep trenches to which more earth is added as the stalks grow, so that the plants are never exposed to sun or air. The top layer of soil is gently removed when the shoots are mature, and they are then cut out of the ground with a special, long bladed, chisel shaped knife. This white asparagus is a great specialty of the town of Mechelen, known as the vegetable garden of Belgium. The most authentic version of this dish must be enjoyed in Belgium, since not enough of the white asparagus is produced for export. In the United States I have made this dish using fresh green asparagus with satisfying results, and recently I've come across

bundles of white asparagus exported from Holland, which are quite good.

3 pounds white asparagus or the freshest local
   asparagus you can get
8 tablespoons (1 stick) unsalted butter
3 large eggs, hard-cooked and peeled
1½ teaspoons fresh lemon juice
¼ cup finely minced fresh parsley
Salt and freshly ground black pepper to taste
Pinch of freshly grated nutmeg

1. Bring a large saucepan of lightly salted water to a boil.

2. Meanwhile, use a vegetable peeler to remove the thick woody skin of each white asparagus stalk from just below the tip to the stem end. If you are using very thin green asparagus, just trim the lower part of each stalk.

3. Bunch the asparagus spears together and trim them to about the same length. Tie the bundle together with kitchen string.

4. When the water boils, lower the heat, add the asparagus, and simmer until they are tender, 15 to 30 minutes depending on the thickness. Cover the pot only if you are cooking white asparagus; do not cover the green as it will lose its fresh color. Remove the asparagus bundle and drain on a kitchen towel. Be careful not to break the delicate asparagus tips.

5. Melt the butter in a small saucepan over low heat. If the hard-cooked eggs are com-

3

pletely cold, plunge them for 1 minute into the asparagus cooking water to reheat and then peel.

6. In a small mixing bowl, mash the eggs with a fork. Add the melted butter, lemon juice, and parsley. Season with salt, pepper, and nutmeg. Stir to mix.

7. Arrange the asparagus on individual plates. Cover each portion with the Flemish sauce, leaving the tips uncovered. Serve immediately while everything is still warm.

Serves 4 to 6

Jeanne's Asparagus

One of the family traditions that I always looked forward to when I was growing up was going to my grandmother Jeanne's to eat the first asparagus of the season.

My grandmother served the tender stalks of white asparagus in a fine porcelain dish alongside of which were a sauceboat filled with melted butter and little silver dishes holding soft-cooked eggs. We ate with our fingers (a rare and delightful treat), dipping the asparagus first in the melted butter and then in the creamy egg yolks. Pure heaven and a very sensuous experience!

Poached Leeks in a Shallot-Parsley Vinaigrette

PREI OP VLAAMSE WYZE
•
POIREAUX A LA FLAMANDE

The noble white asparagus was a delicacy that my great grandmother Marie tasted only a few times in her entire life—at the sumptuous wedding of her cousin and perhaps an occasional funeral gathering. She considered these mysteriously pale stalks as food for *les gens du château* (the people who lived in the castle), that is, for the aristocracy.

But she often prepared a perfectly delicious salad from the leeks she grew in her garden, taking satisfaction in knowing that leeks are good for cleansing the digestive system. Today, because of modern growing methods, most produce, including asparagus, is

available to everyone at reasonable prices. However, this simple leek salad remains a Belgian favorite.

Serve on its own as a salad course, or pair it with some finely sliced smoked fish such as haddock or salmon or with a platter of charcuterie.

8 medium leeks, white parts only
Salt to taste
½ cup Shallot-Parsley Vinaigrette (recipe follows)
¼ cup finely minced fresh parsley
2 large eggs, hard-cooked and peeled, yolks pressed through a sieve and whites finely chopped (optional; see "Mimosa" this page)

1. Bring a large saucepan of lightly salted water to a boil.

2. Meanwhile, trim the leeks and discard the tough outer layers. Rinse them thoroughly under cold running water, splitting the leeks partway down if necessary to remove all the grit.

3. When the water boils, lower the heat, add the leeks, and simmer until they are very tender but still hold their shape, about 25 minutes. Drain the leeks. (Save the broth. It makes a great addition to any soup.)

4. Arrange the leeks in a single layer on a large platter and, while they are still warm, cover them with the shallot vinaigrette. Let cool completely.

5. Before serving, sprinkle with the parsley and the eggs if using.

Serves 4

Mimosa

*O*ne eats as much with his eyes as with the mouth," was my grandmother Jeanne's favorite motto, and this garnish of hard-cooked eggs is a perfect example of her approach to cooking. The look of a dish was never taken for granted.

Cut hard-cooked eggs in half and remove the yolks from the whites. Chop the whites into tiny cubes with a knife. Pass the yolks through a sieve sprinkling the tiny "mimosa flowers" over the whites.

Shallot-Parsley Vinaigrette

VINAIGRETTE MET SJALOTS EN PETERSELIE
•
VINAIGRETTE MAISON AUX ECHALOTES

*T*he combination of shallots and parsley is a happy one and is widely used in Belgian homecooked sauces, salads, and dressings. This zesty dressing keeps well for up to two weeks in the refrigerator.

1 tablespoon Dijon mustard

⅓ to ½ cup red wine vinegar (depending on the acidity of your vinegar)

2 large egg yolks, if making dressing by hand, or 1 whole large egg if making by blender or food processor (see Notes)

1½ cups vegetable oil

3 tablespoons finely minced shallots

2 tablespoons finely minced fresh parsley

Salt and freshly ground black pepper to taste

By hand: Whisk together the mustard, ⅓ cup vinegar, and the egg yolks in a mixing bowl. Whisk in the oil, first a few drops at a time, then by tablespoons, until you obtain a smooth, emulsified sauce. Add the shallots, parsley, salt, and pepper. Taste the dressing and add more vinegar if desired.

By blender or food processor: Combine the mustard, ⅓ cup vinegar, and the whole egg in a blender or food processor. With the engine running, add the oil in a steady, fine stream until it is incorporated. Add the shallots, parsley, salt, and pepper. Taste the dressing and add more vinegar if desired.

Makes 2 cups

Notes: *If you are concerned with the quality of the eggs available to you, it is best not to prepare recipes in which they are left uncooked.*

• *To rescue a vinaigrette that has separated, start all over again with 1 egg yolk and 1½ teaspoons mustard. Use the separated sauce instead of the oil.*

Warm Green Bean and Potato Salad from Liège

WARME LUIKSE SLA
•
SALADE LIEGEOISE

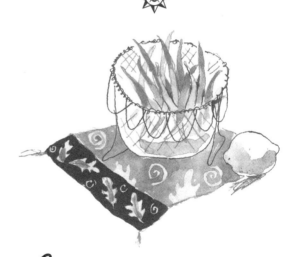

If you were to ask any passerby in Liège what he considers to be the most popular dish in his city, he would probably reply, *"Ah, mais il n'y a rien qu'une bonne salade liégeoise!"* (Ah, but there is nothing like a good *salade liégeoise!*) "But it must be well prepared!" This answer might surprise you, for you would have quickly discovered that Liège abounds in fine restaurants offering specialties of the region, which include crayfish and fresh trout, excellent charcuterie including the local *jambon d'Ardennes,* and a wide variety of game during the hunting season. Yet Belgians are at heart unswervingly faithful to their home cooking. *A salade liégeoise,* prepared with as much care and love as one would lavish on a fancier dish, remains a perennial favorite.

This salad is at its best when it is made with waxy new potatoes and crisp, fresh green beans. It must be assembled while the beans and potatoes are still warm enough to absorb the bacon-vinegar dressing and served immediately. With some good country bread, this robust and simple salad is a meal in itself.

6 to 8 new red potatoes (about ¾ pound),
    scrubbed
Salt to taste
1 pound green beans, trimmed
2 tablespoons unsalted butter or
    vegetable oil
5 ounces slab bacon, cut into
    1 × ¼-inch strips
¼ cup red wine vinegar
2 shallots or 1 small onion,
    finely chopped
¼ cup finely minced fresh parsley
Freshly ground black pepper
    to taste

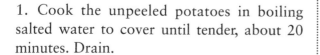

1. Cook the unpeeled potatoes in boiling salted water to cover until tender, about 20 minutes. Drain.

2. Cook the green beans in plenty of boiling salted water until tender but still crunchy, 10 to 15 minutes. Do not cover the pot or they will discolor.

3. When the potatoes are cool enough to handle but still quite warm, peel them and cut each potato into 4 pieces. Combine the potatoes and warm green beans in a salad bowl.

4. Melt the butter or heat the oil in a medium-size skillet over medium heat. Add the bacon strips and sauté until crisp but not too brown, 4 to 6 minutes.

5. Pour the bacon and the rendered fat over the green beans and potatoes.

6. Deglaze the warm skillet with the vinegar and reduce over high heat by two-thirds, 1 minute. Pour over the vegetables and combine well.

7. Season with salt to taste. Sprinkle with the shallots, parsley, and a generous grinding of freshly ground black pepper.

Serves 4

Variation: *A warm dressing of bacon and red wine vinegar is a favorite for many other salads composed of leafy or bitter lettuces and hearty winter vegetables. Try mixing your own blend of curly endive, Belgian endive, grated celery root, finely shredded red cabbage, and tangy apples. Toss it with the bacon-vinegar vinaigrette (described above) and top with garlic croutons.*

Filled Belgian Endive Leaves

APERITIEF HAPJES MET WITLOOF

•

HORS D'OEUVRES VARIES AUX ENDIVES

The lovely pale leaves of the Belgian endive replace crackers and breads in these unusual hors d'oeuvres. You can make these hors d'oeuvres several hours before the arrival of your guests without worrying about soggy crackers, and the delicious, crunchy leaves have virtually no calories!

The boat-shaped leaves will look particularly attractive if you pipe the filling through a pastry bag fitted with a star tip.

Select small, tightly closed heads of Belgian endive to make these appetizers. First, remove the core ends and separate the leaves. Do not rinse them, but wipe with a damp cloth if necessary. Two to three Belgian endives will give you about 20 usable leaves.

Fresh Goat Cheese Filling

6 ounces fresh (soft) goat cheese
1 to 2 tablespoons finely minced fresh herbs of your choice, such as basil, chives, tarragon, parsley, mint, dill, or thyme
Extra-virgin olive oil
Sliced radishes, sprigs of parsley, snipped fresh chives, or diced pimiento, for garnish

1. In a small bowl, mix the goat cheese with the fresh herbs until well blended.

2. Using a pastry bag, pipe the filling into each Belgian endive leaf.

3. Drizzle the filling in each leaf with a few drops of olive oil and garnish with radishes, parsley, chives, or pimiento. Cover and refrigerate until ready to serve.

Makes enough to fill 20 leaves

Roquefort Filling

4 to 5 ounces Roquefort or other blue cheese, at room temperature
8 tablespoons (1 stick) unsalted butter, at room temperature
1 tablespoon Cognac
20 walnut halves, for garnish

1. In a small bowl, mix the Roquefort, butter, and Cognac together to form a smooth paste.

2. Using a pastry bag, pipe the filling into each Belgian endive leaf.

3. Garnish with walnut halves. Cover and refrigerate until ready to serve.

Makes enough to fill 20 leaves

Sauce Gribiche Filling

1 cup Sauce Gribiche (page 316)
1 to 2 ounces (or more) red or
  black caviar

1. Using a small spoon, divide the filling among the Belgian endive leaves.

2. Garnish with a dollop of caviar. Cover and refrigerate until ready to serve.

Makes enough to fill 20 leaves

Smoked Fish Mousse Filling

1½ cups (approximately) Smoked Trout Mousse
  or Smoked Salmon Mousse variation
  (page 36)
20 sprigs fresh dill, for garnish
20 paper-thin slices lemon, for garnish

1. Using a pastry bag, pipe about 1 tablespoon of the fish mousse into each Belgian endive leaf.

2. Garnish with the fresh dill sprigs and lemon slices. Cover and refrigerate until ready to serve.

Makes enough to fill 20 leaves

Salad from the Ardennes

ARDEENSE SALADE
• SALADE D'ARDENNES

This first-course salad combines the bounty of the fertile farms of Flanders with the fine, smoky flavor of *jambon d'Ardennes*. In this country you can substitute a fine imported prosciutto from Parma or any other fine dry-cured or smoked ham.

1 small head romaine or red leaf lettuce (about
   ½ pound)
½ head curly endive or escarole (about
   ½ pound)
2 Belgian endives, cored
12 cherry tomatoes, halved
3 ounces good quality dry-cured ham, such as
   prosciutto, cut into 1 × ¼-inch strips
¾ cup Shallot-Parsley Vinaigrette (page 5)
2 tablespoons unsalted butter
1 tablespoon olive oil
3 slices (½ inch thick) country-style
   white bread
2 cloves garlic, peeled and halved
2 tablespoons minced fresh parsley

1. Rinse and dry the salad greens and
endives. Combine them in a salad bowl with
the tomatoes, ham, and vinaigrette.

2. Heat the butter and oil in a large skillet
over low heat. Add the bread and fry until
lightly browned on each side. Remove and
drain on paper towels. Rub each side with the
cut side of the garlic cloves. Cut into 1-inch
cubes and add to the salad.

3. Sprinkle with the parsley
and serve at once.

Serves 6

My Mother's Potato Salad

MOEDER'S AARDAPPEL SALADE

•

LA SALADE DE POMMES DE TERRE DE MA MERE

What summer picnic or barbecue would be complete without potato salad? This certainly holds true in Belgium, where a man might be tempted to give up the comfort of his dining table for a picnic in the grass, but never ever to give up his beloved potatoes. Served inside or outside, this lovely potato salad will always be welcome.

6 to 8 Red Bliss or Yellow Finn potatoes or
   other new waxy potatoes (about ¾ pound)
1 teaspoon salt
½ cup Shallot-Parsley Vinaigrette
   (page 5), or more to taste
1 tablespoon finely minced fresh parsley

1. Scrub the potatoes under cold running
water. Place in a medium-size saucepan and
cover with cold water. Add the salt and bring
to a boil. Reduce the heat and simmer, covered, until tender, about 20 minutes. Drain.

2. As soon as the potatoes are cool enough to handle, peel them and slice or cube them into a salad bowl. While they are still warm, pour the shallot vinaigrette over them so they can absorb the flavors of the vinaigrette.

3. Sprinkle with the parsley and serve.

Serves 4

Sweet-and-Sour Cucumbers with Chives

ZOET-ZURE KOMKOMMER SALADE MET BIESLOOK
•
CONCOMBRES MARINES A LA CIBOULETTE

This delightfully refreshing summer salad is traditionally served with cold poached fish, Flemish pickled herring, and any smoked fish. It is also my favorite low-calorie addition to any composed salad or buffet table. In the summer months when vegetables are garden-fresh and the cucumber skins are tender and unwaxed, leave the skins on and the seeds in for extra color and flavor.

1 long European cucumber, peeled, seeded, and sliced
½ medium red onion, cut into paper-thin slices
1 cup apple cider vinegar
1½ tablespoons sugar
1 teaspoon salt
Freshly ground black pepper to taste
1 tablespoon finely minced fresh chives

Combine all the ingredients in a nonreactive mixing bowl. Cover and refrigerate for 1 to 2 hours before serving. This salad keeps well, covered and refrigerated, for up to 1 week.

Serves 4 to 6

To Peel or Not to Peel

If your cucumber comes from your garden and you know that it is free of sprays, waxes, or other chemical treatments, you can leave the skin on for added color, flavor, and texture. I often saw my grandmother decorate her cucumbers by pulling a fork lengthwise along the unpeeled cucumber, which produced a beautiful striped effect.

The easiest way to remove the seeds from a cucumber is to slice it in half lengthwise and scoop them out with a teaspoon.

Café Life in Belgium

In the time of Pieter Breughel the Elder, popular social life was centered around the *kroeg*, the bar in the local inn or tavern. His paintings, along with those of David Teniers, Jacob Jordaans, and Adriaan Brouwer, documented and celebrated the conviviality of these gatherings. The drink was beer and the feeling was joyous. These painters portrayed on canvas the notion—held dearest in the heart of every one of my countrymen—that Belgians are masters of the art of enjoying life, and that beer in all its myriad varieties is an integral part of that enjoyment. Beer drinkers, say the paintings of the masters, are happy and gregarious folk. And today, except for the change in fashions, not much has changed. If you wander into one of the older cafés in any city or village, you are likely to feel that you have wandered into one of these paintings, as you see the same laughing faces and the same golden liquid topped with foam. And, of course, there is also the wonderful aroma, the ancient, evocative aroma of hops and yeast, that caused Georges Simenon to declare that, "For me the delicious smell of freshly drawn beer remains the smell of Belgium."

A popular guidebook declares that there is a café on virtually every street corner in Brussels, and goes on to say that all cafés are really taprooms in disguise. Although they serve a small selection of wines and perhaps *genever* (Belgian gin), Belgian cafés serve mostly beer, and always beer at its best and in a variety of choices that staggers the imagination. Without a doubt (and putting modesty aside), Belgium has some of the most refined places in the world in which to drink beer. It also has some of the most intimate, friendly, and entertaining places to drink beer.

Whether we call them cafés, brasseries, beer houses, or *estaminets*, you will find beer drinking establishments in all styles and sizes, from the very old to the quite new, from the traditional to the modern. Some are loud and jovial, others are elegant and restrained. Some have a reputation for attracting gatherings of intellectuals and others are known as artists' cafés. In Brussels you can sample a beer at La Fleur en Papier Doré, where René Magritte was a patron and Max Ernst held an exhibition. What all the

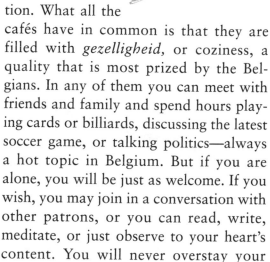

cafés have in common is that they are filled with *gezelligheid,* or coziness, a quality that is most prized by the Belgians. In any of them you can meet with friends and family and spend hours playing cards or billiards, discussing the latest soccer game, or talking politics—always a hot topic in Belgium. But if you are alone, you will be just as welcome. If you wish, you may join in a conversation with other patrons, or you can read, write, meditate, or just observe to your heart's content. You will never overstay your welcome.

Here is a random sampling of the poetic names of the cafés you might visit:

De Dulle Griet in Ghent. The name is taken from the enormous cannon that once helped protect the city.

La Mort Subite in Brussels. The name, which means Sudden Death, does not refer to the effect of drink upon the patrons but to a dice game that was popular in this café.

Den Hopduivel in Ghent. The name means Hop Devil and refers to the blights and pests sent by the devil to plague the farmers who grow the much valued hops. In many rural areas of the hop-growing regions, farmers will burn a straw figure effigy of the Hop Devil during the harvest celebrations.

Vlissinghe in Brugge. The beer is named after a small town just over the Dutch border and people have been enjoying beer here since 1552.

Het Elfde Gebod in Antwerp. "The Eleventh Commandment" is tucked away just under the Cathedral and is jam-packed with plaster angels and saints salvaged from old churches. They look on indulgently while the good beer is sipped in a very friendly atmosphere.

He [Simenon] went on to recount how, on a recent trip to Belgium, he had revisited three of the places where, as a young man, he had drunk beer, and he explained the exact differences between the three bars, the sort of glasses one drank from, the sort of beer they served, how it tasted and the different behaviour of the men and women who served it.

—Patrick Marnham
The Man
Who Wasn't Maigret

Creamy Cucumber Salad with Chervil

ROMIGE KOMKOMMER SALADE MET KERVEIL

•

SALADE DE CONCOMBRES AU CERFEUIL

Another refreshing salad, this one is enlivened by mustard and chervil. If chervil is unavailable, substitute fresh parsley, dill, or even tarragon.

1 long European cucumber, peeled, seeded,
   and cut into thin (⅛ inch) slices
2 teaspoons salt
½ cup heavy (or whipping) cream
1 teaspoon Dijon mustard
Juice of ½ lemon
3 tablespoons finely minced fresh chervil
Freshly ground black pepper to taste
Several fresh chervil sprigs, for garnish

1. Place the cucumber slices in a colander, sprinkle with the salt, and let drain for at least 1 hour.

2. In a small mixing bowl, whisk together the cream and mustard until slightly thickened. Season with the lemon juice, minced chervil, and pepper. Do not add salt as the cucumbers are already salted.

3. Just before serving, toss the cucumber with the creamy mustard dressing, and garnish with sprigs of fresh chervil.

Serves 4 to 6

Autumn Salad with Celery Root and Belgian Endive

HERFST SALADE

•

SALADE D'AUTOMNE

This hearty fall salad is the ideal accompaniment to a charcuterie platter or an assortment of cheeses. Together with some good bread this makes a typical family dinner in Belgium, especially when there has been a three-course, midday summer meal. This salad makes an excellent

14

lunch or light supper, with a minimum of time spent in the kitchen.

1 celery root (celeriac), peeled and cut into ¼-inch slices
4 cups water
Salt to taste
3 ounces mâche (lamb's lettuce) or 1 bunch watercress, stems removed and discarded
2 Belgian endives, cored and sliced into thin rings
Mayonnaise, preferably homemade (page 315)
Freshly ground black pepper to taste

1. Place the celery root slices in a saucepan, cover with the water, and add salt. Bring to a boil, reduce the heat, and simmer until just tender, about 8 minutes. Drain and refresh the celery root under cold running water. (The cooking tones down some of the assertive celery flavor.)

2. Cut the slices of celery root into ¼-inch strips. Mix together with the lettuce and endives in a salad bowl. Dress with just enough mayonnaise to bind the salad. Season with salt and pepper and serve at once.

Serves 4 to 6

Variations: If you like the pronounced peppery flavor of raw celery root, skip the first step of cooking it. Simply peel, slice, and julienne the celery root, then sprinkle with lemon juice to prevent discoloration.

• Try some of this salad spread on a roast beef sandwich.

Celery Root

The gnarled, ugly celery root, also known as celeriac, is a much beloved fall and winter staple in Belgium and many other European countries. It appears both raw and cooked in salads, soups, and vegetable purées. In any guise you choose, it is a delectable vegetable.

Raw celery root has a tendency to discolor once it is peeled. To prevent this, add the peeled celery root to a bowl of cold water into which you have squeezed the juice of ½ lemon.

Vineyard Salad

WYNGAARD SALADE
•
SALADE VIGNERONNE

The climate in Belgium is not particularly suited for growing wine grapes, but the region of Hoeilaart produces excellent deep purple table grapes. Perfect bunches of these grapes, exquisitely wrapped in tissue paper, appear in the market as a luxury item. Mostly these are eaten for dessert, but combined with apples and shallots, they turn an otherwise ordinary green salad into a real feast.

1 head chicory or escarole, rinsed, dried, and cut into bite-size pieces
½ tart green apple, unpeeled, halved, cored, and thinly sliced
1½ cups seedless red grapes, rinsed and halved
6 tablespoons vegetable oil
Salt and freshly ground black pepper to taste
5 ounces slab bacon, cut into 1 × ¼-inch strips
2 tablespoons finely minced shallots
6 tablespoons Spiced Vinegar (page 317) or apple cider vinegar
1 tablespoon finely minced fresh parsley

1. Combine the chicory, apple, and grapes in a salad bowl. Add the oil and mix well. Season with salt and pepper.

2. Fry the bacon in a skillet over high heat until nicely browned, 4 to 6 minutes. Remove with a slotted spoon and drain on paper towels. Sprinkle over the salad.

3. Pour off all but 3 tablespoons of the bacon fat from the skillet. Add the shallots and cook, stirring, over medium heat for 2 minutes. Add the vinegar and bring to a quick boil. Reduce this mixture by one-third. Pour the hot mixture over the salad and toss well. Sprinkle with the parsley and serve at once.

Serves 6

Red Cabbage Salad

RODEKOOLSLA
•
SALADE DE CHOU ROUGE

A fine winter salad to serve with dinner or on a buffet table. The colors are stunning, and the flavors are pleasantly assertive with the sweet-and-sour tang so beloved by Belgians.

1½ cups cider vinegar
2 tablespoons sugar
2 bay leaves
1 sprig fresh thyme
½ head red cabbage (about 1 pound), finely shredded
½ cup vegetable oil
Salt and freshly ground black pepper to taste
1 tart apple, unpeeled, halved, cored, and thinly sliced
½ cup walnut halves, toasted (see "Toasting Nuts," facing page)

16

1. Heat the vinegar with the sugar, bay leaves, and thyme in a small saucepan. Stir until sugar is dissolved. Pour the warm vinegar over the shredded red cabbage in a bowl and toss well. Cover and refrigerate for at least 6 hours.

2. Remove the salad from the refrigerator. The cabbage will be wilted and slightly pickled. Add the oil and mix well. Season with salt and pepper. The salad will keep in the refrigerator up to 2 weeks.

3. Just before serving, discard the bay leaves and thyme. Decorate with apples slices and sprinkle with walnuts.

Serves 6 to 8

Toasting Nuts

Most nuts lose their crunchiness and rich flavor after a while, but they perk up considerably when they are briefly toasted in the oven.

Preheat the oven to 350°F. Spread the nuts out evenly on a baking sheet and bake for 7 to 10 minutes, until you can just start to smell them and they have started to brown. Keep a careful eye on them as they can scorch easily. Let the nuts cool on paper towels before using.

Marie's Red Beet Salad

MARIE'S RODE BIETJES SLA

•

SALADE DE BETTERAVES DE MARIE

Another colorful and very flavorful winter salad, this time made with red beets. The recipe comes from my great grandmother Marie, and, as we say in Flanders, it is a recipe "as old as the street," referring to the centuries-old cobblestones that still line Belgian Roads.

This fine salad is best made a day or two ahead, as the flavors of the beets and onions improve as they marinate in the vinaigrette. The salad will keep up to two weeks in the refrigerator.

In Belgium this salad is often served as a first course or as a light meal with smoked fish, pickled herring, or simply a hard-cooked egg.

4 or 5 small red beets (about 1½ pounds),
   scrubbed clean but unpeeled, with about
   2 inches of the green tops left on
6 tablespoons vegetable oil
2 tablespoons fresh lemon juice
1 small onion, thinly sliced
Salt to taste
Freshly ground black pepper
   to taste
4 cups torn mixed lettuces
2 tablespoons finely minced fresh parsley,
   chives, or chervil

1. Place the beets in a saucepan, cover with cold water, add salt, and bring to a boil. Reduce the heat to a simmer and cook, covered, until the beets are tender, 25 to 40 minutes, depending on their size. Drain and let cool slightly.

2. When the beets are cool enough to handle, peel them and cut into thin slices or ½-inch cubes. Whisk together the oil and lemon juice and pour over the beets while they are still warm. Add the onion slices and season with salt and pepper. Refrigerate until ready to serve.

3. Just before serving, drain off and reserve
   e of the vinaigrette, which will have
   ed a dazzling red. Serve the beets and
   n on a bed of mixed lettuces. Drizzle the
   ved ruby red vinaigrette over the salad
   around the inside edge of the plate for a
   atic effect. Sprinkle with the parsley just
   e serving.

   s 4 to 6

Variation: For a more intense flavor, replace 2 tablespoons of the vegetable oil with walnut oil.

Harvest Salad with Roquefort Toast

HERFST SALADE MET WALNOTEN EN ROQUEFORT
•
SALADE D'AUTOMNE AUX NOIX ET ROQUEFORT

This robust salad makes a wonderful first-course or even a light evening meal on its own. The mingling of crisp greens, walnut-flavored vinaigrette, tart apple, and the rich complex flavor of Roquefort cheese is absolutely heavenly.

Vinaigrette:
¾ cup walnut oil
½ cup corn oil
⅓ cup raspberry or
   cider vinegar
Salt and freshly
   ground black
   pepper
   to taste

Roquefort Toast:

2 to 3 ounces Roquefort or other blue cheese, at room temperature

4 tablespoons (½ stick) unsalted butter, at room temperature

4 to 6 slices firm white bread, lightly toasted

2 tablespoons finely minced fresh chives (optional)

Salad:

4 cups Boston, red leaf, radicchio, and/or watercress leaves, rinsed, dried, and torn into bite-size pieces

2 Belgian endives, cored and leaves separated

1 tart green or red apple, unpeeled, halved, cored, and thinly sliced

¼ cup walnuts, lightly toasted (page 17) and coarsely chopped

1 tablespoon finely minced shallot

1. Preheat the broiler.

2. To make the vinaigrette, whisk together all the ingredients. Set aside.

3. To make the Roquefort toast, cream together the cheese and butter. Spread the mixture on the toasted bread and broil until the cheese has completely melted and becomes bubbly, 1 to 2 minutes. Sprinkle with the chives if using. Cut each toast diagonally into 4 triangles.

4. For the salad, spread the mixed lettuce leaves on a big platter. Arrange the endive leaves, alternating with the apple slices in a sunburst pattern on top of the lettuce leaves. Sprinkle with the walnuts and shallots. Just

before serving, drizzle about 1 tablespoon of the vinaigrette over the salad. Arrange the warm Roquefort toast triangles on the salad. Serve the remaining vinaigrette in a sauceboat on the side. (Keep leftover vinaigrette in a tightly closed container in the refrigerator for up to 1 week.)

Serves 4 to 6

Belgian-Style Fresh Cheese with Herbs and Radishes

PLATTE KAAS MET VERSE KRUIDEN EN RADIJSJES

•

FROMAGE BLANC AUX HERBES ET RADIS

This simple country dish was a favorite of my great grandmother Marie. She always prepared it when we came to visit and served it for *het vieruurtje*—the traditional afternoon snack, which at her house

19

My Hometown, Ghent

I was born and raised in Ghent, once the largest medieval city of Northern Europe after Paris. From my earliest days, I was surrounded by the remains of a glorious past that can be traced back to the 7th century, when St. Amand founded an abbey at the confluence of the Scheldt and Leie Rivers. My first steps were taken on the uneven old cobblestones that still pave the streets of my city.

My father is a natural storyteller, and in Ghent, there are stories everywhere. Both Ghent and Brugge are the centers of Flemish art and represent the flowering of the late Middle Ages. As early as the days of the Roman occupation, 2,000 years ago, Flemish weavers were famous for the quality of their work.

By the 13th century, the cloth trade in Ghent employed upwards of 30,000 people, and long before capitalism or the industrial revolution, all these workers were organized in very strictly delineated guilds. My father often took me to the Vrijdagmarkt (Friday Market), a square where the people of Ghent have organized, rioted, and rebelled since the 14th century. Under the leadership of Jacob van Artevelde (whose statue now stands there), the weavers first made it the place to battle their oppressors. My father loved to tell me stories about the rebellious and courageous men and women of Ghent, who turned their city into an independent city-state during the 14th and 15th centuries.

As a child, one of my favorite destinations in Ghent was the gray and imposing Gravensteen (Castle of the Counts of Flanders) and the ice cream parlor across the way. The castle was built in 1180 and it is said to be one of the strongest fortresses of Western Europe, as well as one of the gloomiest. While enjoying my ice cream, I loved to sit and stare at the strong walls, surrounded by a moat of dark, still water.

We went often to St. Bavon's Cathedral, whose drab exterior always leaves one unprepared for the incredibly rich, art-filled interior. Housed in the Cathedral is one of the "Seven Wonders of Belgium," the twenty-four-panel Adoration of the Holy Lamb by Jan Van Eyck (which was perhaps completed with the assistance of his brother Hubert). It is said that this twenty-four-paneled painting took twelve years to finish. At the other end of the cathedral is an important painting by Peter Paul Rubens, the "Conversion of St. Bavon," a portrayal of a once dissolute and worldly count who renounced his sinful ways in order to seek admission to the monastery, where he was transformed into the saint for whom the cathedral is now named.

It would take a whole book to tell you about all the wonderful things you can see and do in my hometown. The 16th-century Dutch humanist and philosopher Desiderius Erasmus said it best when he wrote, "I do not think that in all of Christianity [the world as he knew it] there is a city that compares with Ghent." I think if he visited the city today, he would still feel the same way.

consisted of *boterhammekes* (sliced buttered bread) and, always, her fragrant and very potent coffee. But her *platte kaas* (fresh cheese) never tasted the same twice. The herbs came from her garden, and her choices depended on what struck her fancy that morning. Some chives, a sprig of chervil, a little garlic, some tarragon, or even a leaf or two of mint would find their way into her *platte kaas*.

All over Belgium, it is a favorite custom on lazy Sunday afternoons for friends to gather at a local café to discuss the latest trip of the Tour de France or the results of the local soccer game while sipping glasses of cool, frothy beer and fortifying themselves with thick slices of dark bread, spread with fresh cheese and radishes.

I serve this lovely fresh cheese on my brunch table along with other spreads, or as an hors d'oeuvre with radishes or other crudités for dipping. The perfect beverage to serve alongside is a good Belgian beer.

2 cups Homemade Fresh Cheese (recipe follows) or 2 cups low-fat cottage cheese mixed with ¼ cup heavy (or whipping) cream in a blender until smooth
1½ teaspoons white wine, champagne, or tarragon-flavored vinegar
1 to 2 tablespoons finely minced shallot or fresh chives
1 tablespoon finely minced fresh parsley
1 tablespoon finely minced fresh chervil or tarragon
Salt and freshly ground black pepper to taste
1 tablespoon walnut or hazelnut oil (optional)
4 to 6 slices good country bread, fresh or toasted
1 bunch red radishes or 1 black radish, trimmed and thinly sliced, or vegetable crudités, such as carrot sticks, celery sticks, cherry tomatoes, cucumber slices, and broccoli and cauliflower florets

1. In a large bowl, whisk together the cheese, vinegar, shallot, parsley, and chervil. Season to taste with salt and pepper. Some walnut or hazelnut oil adds a mysterious flavor.

2. Serve on thick slices of country bread and decorate with thinly sliced radishes, or serve as a dip with crudités.

Serves 4 to 6

Variations: *Mix the cheese together with minced fresh basil, garlic, and finely minced black olives. Spread on rounds of Italian bread and decorate with slices of tomato or cucumber.*

• *Mix the cheese with minced fresh dill, lemon juice to taste, and about ¼ cup diced smoked salmon, smoked trout, or other smoked fish. Serve as a spread or dip.*

Homemade Fresh Cheese

PLATTE KAAS
•
FROMAGE BLANC

Nothing could be easier than making your own fresh cheese to flavor with your own mixture of herbs and seasonings. Allow 3 to 4 days to complete the process.

4 cups milk
1 cup buttermilk

1. In a glass or earthenware bowl, mix together the milk and the buttermilk. Cover with plastic wrap and leave at room temperature (preferably 70 to 80°F) until the mixture thickens. This will take 24 to 48 hours.

2. Line a sieve or colander with a double layer of cheesecloth. Pour the thickened milk mixture into this and let drain over a bowl for at least 12 hours in the refrigerator. The longer the cheese drips, the thicker it will be. Discard the watery liquid (whey). Remove the cheese to a small bowl, cover tightly, and refrigerate until ready to use. The fresh cheese will keep for 3 to 4 days in the refrigerator.

Makes 3 to 3½ cups

Cleaning Cutting Boards and Knives

Herring can leave a clinging fishy odor on wooden boards and knife handles which can't be completely eliminated with soap and water. The only way to neutralize the strong fish odor is to wash everything with salted water. The fishmongers who tend their little wooden stands in the harbors of Belgium still clean everything with seawater when they can.

Smoked Herring and Bean Salad from Ostend

OOSTENDSE SALADE
•
SALADE DES PECHEURS

From the busy port city of Ostend comes the recipe for this favorite fishermen's salad, which combines smoked herring fillets with a tangy white bean salad. To add a colorful note, I often accompany this salad with Marie's Red Beet Salad (see Index).

1 pound dried Great Northern beans or any
white bean, soaked for 12 hours in plenty
of cold water (see Note)

1½ teaspoons Dijon mustard

2 tablespoons mayonnaise, preferably homemade (page 315)

1 small onion, finely chopped

1 clove garlic, finely minced

½ cup finely minced fresh parsley

Salt and freshly ground black pepper to taste

1 hard-cooked egg, peeled

4 smoked herring or kipper fillets, cut crosswise
into ½-inch strips

3 ounces cooked and peeled gray North Sea
shrimp or smallest shrimp available (optional)

1. Drain the beans and place them in a
medium-size Dutch oven. Add enough cold
water to cover the beans by at least 3 inches
and bring to a boil. Reduce the heat to a simmer, cover partially, and cook until tender,
1 to 2 hours depending on the age and size
of the beans. Drain and let the beans cool.

2. For the dressing, mix the mustard and
mayonnaise in a small bowl. Stir in the onion,
garlic, and all but 1 tablespoon of the parsley.

3. Toss the beans together with the dressing
and season to taste with salt and pepper. Be a
little skimpy with the salt because the herring
is salty.

4. Cut the egg in half and separate the white
from the yolk. Mash the egg yolk and white
separately with the tines of a fork.

5. Spoon the bean salad in the center of a
serving platter. Arrange the herring strips over
the beans and sprinkle with the mashed egg
yolk, mashed egg white, and the remaining 1
tablespoon parsley. Decorate with the cooked
shrimp if using.

Serves 4

*Note: You can save time by substituting two
15-ounce cans of white cannellini beans.
Drain and rinse them well in cold water.*

Smoked Herring with Apple-Onion Cream

SALADE MET GEROOKTE HARING, APPELS EN AJUIN

•

HARENGS FUMES A LA CREME D'OIGNONS

This was my grandmother's favorite
way of serving smoked herring fillets.
The apples and onions in whipped
heavy cream provide an excellent counter-
point to the smoky saltiness of the fish. Serve
with fresh buttered bread, new potatoes and
sliced ripe tomatoes.

3 tablespoons heavy (or whipping) cream

3 tablespoons peeled, cored, and
   finely diced apple

1½ tablespoons finely minced onion

2 tablespoons finely minced fresh parsley

1 teaspoon fresh lemon juice

Salt and freshly ground black pepper
   to taste

4 smoked herring or kipper fillets

1 small onion, sliced into thin rings

1. Whisk the cream in a bowl until it just starts to thicken. Add the apple and minced onion, 1 tablespoon of the parsley, and the lemon juice. Mix well and season to taste with salt and pepper.

2. Roll up the herring or kipper fillets and place on individual plates. Serve with a dollop of apple-onion cream and decorate with onion rings and the remaining 1 tablespoon parsley.

Serves 4

Herring: A Taste of History

The lowly herring, considered a poor cousin of the aristocratic turbot, the delicate sole, and even the mundane cod, has in its day been the making and unmaking of several empires. Two facts made the herring of critical importance in European history. One is that until fairly recently herring was the most abundant seafood in the world, and it has fed mankind since prehistoric times. Herring bones have been found in Scandinavian excavations that date back to 3000 B.C.

Second, when a method for preserving fresh herring by layering them with salt in airtight barrels was discovered early in the 14th century, it became possible to transport large quantities of the fish to customers far away from the sea coast. This enabled nations that maintained large herring fleets to profit and thrive. In prosperous times, herring, plentiful and cheap, was the food of the poor; in times of famine, herring could sustain the population at large when little else was available.

In Belgium, as in other European countries, the herring has played an important role for centuries. Many generations of Belgians living along the coast of the North Sea were saved from famine by the abundance of herring caught by their fishing fleets.

Today, alas, the once ubiquitous herring is nowhere near as plentiful in our waters as it was in the past. And because of overfishing and other ecological problems, it appears on the list of species that need to be protected in order not to disappear completely.

Marinated Pickled Herring Fillets

ROLLMOPS
•
HARENGS SAUR A LA DAUBE

———————— ✦ ————————

Rollmops (whether rolled or flat, as in this recipe) is another name for pickled herring, and it is definitely a taste that we Belgians acquired from our neighbors in Scandinavia. No wonder! Fresh herring fillets are delicious when they are marinated for several days in seasoned and flavored vinegar. Many fish stores and even supermarkets sell their own pickled herring, but it is worth it to make your own with either fresh or salted herring fillets.

Serve rollmops as a low-calorie appetizer or with Marie's Red Beet Salad and My Mother's Potato Salad. Or arrange a buffet table that also includes a plate of ripe, sliced tomatoes, Sweet-and-Sour Marinated Cucumbers with Chives, or Creamy Cucumber Salad with Chervil (see Index for all page numbers). Add a loaf of hearty country bread and offer plenty of beer.

12 fresh or salted herring fillets
2 cups white wine vinegar or tarragon-flavored vinegar
1 tablespoon sugar
1 tablespoon olive oil
2 bay leaves
1 sprig fresh thyme
1 tablespoon black peppercorns
1½ teaspoons coriander seeds, crushed
1 carrot, peeled and sliced into thin rounds
2 medium onions, sliced into thin rings
1 lemon, peeled and white pith removed, thinly sliced
2 hard-cooked eggs, finely chopped, for garnish
½ cup finely minced fresh parsley, for garnish

1. If you are using salted herring fillets, place the fillets in a large bowl and cover with cold water or milk. Let stand in the refrigerator, covered, overnight. Drain, rinse, and dry on paper towels.

2. Place the vinegar, sugar, oil, bay leaves, thyme, peppercorns, and coriander seeds in a nonreactive saucepan. Simmer, covered, for 10 minutes. Remove from the heat and let cool.

3. Choose an earthenware or glass casserole at least 4 inches deep. Arrange half the carrot and onions on the bottom and cover with 6 herring fillets. Pour half of the vinegar mixture over the fillets. Top with the remaining carrot, onions, and herring, then pour the remaining vinegar mixture over the fillets. Arrange the lemon slices over the top.

4. Cover the casserole with plastic wrap and let marinate in the refrigerator for at least 2 days or up to 1 week.

5. To serve the pickled herring fillets, you can either arrange them on a platter and garnish with the hard-cooked egg and parsley, or arrange 2 fillets on each plate and then garnish.

Serves 12 as an appetizer or 6 as a light lunch

Tomatoes Stuffed with Shrimp, Crab, and Lobster

TOMAAT MET GRYZE GARNAALKES
•
TOMATES AUX CREVETTES

Whenever you visit my little country, sampling this simple and delectable appetizer is a must and definitely *vaut le détour* (worth going out of your way for, although you will never have to go very far). Since there isn't any substitute for the tiny, delectable North Sea shrimp that are the sole stuffing in Belgium, I have substituted a mixture of shrimp, crabmeat, and lobster meat for a lovely and delicious adaptation. Of course, if you prefer, you can leave out any one or even two of the three ingredients.

This is a very luxurious appetizer and not an inexpensive one, but you can console yourself that it takes only minutes to prepare.

4 firm, ripe, large beefsteak tomatoes
Salt to taste
2 cups cooked, shelled, and diced shrimp, crabmeat, and/or lobster meat
³⁄₄ cup mayonnaise, preferably homemade (page 315)
Freshly ground black pepper to taste
8 to 12 Boston lettuce leaves, rinsed and dried
¹⁄₄ cup minced fresh parsley

1. Cut a thin slice off the top of each tomato and reserve. Carefully scoop out the seeds and pulp of each tomato with a teaspoon. (Save the pulp for a tomato sauce.) Sprinkle the insides of each hollowed-out tomato with a pinch of salt and turn upside down on paper towels to drain.

2. Mix the shellfish with the mayonnaise and season with salt and pepper to taste.

3. Arrange 2 or 3 Boston lettuce leaves on each plate. Place a scooped-out tomato in the center. Sprinkle the inside of each tomato with freshly ground black pepper and fill each tomato with the seafood mixture. Cover with the reserved tomato tops and sprinkle each plate with minced parsley.

Serves 4

Stuffed Tomatoes

GEVULDE TOMATEN
•
TOMATES FARCIES

ipe, juicy beefsteak tomatoes stuffed with a flavorful meat filling and served with an oniony tomato sauce is one of Belgium's favorite summer dishes. These tomatoes are easy to prepare, comforting, and delicious all at once. Served with buttered rice or fresh crusty bread, stuffed tomatoes make a lovely lunch or light supper dish.

4 firm, ripe beefsteak tomatoes
Salt to taste
1 tablespoon unsalted butter
½ medium onion, finely minced
1 clove garlic, finely minced
2 tablespoons tomato paste
1 sprig fresh thyme or ¼ teaspoon
   dried thyme
Freshly ground black pepper to taste
¼ teaspoon sugar, if needed
1 tablespoon finely minced
   fresh parsley

Stuffing:
1 slice (1 inch thick) firm white bread,
   crusts trimmed
½ cup milk
1 tablespoon unsalted butter
½ medium onion, minced
¾ pound lean ground meat (a mixture
   of pork and veal or all beef)
1 clove garlic, finely minced
1 large egg, lightly beaten
1½ tablespoons finely minced fresh
   parsley
Salt and freshly ground black pepper
   to taste
Pinch of freshly grated nutmeg

1. Cut a thin slice off the top (stem end) of each tomato. Use a teaspoon to scoop out the pulp, leaving the walls ¼- to ½-inch thick. Reserve the lids and the tomato pulp. Sprinkle the insides of the scooped-out tomatoes with salt and turn them upside down on a plate to drain.

2. Melt the butter in a medium-size saucepan over medium heat. Add the onion and cook, stirring, until translucent, about 7 minutes. Do not let it brown. Add the garlic, the reserved tomato pulp, the tomato paste, and thyme. Simmer, covered, over low heat for 35 minutes. Season with salt and pepper to taste. If the tomatoes are on the tart side, add the sugar. Purée the sauce in a blender or food processor until smooth. Sprinkle with the parsley.

3. Preheat the oven to 350°F.

4. Prepare the stuffing: Let the bread soak in the milk in a small mixing bowl for about 10 minutes. Melt the butter in a small skillet over medium heat. Add the onion and cook, stirring, until softened but not browned. Squeeze the bread dry and discard the milk. In a large mixing bowl, combine the sautéed onion, bread, ground meat, garlic, egg, and parsley. Season well with salt, pepper, and nutmeg.

5. Generously butter a glass or enameled baking dish just large enough to hold the 4 tomatoes. Fill the tomatoes with the meat stuffing and place the reserved lids on top. Place the tomatoes in the buttered dish and bake for 35 minutes. Reheat the tomato sauce and serve each tomato with some sauce spooned over it.

Serves 4

Variations: *The stuffing for the tomatoes can be varied to your heart's content. See the variations for Meat Loaf, Belgian Style (see Index), for some ideas.*

• *Add a roasted red bell pepper to the tomato sauce when it is being puréed.*

Fried Cheese Croquettes

BELGISCHE KAASKROKETTEN

•

FONDUE BRUXELLOISE

These delectable croquettes will always be associated in my mind with my grandmother's formal dinner parties. I remember well her beautifully set table with fresh flowers and sparkling silver, and these golden cheese croquettes to start the meal. With the first bite, you are in heaven. The outside of the croquette is thin and very crispy; the inside, a luxurious flow of soft, melting cheese. Everyone is happy and the mood is set for the meal to follow. This is another dish that requires an overnight stay in the refrigerator, so allow yourself enough preparation time.

Serve the larger croquettes as a first course with Fried Parsley and a wedge of lemon, or make them bite-size and serve them as appetizers.

Cheese Croquettes:
6 tablespoons (³/4 stick) unsalted butter
1 cup all-purpose flour
1²/3 cups milk
1 cup grated Parmesan cheese
1 cup grated Swiss Emmental cheese
2³/4 cups grated Gruyère cheese
3 large egg yolks
Salt and freshly ground white pepper to taste
Freshly grated nutmeg to taste
Pinch of cayenne pepper

Coating:
3 large egg whites
¹/2 teaspoon salt
1 tablespoon vegetable oil
¹/2 cup all-purpose flour
1 cup dried bread crumbs

Frying and Serving:
Vegetable oil for deep frying
Boston lettuce leaves, for serving (optional)
Lemon wedges, for serving (optional)
Fried Parsley (page 32), for serving (optional)

1. Melt the butter in a medium-size saucepan over medium heat. Add the flour and cook, stirring constantly with a wooden spoon, for a few minutes. Switch to a whisk and gradually whisk in the milk. Continue whisking as you bring the mixture almost to a boil. Reduce the heat and simmer for 5 minutes, stirring occasionally. The sauce should be thick and smooth. Add the cheeses and bring to a boil, stirring constantly.

2. Remove the sauce from the heat. Stir briskly for a few minutes to cool it slightly.

Stir in the egg yolks, one at a time, and season generously with white pepper, nutmeg, and cayenne. Taste before adding salt, as the cheeses are already quite salty.

3. Line a 9-inch-square cake pan with plastic wrap. Pour in the cheese mixture and smooth it with a spatula. Press plastic wrap directly on the surface to prevent a skin from forming. Refrigerate at least overnight or up to 3 days.

4. Prepare the coating: In a medium-size bowl, beat the egg whites with the salt and 1 tablespoon vegetable oil just until frothy. Put the flour and bread crumbs into separate shallow bowls.

5. Unmold the firm cheese mixture onto a lightly floured surface. Cut into 12 rectangles approximately 3 × 2 inches for larger croquettes. For smaller hors d'oeuvres, cut each rectangle in thirds to make 36 pieces; dust your palms with flour and roll each piece into a ball.

6. Coat the croquettes one at a time: Dust each rectangle or ball lightly with flour, dip into the egg white mixture, and coat with the bread crumbs. Cover and refrigerate until ready to fry. (The croquettes can wait several days in the refrigerator or longer in the freezer. Thaw in the refrigerator before frying.)

7. Preheat the oven to 250°F.

8. Heat the vegetable oil in a deep fryer or a wok over medium-high heat to 375°F. Fry the croquettes, a few at a time, until they turn

a rich golden color, 3 to 6 minutes depending on size. Drain on paper towels and keep warm in a low oven until ready to serve.

9. Serve the little walnut-size fritters as hors d'oeuvres, along with a supply of toothpicks. (The larger croquettes are traditionally served as first course on a plate decorated with Boston lettuce leaves, lemon wedges, and Fried Parsley.)

Makes 12 croquettes or 36 walnut-size hors d'oeuvres

A Note About Cheese

Old-fashioned yet still popular, cheese croquettes are usually made with at least two and more often three different cheeses. The classic combination is Parmesan, Emmental, and Gruyère. Recently Belgium has had a revival of small cheese producers which provides us with a wide variety of delicious domestic cheeses. Some cooks have been experimenting with new combinations of cheeses for these croquettes, using the local Pilgrim cheese, Maredsous, aged Gouda, and Bocholt with excellent results. While it is not yet possible to find most of these Belgian cheeses in the United States, you can certainly be creative and select a variety of hard cheeses to create your own combinations.

Shrimp Croquettes

GARNAALKROKETTEN

•

CROQUETTES AUX CREVETTES GRISES

These little fritters are certainly one of the finest appetizers from the traditional Belgian kitchen, and you will find them served in the most opulent restaurants as well as in modest cafés and homes all over Belgium. For a while I thought I could never duplicate them in this country without the very flavorful, tiny North Sea shrimp. But with a little experimentation I achieved quite good results using shrimp available in the United States. Do avoid frozen peeled shrimp, for they have very little flavor and search out instead the freshest shrimp you can find.

This dish must be refrigerated at least overnight, so allow yourself enough preparation time.

Shrimp Croquettes

½ pound smallest unpeeled shrimp available
5 tablespoons unsalted butter
1 small onion, thinly sliced
1¾ cups plus 5 tablespoons milk
½ bay leaf
1 envelope unflavored gelatin
5 tablespoons cold water
⅔ cup all-purpose flour
2 ounces Parmesan or Gruyère cheese, grated
1 large egg yolk
1 tablespoon fresh lemon juice
Salt and freshly ground black pepper to taste
Freshly grated nutmeg to taste
Pinch of cayenne pepper

Coating:

3 large egg whites
½ teaspoon salt
1 tablespoon vegetable oil
½ cup all-purpose flour
1 cup dried bread crumbs

Frying and Serving:

Vegetable oil for deep frying
Boston lettuce leaves (optional)
Lemon wedges (optional)
Fried Parsley (recipe follows, optional)

1. Shell the shrimp and reserve the shells. Chop the shrimp into ¼-inch dice.

2. Melt 1 tablespoon of the butter in a medium-size saucepan over medium heat. Add the onion and cook, stirring, until translucent but not browned, 2 to 3 minutes. Add the shrimp shells and cook for 2 more minutes. Add 1¾ cups milk and the bay leaf and bring to a boil. Reduce the heat and simmer, uncovered, for 15 minutes.

3. Strain the broth through a sieve and discard the solids. Return the broth to the saucepan and heat over low heat. Add the shrimp and poach for 3 minutes. Drain the shrimp and reserve the broth. You should have 1½ cups of broth left.

4. In a small saucepan, sprinkle the gelatin over the cold water. Let stand while you prepare the béchamel sauce.

5. Melt the remaining 4 tablespoons butter in a medium-size saucepan over low heat. Stir in the flour with a wooden spoon. Switch to a whisk and gradually whisk in the reserved broth. Bring almost to a boil, then reduce the heat and simmer, stirring occasionally, until the sauce is smooth and thick, about 7 minutes. Add the grated cheese and bring to almost a boil again.

6. Heat the gelatin mixture over low heat until the gelatin has melted, 1 to 2 minutes. Stir it into the béchamel sauce and mix well.

7. Remove the sauce from the heat and let cool for a few minutes. Whisk the egg yolk and remaining 5 tablespoons milk together, then stir it into the béchamel. Stir in the shrimp, lemon juice, salt, pepper, nutmeg, and cayenne.

8. Line a 9-inch-square cake pan with plastic wrap. Pour in the shrimp mixture and smooth

31

with a spatula. Press plastic wrap directly on the surface to prevent a skin from forming. Refrigerate at least overnight or up to 3 days.

9. Prepare the coating: In a medium-size bowl, beat the egg whites with the salt and 1 tablespoon vegetable oil just until frothy. Put the flour and bread crumbs into separate shallow bowls ready for dipping.

10. Unmold the firm shrimp mixture onto a lightly floured surface. Cut into 3 × 1½-inch rectangles and roll each rectangle into a cylinder for croquettes. For smaller hors d'oeuvres, cut each rectangle in half and roll into a ball.

11. Coat the croquettes one at a time: Dust each cylinder or ball lightly with flour, dip into the egg white mixture, and coat with the bread crumbs. Cover and refrigerate until ready to fry. (At this point the croquettes can wait several days in the refrigerator or longer in the freezer. Thaw in the refrigerator before frying.)

12. Preheat the oven to 250°F.

13. Heat the vegetable oil over medium-high heat in a deep fryer to 375°F. Fry the croquettes, a few at a time, until they turn a rich golden color, about 3 minutes. Drain on paper towels and keep warm in the oven until ready to serve.

14. Serve the little walnut-size fritters as hors d'oeuvres with a supply of toothpicks. The larger croquettes traditionally are served on a plate decorated with Boston lettuce leaves, lemon wedges, and Fried Parsley.

Makes 18 croquettes or 36 walnut-size hors d'oeuvres

Fried Parsley

*D*eep-fried parsley is very crisp and utterly delicious. It is traditionally served with cheese or shrimp croquettes and as a garnish for fish dishes.

2 cups curly parsley leaves, stems
*   removed*
Vegetable oil for deep frying

1. Rinse the parsley leaves under cold running water. Spin dry in a salad spinner and roll in a clean dish towel to dry completely.

2. Heat the oil in a deep fryer or wok over medium-high heat to 375°F. Add the parsley and fry until crisp but not brown, 20 seconds. Remove with a skimmer and drain on paper towels.

Makes about 1 cup

Fishing on Horseback?

Every morning at low tide in Oostduinkerke on the North Sea, a group of older men put on their yellow slickers and heavy boots, mount their enormous Belgian workhorses (horses as big as Clydesdales, weighing a ton or more) and march into the surf, dragging nets to catch the tiny North Sea shrimp. There are days when the surf can be wild, but men and horses battle the sea to catch this famous delicacy.

These fishermen on horseback, known as De Peerdevissers, are following a tradition that began in the late 1400s. It is said to have been originated by older fishermen who no longer had the stamina to brave the wild North Sea in boats. Should you ever get to witness this spectacle, I think you will appreciate the hardiness of these people who view horseback fishing as an occupation for retired older men.

Restaurants in the area serve these shrimp for lunch on the same day they are caught. I assure you that it is one of the great pleasures of life to sit on a sunny terrace with a glass of local beer and a huge platter of fresh shrimp before you. Yes, you have to peel each tiny shrimp before popping it into your mouth. But the rewards are great and Belgians do enjoy prolonging their pleasures.

Bay Scallops on a Bed of Belgian Endives

ST. JACOB SCHELPEN OP EEN BEDJE VAN WITLOOF

•

COQUILLES ST. JACQUES AUX CHICONS

The recipe for this wonderful appetizer comes from my new friend Greet, who is an excellent cook. It is an unusual but very happy marriage of two of my favorite ingredients: salty sweet, lightly caramelized bay scallops and bittersweet, buttery sautéed Belgian endives. Best of all, it is prepared in a snap. Serve it to start a special dinner.

5 or 6 Belgian endives, cored and sliced lengthwise into strips ½ inch long
1 tablespoon confectioners' sugar
1 tablespoon fresh lemon juice, plus additional to taste
Salt and freshly ground black pepper to taste
4½ tablespoons unsalted butter
½ cup heavy (or whipping) cream
1 pound bay scallops

1. In a large mixing bowl, toss the julienned

endives with the sugar, 1 tablespoon lemon juice, salt, and pepper.

2. Melt 1½ tablespoons of the butter in a large skillet over high heat. Add half the endives and cook, stirring frequently, until tender and slightly caramelized, 5 to 7 minutes. Transfer to a sauté pan or wok. Melt another 1½ tablespoons butter in the skillet and cook the second batch of endives.

3. Add the second batch to the first in the sauté pan, add the cream, and simmer until thickened, 8 to 10 minutes.

4. Melt the remaining 1½ tablespoons butter in the first skillet over high heat. Add the scallops and sauté, turning them over with a spatula, until they turn opaque and slightly browned from the caramelized butter in the skillet. This should take no longer than 2 or 3 minutes. Season with salt, pepper, and lemon juice to taste.

5. Arrange the creamed endives on individual plates and top with the sautéed scallops.

Serves 4

Note: *For a special presentation, decorate the outside edge of each plate with minced parsley, finely diced blanched carrots, or diced red peppers.*

Gratin of Belgian Endives

WITLOOF MET HAM IN DE OVEN
•
CHICONS AU GRATIN

This dish is very popular throughout Belgium and always a best-seller on bistro menus. For a light but complete meal, serve it with mashed potatoes and a crisp green salad and have some nice fresh bread on hand to scoop up the delicious sauce.

6 to 8 Belgian endives, cored, stems removed
Juice of ½ lemon
½ teaspoon salt, plus additional to taste
3 tablespoons unsalted butter
4 tablespoons all-purpose flour
3 cups milk
1½ cups grated Gruyère cheese
Freshly ground black pepper to taste
Pinch of freshly grated nutmeg
8 thin slices boiled ham

1. Put the endives in a saucepan with just enough water to cover. Add the lemon juice and the ½ teaspoon salt. Cover, bring to a boil, then reduce the heat and let simmer until the endives are tender, 20 to 25 minutes.

Drain well but reserve 1 cup of the cooking liquid for the sauce.

2. Preheat the oven to 400°F.

3. Melt the butter in a small saucepan over medium heat. Stir in the flour and cook, stirring constantly with a wooden spoon, for 1 minute. Add the milk gradually, stirring with a wire whisk, then add the reserved cooking liquid. Cook, whisking to avoid getting any lumps, until the sauce is smooth and thickened. Let it simmer for 2 to 3 minutes longer. This is important to get rid of the pasty flavor of the flour. Remove from the heat and stir in ¼ cup of the cheese. Season to taste with salt, pepper, and nutmeg.

4. Butter a glass or enameled baking dish large enough to hold the endives in a single layer. Wrap each cooked endive in a slice of ham and place in the prepared dish. Pour the sauce over the endives and top with the remaining ¼ cup cheese. (The dish can be made ahead up to this point and refrigerated or even frozen until you are ready to proceed.)

5. Preheat the broiler.

6. Bake 15 minutes, then finish the dish for 5 minutes under the broiler to brown the cheese. Serve immediately. This is one dish that cannot sit around because the sauce will get watery.

Serves 6 to 8 as an appetizer or 4 as a light meal

Variations: If you omit the ham, this becomes a dish called Belgian Endive in Béchamel and makes a wonderful vegetable accompaniment to many main courses, most particularly to fricandeau *(the Belgian version of meat loaf, see Index). The smooth, cheese-flavored béchamel makes this slightly bitter vegetable more palatable for children.*

• *My favorite variation on this dish is to make a batch of my great grandmother Marie's Buckwheat Pancakes (see Index). Roll up each endive in a ham slice as directed above, spread each roll with 1 tablespoon béchamel, and then roll up each package in a buckwheat pancake. Arrange these in a single layer in a glass or enameled baking dish. Pour the remaining béchamel over the rolls and sprinkle with the remaining cheese. Bake as directed and finish under the broiler. This variation makes a hearty main course that is delicious and satisfying.*

Smoked Trout Mousse with Watercress Sauce

MOUSSE VAN GEROOKTE FOREL MET WATERKERS SAUS

•

MOUSSE DE TRUITE FUMEE AVEC CREME DE CRESSON

2 smoked trout (about ½ pound each)
1½ teaspoons unflavored gelatin
3 tablespoons cold water
2 tablespoons finely minced shallots
1 tablespoon olive oil
1½ teaspoons fresh lemon juice
½ teaspoon paprika
Pinch of cayenne pepper
Freshly ground black pepper to taste
¾ cup heavy (or whipping) cream, whipped to
    soft peaks
Salt if needed
Watercress leaves, for garnish
1 ripe medium tomato, peeled, seeded,
    and diced, for garnish
Watercress Sauce (recipe follows)

The rivers in the hilly south of my country, known as the Ardennes, are abundant with fresh trout, a wonderful fish that can be eaten fresh or smoked. This delicacy is frequently served plain with a squeeze of lemon juice and some boiled new potatoes. It can also be turned into this easy and popular Belgian appetizer to include on a buffet table, a picnic, or an hors d'oeuvres tray. The trout in this recipe can be replaced by other smoked fish such as salmon, eel, or haddock.

1. Remove the skin and all the bones from the smoked trout. Place the fish in the bowl of a food processor and process to a smooth purée.

2. Sprinkle the gelatin over the cold water in a small saucepan. Let stand for 5 minutes to soften. Place the saucepan over low heat and stir until the gelatin is dissolved. Remove from the heat.

3. Add the dissolved gelatin, shallots, oil, lemon juice, paprika, cayenne, and pepper to the puréed trout and process until smooth and well blended. Remove the mixture to a medium-size bowl. Fold in whipped cream and taste and adjust the seasonings.

4. Brush a 2-cup decorative fish mold with oil. (Or substitute a suitable rectangular dish or individual ramekins.) Fill with the mousse

mixture, cover with plastic wrap, and refrigerate for several hours until set. (This dish can be made 1 day ahead up to this point.)

5. To serve, dip the dish in hot water up to the rim for a couple of seconds and invert the mousse onto a platter. Decorate with watercress leaves and diced tomato. Serve with the watercress sauce and toasted white bread or good-quality crackers.

Serve 6 as an appetizer

Variation: You can prepare very elegant-looking hors d'oeuvres with this mousse, or any other fish mousse. Prepare the recipe through step 3, omitting the gelatin. Spoon the mousse mixture into a pastry bag fitted with a star tip and refrigerate until ready to use. (The mousse can be made several days ahead.) Prepare leaves of Belgian endive or cucumber stars (thick slices of cucumber cut into star shapes with a cookie cutter) or scooped-out cherry tomatoes. Pipe the fish mixture into any or all of these vegetables. Decorate with a dollop of caviar, minced-chives, or tiny dill sprigs.

Watercress Sauce

WATERKERS SAUS
•
CREME DE CRESSON

Serve this tasty sauce with the smoked trout mousse (or another fish mousse) or with cold poached salmon.

1½ tablespoons unsalted butter
1 shallot, finely minced
1 large bunch watercress, tough stems discarded, coarsely chopped
2 cups heavy (or whipping) cream
Juice of ½ lemon
1 tablespoon chopped fresh chives
Salt and freshly ground black pepper to taste

1. Melt the butter in a medium-size saucepan over low heat. Add the shallot and watercress and cook, stirring frequently, until softened, 8 to 10 minutes.

2. Transfer the watercress to a blender or food processor, add the cream, and purée. Stir in the lemon juice and chives; season to taste with salt and pepper.

3. Keep refrigerated until ready to serve, up to 2 days.

Makes 2½ cups

Variation: In step two, add a tablespoon or two of bottled horseradish to the sauce for a more piquant flavor.

Jeanne's Chicken Liver Mousse

JEANNE'S KIPPELEVER MOUSSE
•
MOUSSE DE FOIES DE VOLAILLES DE JEANNE

My grandmother called this mousse her *foie gras des pauvres* (the foie gras of the poor). And, indeed, prepared with plump, fresh chicken livers and good-quality butter, the smooth and velvety mixture melts on your tongue, so that for a moment you might be fooled. But unlike foie gras, it is inexpensive and very quick to prepare. Serve it as an hors d'oeuvre on toasted brioche or a good crispy cracker. For an appetizer course, serve the mousse with a few crisp salad greens and Onion-Raisin Marmalade (see Index).

½ pound chicken livers, trimmed, rinsed, and dried
½ cup dry white wine
8 tablespoons (1 stick) unsalted butter, at room temperature
1 tablespoon port or Madeira
1 teaspoon salt
¾ teaspoon coarsely ground black pepper
Pinch of freshly grated nutmeg
Few drops of olive oil

1. Place the chicken livers and white wine in a small saucepan and bring to a boil. Cook over medium heat for 3 to 4 minutes. The chicken livers should feel firm but still be pink in the center.

2. Drain the chicken livers and purée them in a food processor until smooth. For an even smoother texture, force the purée through a fine drum sieve into a bowl. Otherwise remove the purée to a small bowl and add the butter and port, and stir until thoroughly combined. Season with salt, pepper, and nutmeg.

3. Cover the surface of the mousse with a few drops of olive oil to keep it from drying out. Cover with aluminum foil and refrigerate until ready to serve, up to 4 days.

Serves 4 to 6

Variations: *Cover ¼ cup raisins with 5 tablespoons port wine, let stand for 1 hour, and drain. Add the raisins to the purée along with the other seasonings.*

• *Flavor the mousse with some green peppercorns.*

• *Season with a pinch of dried thyme and rosemary or oregano and 2 tablespoons diced roasted red pepper.*

Pork Liver Pâté with Prunes

FYNE VARKENSPASTEI MET PRUIMEN
•
PATE DE PORC AUX PRUNEAUX

The Belgian version of a traditional pork pâté is a masterpiece of smooth texture (imparted by the pork liver) and delicate, heady flavor bestowed by our favorite spices—cloves, nutmeg, allspice, and juniper berries. The sautéed onions, dried fruits, and fortified wine provide a sweet and hearty taste that descends directly from our medieval heritage.

Serve this and other pâtés with cornichons, a good mustard, and a crusty baguette. In Belgium we add a simple salad for a favorite light evening meal. The pâté, served in thin slices, makes an ideal appetizer as well.

¼ cup Cognac or brandy

¼ cup port

10 pitted prunes

¼ cup raisins

4 ounces lard

1 pound fresh pork liver, cut into
 1-inch cubes

½ pound pork butt or shoulder, cut into
 1-inch cubes

1 pound fresh pork belly (see Note),
 cut into 1-inch cubes, or ½ pound
 salt pork fatback, cut into 1-inch cubes
 and simmered for 10 minutes in water to
 remove the salt

2 medium onions, coarsely chopped

½ pound slab bacon, coarsely chopped

2 large eggs, lightly beaten

2 tablespoons all-purpose flour

1 tablespoon (packed) dark brown sugar

2 teaspoons dried thyme

1 bay leaf, finely crumbled

1 tablespoon salt

1 tablespoon freshly ground
 black pepper

½ teaspoon ground ginger

¼ teaspoon freshly grated nutmeg

¼ teaspoon ground allspice

¼ teaspoon ground cloves

6 juniper berries, crushed

½ pound thin sheets fresh pork fatback
 (see Note) or sliced bacon,
 to line the pâté mold

2 bay leaves

2 sprigs fresh thyme

1. Pour the Cognac and port into a small saucepan and heat to lukewarm. Place the

prunes and raisins in a bowl and cover with the Cognac mixture. Let marinate for 1 hour.

2. Melt 2 ounces of the lard in a large skillet over high heat. Add half of the liver, pork, and pork belly (or pork and salt pork substitute) and sear on all sides. Do this in two batches so as not to crowd the pan. The outsides should be browned but the insides still raw. Set aside all the seared meat.

3. In the same skillet, melt the remaining 2 ounces lard over medium heat. Add the onions and cook, stirring, until translucent but not browned, about 10 minutes.

4. Pass all the seared meat, the onions, and the chopped bacon through a meat grinder fitted with a coarse blade. If you wish, you can also grind these ingredients in a food processor; process with on and off pulses to a coarse purée. You'll need to do this in 2 batches. Remove the mixture to a large mixing bowl.

5. Preheat the oven to 325°F.

6. Add the eggs, flour, and sugar to the liver mixture and mix well. Add the raisins and the marinade but reserve the prunes. Add the dried thyme, crumbled bay leaf, salt, pepper, and all the spices; mix well. Sauté a small amount of the pâté mixture and taste it for seasoning. The pâté should be mild but not bland. What you are looking for is a harmonious ensemble of flavors, and no one of the spices should dominate. Remember, too, that you will be serving it cold, which will dull the seasoning.

7. Line a 2-quart terrine or loaf pan with the strips of fresh pork fatback or the bacon slices. Reserve a few for the top of the pâté. Spread half of the meat mixture evenly in the terrine and arrange the reserved prunes over the meat. (They will give the pâté contrast in color, texture, and flavor.) Cover with the remaining meat mixture and decorate the top with the whole bay leaves and fresh thyme sprigs. Cover the surface with strips of pork fat or bacon arranged in a lattice pattern. Cover tightly with aluminum foil and place the terrine lid on top. If you are using a loaf pan that has no lid, cover with a double layer of foil.

8. Place the terrine in a roasting pan. Add enough hot water to come two-thirds of the way up the sides of the terrine. Bake until a meat thermometer reads 160°F, 1½ to 2 hours. Check on the water in the roasting pan from time to time and add more if needed.

9. Remove the pâté from the water bath and allow it to cool to lukewarm. Remove the lid but leave the foil in place. Set a 5-pound weight on top of the foil (canned goods are excellent) to compress the pâté and make for

perfect slices. Refrigerate with the weight on at least 12 hours and up to 3 days before serving.

10. You can serve directly from your terrine mold, but remove the first slice in the kitchen to make it easier to slice and serve at the table. It is also attractive to remove the pâté from the pan. Set the pan over a hot burner for a few seconds to loosen the bottom. Run a knife around the sides of the pâté and turn it upside down on a platter. Remove excess fat, cut into slices, and serve.

Serves 8 to 10

Notes: *Fresh pork belly, also called sowbelly, is the cut that gives the smoothest texture to a pâté. This cut is hard to find in American markets, but it is worth seeking out in ethnic neighborhoods or pleading with your butcher to get some for you. In this recipe it can be substituted for with a combination of pork butt or shoulder and salt pork.*

Fresh pork fatback, which your butcher can slice into thin sheets, is ideal for lining a pâté mold. Unfortunately, it too is not easy to come by in American markets. Sliced bacon can be substituted for it. If you wish to avoid the smoky flavor of the bacon, blanch the slices for 10 minutes in simmering water.

My Grandmother's Terrine

GROOTMOEDER'S KIPPELEVER EN APPEL PATE
•
TERRINE AUX FOIES DE VOLAILLE ET POMMES

It took me several attempts and a great deal of patience to extract this recipe from my grandmother with all the ingredients measured out, but it was certainly worth waiting for. This is a wonderfully rustic, yet elegant terrine prepared with readily available ingredients. The layered slices of the terrine are very pretty. For an appetizer, arrange the slices on plates along with a colorful variety of lettuces and a few slices of poached pears.

Spread any leftover terrine on toast triangles and top with a teaspoon of Onion-Raisin Marmalade (recipe follows) or use it to make some of the best sandwiches you have ever had.

Allow two days to prepare this terrine: one to marinate the chicken livers and another to make the terrine.

Marinade:

¼ cup Cognac

2 tablespoons port

2 tablespoons medium dry sherry

½ teaspoon dried thyme

1 bay leaf, crumbled

1 tablespoon finely minced fresh parsley

1 clove garlic, smashed

½ teaspoon sugar

¼ teaspoon ground cloves

¼ teaspoon ground allspice

¼ teaspoon ground ginger

Pinch of freshly grated nutmeg

1 tablespoon olive oil

Terrine:

1¼ pounds chicken livers, trimmed

2½ tablespoons unsalted butter

1 large onion, coarsely chopped

Salt and freshly ground black pepper to taste

2 tart apples, peeled, cored, and thinly sliced

½ pound fresh pork belly (fatback, see Note,
    page 41), coarsely ground, or ½ pound salt
    pork, blanched for 10 minutes, coarsely ground

½ pound pork butt or shoulder, coarsely ground

½ pound lean slab bacon, coarsely ground

1 large egg, lightly beaten

3 tablespoons all-purpose flour

1 tablespoon salt

1 teaspoon freshly ground black pepper

1 teaspoon dried thyme

½ teaspoon ground mace or nutmeg

1 bay leaf, crushed to a fine powder

½ pound thin sheets fresh fatback or sliced bacon

⅓ cup shelled hazelnuts or pistachios

2 bay leaves

1 sprig fresh thyme

1. In a medium-size bowl, mix all the ingredients for the marinade. Rinse and dry the chicken livers. Add them to the marinade and toss to be sure they are well covered with the marinade. Cover and refrigerate overnight.

2. Melt 1 tablespoon of the butter in a large heavy skillet over low heat. Add the onion and cook, stirring, until softened but not browned, 5 to 7 minutes. Season with salt and pepper to taste and set aside.

3. Melt the remaining 1½ tablespoons butter in the same skillet over medium heat. Add the apples and sauté to soften, 3 to 4 minutes. Set aside.

4. Drain the chicken livers but reserve the marinade. Select 4 of the best-looking livers and set aside. Purée the remaining livers together with half the apple slices in a food processor. The texture will be rather liquid.

5. In a large mixing bowl, combine the ground pork fat, meat, and bacon with the puréed liver mixture and the cooked onions. Use a large wooden spoon to beat in the egg, flour, 1 tablespoon salt, 1 teaspoon pepper, the thyme, mace, crushed bay leaf, and two-thirds of the marinade (about ¼ cup). Continue mixing until everything is well blended.

6. Sauté a small amount of the terrine mixture and taste it for seasoning. Remember that you will be serving it cold, which will dull the taste somewhat. The terrine should be well seasoned.

7. Preheat the oven to 325°F.

8. Line the bottom and sides of a 2-quart terrine or loaf pan with sheets of fresh pork fatback or the bacon slices. Spread half the meat mixture in the bottom of the terrine. Make a layer of half the remaining apple slices, then a layer of half the nuts. Arrange the reserved chicken livers in a line down the center of the terrine. Cover with half the remaining meat mixture. Follow with a layer of the rest of the apple slices. Finally add the rest of the meat mixture. Press the surface firmly with the back of a wooden spoon. Sprinkle the remaining nuts over the surface and press them gently into the mixture. Decorate the top with the whole bay leaves and sprig of fresh thyme. Cover tightly with aluminum foil and cover with the lid if you have one. If not, cover with two thicknesses of aluminum foil.

9. Place the terrine in a roasting pan. Add enough hot water to come two-thirds of the way up the sides of the terrine. Bake until a meat thermometer reads 160°F, 1½ to 2 hours. Check on the water in the roasting pan from time to time and add more if needed.

10. Remove the pâté from the water bath and allow it to cool to lukewarm. Remove the lid but leave the foil in place. Set a 5-pound weight on top of the foil (canned goods are excellent) to compress the pâté and make for perfect slices. Refrigerate with the weight on for at least 12 hours up to 3 days before serving.

11. You can serve directly from your terrine mold but remove the first slice in the kitchen to make it easier to slice and serve at the table. It is also attractive to remove the pâté from the pan. Set the pan over a hot burner for a few seconds to loosen the bottom. Run a knife around the sides of the pâté and turn it upside down on a platter. Remove excess fat, cut into slices, and serve.

Serves 8 to 10

Liège

The great bustling city of Liège, known as La Cité Ardente, (the hot-blooded city), is considered to be the capitol of Wallonia, the French-speaking, southern half of Belgium. So much is francophile Liège influenced by Paris that many Belgians feel that visiting Liège is almost as good as going abroad. Georges Simenon, the great psychological crime novelist, was born in Liège and lived there throughout his early years. Later, he easily transplanted the cafés and streets of Liège to Inspector Maigret's Parisian haunts as well as setting many of his books in this city.

Liège is also the gateway to the Ardennes, and much of its cuisine is enriched by ancient recipes for game. So distinct is the cuisine of Wallonia that it deserves a cookbook it's own. Yet some dishes from this region have become so popular that they are now considered national Belgian dishes.

Onion-Raisin Marmalade

MARMELADE VAN AJUIN
EN ROZYNTJES

•

CONFITURE D'OIGNONS
ET DE RAISINS

---

1 medium-large onion (about ½ pound),
    thinly sliced
½ cup raisins or currants
¼ cup sugar
1¼ cups hearty red wine, such as a Burgundy
⅓ cup port
1 stick cinnamon (2 inches long)
Pinch of ground allspice
½ teaspoon salt
½ teaspoon freshly ground black pepper

1. Combine all the ingredients in a stainless steel or enameled saucepan. Cook, covered, over medium-low heat for 30 minutes. Uncover and continue cooking, stirring occasionally, until the mixture is as thick as marmalade, another 45 to 60 minutes. Transfer the marmalade to a bowl and let cool.

2. Serve with pâtés and terrines. The marmalade will keep for several weeks in the refrigerator in a tightly closed jar.

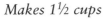

Makes 1½ cups

Leek Tart

POREI TAART

•

FLAMICHE

The *flamiche* that we are familiar with today is most often flavored with leeks and sometimes also with smoky bacon. Some cooks like to sauté the leeks with a little white wine, while others follow the old recipes from the monasteries and cook their leeks in dark Abbey beer. The beer imparts a very original and quite Flemish flavor to this wonderful tart.

Basic Flemish Pie Crust (recipe follows)
2 tablespoons unsalted butter
4 large leeks, white and light green parts only,
    rinsed well and sliced into 1-inch thick rings
Salt and freshly ground black pepper to taste
2 tablespoons white wine or dark abbey beer,
    such as Orval or Trappist (optional)
3 ounces slab bacon, cut into 1 × ¼-inch strips
    (optional)
3 large eggs
1 cup half-and-half
Pinch of freshly grated nutmeg
1 ounce Belgian Gouda or Gruyère cheese,
    grated

1. Line a 10-inch porcelain pie plate or a deep tart pan with a removable bottom with the dough. Trim and crimp the edges. Prick the bottom all over with a fork and line the dough with a sheet of aluminum foil. Fill with dried beans or rice or pie weights to keep the dough flat and refrigerate for 30 minutes.

2. Preheat the oven to 400°F.

3. Bake the pastry for 10 minutes. Remove the pie weights and foil and bake the pastry for another 10 minutes. The crust should be set (cooked halfway through) but not browned. Remove from the oven and let cool while you prepare the filling.

4. Reduce the oven heat to 350°F.

5. Melt the butter in a medium-size saucepan. Add the leeks, salt, pepper, and the wine if using. Cook the leeks, covered, over medium heat for 15 minutes. Do not let them brown.

6. If using the bacon, sauté the bacon strips in a skillet for 5 minutes over high heat to render some of the fat.

7. In a mixing bowl, lightly beat the eggs together with the half-and-half. Season to taste with salt, pepper, and nutmeg.

8. Drain the leeks and spread them over the bottom of the pie crust together with the bacon. Pour the egg mixture over the leeks and sprinkle the grated cheese over the top.

9. Bake until the custard is set and a knife inserted in the middle comes out clean, 20 to 25 minutes. Let the tart set for 10 to 15 minutes before serving. Cut into wedges and serve. The tart is best eaten while it is still warm.

Serves 6 to 8 as an appetizer

Variations: Substitute 1 pound puff pastry for the pie pastry. Roll it out ⅛-inch thick but do not prebake it. Add the filling ingredients just as for pie pastry and bake as directed.

• *In the region of Mechelen (Malines) where the tender, delicate white asparagus is cultivated, asparagus tips are substituted for the leeks, and smoked salmon or a handful of North Sea shrimp is substituted for the bacon. It makes an extravagant and delicious quiche.*

Basic Flemish Pie Crust

KRUIMELDEEG
•
PATE BRISEENS

This is a homey, all-purpose type of crust, suitable for quiche and other single-crust savory pies. You can make the dough when you feel like it and keep it on hand in the refrigerator for 2 to 3 days or in the freezer up to several months.

The easiest and quickest way to prepare a pie crust is in your food processor, where it is only a matter of a few minutes work. The first time I demonstrated this to my grandmother her eyes first widened with astonishment, then she quickly declared that the crust could not possibly meet her high standards. In fact it did, and she agreed that this was truly progress, but she continues to make her own pâte brisée by hand.

If you are making pie crust by hand, you should work quickly so the heat from your fingers does not melt the butter. Either way, do not overwork the dough or the pie crust will be tough.

2 cups all-purpose flour
8 tablespoons (1 stick) unsalted butter,
 chilled and cut into small cubes
1 large egg
½ teaspoon salt
⅓ cup ice-cold water

By food processor:

1. Measure the flour into the bowl of food processor and pulse on and off for a few seconds.

2. Add the butter, egg, and salt and pulse the machine on and off a few times until the mixture has a very coarse texture and the pieces of butter are about the size of small peas.

3. With the food processor on, add the water through the feed tube a little at a time until the dough just holds together. (Do not let the dough form into a ball or it will be overworked and tough.) Stop immediately. Scrape the dough from the processor.

By hand:

1. Sift the flour onto your work surface. Make a well in the center.

2. Into the well, add the butter, egg, and salt. Use your fingertips to blend the flour into the butter and egg until the mixture has a very coarse texture and the pieces of butter are about the size of small peas.

3. Add the water a little at a time, blending with your fingertips until you have a dough that you can knead. Knead very briefly.

Either method:

4. Shape the dough into a thick disk. Wrap in plastic wrap. Refrigerate at least 1 hour.

5. When the dough is chilled, roll it out ⅛ inch thick on a lightly floured surface with a lightly floured rolling pin or between two sheets of plastic wrap or parchment paper. If the dough is still a little sticky, let it harden in the freezer for a few minutes. Do not work with sticky dough.

6. Drape the dough loosely on your rolling pin and unroll it onto the pie plate without stretching the dough. Pat it gently into place with your fingers. Trim away the excess so that the dough is just slightly bigger than the pie plate. Make a fluted edge by pinching the edges of the dough with your fingers or press the edges all around with the tines of a fork.

Makes one 9- to 11-inch pie crust.

Ham and Belgian Endive Tart

BRABANTSE QUICHE
•
QUICHE AUX ENDIVES ET JAMBON

After decades of enjoying all sorts of quiches, some of us are difficult to surprise with yet another variation. Still, I think that the Brabantse quiche with its rich filling of sweet cooked endives, ham, and Gouda cheese will delight and satisfy quiche lovers. In Belgium these ingredients are a classic combination, and once you've experienced it, you will understand why it is such a happy one.

Basic Flemish Pie Crust (page 45)
2 tablespoons unsalted butter
3 to 4 Belgian endives (about 1½ pounds), cored and sliced lengthwise into thin slivers
Salt and freshly ground black pepper to taste
½ teaspoon confectioners' sugar
½ teaspoon fresh lemon juice
2 large eggs
1 cup half-and-half
Freshly grated nutmeg to taste
5 ounces boiled or baked ham, cut into ½-inch cubes
2 ounces Belgian Gouda or Gruyère cheese, grated
1 tablespoon chopped fresh chives or parsley

1. Line a 10-inch porcelain pie plate or a deep tart pan with a removable bottom with the dough. Trim and crimp the edges. Prick the bottom all over with a fork and line the dough with a sheet of aluminum foil. Fill with dried beans or rice or pie weights to keep the dough flat and refrigerate for 30 minutes.

2. Preheat the oven to 400°F.

3. Bake the pastry for 10 minutes. Remove the pie weights and foil and bake the pastry for another 10 minutes. The crust should be set (cooked halfway through) but not browned. Remove from the oven and let cool while you prepare the filling.

4. Reduce the oven heat to 350°F.

5. Melt the butter in a large heavy skillet. Add endives, salt, pepper, and sugar; sprinkle with the lemon juice. Cook, covered, over medium heat until the endives are soft and lightly caramelized, about 20 minutes. Stir from time to time to make sure the endives do not burn.

6. In a mixing bowl, lightly beat the eggs together with the half-and-half. Season to taste with salt, pepper, and a generous grating of nutmeg.

7. Spread the endives and the ham over the bottom of the pie crust. Pour the egg mixture over and sprinkle with the cheese and then the chives.

8. Bake until the custard is set and a knife inserted in the middle comes out clean, 20 to 25 minutes.

9. Let the quiche set for 10 to 15 minutes before serving. Cut into wedges and serve while still warm.

Serves 6 to 8

Quiche or Flamiche?

In the United States quiche is a relative newcomer, but it appeared in Flanders as early as 1385, around the time of the annexation of the "low countries" (what is Belgium and most of Holland today) by the Burgundian dukes. In the following hundred years, the arts flourished in Flanders as never before. This was the age of the Flemish painters Memling, Van der Weyden, and Van Eyck, as well as a time of giant festivals, tournaments, jousts, banquets, and ceremonies.

What is not quite clear is why the quiche, which is said to have come from Burgundy, is called flamiche (Flemish). Could it be that the princes of Burgundy brought this savory tart back to their own homeland and simply appropriated the credit for its invention? I suppose that we will never resolve this issue.

What we do know is that originally flamiche was made with leftover bread dough and baked in the gradually cooling wood oven after the day's loaves were done. The favored fillings were savory and cheese based, but sweet fillings were popular as well. Flamiche was, and continues to be, the kind of food that lends itself to improvisation, and chefs today continue to delight and surprise with their imaginative creations.

Quiche with Gorgonzola and Asparagus

QUICHE MET GORGONZOLA EN ASPERGES

•

QUICHE AU GORGONZOLA ET ASPERGES

This is definitely a nouvelle cuisine creation, as it pairs Italian Gorgonzola or French Roquefort with one of Belgium's most beloved vegetables—asparagus. I have replaced the heavy cream called for in the original recipe with the fresh cheese, *platte kaas*, that my great grandmother used to make, and the result is a light, airy custard that is a perfect foil for the sharp cheese and the tender green taste of the asparagus.

Serve it warm as an appetizer or first course, or as a light meal accompanied by a crunchy salad.

1 pound asparagus, peeled and tied in a bundle with kitchen string
Basic Flemish Pie Crust (page 45)
1⅓ cups Homemade Fresh Cheese (page 22)
¼ pound Gorgonzola or Roquefort cheese
3 large eggs
1 tablespoon finely minced fresh chives
Freshly ground black pepper to taste

1. Bring a large pot of salted water to a boil. Add the asparagus and cook 1 minute. Remove the asparagus, drain, and let cool slightly. Cut into 2-inch pieces and set aside.

2. Line a 10-inch porcelain pie plate or a deep tart pan with a removable bottom with the dough. Trim and crimp the edges. Prick the bottom all over with a fork and line the dough with a sheet of aluminum foil. Fill with dried beans or rice or pie weights to keep the dough flat and refrigerate for 30 minutes.

3. Preheat the oven to 400°F.

4. Bake the pastry for 10 minutes. Remove the pie weights and foil and bake for another 10 minutes. The crust should be set (cooked halfway through) but not browned. Remove from the oven and let cool while you prepare the filling.

5. Reduce the oven heat to 350°F.

6. Mix together the fresh cheese and Gorgonzola either in a food processor or in a mixing bowl with a fork. Add the eggs, one at a time, mixing until they are well blended. Stir in the chives and pepper. The Gorgonzola or Roquefort is usually salty enough to flavor the whole dish.

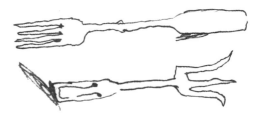

7. Arrange the asparagus over the bottom of the pie crust and pour the cheese mixture over it. Bake until the custard is set and a knife inserted in the middle comes out clean, 25 to 30 minutes.

8. Let the quiche set for 10 to 15 minutes. Cut into wedges and serve while still warm.

Serves 6 to 8

Variation: For special occasions I love to make this quiche in individual servings. Pre-bake the pastry in individual 1½- to 2-inch tartlet pans lined with aluminum foil and filled with dried beans or rice or pie weights for 5 minutes. Remove the foil and pie weights and bake for 2 minutes longer. Fill each tartlet pan two-thirds full with the cheese mixture and garnish each one with an asparagus tip. Bake until a knife inserted in the center comes out clean, 7 to 12 minutes, depending on the size of the pan.

These very elegant hors d'oeuvres can be made in advance and warmed in the oven before serving.

Soups

Soups

For centuries in deep rural Flanders, hearty soups reflecting the fruits of the season were the basis of most people's daily ration of food. From the Middle Ages through the Renaissance and into the 20th century, soup remained the soul of the midday meal. Paintings depicting daily life often included scenes of happy people eating their soup.

To this day, I don't know of any country that celebrates soup as much as Belgium and I believe they have some of the greatest soups of the world. Belgian soups range from the simple to the sophisticated. Some, like the aristocratic white asparagus soup, make a sublime beginning to a sumptuous meal; others, like the earthy and chunky *hutsepot*, enriched with beef, pork, or lamb, could feed a family for days. There are smooth purées of spinach, cauliflower, carrots, and tomatoes rich in taste and flavor but

> *Men especially feel deprived if their dinner does not start with soup, and I've seen strong men being pitiful about this.*
>
> —*Nika Hazelton*
> The Belgian
> Cookbook

healthfully thickened only with potatoes. Traditional *waterzooi*, a specialty of my own hometown of Ghent, is said to have been one of King Charles V's favorite meals back in the 1600s. The very Belgian *waterzooi*, not quite a soup and not quite a stew, is one of the few medieval dishes that has survived into modern times. There are restaurants in Ghent that specialize in preparing and serving mostly *waterzooi*. Other very specifically Belgian soups include the milk and buttermilk soups, *taatjespap* for one, that are part of our Lenten traditions. And from the North Sea, we have the many bouillabaise- and chowder-style soups made with the excellent fish and shellfish of that region.

It is no wonder, then, that most Belgians eat soup every day, whether at home or in cafés, bistros, and restaurants, and that a proper meal must always include a plate of good, carefully prepared soup.

Marie's Chicken Broth

MARIE'S KIPPEBOUILLON
FOND DE VOLAILLE

Making your own chicken broth is definitely worth the bit of extra work required. With a little planning, you can have the ingredients on hand in your freezer to make a stock whenever you have a few spare minutes. It's easy to make a habit of saving chicken parts in the freezer, accumulating necks, backs, wing tips, and gizzards, until you are ready to make a stock. Save chicken livers for pâté and never add them to chicken broth, for they will impart an unpleasant, bitter flavor.

The rewards of homemade broth, of course, are many. As the foundation of any number of sauces, stews, and soups, it will enhance the flavor of all these dishes. In much of today's "light" cooking, a well-reduced and defatted chicken broth often replaces butter and/or cream.

2 pounds chicken parts (necks, backs, and gizzards not including the liver), or 1 chicken (about 3 pounds) cut into pieces, well rinsed
3 quarts cold water
1 large onion, peeled and halved
4 whole cloves
2 carrots, peeled and cut into thirds
3 ribs celery, cut into 3-inch lengths
1 leek, trimmed, rinsed well, and cut into chunks
1 tablespoon black peppercorns
Bouquet garni: 1 sprig fresh thyme or ¼ teaspoon dried thyme, 3 sprigs parsley, and 2 bay leaves tied together with kitchen string or in a piece of cheesecloth

1. Place the chicken parts in a large stockpot, cover with the cold water, and bring to a boil over high heat. Boil gently for 5 minutes and skim off as much of the fat and foam as you can.

2. Stud the onion halves with the cloves and add them to the pot with the carrots, celery, leeks, peppercorns, and bouquet garni. Reduce the heat and simmer, uncovered, for 3 to 4 hours. Skim occasionally to remove as much fat as possible.

3. Strain the broth into a large bowl or pot and discard the chicken parts and vegetables. (All the flavor will have cooked out of them.) Taste the broth; if you would like to reduce it further for a stronger taste, return it to the pot and cook over high heat to the desired strength.

4. Cool the broth as quickly as possible. I usually plunge the bowl or pot that is holding

53

the broth into an ice bath in my sink. This cools the soup quickly and prevents the broth from spoiling.

5. Cover and refrigerate when cool. Any remaining fat will congeal on the surface when the broth has been refrigerated overnight and can be easily removed. Chicken broth will keep in the refrigerator for 3 to 4 days or in the freezer for up to 6 months.

Makes 2 quarts

Note: *I never add salt when preparing broth, thereby preventing it from becoming too salty while it reduces. Salt may be added when the broth is completely finished but I generally don't add salt until the broth has been added to the finished dish.*

Grandmother's Trick

Be a kitchen-smart cook and prepare a meal while you are making broth.

Poach a whole chicken for later use (as in a chicken salad, for example) by adding it to your broth for the last hour of cooking. When it is tender, remove it carefully and set aside. Proceed with the broth recipe as directed.

Your poached chicken will be tender, juicy, and full of flavor, and at the same time, will have contributed its own flavor to the broth.

Marie's Beef Broth

MARIE'S VLEESBOUILLON
•
FOND BLANC DE BOEUF

In the Flemish countryside of my great grandmother Marie's day, the farm wife often started her bouillon in the evening, letting it simmer through the night on top of the slowly dying wood stove. Nothing was ever wasted, not even the heat of the stove.

Times have changed and the wood stove is mostly gone, but every serious home cook still appreciates the value of homemade beef broth. The beginning of winter is a particularly good time to go through the rituals of making quantities of beef broth to "stock up" your freezer for the many winter soups and stews that require this flavorful base.

3 pounds beef shank or stewing beef
2 pounds beef or veal bones
6 quarts cold water
3 leeks, trimmed, rinsed well, and sliced
2 medium onions, quartered
2 ribs celery, cut into thirds
2 tablespoons tomato paste
1 tablespoon black peppercorns
Bouquet garni: 1 sprig fresh thyme or
¼ teaspoon dried thyme, 3 sprigs parsley, and
2 bay leaves tied together with kitchen string
or in a piece of cheesecloth

Bouillon on Schedule

My great grandmother was what we called a sacré petit bout de femme (a tough little woman), and she was not only extremely well organized but also very stubborn. There was just one right way to do things and that was her way. She'd say "If you want to serve lunch at one, you'd better start your bouillon before nine if you haven't done it the night before." A big kettle was filled with water, a nice beef shank was added to all the leftover bones, necks, and chicken parts from the previous day. In went carrots, celery, leeks, and a big onion studded with cloves, along with a handful of herbs. Around eleven, and no earlier, it was time to have another cup of coffee while fortifying the soup with a juicy piece of beef, or an oxtail, or, if it was the end of the month and the household budget very tight, a small slab of fresh bacon. The broth might be served for lunch with boiled potatoes, a sweet caramelized onion sauce, and the vegetables she would

have picked in her potager (kitchen garden) that same morning.

The leftover meats were served the next day with mustard and pickled cornichons, poached cauliflower dressed with shallot and parsley mayonnaise, or simply sliced tomatoes. Once a week she baked all her own bread—large, crusty wheels of whole-grain country bread. She would hold the wheel of bread against her breast, making the sign of the cross with her knife to bless the bread and thank the Lord before slicing it, as was the custom in the Catholic countryside.

But my great grandmother's best culinary secret was using the broth as the basis of her vegetable soups—soups with tomatoes or peas or leeks. The vegetables varied according to what was currently available in her garden. Only the potatoes she added for thickening and consistency were a constant ingredient.

Bread, soup, vegetables, and a little meat was the daily diet she and her family lived and thrived on. Today we know that it is one we could all follow to advantage.

1. Place the meat and bones in a large stockpot, add the cold water, and bring to a boil over high heat. Let boil for 10 minutes, skimming off as much foam and fat as possible from the surface of the liquid.

2. Reduce the heat and add the leeks, onions, celery, tomato paste, peppercorns, and bouquet garni. Simmer, uncovered, over low heat for 4 to 5 hours, skimming occasionally.

3. Strain the broth through a fine-meshed sieve into a large bowl or pot and discard the solids. Allow the broth to cool as quickly as possible. (I usually plunge the bowl or pot that is holding the broth into an ice bath in my sink. This cools the soup quickly and prevents the broth from spoiling.) Refrigerate the broth overnight and

remove the fat that will have congealed on the surface. Keep in the refrigerator for 3 to 4 days or up to 6 months in the freezer.

Makes 3 to 4 quarts

Fish Broth

VISBOUILLON
•
FUMET DE POISSON

*L*ike chicken and meat broths, fish broth is wonderful to have on hand for a great variety of fish soups, stews, and sauces. It is much quicker to make than chicken or meat broth, but I still prefer to do it ahead and freeze it, so as not have the extra step when I want to make a special fish dish.

The backbones of flounder and sole are said to make the very best fish stock, but the bones from almost any white nonoily fish will be good. Avoid using the bones and trimmings from any dark-fleshed oily fish, such as mackerel or bluefish, as they will have a very strong and unpleasant flavor.

3 tablespoons unsalted butter

2 medium onions, coarsely chopped, or
    2 leeks, white and pale green parts only,
    trimmed, rinsed well, and sliced

1 rib celery, sliced

2 pounds fish bones, heads, tails, and trimmings
    from white-fleshed, nonoily fish, such as sole,
    flounder, or cod

2 quarts cold water

2 cups dry white wine

½ lemon, peeled to remove all the white pith
    and sliced

2 teaspoons salt

1 tablespoon black peppercorns

Bouquet garni: 1 sprig fresh thyme or
    ¼ teaspoon dried thyme, 3 sprigs parsley, and
    2 bay leaves tied together with kitchen string
    or in a piece of cheesecloth

1. Melt the butter in a large stockpot over medium heat. Add the onions and celery; cook, stirring, until softened, about 5 minutes. Add the fish bones, heads, tails, and trimmings; cook, stirring, for another 5 minutes.

2. Add the cold water, wine, lemon, salt, peppercorns, and bouquet garni. Bring slowly to a boil, skimming frequently. Reduce the heat and simmer, uncovered, for 20 minutes.

3. Strain the broth into a large bowl or pot, discarding all the solids. Cool the broth as quickly as possible. (I usually plunge the bowl or pot into an ice bath in my sink. This cools the soup quickly and prevents the broth from spoiling.) Refrigerate for 2 to 3 days or freeze for up to 6 months.

Makes about 2 quarts

Variation: Shrimp shells and/or lobster shells may be added to the fish bones for a more intense seafood flavor.

• *A handful of mushrooms or mushroom stems cooked with the onion and celery will deepen the flavor of the broth.*

My Mother's Cream of Tomato Soup

TOMATEN ROOMSOEP
•
CREME DE TOMATES

This lovely soup has achieved a very lofty status in Belgium. In the last century it has become a symbol of opulence and festivity, and no great occasion, wedding dinner, anniversary, or other special celebration is complete without it. And no wonder, for it is as different from ordinary tomato soup as it is possible to be. Smooth and creamy, it has little bits of fresh tomato to

enliven it, and the rich flavor of Madeira or Cognac provides a suave and sophisticated undertone. There is no better starter for a fine meal and you can easily make it a day ahead. My mother's version of this soup is the best I have ever had.

5 tablespoons unsalted butter
1 medium onion, finely chopped
1 carrot, peeled and finely chopped
2 pounds ripe tomatoes, peeled, seeded, and
    coarsely chopped, or 1 can (28 ounces) whole
    tomatoes with their juices, coarsely chopped
1½ teaspoons sugar
Pinch of cayenne pepper
Salt to taste
4 tablespoons all-purpose flour
3½ to 4 cups beef or chicken broth, preferably
    homemade (page 54 or 53)
¾ cup heavy (or whipping) cream
2 to 4 tablespoons Madeira or Cognac,
    or more to taste
Freshly ground black pepper
    to taste

Garnish:
1 tablespoon unsalted butter
1 ripe tomato, peeled, seeded, and cut into
    small cubes
Finely minced fresh chives, chervil, or parsley

1. Melt 2 tablespoons of the butter in a large soup kettle over medium heat. Add the onion and carrot and cook, stirring occasionally with a wooden spoon, until softened but not browned, 8 to 10 minutes.

2. Add the tomatoes, sugar, cayenne, and a little salt. Cook gently over low heat for 20 minutes, stirring occasionally. Let the tomato mixture cool slightly, then purée it in a blender or food processor or press it through a food mill. Set aside.

3. Melt the remaining 3 tablespoons butter in the soup kettle over low heat. Sprinkle the flour over the melted butter and stir until smooth. Gradually add the broth while stirring constantly with a wire whisk. Continue to cook until you have a thick, velvety white sauce the consistency of heavy cream. Still whisking, let it boil up once or twice to get rid of any pasty flour taste.

4. Remove the soup from the heat and whisk in the tomato mixture. Let rest until just before serving. (The soup may be prepared a day ahead up to this point. Cool to room temperature and refrigerate covered.)

5. Gently reheat the tomato soup but be careful not to let it come to a boil. Stir in the cream and Madeira. Season to taste with salt and pepper. The soup can be reheated later but do not let it come to a boil or the cream will curdle.

6. Prepare the garnish: Melt the butter in a small skillet over medium heat. Add the tomato and sauté for 1 minute. Season with salt and pepper and stir into the hot tomato soup. Sprinkle with the minced fresh herbs and serve at once.

Serves 6

How to Peel and Seed Tomatoes

Core each tomato and make an X with a small knife on the bottom. Drop each tomato into a pot of boiling water and remove with a slotted spoon after 20 to 30 seconds. Immediately hold each tomato under cold running water to stop them from cooking. Peel away the skin. Slice each tomato in half horizontally and squeeze lightly in your palm to extract most of the seeds and juices.

Tomato Soup with Little Meatballs

TOMATENSOEP MET BALLEKES
•
SOUPE AUX TOMATES ET QUENELLES DE VIANDE

This soup, one of my grandmother Jeanne's specialties, is a wonderful combination of delicate flavor and satisfying heartiness.

It is a favorite at family dinners, but my grandmother always said she had to ladle it out with a fair and watchful hand to make sure that the delicious little meatballs were evenly distributed.

Soup:
2½ tablespoons unsalted butter
1 medium onion, coarsely chopped
1 leek, white and pale green parts only, trimmed, rinsed well, and coarsely chopped (double the amount of onion if no leeks are on hand)
1 carrot, peeled and chopped
1 cup coarsely chopped celery
3½ cups beef broth, preferably homemade (page 54)
2 pounds ripe tomatoes, peeled, seeded, and coarsely chopped, or 1 can (28 ounces) peeled whole tomatoes
1 large baking potato, peeled and cut into 1-inch cubes
2 tablespoons minced fresh parsley
1 bay leaf
1 to 1½ teaspoons sugar, if needed
Salt and freshly ground black pepper to taste
½ cup heavy (or whipping) cream or whole milk (optional)

Meatballs:
6 ounces ground veal or a mixture of ground veal and pork (see Note)
1 tablespoon minced fresh parsley
Pinch of freshly grated nutmeg
¼ teaspoon salt, or to taste
Freshly ground black pepper to taste

1. For the soup, melt 1½ tablespoons of the butter in a large saucepan over medium heat. Add the onion, leek, carrot, and celery; cook, stirring, until the vegetables are softened, about 10 minutes. Do not let them brown.

2. Add the beef broth, tomatoes, potato, parsley, and bay leaf. Bring to a boil and reduce the heat to low. Cover and simmer until the vegetables are very soft, 40 to 50 minutes.

3. Remove from the heat and allow the soup to cool slightly. Discard the bay leaf, then purée the soup in batches in a blender or food processor. Return the puréed soup to the saucepan and taste for seasoning. Add a little sugar if necessary. This will depend on the acidity of the tomatoes. The soup should taste smooth, neither acidic nor sweet. Add salt if necessary and a generous grinding of black pepper.

4. While the soup is simmering, prepare the meatballs: Bring a large pot of salted water to a boil. Mix the ground meat with the parsley, nutmeg, salt, and pepper until combined. Coat the palms of your hands with flour and shape the meat into little balls the size of marbles. You should have about 20 meatballs. Drop the meatballs into the boiling water and poach until they float to the surface, 2 to 3 minutes. Remove the meatballs with a slotted spoon and set aside.

5. When ready to serve, heat the soup but do not let it boil. Whisk in the cream if using and the remaining 1 tablespoon butter. If you are dieting, forget this final step. The soup will still be delicious. Add the meatballs to the soup just before serving, and make sure that

everyone gets a fair share of delicious "marbles" in their plate.

Serves 6

Note: *In Belgium, ground meat is very popular and turns up in many home-cooked specialties. Usually every butcher prepares several different mixtures of ground meat—veal, pork, and beef;*

pork and beef; or veal and pork as is usually called for in this soup. Feel free to use whatever ground meat is available in your market and to experiment with your own combinations.

Variation: *These same meatballs can also be served in Chervil Soup, Flemish Carrot Soup, or simply in homemade chicken broth (see Index for page numbers).*

Tips on Making Soup

*Y*ou don't have to be a gourmet chef nor do you need to have a fat wallet to make great soups. Most soups improve when reheated, so you lose nothing by preparing your soups ahead of time and gain, instead, a treasure trove of instant meals.

1. Keep your soup at a simmer. Don't let it boil or you will end up with a cloudy soup and an altered flavor. This is especially important when reheating soup. Soups that are thickened with potatoes get an off flavor if they are boiled. Soups with cream or eggs in them will curdle if they are boiled.

2. Respect the cooking times indicated in the recipes. Vegetables should be soft but not soggy and overcooked.

3. Nothing beats the flavor of vegetables cooked in fresh butter. The quantity of butter in my recipes has been reduced to a minimum, only enough to add a suave flavor to certain soups. If you wish, a mild-flavored vegetable oil, like safflower or canola, can be substituted. I would stay away from olive oil, as its strong taste would alter the Flemish character of the soups.

4. A good stock—beef, chicken, or fish—is the foundation of many soups. It profoundly affects the flavor and character of the whole soup. It is not difficult to make in quantity and keep on hand in your freezer. But if you have no homemade stock and don't have time to make some, you can still make a perfectly good soup with a good-quality canned broth or with bouillon cubes. I prefer Knorr bouillon cubes to all others and dissolve 1 bouillon cube in 4 cups water. The flavor of this diluted bouillon doesn't overpower the natural, delicate flavors of the vegetables and herbs. Don't forget that canned broth and bouillon cubes are usually very highly salted. Add your salt and pepper at the end and taste frequently while doing so.

5. All soups will keep for 3 to 4 days in the refrigerator. Simply reheat and serve. If freezing, label the freezer container with the name of the soup and the date. Cream soups should be frozen before adding the cream or any herb garnish. Once the soup is thawed and reheated, proceed with the step calling for the cream. An herb garnish can be added before serving.

Cream of Belgian Endive Soup

B R A B A N T S E
W I T L O O F R O O M S O E P
•
C R E M E   D ' E N D I V E S

The Belgian endive originated in Brussels and is raised today with meticulous care and patience on small family farms in Brabant. A well-tended acre will produce 10,000 pounds of Belgian endives in one season. The season for Belgian endive lasts from October through May. During that time it is prepared in a variety of ways, but one of the most unique is this suave, velvety soup. It makes an ideal beginning to a special-occasion dinner, and despite its elegant taste and appearance, it is extremely easy to make and even can be made a day ahead.

2 tablespoons unsalted butter
1 medium onion, finely diced
1 medium leek, white and pale green parts only, rinsed well and sliced into thin rounds
1 rib celery, trimmed and diced
4 large Belgian endives, cored and coarsely chopped
1 tablespoon all-purpose flour
4 cups warm chicken broth, preferably home-made (page 53)
⅛ teaspoon freshly grated nutmeg
Salt and freshly ground black pepper to taste
½ cup heavy (or whipping) cream
2 tablespoons minced fresh chives, for garnish

1. Melt the butter in a heavy soup pot over medium heat. Add the onion, leek, celery, and endives and cook, stirring, until the vegetables are wilted but not browned, 3 to 5 minutes. Stir in the flour, shaking the pan to coat the vegetables evenly, and cook, stirring constantly, for 1 minute.

2. Pour the warm chicken broth over the vegetables and stir well. Simmer, covered, until the vegetables are tender, about 30 minutes. Add the nutmeg, salt, and pepper.

3. Transfer to a bowl and let cool slightly. Purée the soup in batches in a blender or food processor and return it to the soup pot. (The soup can be made ahead up to this point. Covered, it will keep in the refrigerator for 1 or 2 days. Reheat before proceeding.) Gradually stir in the cream and heat through, but do not boil.

4. Garnish with the chives and serve hot.

Serves 4 to 6

Flemish Carrot Soup

WORTELSOEP OP Z'N VLAAMS
•
SOUPE DE CAROTTES A LA FLAMANDE

A healthy and delicious soup flavored with the favorite Flemish trio: leeks, thyme, and bay leaf. As carrots are available year round, you don't need to wait for the right season to make this soup.

3 tablespoons unsalted butter
3 medium leeks, white and light green parts
    only, rinsed well and sliced into thin rings
1 large onion, sliced
2 cups chicken broth, preferably homemade
    (page 53)
4 cups water
1½ pounds carrots, peeled and cut into
    1-inch slices
1 large baking potato, peeled and cubed
1 tablespoon fresh thyme or 1½ teaspoons
    dried thyme
1 bay leaf
1 cup milk, plus additional if needed
Salt and freshly ground white pepper to taste
2 tablespoons minced fresh parsley
Croutons, flavored with parsley and thyme
    (page 75)

1. Melt the butter in a heavy soup pot over medium heat. Add the leeks and onion; cook, stirring until softened but not browned, about 10 minutes.

2. Add the chicken broth, the water, carrots, potato, thyme, and bay leaf. Simmer, covered, until the vegetables are very soft, 35 to 40 minutes. Remove from the heat and let cool a little. Discard the bay leaf.

3. Purée the soup in small batches in a blender or food processor. Return to the soup pot and stir in the milk (add a little more if the soup is too thick). Season with salt and pepper. Reheat the soup and serve sprinkled with minced parsley. Pass a bowl of freshly made croutons at the table.

Serves 4 to 6

Variations: *This soup is also good made with pumpkin or butternut or acorn squash. Peel 1½ pounds pumpkin or squash and cut into cubes. Use in place of the carrots.*

• *You can substitute 1 bunch scallions for the leeks.*

• *For a delicious variation, leave out the leeks and cook 5 minced garlic cloves with the onion. Add 2 roasted, peeled, and diced red bell peppers with the carrots. The result is a very vivid and intensely flavored soup.*

Soup at Sea

*I*n many ways the daily soups of my childhood are as much a part of my heritage as the finely carved oak bride-trunk and the sturdy old Flemish dresser that now decorate my mother's room. From generation to generation, the recipes evolved so that today my great grandmother's beef broth is sometimes replaced by a lighter chicken stock, or even by water alone, but the basic principles remain the same.

Soup is the backbone of all family meals. My grandmother Jeanne and my mother, Anny, are renowned for their delicious soups. As for me, there is no doubt that soups are among my favorite foods, and, in fact, there have been times when soup has saved my life.

I have loved sailing from the time I was a little girl. In 1984 I was in love with a man who was also an avid sailor. So we set out on a great adventure. We left Belgium on a 33-foot sailboat, and for the next three years we roamed around the world. We stopped in many places, living for a time in Africa, South America, and the Caribbean. But there were long periods when we were far out to sea and there were days when the sea got so rough and my poor stomach so upset that a light soup was the only food that would give me any relief. On land, wherever in the world I may be cooking, I always start with soup when I plan a menu because I know that soup will never let me down.

Leek and Potato Soup

PREI SOEP
•
SOUPE AUX POIREAUX

*A*nother farmhouse classic in which two humble ingredients combine to make a sublime soup. Nothing is simpler to make, and no other soup provides the same soothing comfort and infallibly delicious taste.

3 tablespoons unsalted butter
5 large leeks, white and light green parts only, rinsed well and sliced into thin rounds
1 pound baking potatoes (2 large), peeled and cubed
5 cups chicken broth, preferably homemade (page 53)
1 cup milk
Salt and freshly ground white pepper to taste

1. Melt the butter in a medium-size soup pot over low heat. Add the leeks and cook, stirring occasionally, for 15 minutes. The leeks should be softened but not browned. Remove ¾ cup of the cooked leeks and reserve.

2. Add the potatoes and chicken broth to the remaining leeks. Bring to a boil and reduce the heat. Simmer, covered, until the vegetables are soft, 20 to 25 minutes.

3. Let the soup cool slightly, then press through a food mill or purée in batches in a blender or food processor. Return the purée to the soup pot and stir in the milk. Add the reserved leeks. Reheat slowly but do not let the soup boil. Season with salt and pepper. Serve hot in warmed soup plates.

Serves 6

Cream of White Asparagus Soup from Mechelen

MECHELSE ASPARAGUS SOEP
•
VELOUTE AUX ASPERGES DE MALINES

White asparagus, with its mild and very delicate flavor, is the prime ingredient of this very luxurious soup, and there is really no substitute for it. For years white asparagus has been all but impossible to find in the United States except processed in cans. I am happy to see that increasing numbers of specialty grocers are carrying white asparagus imported from Holland, and I hope that in years to come American growers will start to produce a local variety of this great delicacy. So be on the lookout for these pale beauties and celebrate spring as we do in Belgium with royal cream of asparagus soup.

1½ pounds white asparagus
6 tablespoons (¾ stick) unsalted butter
6 cups chicken broth, preferably homemade (page 53)
2 cups boiling salted water
3 tablespoons all-purpose flour
Salt and freshly ground white pepper to taste
½ cup heavy (or whipping) cream
1 large egg yolk
2 tablespoons finely minced fresh chervil, plus a few chervil leaves for garnish

64

1. Peel the asparagus stalks meticulously with a sharp vegetable peeler. Break off the tips and reserve them. Cut the stalks into 1-inch pieces.

2. Melt 4 tablespoons of the butter in a large heavy saucepan over medium heat. Add the asparagus stalks and cook, stirring frequently, for 5 minutes. Add 2 cups of the chicken broth and simmer, covered, for 20 minutes.

3. Remove from the heat and let cool a little. Pass through a food mill or purée in batches in a blender or food processor and set aside.

4. Cook the asparagus tips in the boiling salted water until just tender, 2 to 3 minutes. Drain, refresh the asparagus tips under cold running water, and reserve.

5. Melt the remaining 2 tablespoons butter in a large saucepan over medium heat. Sprinkle the flour over the melted butter and stir with a wooden spoon until smooth. Switch to a wire whisk and gradually stir in the remaining 4 cups chicken broth. Bring to a boil, stir once more, and remove from the heat.

6. Stir the asparagus purée into the soup base. Season to taste with salt and pepper. (The soup can be prepared ahead up to this point. Cover and refrigerate until needed.)

7. To serve the soup, whisk together the cream and egg yolk. Gently reheat the soup and stir in the cream mixture and the chervil. Do not let the soup come to a boil or it will curdle. Add the asparagus tips to the soup, heat through gently, and serve. Be sure to garnish each soup plate with a few chervil leaves.

Serves 4 to 6

Variation: You can make this soup using the more readily available green asparagus. It will be a totally different soup in color, flavor, and consistency, but delicious nonetheless. Thin, young asparagus will not need to be peeled, but thicker stalks should be to avoid having stringy soup.

The Best Is from Belgium

The Flemish town of Mechelen and its environs are famous for producing two of the three best-known Belgian vegetables—white asparagus and witloof, or Belgian endive. Cultivated asparagus has always been considered a vegetable for the privileged few, and white asparagus is the stalk of choice throughout Belgium and the rest of Europe. It is harvested throughout the months of May and June up to the 21st, the longest day of the year and the beginning of summer.

If you visit Belgium during the asparagus season, you will find that discriminating diners in restaurants will always inquire if the asparagus being served is Belgian asparagus. If it is not, they will usually pass it up.

Chervil Soup

KERVEL SOEP
•
POTAGE AU CERFEUIL

The delicate, clear flavor of chervil, a taste that falls somewhere between parsley and tarragon, perfumes this lovely soup which is traditionally served to herald spring.

3 tablespoons unsalted butter
2 large ribs celery, sliced
1 medium leek, white and pale green parts only, rinsed well and sliced
1 medium onion, sliced
1 small baking potato, peeled and cubed
4 cups beef or chicken broth, preferably homemade (page 54 or 53)
1 cup finely shredded fresh chervil leaves and stems, plus chervil leaves for garnish (see Note)
Salt and freshly ground white pepper to taste

1. Melt the butter in a medium-size soup pot over low heat. Add the celery, leek, and onion; cook, stirring occasionally, until translucent but not browned, about 10 minutes.

2. Add the potato and broth. Bring to a boil and reduce the heat. Simmer, covered, until the vegetables are very soft, 25 minutes.

3. Add the shredded chervil and simmer for another 10 minutes. Remove from the heat and let cool slightly. Purée the soup in batches in a blender or food processor. Return to the pot and reheat gently. Season the soup with salt and pepper. Garnish each soup plate with chervil leaves.

Serves 4

Chervil

Chervil, which is often hard to find in the United States, is almost the national herb of Belgium. It is one of the classic fines herbes, along with parsley, tarragon, and chives. It grows profusely in kitchen gardens and in pots on windowsills. It is a lovely herb and not at all difficult to grow from seed, if you remember to plant it in a spot that has some shade and don't allow the soil to get too dry.

Variations: For a much richer soup and a very elegant start to a formal dinner, whisk ½ cup heavy cream with 1 egg yolk together and stir into the hot soup. Do not boil or the egg and cream will curdle.

• In Belgium, mothers serve this soup with little veal meatballs (page 58) floating in it as an extra treat for children.

Cream of Spinach with Sorrel

SPINAZIE SOEP MET ZURKEL

•

CREME D'EPINARDS A L'OSEILLE

The unusual deep-green color and vitamin-rich goodness make this soup the classic choice for spring and early summer menus. As in many Belgian "cream" soups, no cream is used; instead the creamy texture comes from the puréed potatoes. The taste is very pure, clear, and appealingly tangy from the fresh sorrel.

1 pound fresh spinach, rinsed well, stems removed and discarded
2 medium baking potatoes (about ¾ pound), peeled and cubed
5 cups water
2 cups chicken broth, preferably homemade (page 53)
Salt and freshly ground white pepper to taste
Freshly grated nutmeg to taste
2 large egg yolks
1 tablespoon unsalted butter
2 ounces (a large handful) sorrel leaves, rinsed, stems removed, leaves finely shredded

1. Place the spinach, potatoes, water, and chicken broth in a heavy nonreactive soup pot. Bring to a boil and reduce the heat. Simmer, partially covered, until the potatoes are very soft, 20 minutes.

2. Remove from the heat and season with salt, pepper, and nutmeg. Let the soup cool slightly, then purée in batches in a blender or food processor. Taste for seasoning again.

3. In a small bowl, beat the egg yolks with a ladleful of the warm soup. Stir the egg yolk mixture gradually into the soup together with the butter. Reheat the soup over very low heat. Do not allow it to come to a boil or you will end up with scrambled eggs.

4. Arrange the shredded sorrel in the bottom of 6 soup plates and ladle the hot soup over the sorrel. Serve at once.

Serves 6

Variations: *If you cannot find fresh sorrel, reserve a handful of the youngest, tenderest spinach leaves after they are washed. Remove the stems and shred them very fine. Arrange in soup bowls as you would the sorrel and pour the hot soup over the shredded spinach.*

• *For a richer soup in which the tartness of the spinach and the sorrel is smoothed out, add only 4 cups of water in step 1. In step 3, mix 1 cup heavy (or whipping) cream or half-and-half with the eggs, then proceed with the rest of the recipe.*

Sorrel

In the United States, sorrel is usually considered an herb, but it is really a leafy green vegetable not unlike spinach. It is much prized in Belgium for its tart, acidic taste, and we grow it in our kitchen gardens right next to the spinach. In the kitchen, sorrel and spinach are often mixed together in one dish—the sorrel leaves give the tamer spinach an extra lemony zing. Sometimes you can find canned sorrel in specialty stores, but if you cannot find any sorrel, simply replace the quantity called for with the same amount of spinach leaves and an additional half lemon's worth of juice.

Creamy Lettuce Soup

ROMIGE SLASOEP
•
CREME DE LAITUES

This is a delightful summer soup to make when Boston lettuce is plentiful. If you have never tasted the delicate flavor of a lettuce soup, you are in for a treat.

2 heads Boston lettuce
3 tablespoons unsalted butter
8 scallions, trimmed and thinly sliced into rounds
1 tablespoon all-purpose flour
2 teaspoons sugar
Salt and freshly ground black pepper to taste
Pinch of freshly grated nutmeg
6 cups chicken broth, preferably homemade (page 53)
2 large egg yolks
3/4 cup heavy (or whipping) cream

1. Discard the dark outer leaves of each lettuce. Separate the lettuce leaves and rinse thoroughly under cold running water. Cut the lettuce leaves into thin strips.

2. Melt the butter in a heavy soup pot over low heat. Add the scallions and shredded lettuce and cook, stirring frequently, until completely wilted, 5 to 7 minutes. Remove about 1/3 cup shredded lettuce and reserve for a final garnish.

3. Sprinkle the flour and sugar over the vegetables and mix well. Season with salt, pepper, and nutmeg. Stir in the chicken broth and simmer, covered, for 30 minutes.

4. Let the soup cool slightly, then press through a food mill or purée in batches in a blender or food processor. Return the puréed soup to the soup pot.

5. Bring the soup to a quick boil and remove from the heat. In a small bowl, mix the egg yolks with the cream and stir in a ladleful of the hot soup. Gradually whisk the egg mix-

ture into the soup. Stir in the reserved lettuce, taste for seasoning, and serve. If you need to reheat the soup at any point, do not let it come to a boil or it will curdle.

Serves 4 to 6

My Grandmother's Cream of Cauliflower Soup

GROOTMOEDER'S BLOEMKOOL SOEP

•

CREME DE CHOU-FLEUR DE MA GRAND-MERE

A beautiful snowy white soup to cheer up a dreary winter day with its sweet and spicy flavors. My mother always said that the fresh bright green herbs that are swirled into the soup at the last minute were a happy reminder that spring is *de lente staat voor de deur* (just behind the door).

1 medium cauliflower
3 tablespoons unsalted butter
1 large onion, thinly sliced
1 medium leek, white and light green parts only, rinsed well and thinly sliced
2 cups chicken broth, preferably homemade (page 53)
½ teaspoon ground mace, or freshly grated nutmeg to taste
¼ to ½ teaspoon freshly ground white pepper
2½ cups milk
Salt to taste
2 tablespoons finely minced fresh chives, chervil, or parsley, for garnish

1. Trim the outer leaves of the cauliflower and discard. Separate the cauliflower into florets, discarding the thick core. Reserve 12 of the smallest florets (about the size of your thumb) for garnishing the soup.

2. Melt the butter in a heavy soup pot over low heat. Add the onion, leek, and cauliflower florets and cook, stirring, until softened but not browned, about 10 minutes.

3. Add the chicken broth, mace, and pepper. Bring to a boil and reduce the heat. Simmer, covered, until the vegetables are soft, about 30 minutes.

4. Bring some lightly salted water to a boil in a small saucepan, add the reserved florets, and boil over high heat until just tender, 10 minutes. Drain but save the liquid to thin the soup if it is too thick.

5. Let the soup cool slightly and purée in batches in a blender or food processor.

Return the puréed soup to the pot and add the milk. Season with salt and adjust the other seasonings. If the soup is very thick, add some of the reserved cooking water. Add the reserved florets.

6. Just before serving, reheat the soup very slowly but do not boil. In a small cup or bowl, mix ¼ cup of the hot soup with the minced chives. Ladle the soup into warmed soup plates and use a teaspoon to swirl a spiral of the fresh herb mixture in each plate of soup.

Serves 4

Independence!

From the time that the Roman legions conquered and ruled the Celtic tribe of the Belgae more than 2,000 years ago, Belgium has been fought over and ruled by Frankish overlords, French dukes, Spanish kings, Austrians, and finally, in 1815, the Dutch. But the Belgians were never compliant and there have been revolts too numerous to count all through the ages. The final revolution for independence was instigated by an evening at the opera in Brussels on August 25, 1830. An aria appropriately called "Sacred Love of Our Fatherland," brought the audience to its feet and sent them storming out into the night to throw off the yoke of their Dutch oppressors. A year later, Belgium had crowned its first king, Leopold of Saxe-Coburg, and it has been a fully independent state since then.

Celery Root Soup

KNOLSELDERROOMSOEP
•
POTAGE AUX DEUX CELERIS

Celery root, also known as celeriac, is a root vegetable with an intense celery flavor that is much prized in Belgium. It is most often eaten raw, julienned and tossed with a remoulade dressing. Here it is paired with celery ribs to make a kind of double celery soup, which everyone finds utterly delicious. It is a perfect soup for the fall and winter months, when root vegetables have the sweetest flavor and few other fresh vegetables are available.

3 tablespoons unsalted butter
2 large celery roots (celeriac; about 1 pound each), peeled and cut into 1-inch cubes
6 ribs celery, coarsely chopped
1 medium onion, sliced
5 cups water
5 cups chicken broth, preferably homemade (page 53)
2 medium baking potatoes, peeled and cubed
1 bay leaf
¼ cup finely chopped fresh parsley
1 cup milk or heavy (or whipping) cream
Salt and freshly ground white pepper to taste
Finely chopped fresh chives, for garnish
Croutons (page 75)

1. Melt the butter in a heavy soup pot over medium heat. Add the celery root, celery, and onion and cook, stirring until the vegetables are slightly softened, about 10 minutes.

2. Add the water, chicken broth, potatoes, bay leaf, and parsley. Bring to a boil and reduce the heat. Simmer, partially covered, until the vegetables are very soft, 45 minutes.

3. Remove the soup from the heat and let cool a little. Press the soup through a food mill or purée in batches in a blender or food processor. (If you are a purist, strain the soup through a very fine sieve.) Return the puréed soup to the soup pot.

4. Stir in the milk and season to taste with salt and pepper. Reheat before serving but do not bring to a boil or the soup will curdle. Garnish each soup plate with chives and croutons.

Serves 8

Variation: *For a special occasion, sprinkle about 1 tablespoon crumbled Roquefort in each soup plate before serving.*

Cream of Brussels Sprouts Soup

SPRUITJESROOMSOEP
•
POTAGE AUX CHOUX
DE BRUXELLES

The sweetness of the leeks and onions combined with the pervasive scent of nutmeg make this a sumptuous winter soup, which can happily serve as a quick lunch on the run, or as a first course for a formal dinner.

3/4 pound small Brussels sprouts
Salt to taste
3 tablespoons unsalted butter
1 leek, white and light green parts only, rinsed well and thinly sliced, or 1 medium onion, thinly sliced
1 rib celery, sliced
Freshly ground white pepper to taste
Pinch of freshly grated nutmeg
1 large baking potato, peeled and cubed
8 cups beef broth, preferably homemade (page 54)
3 cups water
1 cup milk
½ cup heavy (or whipping) cream
2 large egg yolks

1. Prepare the Brussels sprouts: Remove any damaged outer leaves and trim the base. Remove 6 sprouts and cook them in plenty of boiling salted water for 10 minutes. Plunge the sprouts into cold water to stop them from cooking, drain, and reserve for garnish.

2. Melt the butter in a large soup pot over medium heat. Add the remaining sprouts, the leek, and celery; cook, stirring occasionally, until softened but not browned, 5 to 7 minutes. Season with salt, pepper, and nutmeg. Add the potato and pour in the stock, water, and milk. Simmer the soup, uncovered, until the Brussels sprouts are very tender, about 45 minutes.

3. Let the soup cool slightly and purée in batches in a blender or food processor. Return the purée to the soup pot and bring to a quick boil. Remove from the heat.

4. In a small bowl, mix together the cream and egg yolks. Mix in a ladleful of the hot soup and stir the egg mixture into the soup. Taste and adjust the seasoning. If the soup seems too thick, add a little more milk.

5. Quarter the reserved Brussels sprouts lengthwise and reheat them gently in the soup. Do not let the soup boil or it will curdle.

Serves 6

Flemish Onion Soup with Cheese

AJUIN SOEP MET KAAS
•
CREME D'OIGNONS AU FROMAGE

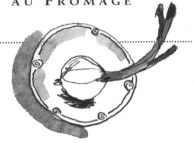

*I*n the old days, this was the soup that fed families at the end of the month. When there was nothing else left, there were always a few onions, potatoes, a bit of cheese, and a loaf of bread. Marrying the natural sweetness of cooked onions with the creamy texture of potatoes, this satisfying soup is a classic of Flemish country cooking and perfectly exemplifies my grandmother's dictum that if you are clever, you can live like a king on a beggar's purse.

4 tablespoons (½ stick) unsalted butter

2 pounds yellow onions, thinly sliced

2 large baking potatoes (about 1½ pounds) peeled and cubed

4 cups water

1 bay leaf

1 cup milk

Salt and freshly ground white pepper to taste

Freshly grated nutmeg to taste

3 tablespoons minced fresh chives (optional)

Croutons (page 75) (optional)

¾ cup grated Gruyère cheese

1. Melt the butter in a heavy soup pot over low heat. Add the onions and increase the heat to medium. Cook, stirring occasionally, until translucent, 10 minutes. Let the onions brown *slightly* for a more pronounced flavor.

2. Add the potatoes, water, and bay leaf. Bring to a boil and reduce the heat. Simmer, covered, until the potatoes are soft, 20 to 25 minutes.

3. Discard the bay leaf and let the soup cool slightly. Press the soup through a food mill or purée in batches in a blender or food processor until smooth.

4. Return the purée to the soup pot and gradually stir in the milk. Season with salt, pepper, and nutmeg.

5. Reheat the soup gently before serving. Do not let it boil. Serve hot in warmed soup plates. If desired, sprinkle with chives and float croutons in each soup plate. Place the grated cheese in a pretty bowl and pass at the table.

Serves 6

Variation: My mother, who is always ready to experiment with nontraditional seasonings, adds 1 tablespoon curry powder to the onions as they are being cooked in butter, making for a delicious variation.

Saving Up for Soup

In my great grandmother Marie's day, there was no such thing as chicken parts, all ready to use from the supermarket. When she made chicken broth, she used an old hen, one that was too old to lay eggs and too tough to cook any other way. As there were only a few hens at any given time that could be used this way, making chicken broth was always a special occasion, and the resulting broth was valued and much appreciated.

Today I make chicken broth on a regular basis so as to always have some around for making soups. I keep a plastic bag in the freezer where I save up various chicken parts—necks, gizzards, hearts, wing tips, and bones—until I have enough to make my broth. Because I am very frugal, I always buy a whole chicken and cut it and bone it myself. Sometimes I do as Marie did in her day and add a pig's foot or a veal knuckle to give my chicken broth a velvety body and consistency and to impart added flavor.

Flemish Split Pea Soup with Ham Hock

VLAAMSE ERWTENSOEP
MET HESPEKNUIST
•
POTAGE SAINT-GERMAIN

Throughout Belgium, this is a favorite winter soup, and many farm families traditionally eat it once a week as a satisfying and hearty one-dish meal. In the northern villages and across the Dutch border, pea soup is often served with a smoked sausage, which is sliced and reheated in the soup. For a comparable taste you can substitute kielbasa.

2 pounds dried split green peas
4 medium leeks
6 tablespoons (³/4 stick) unsalted butter
Salt and freshly ground pepper
   to taste
2 carrots, peeled and diced
2 ribs celery, diced
1 large onion, diced
3½ quarts water
1 smoked ham hock or 1 meaty
   ham bone
4 sprigs fresh parsley
3 sprigs fresh thyme or ½ teaspoon
   dried thyme
2 bay leaves
1 cup milk
Croutons (recipe follows)

1. Pick over the split peas to remove any grit and stones. Rinse them well. In Belgium, we like to soak split peas overnight in cold water to cover by at least 4 inches. (In a warm kitchen, refrigerate the soaking peas.) You can skip the soaking if you wish and increase the cooking time by 30 minutes.

2. Remove the white and light green parts from 2 of the leeks. Trim, rinse well, and slice into thin rounds. Melt 2 tablespoons of the butter in a small skillet over low heat. Add the sliced leeks and cook, stirring occasionally, for 15 minutes. The leeks should remain slightly crunchy. Season with a little salt and pepper and reserve.

3. Trim and discard the dark green parts of

the remaining leeks. Rinse the light green and white parts thoroughly and cut into thin rounds.

4. Melt the remaining 4 tablespoons butter in a heavy soup pot over low heat. Add the uncooked leeks, carrots, celery, and onion; cook, stirring, until the vegetables are softened but not browned, about 10 minutes.

5. Drain the split peas and add them to the pot together with the water, the ham hock, parsley, thyme, and bay leaves. Bring to a boil and reduce the heat. Simmer, covered, until the peas are very soft, 1½ to 2 hours. Stir the soup occasionally to prevent the vegetables from sticking on the bottom.

6. Remove the soup from the heat and let cool slightly. Remove the bay leaves and ham hock. Season the soup with salt and pepper to taste. Purée the soup in batches in a blender or a food processor for a very smooth soup. For a more rustic soup, pureé only part of the soup or skip this step altogether.

7. Remove the meat from the cooked ham hock and shred or slice it into bite-size pieces. Add the meat and reserved cooked leeks to the soup. Stir in the milk.

8. Reheat gently but do not boil or the soup will curdle. Serve with croutons.

Serves 8

Variations: If you don't have time to soak the peas overnight, increase the cooking time by 30 to 45 minutes.

• A chunk of Canadian bacon or other lean smoked bacon can be substituted for the ham hock.

• For a vegetarian version, omit the ham hock altogether. The soup will be lighter tasting but still satisfying.

Croutons

4 to 6 slices firm white bread
2 tablespoons unsalted butter
1 tablespoon finely minced garlic
1 tablespoon finely minced fresh parsley
*1 teaspoon fresh thyme or ½ teaspoon
   dried thyme*

1. Remove the crusts from the bread and cut the bread into ½-inch cubes.

2. Melt the butter in a large, heavy skillet over medium heat and add the bread cubes and garlic. Sauté until the bread cubes are a nice golden color all over. Be sure to turn them frequently with a spatula, so they do not burn. Toss the bread cubes with the parsley and thyme and serve.

Serves 8 as a garnish for soup

Hearty Winter Vegetable Soup

HUTSEPOT SOEP
•
POTAGE D'HIVER

Winter always seems harsher in the country, so it isn't surprising that our country women prepare the most comforting soups to provide an antidote to a landscape of frozen earth, naked trees piercing slate-colored winter skies, and a darkness that falls at four in the afternoon. *Hutsepot* is the most traditional of Belgium's country soups, and like Italy's minestrone and Russia's borscht, it has sustained hungry country folk for centuries.

4 ounces lean slab bacon, cut into
    1 × ½-inch strips
1 medium onion, cut into ¼-inch dice
1 cup trimmed and halved Brussels sprouts
1 cup diced (¼ inch) peeled carrots
½ cup diced (¼ inch) peeled celery root (celeriac)
½ cup diced (¼ inch) peeled turnips
½ cup diced (¼ inch) peeled potatoes
5 cups beef or chicken broth, preferably
    homemade (page 54 or 53)
Salt and freshly ground black pepper to taste
2 tablespoons finely minced fresh parsley

1. Cook the bacon in a heavy soup pot over medium heat to render the fat, about 5 minutes. Add the onion and cook, stirring occasionally, for another 5 minutes.

2. Add the remaining vegetables and the broth. Bring to a boil and reduce the heat. Simmer, covered, for 20 to 25 minutes. The vegetables should be cooked but not so soft that they lose their shape.

3. Season with salt and pepper and sprinkle generously with parsley just before serving.

Variation: For a lighter taste, substitute 1½ tablespoons butter for the bacon.

Fish Stew from the North Sea

NOORDZEE VISSOEP
•
LA BOUILLABAISSE
DE LA MER DU NORD

This is an exquisite fish stew that can be best described as a bouillabaisse from the North Sea. The original version is prepared with a flavorful fish broth, but cooking in the United States made me realize how difficult it can be to find fresh fish bones and heads. So in this version I made use of the shellfish, which are widely available, to make a very quick broth. The result is delightful, and, I whisper to say this, even more flavorful than the original.

The final presentation of this bouillabaisse is very colorful and beautiful, making it a wonderful company dish, but the total preparation time need not be longer than 1 hour. You can save even more time by slicing the vegetables rather than cutting them into the more time-consuming julienne.

Serve this bouillabaisse with a tossed green salad and herbed garlic bread (recipe follows).

Mussel Broth:
1½ tablespoons unsalted butter
1 medium onion, sliced
1 rib celery, sliced
2 leeks, green parts only (save the white parts for the fish stew), rinsed well and sliced
Shrimp shells from 12 to 18 medium shrimp
1 teaspoon dried thyme
1 bay leaf
3 parsley sprigs
1½ cups dry white wine
1 cup water
2 pounds small mussels, thoroughly cleaned and bearded (page 93)

Fish Stew:
3 tablespoons unsalted butter
2 leeks, white parts only, rinsed well and julienned or thinly sliced
1 large carrot, peeled and julienned or thinly sliced
1 celery root (celeriac; in the winter), or 1 small fennel bulb (in the summer), julienned or thinly sliced
1 tablespoon minced shallots
1 clove garlic, minced
1 cup heavy (or whipping) cream
½ teaspoon dill seeds
½ teaspoon dried thyme
1 bay leaf
Pinch of saffron threads
Pinch of cayenne pepper
1 large ripe tomato, peeled, seeded, and diced into ¼-inch cubes
Salt and freshly ground black pepper to taste
8 to 12 littleneck clams (2 per person), scrubbed
1¼ pounds monkfish, cod, hake, or red snapper fillet (or a combination of several white firm-fleshed fish), skin removed, cut into 1-inch cubes
12 to 18 medium shrimp, peeled, shells reserved for the broth
½ pound bay scallops
2 tablespoons finely minced fresh parsley

Herbed Garlic Bread Belgian Style (recipe follows)

1. Prepare the mussel broth: Melt the butter in a large soup pot over medium-low heat. Add the onion, celery, and green slices of leeks and cook, stirring occasionally, until

softened but not browned. Add the shrimp shells, thyme, bay leaf, parsley sprigs, wine, and the water and bring to a boil. Add the mussels, cover the pot, and cook the mussels over high heat until all the mussels are open, 4 to 6 minutes. Remove from the heat and let cool a little. Remove the mussels from the pot, discarding any that haven't opened. Remove the mussels from their shells but leave 1 mussel with shell attached per person.

2. Strain the broth through a sieve lined with cheesecloth. There should be about 2 cups mussel broth. Reserve.

3. Prepare the fish stew: In a large enameled Dutch oven, melt the butter over medium heat. Add the leeks, carrot, celery root, shallots, and garlic, and cook, covered, until the vegetables are soft, 10 to 15 minutes. Check on them from time to time to make sure they do not brown. Stir in a little water if necessary.

4. Add the mussel broth, cream, dill seeds, thyme, bay leaf, saffron, and cayenne pepper. Simmer over low heat for another 10 minutes. Do not boil or the cream will curdle. Add the tomato, salt, and pepper; cook for 1 minute more. (You can prepare the dish in advance up to this point.)

5. Just before serving, reheat the broth over medium heat and add the fish and shellfish in the order of cooking times: Start with the clams; cook, covered, for 2 to 3 minutes. Add the fish and the shrimp; cook for another 2 minutes. Add the scallops and cook for 2 minutes longer. Finally, add the cooked mussels, including those in the shell; cook just

long enough for the mussels to heat through. Discard any clams that haven't opened.

6. Serve in deep soup plates, making sure there is a clam and a mussel in the shell in each plate. Sprinkle each plate of *vissoep* generously with minced parsley. Serve with the herbed garlic bread.

Serves 4 as a main course or 6 as a first course

Note: *Fish and shellfish should never be overcooked, for their delicate flesh will turn tough and chewy.*

The Way to a Man's Heart

"*Do you want to keep your man strong and happy? Then feed him well,*" *my great grandmother told her daughter. She fervently believed that every divorce was caused by the wife's inability to cook. Even today the expression "The way to a man's heart is through his stomach" is commonplace in Belgium, where home cooking is not a dying art but rather a proud accomplishment. Cooking for the family may have become slightly simplified to adjust to the pressures of modern living, but even working women organize their time to include the planning and cooking of proper meals for their families.*

Herbed Garlic Bread, Belgian Style

8 tablespoons (1 stick) unsalted butter,
   at room temperature
2 teaspoons finely minced garlic
1½ tablespoons finely minced fresh parsley
   or chervil
1 teaspoon minced fresh thyme or tarragon
Salt and freshly ground black pepper to taste
1 large French or Italian loaf or 2 smaller loaves

1. Preheat the over to 375°F.

2. In a small bowl, mix together the butter, garlic, herbs, salt, and pepper well. Slice the bread 1 inch thick but do not cut all the way through the bottom of the loaf. Spread approximately 1 to 2 teaspoons of the garlic butter in between each cut.

3. Wrap the bread in aluminum foil and bake about 10 minutes. Serve immediately.

Serves 4

Cream of Squash Soup with Mussels

POMPOENSOEP MET MOSSELS
•
CREME DE COURGE AUX MOULES

This is a dish I created using one of my favorite ingredients from the New World—sweet and creamy butternut squash or pumpkin—but keeping a traditional Belgian mussel soup in mind. This colorful soup makes a festive light first course for a special dinner or luncheon.

1 butternut squash (2½ to 3 pounds),
   or an equivalent wedge of pumpkin
2 tablespoons unsalted butter
1½ cups water
1 cup dry white wine
2 tablespoons finely chopped shallots
2 sprigs fresh thyme or pinch of dried thyme
2 pounds mussels, thoroughly cleaned and
   bearded (page 93)
1 cup heavy (or whipping) cream
Salt and freshly ground black pepper to taste
Fresh chervil leaves, minced chives,
   or minced parsley, for garnish

1. Peel and seed the squash and cut into ½-inch cubes.

2. Melt the butter in a heavy soup pot over medium heat. Add the squash and cook, stirring occasionally, for 2 to 3 minutes. Add 1 cup of the water and cook, covered, until the squash is soft enough to be puréed, about 20 minutes. Check from time to time to see if you need to add a little more water to be sure the squash doesn't burn. Set aside.

3. In a large pot, bring the wine and remaining ½ cup water to a boil. Reduce the heat to low, add the shallots and thyme, and simmer for 5 to 6 minutes. Add the mussels, increase the heat to high, and cover the pot. Steam the mussels until the shells have opened, 4 to 6 minutes depending on the size of the mussels. Shake the pot 2 or 3 times while they are steaming to toss the mussels around. Remove from the heat and transfer the mussels to a large bowl with a slotted spoon. Let cool. Discard any mussels that haven't opened.

4. Remove the mussels from their shells and cover with plastic wrap until ready to use. Strain the cooking liquid through a sieve lined with cheesecloth or a paper coffee filter.

5. In a blender or food processor, purée the squash with its liquid and the mussel cooking liquid. (The soup can be prepared in advance up to this point.)

6. Reheat the squash purée in the soup pot. Stir in the cream. If the soup seems too thick to you, add a little water or milk to thin it. Reheat the mussels briefly in the soup but do not boil. Season with salt and pepper. Sprinkle each serving of hot soup with fresh chervil leaves.

Serves 4

Variations: *For a more festive presentation, leave 4 mussels per person on the half shells and float these in the soup. The blue-black shells make a colorful contrast with the orange soup speckled with green herbs.*

• *For a less caloric soup that is equally delicious, substitute a light chicken broth for the heavy cream.*

Flemish Potato Buttermilk Soup

TAATJESPAP OR STAMPERS

Belgium is predominantly a Catholic country, and for centuries Friday has been considered a fasting day, which means that one abstains from meat and takes only light meals. The one-day fast is to give the stomach a little rest, in order that the spirit, less burdened, might be free to contemplate one's mortal and moral condition and (presumably) to repent. A typical Friday meal in rural Belgium might well consist of fish or one of the traditional milk-based soups, of which *taatjespap* is just one example.

In my great grandmother Marie's day, unless you happened to live by the North Sea, fish was a rare and expensive commodity, a luxury food for prosperous villagers only. Marie could never afford it, so for her, Friday was *taatjespap* day. Every week she prepared the tangy, smooth mixture of buttermilk and potatoes, heavily scented with nutmeg and flavored with hazelnut-brown butter. Her recipe, passed from mother to daughter, is now for the first time mine to write down and perhaps save from eventual extinction.

Taatjespap, you see, is the kind of unpretentious, homey, comfort food of which Belgians in exile dream. It is in fact the very embodiment of our longing and homesickness, the food of our childhood, the one thing we simply cannot get abroad and the first thing for which we ask when we return home. Non-Belgians either love it or hate it, but if you care about someone who is homesick for *taatjespap*, make them this. Nothing else will do.

Serve *taatjespap* with an earthy wholewheat bread and some young Gouda cheese.

8 large baking potatoes, peeled and cubed
1 tablespoon salt, plus additional to taste
2 quarts buttermilk
1 tablespoon cornstarch
2 tablespoons cold water
Freshly ground black pepper to taste
Freshly grated nutmeg to taste
8 tablespoons (1 stick) unsalted butter

1. Place the potatoes, 1 tablespoon salt, and enough cold water to cover the potatoes in a large soup pot. Bring to a boil and reduce the heat to medium. Cook, covered, until the potatoes are very soft, 20 to 25 minutes. Drain the potatoes. Press through a food mill or ricer or mash them with a potato masher.

2. Heat the buttermilk slowly in a medium-size saucepan over medium heat. Dissolve the cornstarch in the cold water and stir into the hot buttermilk with a large wooden spoon. Over medium heat, stir constantly, tracing a large number 8 with your wooden spoon. Bring to a boil and remove from the heat.

3. Stir in the mashed potatoes a little at a time. The final soup should be quite thick. Season with salt and pepper to taste and finish with a generous grinding of nutmeg.

4. Just before serving, melt the butter in a small saucepan over low heat and cook until it turns a hazelnut-brown color, about 20 minutes. Reheat the soup but do not let it boil. Drizzle the browned butter over the soup and serve.

Serves 6

Buttermilk Soup with Apples

KARNEMELK SOEP MET APPELKES

SOUPE AU LAIT BATTU ET POMMES

This is another very ancient recipe, certainly dating back to the Middle Ages. The sweet and tart flavors of the soup reflect a time when sugar was used as a seasoning and was just as precious as pepper and other spices. It was from that time also that *pap* (sweet milk soup) became associated with biblical images of the land of milk and honey. It was food for fasting days and a reminder of the better world to come. But it is definitely a Flemish way of fasting, as this buttermilk soup is really a treat, one that is especially beloved by children.

½ cup all-purpose flour
4 cups buttermilk
1 large Granny Smith apple, peeled, cored, and thinly sliced
1 tablespoon granulated sugar
Pinch of salt
A small bowl of dark brown sugar, for serving

1. In a small bowl, mix the flour with about ¾ cup buttermilk. The mixture should look

like a thick white sauce. Transfer to a heavy soup pot and whisk in the remaining 3¼ cups buttermilk. Bring to a boil over medium heat, whisking constantly. Reduce the heat to low and cook for another 8 to 10 minutes, stirring all the while.

2. Add the apple slices, sugar, and salt; continue to cook, stirring, for another 5 minutes.

3. Serve hot with brown sugar on the side.

Serves 4

Ingelmunster

When my mother was growing up, Ingelmunster was a typical small Belgian village. In the center was the church around which everything was organized. There was one café, one butcher shop, one village baker, and one other store, which was called kruidenierswinkel, *or the spice store. There one could buy everything else that was necessary for life.*

Throughout my childhood I heard the story of how one Friday when my mother was a small girl, her mother found that the nutmeg grater was empty. She sent little Anny to the kruidenierswinkel *with a short shopping list. Happy and excited, Anny ran over the cobblestone streets. From the moment she passed through the shop's doorway and stepped down into the dimly lit room, she felt as if she had walked into the magic cave of Ali Baba. Coming in from the bright sunshine, she could see almost nothing at first, but her nose and lungs filled with the thick smell of spices mingled with the pungent cheeses, sweets, and other delicacies. The shop was small and very crowded with canned goods, household items, boots, buckets, brooms, brushes, and toys—*

everything stacked in piles or hanging suspended from the ceiling. It was the most seductive place imaginable, and no modern department store could ever hope to duplicate this wonderful atmosphere.

When her eyes finally became accustomed to the dim light, Anny could see that she was alone. The shopkeeper was nowhere to be seen. At last she heard a woman's voice coming from the back of the shop. "Come here, little girl. You will have to stir my taatjespap.*" The woman placed Anny's small hand around the handle of the wooden spoon. "Here, like so," she said as she showed her how to trace a figure eight through the thickening soup. And Anny had to stir the soup while the shopkeeper gathered the items on her mother's list.*

The moral of this story, when my mother told it, is that when the taatjespap *is thickening, you must not stop stirring for even a minute. But I have taken quite another lesson from it—be careful not to lose the good things from the past. All over Belgium the small village* kruidenierswinkeltjes *are being replaced by supermarkets. Only in the remote villages of the Flanders countryside and in the Ardennes will you still find an old-time* kruidenierswinkel *like the one that enchanted my mother when she was a little girl.*

Milk Soup from the Ardennes

ARDEENSE SOEP
•
SOUPE AU LAIT ARDENNAISE

2 tablespoons unsalted butter

3 leeks, white parts only, rinsed well and sliced into thin rings

1 large onion, coarsely chopped

4 to 6 escarole leaves, coarsely chopped

4 cups milk

3 medium baking potatoes, peeled and cut into ½-inch cubes

Salt and freshly ground black pepper to taste

2 tablespoons minced fresh parsley

Another delicious milk-based soup, this one is popular in the southern villages of the country. Traditionally the soup is served with thick slices of peasant-style bread that have been toasted in a hot oven. If you are lucky, your host will slice some of the home-cured ham he might have hanging from the ceiling or let you taste his homemade pâtés and smoked *saucisses*.

But you can easily make this soup for yourself right at home, as all the ingredients are readily available in the United States. Add a mixed green salad and a loaf of bread, and you have a wonderful, unpretentious evening meal.

1. Melt the butter in a heavy soup pot over medium heat. Add the leeks, onion, and escarole; cook, covered until the vegetables are softened but not browned, 5 to 10 minutes.

2. Add the milk and the potatoes, and season with salt and pepper. Simmer, covered, until the potatoes are very soft and start to fall apart, about 30 minutes. You can serve this chunky soup as is—country style—or purée it in a blender or food processor for a more elegant presentation.

3. Serve hot, sprinkled with minced parsley.

Serves 4

Fish and Shellfish

The Belgian Coast

A FISH LOVER'S PARADISE

The Belgian coast, 65 kilometers (40 miles) of some of the widest, whitest beaches in the world, stretching between France and the Netherlands along the North Sea, is a mass of paradoxes and seeming contradictions. It is a resort area crammed with hotels, casinos, restaurants, and amusement parks. At the same time it is an area of old, picturesque fishing villages that seem untouched by time. It is crowded with Belgians on vacation or on a weekend outing for *een dagje aan zee* (a day at the beach), as well as with visitors from France, Holland, England, Germany, and the rest of Europe. Yet there are also endless vistas of uncrowded beaches where one can walk in solitude looking at nothing but sand and sea and sky. It has many of the most luxurious three-star restaurants in all of Belgium, where renowned chefs create cuisine fit for the gods and feed some of the most affluent diners in all of Europe. At the same time, there are hundreds of small seaside restaurants cooking up the best of Belgium's bourgeois cuisine so that every one can enjoy their *moules-frites* or sugar waffles or dozens of other specialties.

Fishing is still very much a family business, and sons follow their fathers, generation after generation. The fishermen go out to sea for days and sometimes weeks at a time, always facing the unpredictable and capricious weather of the North Sea. But when they return, their boats are loaded with sparkling, squirming seafood—cod, ray, turbot, Dover sole, sea eel, flounder, mackerel, crabs, shrimp, and langoustines. Small stands line the harbor where the women of the family, their faces almost as red from the wind and sun as their rubber boots, clean and sell the catch of the day. The marketplace is as lively as the sea itself with the fresh catch splashing in buckets and baskets at each of the fishing stalls.

Seduced by the Sea

I, too, was seduced by the mysterious powers exerted by the sea. My sweetheart and I sailed off in a small boat for a three-year voyage that took us to the Canary Islands, Madeira, Africa, Brazil, and all around the Caribbean. When our money ran out, I found work as a chef. Of course, we met many people, some of them from New York, and one of them offered me a job. Alas, my sweetheart and I parted company, but I found a new life in the United States.

86

No wonder that Belgians are known to be among the biggest fish eaters in Europe. With all this bounty available to us, we have developed an extensive and refined seafood cuisine.

Belgian Steamed Mussels

GESTOOMDE MOSSELS
•
MOULES MARINIERE

Moules marinière, is a delicious dish all on its own, save for a loaf of fresh crusty bread to dip into the flavorful broth. But I urge you to try the classic Belgian meal of *moules-frites:* a bowl of *moules marinière* and a plate of crispy, golden Belgian fries. The mussels are a snap to prepare, and the Belgian fries (see Index) are easily mastered as well. To experience the truly Belgian addiction, make sure to serve a small bowl of homemade mayonnaise, strongly flavored with mustard, to dip your *frites* in and a fresh pint of beer to wash it all down.

3 tablespoons unsalted butter
2 large shallots or 1 medium onion, finely chopped
2 ribs celery, finely chopped
4 to 6 pounds mussels, thoroughly cleaned and bearded (page 93)
1 teaspoon fresh thyme or ½ teaspoon dried thyme
1 bay leaf
2 tablespoons finely chopped fresh parsley
Freshly ground black pepper to taste
1½ cups dry white wine

1. Melt the butter in a pot large enough to hold all the mussels over medium heat. Add the shallots and celery; cook, stirring occasionally until the vegetables are softened but not browned, about 5 minutes. Add the mussels, sprinkle with the thyme, and add the bay leaf, 1 tablespoon parsley, and a generous grinding of black pepper. Pour the white wine over the mussels and cover the pot tightly.

2. Bring to a boil over high heat and steam the mussels in the covered pot until they open. This will take from 3 to 6 minutes, depending on the size of the mussels. Be careful not to overcook the mussels, as this will toughen them. As soon as most of the mussels have opened, take them off the heat. Shake the pot several times to toss the mussels with the buttery vegetables. Discard any mussels that have not opened.

3. Spoon the hot mussels into soup plates along with some of the broth. Sprinkle with the remaining 1 tablespoon parsley just before serving.

Serves 4 as a generous main course or 6 as a first course

Note: *Strain any leftover cooking liquid and keep frozen for later use. This flavorful broth is a lovely base for soups and fish sauces.*

Variations: *A very Belgian twist is to replace the wine with a Belgian beer, such as Gueuze, or with a strong Duvel.*

• *For an American twist, replace the mussels with littleneck or steamer clams.*

An Old Custom

My grandmother used to put a silver spoon on top of her mussels to check their freshness. If her little spoon turned black, she would throw them all out. The same silver spoon turned up when she went picking mushrooms. If the spoon turned black, there were poisonous mushrooms in her basket. Today, this magic little silver spoon is still my favorite dessert spoon but nothing more . . . although I often wonder.

Mussels Steamed in Their Own Juices

MOSSELS GEKOOKT IN HUN EIGEN NAT
• MOULES CUITES A SEC

I always tell the students in my cooking classes that if they want to save time and effort, they must learn to be kitchen smart. A few minutes spent cleaning and cooking a batch of mussels will give you the means to produce elaborate-looking meals at the drop of a toque. Any leftover broth can be frozen and used as a base for soups and sauces. Add the mussels to chowders, pasta dishes, or the top of a pizza, or turn a bit of leftover rice into an impressive rice and mussel salad. You can also use the reserved mussels to prepare Mussels with a Dijon Mustard Vinaigrette, Mussels with Snail Butter (remember to save the same amount of half shells as you have mussels), Sautéed Mussels, or Mussels Grilled en Brochette (recipes follow).

Mussels

1. Place cleaned and bearded mussels (page 93) in a tall soup pot with a tight-fitting lid. Do not add any liquid or seasoning. Cover the pot and cook over high heat for 4 to 6 minutes. Shake the pan vigorously a few

times to move the mussels around. When the mussels have opened and released their juices, remove the pan from the heat, uncover the pot, and allow the mussels to cool. Discard any that haven't opened.

2. Remove the mussels from their broth. Strain the broth through cheesecloth or a paper coffee filter to remove any sand or grit. Remove the mussels from their shells and cover with the broth. Refrigerate until you are ready to use the mussels in the recipe of your choosing.

Mussels with Snail Butter

M O S S E L S   M E T   L O O K B O T E R

•

M O U L E S   A   L ' E S C A R G O T

This dish was created in Belgium during one of their many gastronomic competitions and has since become a classic. The French may be fanatical about their snails in garlic butter, but in Belgium we

have adapted this same technique to prepare our beloved mussels.

Serve these mussels as a flavorful, easy-to-prepare, and inexpensive appetizer. Be sure to accompany them with a crusty baguette to mop up the juices.

30 large mussels, thoroughly cleaned and bearded (page 93)
2 cups coarse or kosher salt
8 tablespoons (1 stick) unsalted butter, at room temperature
2 cloves garlic, very finely chopped
2 tablespoons finely chopped shallots
2 tablespoons finely chopped fresh parsley
1 tablespoon finely chopped fresh tarragon or a pinch of dried tarragon
A few drops of fresh lemon juice
Salt and freshly ground black pepper to taste
¼ cup dried bread crumbs

1. Steam the mussels in their own juices (page 88). When the mussels are cool enough to handle, discard the empty shell of each mussel, leaving only mussels on the half shell. Discard, too, any mussel that hasn't opened.

2. Spread the salt in a shallow baking dish large enough to hold the mussels in a single layer. Arrange the mussels on the salt.

3. Cream the butter in a small bowl. Add the garlic, shallots, parsley, tarragon, lemon juice, salt, and pepper. Mix well.

4. Preheat the broiler.

5. Dab about ½ teaspoon of the garlic butter on each mussel, then sprinkle with the bread crumbs. Place the mussels under a very hot broiler until the butter is bubbling and the crumbs have browned slightly, 2 to 3 minutes. Serve immediately.

Serves 4 as an appetizer

Variation: Serve mussels nestled in mushroom caps. Stem large mushrooms, wipe the caps clean, and brush with melted butter. Place the caps, stemmed side up, in a buttered baking dish, season with salt and pepper, and bake in a 400°F oven until tender but still firm, about 10 minutes. Depending on the size of your mushrooms, place 1 or 2 shelled mussels into each cap, add the garlic butter, and sprinkle with the bread crumbs. Before serving, run under a hot broiler for 2 to 3 minutes until nicely browned on top.

Gloves from the Sea

The beards, or byssus threads, on the mussels are made of extremely tough material. In ancient Greece these beards were collected and woven into gloves for fishermen. The gloves were stronger than any from a man-made fiber, and as long as they were stored in buckets of seawater, they were so durable that they could be passed on from generation to generation.

Sautéed Mussels

GEBAKKEN MOSSELS
OP Z'N VLAAMS
•
MOULES SAUTEES
A LA FLAMANDE

This quick and easy recipe makes a delicious meal. It is my mother's favorite way to use any leftover cooked mussels. Serve with a fresh cucumber, lettuce, and tomato salad and plenty of good bread.

60 mussels, thoroughly cleaned and bearded (see page 93)
6 tablespoons (¾ stick) unsalted butter or olive oil
6 tablespoons finely chopped shallots
3 slices firm white bread, crusts trimmed and cut into ½-inch cubes
1 tablespoon finely chopped garlic
Pinch of dried thyme
3 tablespoons finely chopped fresh parsley
4 lemon wedges

1. Steam the mussels in their own juices (see page 88). When the mussels are cool enough to handle, discard the shells and any mussels that haven't opened.

2. Melt the butter in a large skillet over high heat. Add the shallots and bread cubes; cook, stirring constantly, for 1 or 2 minutes. Add the garlic, mussels, and thyme; cook, stirring constantly, until the bread cubes are nicely browned and crusty and the mussels are heated through, about 2 minutes longer.

3. Sprinkle with the fresh parsley and serve at once, accompanied by the lemon wedges.

Serves 4

Mussels Grilled en Brochette

MOSSELSPITJES
•
MOULES EN BROCHETTE

In the summertime, search out the largest mussels possible to make these surprisingly tasty grilled mussels. I like to serve these with a Gribiche sauce (see Index) and an onion and tomato salad.

You can turn this meal into a real seafood extravaganza by including some scallops and shrimp on the skewers and additional skewers of fish wrapped in bacon (see Fish and Shellfish Brochettes, page 106).

2 or 3 pounds large mussels, thoroughly cleaned and bearded (page 93)
2 large eggs
1 cup dried bread crumbs
1 teaspoon dried thyme or savory
1 teaspoon finely chopped fresh parsley
Freshly ground black pepper to taste
Small bunch fresh thyme sprigs, tied together to make a brush (optional)
¼ cup melted unsalted butter or olive oil

1. Steam the mussels in their own juices (page 88). When they are cool enough to handle, discard the shells (see Note).

2. In a small bowl, beat the eggs until blended. In another bowl, mix the bread crumbs with the thyme, parsley, and pepper.

3. Dip each mussel first in the egg mixture, then roll in the seasoned bread crumbs. Thread the mussels on 8 skewers and let rest for 10 minutes.

4. Prepare a charcoal grill or preheat the broiler.

5. Using the thyme sprig brush if desired, brush the mussels with the melted butter. Grill or broil the mussels for 2 minutes on each side until nicely browned. Keep the grilled mussels moist by brushing them once more with the melted butter. Serve immediately.

Serves 4

Mussels

My great grandmother Marie used to tell me that mussels were "good for you, full of the strength of the sea." Everyone who lives in Belgium has a close relationship with the sea, because no matter where you are in this small country, it is never very far away.

My great grandmother was right, for mussels are good for you. In fact, in many ways they are the perfect food—full of protein, vitamins, and minerals, and extremely low in fat and cholesterol. When we eat mussels in Belgium, the mussels are the main course. Not the appetizer, not the first course, but the main meal. In many of the cozy little restaurants that dot the harbors along the North Sea, the whole pot of mussels is brought, steaming-hot, to the table, along with a big empty bowl for the shells. Everybody digs in and helps themselves for a jolly family-style meal.

Everywhere you go in Belgium—in homes, in restaurants, in roadside stands, all along the sea coast—you will encounter *les moules-frites,* mussels steamed in wine with aromatic herbs and vegetables and served in the shell, accompanied by a mound of crispy fried potatoes. This classic and delicious combination comes as close as anything to being Belgium's national dish. Some of the most famous *moules-frites* restaurants are in the very center of Brussels, our capital city. In a casual atmosphere, you can dispense with silverware altogether and use a double empty shell to pluck mussels out of their shells and to spoon up the broth. And everyone knows that fried potatoes are best eaten with the fingers. On the other hand, the beautiful blue-black mussels, swimming in their aromatic broth and served forth in deep bowls, are a great first course at any dinner party, no matter how formal.

Although mussels are abundant in America, they are not yet as popular as they have always been in Europe. Like oysters, mussels are at their peak during the cool weather, and according to an old fisherman's saying, they should be eaten only during those months that have the letter "r" in their name.

Mussels are inexpensive and very easy to cook. If you are lucky enough to have access to the seashore where you are sure the waters are unpolluted, you can gather them yourself. Otherwise buy them fresh and still alive at a reputable seafood market.

BUYING MUSSELS

The most important thing to know about mussels is that they must be alive when you buy them and they must remain alive until you cook them. As soon as mussels die, they start to spoil, and you want to prevent that from happening.

Live mussels are sold either by the quart or by the pound. You can figure that there are 16 to 20 mussels in a pound, and about 1½ pounds, or 24 to 30 mussels, in a quart. I usually count on 1 quart of mussels per person for a main course. This allows for some of the inevitable discards without worrying if there will still be enough. Whether you are buying mussels or gathering them, remember that live mussels keep their shells tightly closed. Do not pick any that are already opened.

STORING MUSSELS

When you get home, store the mussels in the refrigerator, but remember that the mussels are *alive* and that they must be able to breathe. If they are in a plastic bag, puncture the bag in several places to make air holes and place the bag on a bed

of ice in a large bowl. Never put them in ice water or in the vegetable compartment of your refrigerator.

CLEANING MUSSELS

This is not nearly as complicated a procedure as it has been made out to be. The only equipment you really need is plenty of water and a small sharp knife. Rinse the mussels under cold running water, scrubbing them with a brush to remove sand and seaweed. Use your knife to scrape away any encrusted dirt and to cut away the beard. Live mussels will open slightly when exposed to temperature changes. If you come across a mussel that has opened, tap it smartly on your work surface. If the mussel reacts by closing its shell, it is alive and safe to be consumed. Do cook the mussels as soon as possible after they are cleaned. They can wait in the refrigerator for one hour, but not a moment longer.

Mussels with a Dijon Mustard Vinaigrette

MOSSELS MET VINAIGRETTE

MOULES VINAIGRETTE

You can improvise with the flavorings in this dish, using any fresh herbs you have on hand. Serve as a first course with a crusty bread, or add a green salad for a wonderful lunch.

2 pounds mussels, thoroughly cleaned and bearded (page 93)
½ cup vegetable oil
2 tablespoons red wine vinegar
2 teaspoons Dijon mustard
2 to 3 shallots, finely chopped
1 tablespoon finely chopped fresh parsley
Salt and freshly ground black pepper to taste

1. Steam the mussels in their own juices (page 88). When they are cool enough to handle, discard the shells and any mussels that haven't opened.

2. In a small bowl, whisk together the oil, vinegar, and mustard.

3. Combine the mussels with the shallots, vinaigrette, and parsley, tossing all the ingredients together. Season to taste with salt and pepper. Chill in the refrigerator until ready to serve.

Serves 4

Variation: For mussels in mayonnaise dressing, substitute ½ cup Homemade Mayonnaise (page 315) for the vinaigrette.

The Town of Waters

Nestled in the hills of the Ardennes, surrounded by expanses of forest, meadows, and heaths, is the town of Spa, which became world-famous for its healing waters. The Romans came here to take the waters and named the town with a word derived from the Latin spagare, *which means to bubble up. The Romans were followed over the centuries by a succession of crowned heads, including Marguerite de Valois, Christina of Sweden, and Peter the Great. During the 18th and 19th centuries, Spa became the place where international high society went to be cured of everything from circulatory diseases and intestinal disorders to gout and rheumatism. While restoring their health, they could while away the time gambling at the many casinos. In the end, "Spa" became a synonym for health resorts everywhere.*

Gratin of Mussels on a Bed of Spinach

GEGRATINEERDE MOSSELS MET SPINAZIE

•

MOULES GRATINEES AUX EPINARDS

This is my mother's favorite mussel dish and a fine example of her cooking philosophy: Take simple, inexpensive ingredients and turn them into a luxurious dish fit for a king. My mother always serves this with mashed potatoes. For a special occasion she pipes the mashed potatoes through a pastry bag with a star tip to make a lovely crown around the spinach and mussels.

1 cup dry white wine
2 shallots or 1 medium onion, finely chopped
2 ribs celery, finely chopped
1 teaspoon fresh thyme or ½ teaspoon dried thyme
1 bay leaf
1 tablespoon finely chopped fresh parsley
Freshly ground black pepper to taste
6 pounds mussels, thoroughly cleaned and bearded (page 93)
2 tablespoons Cognac
4 tablespoons (½ stick) unsalted butter
3 tablespoons all-purpose flour
¾ cup heavy (or whipping) cream or milk
Pinch of cayenne pepper
Fresh lemon juice to taste
3 pounds spinach, thoroughly rinsed and stems removed, or 3 packages (10 ounces each) frozen chopped spinach, thawed and squeezed to remove excess moisture
Salt to taste
1 cup grated Gruyère cheese

1. Prepare the mussels: Place the wine, shallots, celery, thyme, bay leaf, parsley, and a generous grinding of black pepper in a pot large enough to hold the mussels. Bring to a boil and add the mussels. Cover the pot tightly. Return to a boil over high heat and steam the mussels in the covered pot for 4 to 6 minutes until they all open. Shake the pot from time to time to redistribute the mussels.

2. With a skimmer or a slotted spoon, transfer the mussels to a large bowl, discarding any that haven't opened. When they are cool enough to handle, take the mussels out of their shells, cover, and set aside.

3. Strain the cooking liquid into a smaller saucepan, leaving behind any sandy residue. Add the Cognac and bring to a boil. Cook over high heat until the liquid is reduced to 1 cup, about 2 minutes.

4. Melt 2 tablespoons of the butter in a medium-size saucepan over low heat and stir in the flour. Little by little, add the reduced liquid, stirring constantly with a wooden spoon. Let simmer for 2 minutes. Stir in the cream and return to a boil. Taste and season with cayenne pepper and a few drops of lemon juice. You will probably not need any salt because the juices from the mussels are full of seawater and already very salty.

5. Melt the remaining 2 tablespoons butter in a large skillet over high heat. Add the spinach and cook, stirring constantly, until wilted or heated through if frozen, 2 to 4 minutes. Season with salt and pepper to taste.

6. To assemble the dish, divide the spinach evenly among 6 individual casseroles or purchased scallop shells, or put it all into a medium-size gratin dish. Arrange the mussels on top of the spinach and cover everything with the white sauce. Sprinkle with the grated cheese. Keep covered in the refrigerator until ready to serve.

7. Preheat the oven to 400°F and the broiler, if it is a separate element.

8. Bake, uncovered, until the sauce is hot and bubbly, 10 to 15 minutes. Then broil about 2 inches from the heat until the cheese is melted and browned. Serve at once.

Serves 6

Aunt Lucette's Waterzooi of Scallops

TANTE LUCETTE'S WATERZOOI VAN ST. JACOBS SCHELPEN
•
WATERZOOI DE COQUILLES ST. JACQUES DE MA TANTE LUCETTE

My Aunt Lucette, an excellent cook, is famous among our friends and family for this delicate and wonderful *waterzooi* of scallops, her own variation on the traditional *waterzooi* of fish. These scallops make a superb appetizer, or a light lunch or supper dish. They are very easy to make, and most of the preparation can be done in advance. I like to serve the scallops with herbed garlic bread (see Index).

3 tablespoons unsalted butter

2 shallots, finely chopped

2 cloves garlic, finely chopped

3 large leeks, white and light green parts only,
    rinsed well and cut into matchstick-size strips

3 medium carrots, peeled and cut into
    matchstick-size strips

3 ribs celery, cut into matchstick-size strips

3 tablespoons finely minced fresh parsley

2 bay leaves

2 sprigs fresh thyme or large pinch dried thyme

½ cup water

½ cup dry white wine

½ cup heavy (or whipping) cream

Salt and freshly ground black pepper to taste

1½ pounds scallops (4 to 6 large sea scallops or
    6 to 8 bay scallops per person)

1. Melt the butter in a medium-size saucepan over medium heat until it foams. Add the shallots, garlic, leeks, carrots, and celery and cook, stirring frequently, until softened slightly but not browned, about 5 minutes.

2. Add 1 tablespoon of the parsley, the bay leaves, thyme, water, and wine. Bring to a boil and reduce the heat to a simmer. Stir in the cream and simmer, covered, for 10 minutes. Season with salt and pepper. (You can prepare the dish in advance up to this point.)

3. Just before serving, reheat the broth and vegetables to a simmer and add the scallops. Poach at a simmer, uncovered, until the scallops turn opaque, 1 to 3 minutes, depending on the size of the scallops. Do not overcook or let the liquid come to a boil, or the delicate flesh will toughen. Serve immediately in soup bowls, sprinkling each portion with the remaining 2½ tablespoons of parsley.

Serves 4

Waterzooi of Fish in the Manner of Ghent

GENTSE WATERZOOI VAN TARBOT
•
WATERZOOI DE POISSONS A LA GANTOISE

For centuries, two rivers, the Schelde and the Leie, which come together at Ghent, have supplied my hometown with pike, perch, and other freshwater fish. With this abundance of fish at the doorstep, one of the centuries-old specialties of Ghent has been this *waterzooi* of fish. Today river fish are no longer abundant, and the *waterzooi* is most often prepared with fish from the North Sea. For more information on *waterzooi*, see page 113.

3 tablespoons unsalted butter

4 leeks, white and light green parts only, rinsed
well and julienned

2 shallots, finely minced

2 carrots, peeled and julienned

½ celery root (celeriac), peeled and julienned

4 cups Fish Broth (page 56)

1 cup dry white wine

1 tablespoon fresh thyme or 1 teaspoon dried
thyme

1 bay leaf

Pinch of saffron threads

Salt and freshly ground black pepper
to taste

2 pounds fillet of firm-fleshed white fish, such
as turbot, cod, monkfish, or halibut, cut into
1-inch cubes

1½ cups heavy (or whipping) cream

3 large egg yolks

2 tablespoons finely minced fresh parsley
or chervil

1. Melt the butter in a large Dutch oven over
medium heat. Add the leeks, shallots, carrots,
and celery root and cook, stirring frequently,
until the vegetables have softened slightly but
are not browned, about 5 minutes.

2. Pour in the fish broth and wine. Add the
thyme, bay leaf, and saffron. Simmer, covered, over medium heat for 10 minutes. Season with salt and pepper. (You can prepare
the dish in advance up to this point.)

3. Before serving, bring the broth and vegetables to a simmer over medium heat. Add the
fish and poach, uncovered, in the simmering
broth until just done, about 10 minutes.

Remove the fish with a slotted spoon and
keep warm.

4. Whisk the cream and egg yolks together,
then gradually whisk in a ladleful of hot
broth to temper the egg mixture. Slowly stir
the egg mixture into the hot broth. Return the
fish to the broth and reheat over very low
heat if necessary. Do not allow it to come to a
boil or the sauce will curdle.

5. To serve, arrange the vegetables in the bottom of heated soup plates. Spoon the fish on
top and ladle plenty of sauce over the fish and
vegetables. Sprinkle with parsley and serve.

Serves 4

Eels
in Green Herb Sauce

PALING IN'T GROEN
•
ANGUILLES AU VERT

The landscape of Flanders is crossed by
many rivers and dotted with peaceful
green oases created by lovely lakes. In
my grandmother Jeanne's region there is a
lake called Donkmeer that is famous for
its eels. Jeanne and her artist companion,

98

Desmet, spent many afternoons walking along the borders of this lake, ending their walk with dinner at one of the many restaurants specializing in preparing this delicate fish. It was in one of these restaurants that the unique dish *anguilles au vert* was created. It has remained a particularly popular dish because of its subtle flavors and fresh green color.

I can just imagine the enterprising author of this dish wandering about her garden, looking for inspiration to prepare this long-bodied fish. She picks a handful of spinach, some sorrel, some tarragon, and mint...and the rest is history. Now every chef has her own secret ingredient—a certain herb that grows in his or her own garden. I don't know where Jeanne got this recipe, but it is the one she has passed on to me and it is excellent.

2 pounds eels, skinned and sliced crosswise into
*   3-inch pieces (see box, page 100)*
2 tablespoons unsalted butter
Salt and freshly ground black pepper to taste
⅔ cup dry white wine
5 shallots, finely chopped
2 cups (packed) very finely chopped fresh spinach
1½ cups (packed) very finely chopped fresh sorrel
½ cup (packed) very finely chopped fresh chervil
1 cup (packed) very finely chopped parsley leaves
1 sprig fresh tarragon
7 fresh leaves from lemon balm or mint
1 tablespoon potato starch
¼ cup cold water
Juice of ½ lemon

1. Rinse the eels carefully under cold running water to remove any traces of blood and run your fingers along the back of the fish to make sure that all the little bones from the fins are removed. Use tweezers to remove any that remain.

2. Melt the butter in a skillet large enough to hold the eel pieces without crowding over high heat. Add the eel and sauté on all sides until firm to the touch but not browned, 2 to 3 minutes. Season with salt and pepper. Add the wine, shallots, spinach, sorrel, chervil, parsley, tarragon, and lemon balm. Bring to a boil and reduce the heat. Simmer, covered, for 3 to 4 minutes.

3. Mix the potato starch with the cold water and gently whisk into the sauce to thicken it. Boil for 1 minute, then remove from the heat. Adjust the seasonings and add lemon juice to taste. Serve hot as an entrée or at room temperature as an appetizer.

Serves 4

Lemon Balm

*L*emon balm, or citronelle *in French, is a member of the mint family. In Belgium it is often grown in the kitchen garden. My great grandmother Marie grew it in great masses in a corner of her herb garden. It is much appreciated for its health-giving qualities and its lovely lemony taste.*

About Eels

Eels have a texture similar to salmon. Their whitish meat cooks up juicy and firm. Although eels are plentiful in America, they are not nearly as popular as they are in Europe. Most eels are sent directly to smokehouses and sold after they have been smoked. You can ask your fishmonger to order fresh eels for you if he does not normally carry them. Eels should be alive when you buy them. Ask your fishmonger to clean and skin them for you, as it takes practice to skin these extremely slippery creatures. When the central bone is removed, the meat separates into two fillets. They should be eaten on the day they are cleaned.

Eels in Cream Sauce

PALING IN ROOMSAUS
•
ANGUILLES A LA CREME

Belgians, along with their Scandinavian and Dutch neighbors, are inordinately fond of the sinuous long-bodied eels. In the United States, eels are regarded with some suspicion, but any adventurous seafood lover will appreciate this delicate, fine-flavored dish. In Belgium, this eel dish is prepared for special occasions and celebrations. Appropriate accompaniments would be some fresh peppery watercress and a generous serving of Belgian Fries (see Index).

2 pounds eels, skinned and sliced crosswise into 2-inch pieces
6 cups water
1 shallot, quartered
1 leek, white and light green parts only, rinsed well and sliced
1 bay leaf
¼ teaspoon freshly ground black pepper, plus additional to taste
Pinch of cayenne pepper
3 tablespoons unsalted butter
2 tablespoons all-purpose flour
¼ cup dry white wine
½ cup heavy (or whipping) cream
1 large egg yolk
Salt to taste
½ pound white mushrooms, cleaned, stemmed, and halved
1 tablespoon fresh lemon juice
2 tablespoons finely minced fresh parsley

1. Rinse the eels carefully under cold running water to remove any traces of blood and run your fingers along the back of the fish to make sure that all the little bones from the fins are removed. Use tweezers to remove any that remain.

2. In a large stockpot, bring the water to a boil. Add the shallot, leek, bay leaf, ¼ tea-

spoon pepper, and pinch of cayenne. Reduce the heat and simmer, covered, for 20 minutes. Add the eel pieces and poach, uncovered, at a gentle simmer for 10 minutes.

3. Remove the eel pieces from the poaching liquid and set aside. Strain the liquid and reserve ¾ cup. The rest can be frozen for later use in soups or sauces.

4. For the sauce, melt 2 tablespoons of the butter in a medium-size saucepan over medium heat. Add the flour and stir it in with a wire whisk. Gradually whisk in the reserved poaching liquid and the white wine. Bring to a boil and boil for 2 minutes, whisking constantly. Remove from the heat. Mix the cream together with the egg yolk. Beat in a ladleful of the hot sauce to temper the egg yolk, then whisk the egg mixture into the sauce. Season to taste with salt and pepper.

5. Melt the remaining 1 tablespoon butter in a medium-size skillet over medium heat. Add the mushrooms and cook until slightly browned and tender, about 8 minutes. Add the lemon juice and season to taste with salt and pepper. (You can prepare the dish in advance up to this point.)

6. Just before serving, add the eel and mushrooms to the sauce and heat through over low heat. Do not let the sauce come to a boil or it will curdle. Sprinkle with the parsley and serve.

Serves 4

Fillet of Cod with Mustard and Gingered Carrots

KABELJAUW MET TIERENTEYN EN WORTELKES

•

CABILLAUD A LA GANTOISE

This is my own recipe using three favorite ingredients of my hometown of Ghent—delicate white codfish, pungent Tierenteyn mustard, and sweet, fresh carrots.

Serve with steamed asparagus or broccoli, depending on the season, and accompany with sautéed new potatoes.

2 tablespoons unsalted butter
1 tablespoon finely minced fresh ginger
4 carrots, peeled and cut into matchsticks
Salt and freshly ground black pepper to taste
¼ cup water
4 codfish or halibut fillets (1 inch thick, about 5 ounces each)
½ cup dry white wine
1 cup heavy (or whipping) cream
1 to 2 tablespoons pungent mustard, such as Tierenteyn or Dijon
2 tablespoons finely minced fresh chervil or parsley, plus a few sprigs for garnish

1. Preheat the oven to 350°F.

2. Melt the butter in a small saucepan over medium heat. Add the ginger and sauté for 1 minute. Add the carrots, season with salt and pepper, and pour in the water. Cover and simmer until tender, 10 to 15 minutes. Add a little more water if necessary to prevent the carrots from burning.

3. Arrange the carrots in a ovenproof baking dish just large enough to comfortably hold the fish. Arrange the fish on top of the carrots, add the wine, and season lightly with salt and pepper. Cover tightly with aluminum foil and bake until the fish is just done, about 15 minutes.

4. While the fish is baking, reduce the cream to ½ cup in a small saucepan over medium-high heat.

5. Carefully remove the fish to a warmed serving platter. Combine the reduced cream with the mustard and mix together with the carrots. Taste and adjust the seasonings. Spoon the carrots and sauce over the fish and sprinkle with the minced chervil. Garnish with a few chervil sprigs and serve.

Serves 4

Fillet of Cod Flemish Style

KABELJAUW OP Z'N VLAAMS
•
CABILLAUD A LA FLAMANDE

One of the many advantages of preparing fish is its quick cooking time. No matter how busy you are, you can have a wonderful meal prepared in under half an hour. This recipe is a Flemish classic with its bold, forthright flavors and simplicity of preparation. Serve it with potato *stoemp*, mashed potatoes, or, for a more lavish meal, leek and potato pancakes (see Index for recipes).

4 tablespoons (½ stick) unsalted butter
1 large onion, thinly sliced
Salt and freshly ground black pepper
* to taste*
5 tablespoons finely minced fresh parsley
3 tablespoons finely minced fresh chives
1½ pounds center-cut cod fillet, or
* 4 individual steaks of cod, scrod, or*
* halibut (5 to 6 ounces each)*
4 slices fresh lemon, peel and pith
* removed*
1 bay leaf
1 sprig fresh thyme or ½ teaspoon
* dried thyme*
⅔ cup dry white wine

1. Preheat the oven to 350°F.

2. Melt the butter in a medium-size skillet over medium heat. Add the onion and cook, stirring occasionally, until softened and lightly browned, about 8 minutes. Season with salt and pepper.

3. Arrange half the onion in an ovenproof baking dish just large enough to comfortably hold the fish. Sprinkle half the parsley and chives over the onion. Arrange the fish fillet or steaks over the onion and season lightly with salt and pepper. Cover with the remaining onion, parsley, chives, the lemon slices, bay leaf, and thyme. Pour in the wine and bake until the fish is just done, about 20 minutes.

Serves 4

Nettles

In the springtime, Jeanne would always add a handful of tender white nettles to the green herbs in her recipe for Eels in Green Herb Sauce (page 98). Nettles are prized for their flavor, but above all they are considered to be a tonic for cleansing the blood. Every spring Jeanne's mother had made nettle soup as a spring tonic for the entire family, and it was as much a part of life in the country as the traditional spring cleaning of the house.

Fillet of Sole with Leeks and Chervil Butter

TONG FILLETS MET KERVELBOTER OP EEN BEDJE VAN PREI

•

SOLES AUX POIREAUX ET LE BEURRE DE CERFEUIL

The refined, delicate flavors of leeks and chervil are perfect accompaniments to the sweet-fleshed Dover sole. At the risk of sounding like a real chauvinist, I must say that the sole that comes from the North Sea is superior in taste and texture to any other sole I have ever had. Unfortunately, due to overfishing and pollution, these wonderful flat fishes, along with the tiny gray shrimp, are fast becoming a rarity, and therefore, are very expensive whenever they are available.

Occasionally, you can find real Dover sole stateside that has been flown in fresh. It is worth trying if you can afford it. Otherwise, substitute the freshest sole available at your fish market. Incidentally, my grandmother taught me years ago that the smaller fish were firmer and more flavorful, so you might keep this in mind when you choose your sole.

8 tablespoons (1 stick) unsalted butter, at room
    temperature
1 tablespoon fresh lemon juice
½ cup finely minced fresh chervil leaves, plus a
    few whole leaves for garnish
Salt and freshly ground black pepper to taste
5 leeks, white and light green parts only, rinsed
    well and thinly sliced
½ cup water
8 sole fillets (1½ to 2 pounds total)
1 tablespoon vegetable oil
1 tablespoon finely minced shallots
½ cup dry white wine or ⅓ cup dry vermouth
¼ pound cooked peeled shrimp, the smallest
    available

1. Combine 6 tablespoons of the butter with
the lemon juice, minced chervil, salt, and pepper in a small bowl. Cover with plastic wrap
and place in the coldest part of the refrigerator for several hours or overnight. The butter
must be cold and hard.

2. Preheat the oven to 375°F.

3. Melt the remaining 2 tablespoons of butter in a medium-size saucepan over medium
heat. Add the leeks and cook for 1 minute.
Add the water, cover the pan, and simmer
over low heat for 20 minutes. Check the leeks
a few times and add more water if necessary
to prevent them from browning. Season with
salt and pepper to taste. Remove from the
heat and set aside.

4. Lightly salt the sole fillets. Roll up each fillet and secure it with a toothpick.

5. Heat the vegetable oil in a small skillet
over medium heat. Add the shallots and cook
until softened, 3 minutes. Spoon the shallots
into an ovenproof baking dish just large
enough to hold the fish and arrange the fish
over the shallot. Add the wine and season
with salt and pepper. Cover the dish tightly
with a sheet of buttered aluminum foil and
bake for 10 minutes. Remove the fish to a
warmed platter and set aside.

6. To finish the sauce, pour the cooking liq-
uids from the fish into a small saucepan and
cook over high heat until reduced to about 3
tablespoons. Off the heat, whisk in the cold
chervil butter, 1 tablespoon at a time, until
completely incorporated and the sauce is
thick and creamy. Stir in the shrimp and
adjust the seasonings if necessary.

7. Reheat the leeks if necessary and arrange
them around the fish. Spoon the chervil
butter sauce over the fish, garnish with the
chervil sprigs, and serve.

Serves 4

Snipping Herbs

My great grandmother used to
say that the delicate perfume
of tiny chervil leaves disperses very
quickly. She insisted that the best
way of mincing chervil or any
other herb was with very sharp
little scissors, and always at the
last minute.

Sautéed Monkfish on a Bed of Belgian Endives in Beer Sauce

ZEEDUIVEL OP EEN BED VAN
WITLOOF EN GUEUZE

•

LOTTE AUX ENDIVES
A LA BIERE

The firm-fleshed, sweet monkfish is very highly regarded in Belgium. Here I have prepared it with beer and Belgian endives to make an original, full-flavored dish. While braising endives in beer is not new or unusual, the idea of pairing a vegetable infused with the strong flavor of beer with the delicate taste of fish is an example of the bold and exciting combinations to be found in Belgian nouvelle cuisine.

2 pounds monkfish fillet, cut into 1-inch chunks
¼ cup all-purpose flour
Salt and freshly ground black pepper to taste
4 tablespoons (½ stick) unsalted butter, plus additional if needed
2 tablespoons finely minced shallots
1 cup Belgian beer, preferably Gueuze or Blanche de Bruges
¾ cup heavy (or whipping) cream
4 Belgian endives, cored, sliced into thin julienne
1 tablespoon fresh lemon juice
2 teaspoons confectioners' sugar
1 ripe tomato, peeled, seeded, and finely diced, for garnish
Several sprigs fresh chervil or 1 tablespoon finely minced fresh parsley, for garnish

1. Dust the pieces of monkfish with the flour and season with salt and pepper.

2. Melt 2 tablespoons of the butter in a large skillet over high heat. Add the fish, reduce the heat to medium, and sauté until browned on all sides, 5 to 7 minutes.

3. Take the fish out of the skillet and keep warm. If the skillet is dry, add 1 tablespoon more butter to the skillet and melt over high heat. Add the shallots and cook for 1 minute. Pour in the beer and cook, stirring constantly for 1 minute. Add the cream and plenty of coarsely ground black pepper; continue cooking over high heat until reduced by half. Taste and adjust the seasonings.

4. Place the endives, lemon juice, and sugar in a bowl and toss to mix well.

5. Melt the remaining 2 tablespoons butter in a second large skillet over medium heat. Add the endives and cook, stirring frequently, until slightly browned and caramelized, 6 to 7 minutes.

6. Serve the fish on a bed of the caramelized endives. Spoon the sauce over the fish and decorate with the diced tomato and sprigs of chervil.

Serves 4

Fish and Shellfish Brochettes

VIS BROCHETTES
•
BROCHETTES DE POISSONS
ET FRUITS DE MER

rapping fish or sea scallops in a thin slice of bacon is a typical Belgian touch to what other-

wise would be ordinary broiled or grilled fish. The bacon keeps the fish moist and imparts a wonderful smoky flavor to the fish. Serve with a bowl of Gribiche sauce (see Index), good crusty bread, and a salad, and you have a very quick and easy dinner. If you are using bamboo skewers to hold the brochettes, soak them first in cold water.

1½ pounds firm-fleshed fish fillets, such as cod-
fish, monkfish, or sea bass, cut into 16 pieces,
or 16 scallops
16 paper-thin slices smoked bacon
1 large red or yellow bell pepper, stemmed,
seeded, and cut into 1-inch chunks
Lemon wedges for serving

1. Prepare a charcoal grill or preheat the broiler.

2. Wrap each piece of fish or scallop in a thin slice of bacon. Alternately thread the wrapped fish chunks and bell pepper chunks onto 8 skewers.

3. Grill the fish over a hot fire or under a hot broiler, turning the skewers a few times, until the fish is just opaque, 8 to 10 minutes.

4. Serve immediately with lemon wedges.

Serves 4

The Fish Market in Brugge

In the Middle Ages, fish and meat could be sold only in special markets that were built for this purpose. They were ornate gothic structures that are still a wonder to behold. The purest example of such a market still exists in the medieval city of Brugge. Go early in the morning and experience a trip back in time. The streets are quiet at sunrise, the silence broken only by the bells from the many church towers, but the fish market is bustling with business and activity. Buckets and baskets of splashing fish are everywhere, for in Belgium we firmly believe that fish have to be alive to be fresh, and no shopper worth his salt would consider the purchase of a fish who wasn't energetically floundering about. Somehow a fish purchased here, among the ancient stone counters and colonnades bearing witness to a glorious past, always tastes better to me than any other.

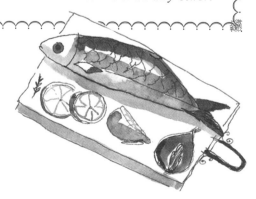

Baked Fresh Herring Packets

GEVULDE HARING IN PAPILLOTE

•

HARENGS EN PAPILLOTE

Cooking *en papillote*, that is, in paper packages or, more easily, in aluminum foil, is an easy, neat, and flavorful method for cooking whole fish. The aluminum package preserves all the tasty juices, and there is absolutely no mess to clean when the cooking is done.

If you can find a source for fresh herring in the spring and early summer, this is a wonderfully simple way to prepare them. The pure and clear flavors of the fish baked with butter and chopped fresh herbs make this a seasonal dish worth seeking out. In the Ardennes, where the rivers are abundant with trout, cooks prepare them in the same way. Another interesting substitute is mackerel. Serve the fish accompanied with new potatoes and lemon slices.

Weather permitting, cook the fish in their pouches on your outdoor grill, and slip a few potatoes wrapped in aluminum foil to cook in the hot coals.

4 tablespoons (½ stick) unsalted butter, at
   room temperature
3 scallions, white and green parts, thinly
   sliced
2 tablespoons finely minced shallots
2 tablespoons finely minced fresh chervil
3 tablespoons finely minced fresh chives
3 tablespoons finely minced fresh parsley
1½ tablespoons finely minced fresh tarragon
4 fresh herrings, gutted and cleaned but
   left whole
Salt and freshly ground black pepper to taste

1. Preheat the oven to 375°F.

2. Mash the butter with a fork in a small
bowl and mix in the scallions, shallots, and
all the herbs.

3. Season the fish
both inside and
out with salt and
pepper. Fill the
cavities of the
fish with the but-
ter mixture and
close each one with a
toothpick.

Fresh Herring

*M*ost herring is quickly
preserved either by salting or
smoking, and a meal of freshly
caught herring is a rare treat
indeed. In the United States it is
almost impossible to find fresh
herring in the market, and you
must seek out a friendly fisherman
to supply you from his catch. But
even in Belgium, fresh herring,
once so common that the smell of
herring frying in butter was invariably associated with the cooking of
the poor, is now hard to come by.

4. Arrange each fish in the center of a sheet
of buttered aluminum foil. Bring up the edges
of the foil all around and fold tightly to seal
in all the juices.

5. Bake 30 minutes. Serve the fish in the
pouch. Open the pouches carefully; they are
steaming hot inside.

Serves 4

Poultry and Game

Poultry

When the French king Henry IV promised his people that even the poorest peasant in his kingdom should enjoy a chicken in his pot (*une poule-au-pot*) every Sunday, the citizens of Belgium took his words very much to heart. For hundreds of years it has been a tradition to feast on a flavorful poached chicken on Sundays after mass. A chicken-in-the-pot dinner appealed to both the taste buds and the thrifty nature of the country folk. An older bird, finished with her egg-laying days and too tough to prepare in any other manner, could be slowly poached with a selection of aromatic vegetables to flavorful tenderness. Roast chicken, on the other hand, was considered the height of luxury. It required the sacrifice of a younger bird and the expenditure of a large blast of fuel, and offered no bonus in the form of broth.

In rural areas, many Belgians continue to raise a few chickens and rabbits for special occasions, just as they did in my great grandmother's day. The birds are allowed to roam around in the backyards and orchards as they have always done, scratching for their own food and clucking away to their hearts' content. As a result they produce a darker, juicier, and more flavorful meat.

For the rest of us, times have changed dramatically. Today chicken is one of the least expensive meats in the market, but most chickens have nowhere near the flavor and texture of their barnyard-raised relatives. Their flesh is full of chemicals and hormones, and the conditions in which they are raised make them susceptible to many diseases and infections, so we must take in how we handle and cook them.

I know what my great grandmother would do in this situation. She would insist on quality even if a slightly higher price meant cutting down on quantity. So, speaking for Marie Baekelandt, I urge you to seek out free-range chickens, which are becoming widely available. The extra expense is well worth it. In the larger cities you can also seek out kosher chickens, which are raised naturally and are always sold at the peak of freshness. The two qualities to insist on with your butcher or grocer are that the poultry be fresh and free of chemicals and hormones. If the poultry also has been raised in a way that allows the birds some freedom of movement and a generally happy (by a chicken's standards) existence, all the better. And, remember, the more we consumers insist on quality, the more grocers and butchers will carry the poultry we want.

Poached Chicken with Veal Dumplings and Rice

SOEPKIP MET BALLEKES EN RYST
•
POULE AU RIZ

Tender poached chicken, light-as-air dumplings, all swimming in a tart lemon sauce with mushrooms—this is a classic and popular Sunday dinner. It is a sumptuous and simple traditional staple.

Chicken:
1 stewing hen or roasting chicken (4 to 6 pounds), all visible fat removed, rinsed, and patted dry
Salt and freshly ground black pepper to taste
1 onion, peeled and halved
4 whole cloves
2 leeks, white and pale green parts only, rinsed well and sliced into ½-inch rounds
2 carrots, peeled and cut into 1-inch chunks
2 ribs celery, cut into 1-inch chunks
1 clove garlic
Bouquet garni: 3 sprigs parsley, 1 bay leaf, and 2 springs fresh thyme tied together with kitchen string
5 black peppercorns

Veal Dumplings:
½ pound ground veal
1 tablespoon all-purpose flour
Pinch of freshly grated nutmeg
1 tablespoon minced fresh parsley and/or chervil
Salt and freshly ground black pepper to taste

Velouté Sauce:
3 tablespoons unsalted butter
½ pound white mushrooms, cleaned, trimmed, and halved
2 tablespoons all-purpose flour
2 large egg yolks
¼ cup heavy (or whipping) cream
Juice of ½ lemon

2 tablespoons minced fresh chervil or parsley, for garnish
Rice Pilaf (recipe follows)

1. Season the cavity of the chicken with salt and pepper. Place the bird in a tall soup pot and cover entirely with cold water. Bring slowly to a boil over medium heat. Skim all the foam off the surface and reduce the heat to a gentle simmer.

2. Stud the onion halves with the cloves and add to the pot with the leeks, carrots, celery, garlic, bouquet garni, and peppercorns. Partially cover the pot and simmer until the chicken is very tender and falling off the bone, about 1½ hours.

3. Prepare the dumplings: Mix the ground veal, flour, nutmeg, parsley, salt, and pepper in a mixing bowl. Dust the palms of your

hands lightly with flour and form the mixture into little balls the size of marbles. Set aside.

4. Remove the chicken from the broth and transfer to a large plate. Allow the chicken to rest until cool enough to handle. Strip off the skin and remove the meat from the bones. Discard the skin and bones. Shred the meat into bite-size pieces.

5. Strain and degrease the broth; reserve 2 cups of broth for the sauce. Discard the solids.

6. Heat the remaining broth in a medium-size pot over medium heat. Add the veal dumplings and poach until they are firm and float lightly to the top, 3 to 4 minutes. Remove the dumplings and set aside. Save the remaining broth to cook the rice.

7. Prepare the sauce: Melt the butter in a medium-size heavy saucepan over medium heat, until foamy. Add the mushrooms and cook, stirring, until lightly browned, 3 minutes. Sprinkle the flour over the mushrooms and stir well with a wooden spoon until the flour is absorbed. Gradually pour in the 2 cups reserved chicken broth, stirring constantly; cook, stirring constantly, until the sauce is smooth and thick. Bring to a quick boil, reduce the heat to low, and simmer for 15 minutes. Season to taste with salt and pepper. Remove from the heat.

8. Whisk together the egg yolks, cream, and lemon juice in a small mixing bowl. Gradual-

ly whisk a ladleful of sauce into the egg mixture, then very gradually whisk this mixture into the sauce. Do not boil the sauce after this point or the egg yolks will curdle. Add the chicken pieces and the cooked veal dumplings and heat through over very low heat. Garnish with the chervil and serve with Rice Pilaf.

Serves 6

Rice Pilaf

2 tablespoons unsalted
   butter
1 small onion,
   finely chopped
1½ cups long-
   grain rice
3 cups reserved chicken poaching broth or water

1. Melt the butter in a medium-size saucepan over medium heat. Add the onion and cook, stirring occasionally, until translucent but not browned, about 5 minutes. Add the rice and stir with a wooden spoon until the rice is thoroughly coated with the butter.

2. Add the chicken broth and bring to a quick boil. Reduce the heat to low, cover the pot, and cook until the rice has absorbed all the liquid, 20 to 25 minutes. Turn off the heat but keep covered until ready to serve.

Serves 6

Waterzooi of Chicken

GENTSE WATERZOOI VAN KIP
•
WATERZOOI DE POULET A LA GANTOISE

*W*aterzooi, a confusion of a soup with a stew, in which the main ingredient (it can be made with chicken, rabbit, or fish) is poached in a creamy broth with aromatic vegetables, is a famous classic of Belgian cuisine and an all-time favorite in many households. Throughout Flanders, one can find as many variations of *waterzooi* as there are church towers on the horizon. One of the most delicate versions, the *waterzooi* of freshwater fish (see Index), originates in my hometown of Ghent, where two commercially important rivers, the Leie and the Schelde, have provided the main ingredients from time immemorial.

The ideal chicken for *waterzooi de poulet* is an older stewing hen whose flesh is rather tough but much more flavorful than a younger bird's. These are not always available in the United States. If you can't find one, choose a large roasting chicken instead and remember that the chicken will probably be tender in half the cooking time.

With a roasting chicken, do use a good chicken broth for the liquid, to compensate for the loss in flavor.

Waterzooi de poulet is usually served as a meal in itself, although it can certainly be preceded by a light appetizer and it won't disagree with the presence of a crisp green salad. Typically *waterzooi* is served hot, ladled into deep plates and accompanied by thick slices of country bread or a crusty baguette. The delicate balance between soup and sauce is what gives this dish its originality.

Waterzooi is easy to prepare and an excellent dish for entertaining as it can be prepared almost entirely ahead of time (see Note).

1 stewing or roasting chicken (3 to 4 pounds)
Salt and freshly ground black pepper to taste
2 bay leaves
3 or 4 sprigs fresh parsley
2 large sprigs fresh thyme or ½ teaspoon dried thyme
3 tablespoons unsalted butter
2 medium onions, coarsely chopped
4 to 6 cups chicken broth, preferably homemade (page 53), or water
4 large carrots, peeled and sliced into ¼-inch rounds
5 medium leeks, white parts only, rinsed well and sliced into ½-inch rounds
2 medium ribs celery, sliced into ½-inch rounds
4 large baking potatoes, peeled and cut into ½-inch cubes
1 cup heavy (or whipping) cream
2 large egg yolks
½ cup finely minced fresh parsley or chervil, for garnish

113

1. Pull away and discard any excess fat from the cavity. Rinse the bird inside and out. Season with salt and pepper and place 1 bay leaf, 2 sprigs parsley, and 1 sprig thyme in the chicken's cavity.

2. Melt the butter in a heavy Dutch oven over medium heat. Add the onions and cook, stirring occasionally, until translucent but not browned, about 5 minutes. Place the bird, breast side up, in the Dutch oven and add enough chicken broth or water (or half water and half chicken broth) to partially, cover the chicken (by about two-thirds). Cover and simmer gently over low heat for 30 minutes.

3. Skim the surface of the broth to remove any foam and fat. Add the carrots, leeks, and celery to the pot. Tie the remaining parsley, thyme, and bay leaf together with kitchen string to make a bouquet garni and add it to the broth. Cover and regulate the heat to maintain the liquid at a slow simmer for another 30 minutes.

4. Add the cubed potatoes to the simmering chicken broth and cook until the potatoes are done and the chicken is very tender, 20 to 30 minutes.

5. Remove the chicken from the broth and transfer to a large plate. Discard the bouquet garni. Allow the chicken to rest until it is cool enough to handle. Strip off the skin and use your fingers to remove the meat from the bones. Discard the skin and bones. Shred the meat into bite-size pieces.

6. Beat the cream and egg yolks together in a mixing bowl. Place the Dutch oven over medium heat. Stir a ladleful of hot broth into the egg mixture to temper it, then gradually stir this mixture into the broth and vegetables. Cook, stirring constantly, over low heat until the sauce thickens. Do not allow to boil or the sauce will curdle. Return the chicken pieces to the broth. Taste for seasoning and add salt and pepper if necessary. Garnish with plenty of fresh chopped parsley or chervil.

7. Serve in heated bowls, making sure that everyone gets equal amounts of chicken, vegetables, and broth.

Serves 4 to 6

Note: Waterzooi *can be prepared almost entirely in advance, and as with other stews and ragouts, the delicate flavors of this broth are enhanced by sitting overnight in the refrigerator. The day before you plan to serve the dish, prepare the recipe through step 5. Let cool completely and refrigerate the broth and vegetables separately from the chicken.*

The following day, before serving, reheat the chicken in the broth. Prepare the egg yolk and cream mixture and proceed with the last steps of the recipe. (The chicken may remain in the broth).

Spur of the Moment

My grandmother Jeanne told me an anecdote about the time her sister dropped in unexpectedly (à l'improviste) *with some of her Parisian friends.* "You know me, chèrie," *she said,* "my door is always open and there is always something to eat in my home. But les Parisiens, *one can't serve them just anything! I had a perfectly good* waterzooi *on my menu for that evening, and happily I remembered the basket of fresh, green asparagus that Kamiel, my gardener, had offered me that same morning. Voilà, I was saved.*

"*I simmered the asparagus stalks in a little chicken broth until they were very tender and put them through the blender. This thick purée added a wonderful flavor and a pretty green color to my* waterzooi. *The asparagus tips were briefly poached and added to the* waterzooi *for a final, elegant touch. A fresh tablecloth, a few roses on the table, a good bottle of white wine . . . it was a feast!* Les Parisiens *were impressed.*"

Jeanne's lesson to me was that once you have mastered the technique of a certain dish, the possibilities for creative adaptation are endless. My Aunt Lucette became famous in the family for her version of waterzooi *of scallops (see Index), and my mother often prepares a wonderful Mediterranean fish* waterzooi.

Chicken with Vegetables

KIP MET LENTEGROENTJES
•
FRICASSEE DE POULET PRINTANIERE

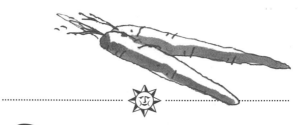

This chicken and vegetable dish, a variation on the classic *waterzooi*, is a delightful simple one-dish meal in which you can substitute whatever vegetables are in season. In autumn, make it with the first small turnips of the season, a handful of woodsy mushrooms, some shredded Savoy cabbage, and a little bit of bacon to add a smoky flavor. In the summer add some chopped ripe tomatoes and a small handful of fresh basil.

I sometimes prepare this dish in my crockpot. I set it on low and go about my business for several hours—gardening, walking, or bike riding. When I return, the house is full of mouth-watering aromas that promise a delicious dinner.

Serve this chicken dish with steamed new potatoes or with a crisp country loaf to mop up the sauce.

2 tablespoons unsalted butter

3 leeks, white and pale green parts only, rinsed
    well and sliced into ¼-inch rounds

3 carrots, peeled and cut into 1-inch chunks

10 pearl onions or 5 shallots, peeled
    and halved

1 whole roasting chicken (about 4 pounds),
    rinsed, patted dry, all visible fat removed

Salt and freshly ground black pepper
    to taste

1½ cups chicken broth, preferably
    homemade (page 53)

Bouquet garni: 3 sprigs parsley, 1 bay leaf,
    and 2 sprigs fresh thyme tied together
    with kitchen string

1 sprig fresh tarragon or ½ teaspoon dried
    tarragon

1 pound snow peas or green beans, trimmed

1 pound fresh green peas, shelled, or 1 package
    (10 ounces) thawed frozen peas

½ head broccoli, divided into florets

Beurre manié: 1½ tablespoons all-purpose flour
    blended with 1 tablespoon unsalted butter
    (optional)

1. Preheat the oven to 350°F.

2. Melt the butter in a large enameled Dutch
oven over low heat. Add the leeks, carrots,
and onions; cook, stirring occasionally, until
softened but not browned, 7 to 10 minutes.

3. Season the cavity of the chicken with salt
and pepper. Place the chicken on the vegetables. Add the chicken broth, bouquet garni,
and tarragon. Bring to a boil on top of the
stove. Cover tightly and bake for 30 minutes.

4. Add the green beans if you are using them
and bake, covered, for another 30 minutes.
Add the snow peas, if using, broccoli, and
fresh or frozen peas. Bake, uncovered, until
the vegetables are tender, about 7 minutes.

5. Carve the chicken and arrange on a platter
surrounded by the vegetables. Discard the
bouquet garni and the tarragon from the
sauce. If the sauce seems too thin to you,
whisk in the *beurre manié* and bring to a
quick boil, whisking constantly. Pour the
sauce over the chicken and vegetables.

Serves 4 to 6

Op Zyn Brussels

*M*any chicken recipes in
Belgium include the phrase
op zyn Brussels (in the manner of
Brussels) as part of the name. This
refers to the typical use of endives
and/or beer, particularly lambic
beer, as ingredients, and to the
chicken itself. Mechelse koekoek,
the chicken raised in the environs
of Brussels, and also known as
coucou, is famous for its quality all
over Belgium. This chicken is carefully barnyard reared, grain-fed,
and always sold fresh. In the
United States, look for free-range
chicken for comparable quality.

Chicken Braised in Beer with Belgian Endives

MECHELSE KOEKOEK
OP ZYN BRUSSELS
•
COUCOU DE MALINES AUX
CHICONS

This popular one-dish meal is a Sunday lunch favorite and is typically made as soon as the first endives of the season come to market (the season runs from September through April). A more elegant variation of this meal is to roast a whole chicken, braise the endives separately, and serve the two together (see Index for recipes). But my favorite has always been to braise the cut-up chicken and endives together in Belgian beer so that they can exchange their complementary bittersweet flavors to make a truly enticing dish. Traditionally this is served with steamed potatoes, and except for some good country bread to mop up the wonderful sauce, you need not serve anything else.

1 roasting chicken (3 to 3½ pounds), cut into
    serving pieces, rinsed and patted dry, all
    visible fat removed
Salt and freshly ground black pepper to taste
2 tablespoons all-purpose flour
1 tablespoon unsalted butter, plus additional
    if needed
1 tablespoon vegetable oil
4 to 5 Belgian endives, cored and halved
4 teaspoons sugar
Juice of ½ lemon
Pinch of freshly grated nutmeg
1½ tablespoons finely minced shallots
¼ cup Belgian beer, such as Duvel
    or any dark ale
½ cup crème fraîche or heavy (or whipping)
    cream
3 tablespoons minced fresh parsley, for garnish

1. Season the chicken with salt and pepper. Coat with flour and shake off any excess.

2. Heat the butter and oil in a large heavy Dutch oven and brown the chicken pieces on all sides. Watch your pot carefully and take care not to burn the butter or the sauce will be bitter. Transfer the chicken pieces to a platter and set aside.

3. Sprinkle the endives with the sugar, add half the lemon juice, and season with salt,

pepper, and nutmeg. Sauté the endives in the chicken drippings over fairly high heat so that the endives are quickly browned and caramelized on both sides, 5 to 7 minutes. You might have to add a little extra butter to the drippings.

4. Add the shallots and cook for 1 minute. Add the beer and arrange the chicken pieces over the vegetables. Cover and simmer over low heat for 15 minutes.

5. Add the crème fraîche and bring to a quick boil. Reduce the heat, cover the pot, and simmer until the chicken is cooked through, 15 to 20 minutes. The cooking time will depend on the size of your chicken pieces. The meat should be tender.

6. Check the seasoning and add the remaining lemon juice. Remove the chicken and endives to a warmed platter.

7. Skim as much fat as possible from the sauce and boil over high heat until reduced by about one-third, about  2 minutes. Pour some of the sauce over the chicken and sprinkle generously with freshly chopped parsley. Serve the remaining sauce on the side.

Serves 4

Variation: For special occasions, pheasant, guinea hen, or other game birds can be substituted with equally delicious results.

Chicken Braised in Belgian Beer

KIP MET RODENBACH

•

POULET A LA BIERE RODENBACH

*C*hicken braised in beer is one of the many hearty and satisfying one-dish meals at which Belgian home cooks particularly excel. It can be prepared in advance, and the flavor usually improves overnight in the refrigerator.

In this recipe, the very authentic Belgian flavor comes from the beer. I have made this with Rodenbach and Trappist Abbey beer as well as Duvel. All are marvelous, with intriguing differences. If you cannot find a Belgian beer, substitute a good full-flavored domestic brand. My grandmother Jeanne used to add a small glass of *genever* (Belgian gin) to all her beer stews, and, indeed, it adds a wonderful depth of flavor. Should you visit Belgium one of these days, do remember to bring home a bottle of this special gin, which, alas, is not yet available in the United States.

Serve the braised chicken with boiled potatoes, braised endives, Savoy cabbage, or any other seasonal vegetable.

1 roasting chicken or capon (4 to 6 pounds), cut into 8 serving pieces, rinsed and patted dry, all visible fat removed

Salt and freshly ground black pepper to taste

1 tablespoon vegetable oil

2 tablespoons unsalted butter

15 pearl onions or 7 shallots, peeled

12 large white mushrooms, cleaned, trimmed, and quartered

1 teaspoon sugar

1 clove garlic, finely minced

3 carrots, peeled and cut into 1-inch chunks

1½ tablespoons all-purpose flour

1 bottle (12 ounces) Belgian beer, preferably Rodenbach

½ cup beef broth, preferably homemade (page 54) or veal broth

1 teaspoon dried thyme or 1 sprig fresh thyme

Bouquet garni: 1 large bay leaf and 3 sprigs parsley tied together with kitchen string

½ cup heavy (or whipping) cream (see Note)

1 tablespoon finely minced fresh parsley, for garnish

Bouquet Garni

*P*arsley, thyme, and bay leaves, tied together with kitchen string when fresh or tied in a piece of cheesecloth when dried, are indispensable for flavoring broths, stews, and sauces.

My great grandmother Marie had her own way of doing things and never varied from her routine. She peeled an onion, cut it in half, and stuck each half with 2 cloves. She tied parsley, thyme, and bay leaves to a piece of celery rib with some kitchen string to make a bouquet garni. Aesthetics were always a part of her skills—the clove-studded onion and the herb bouquet were pretty—but practicality was always a factor as well—the bouquet was easy to remove and discard when the stock was complete.

1. Season the chicken pieces generously with salt and pepper.

2. Heat the oil and 1 tablespoon of the butter in a large enameled Dutch oven over medium heat until hot but not smoking. Add the chicken pieces, a few at a time, and sauté over medium-high heat until golden brown on

both sides, about 10 minutes. Carefully regulate the heat so the chicken browns but the butter does not burn. Brown all the chicken pieces and set aside.

3. Add the remaining 1 tablespoon butter to the Dutch oven over medium heat. Add the onions and mushrooms; cook, stirring frequently, until they begin to brown slightly, 5 to 7 minutes. Sprinkle with the sugar, add the garlic, and cook for 1 minute longer, shaking the pan constantly.

4. Add the carrots. Sprinkle the flour over the vegetables and stir with a wooden spoon making sure that the flour and butter are well blended. Add the beer and broth and stir with the wooden spoon, scraping up all the little brown bits on the bottom of the pan. Add the chicken pieces, thyme, and bouquet garni.

5. Cover the pan and simmer over low heat until the chicken is tender, 40 to 50 minutes.

6. Discard the bouquet garni. Remove the chicken and set aside. Reduce the sauce over high heat by one-third, about 5 minutes. Add the cream and reduce further until the sauce is smooth and nicely thickened. Taste and adjust the seasoning. Return the chicken to the pot and carefully turn the pieces over in the sauce so that every bit of chicken is coated. Sprinkle with the fresh parsley and serve.

Serves 4 to 6

Note: For a lighter dish, replace the cream in this recipe with more stock.

Braised Chicken with Tomatoes and Mushrooms

GESMOORDE KIP MET TOMATEN EN CHAMPIGNONS
•
POULE A LA TOMATE ET AUX CHAMPIGNONS

This straightforward and delicious braised chicken is a perennial favorite in many Belgian households. My mother always serves this dish with generous portions of golden, crunchy Belgian fries and a large green salad. Whenever you have access to fresh herbs, such as basil, savory, or rosemary, you can add these along with the tomatoes for extra flavor.

3 tablespoons olive oil

1 whole roasting chicken (3 to 4 pounds), cut
into 8 serving pieces, rinsed and patted dry,
all visible fat removed

Salt and freshly ground black pepper to taste

1 teaspoon paprika

2 medium onions, coarsely chopped

½ pound mushrooms, cleaned, trimmed, and
halved or left whole if very small

2 large cloves garlic, finely minced

1 tablespoon all-purpose flour

1¼ cups dry white wine

2 ripe large beefsteak tomatoes, peeled, cored,
seeded, and chopped; or 1½ cups canned
plum tomatoes, drained and chopped

2 tablespoons tomato paste

2 teaspoons fresh thyme or ¾ teaspoon dried
thyme

1 bay leaf

1 tablespoon finely minced fresh parsley, for
garnish

1. Heat the oil in a large enameled Dutch
oven over medium heat. Sear the chicken
parts, without crowding, until golden brown
all over, about 10 minutes. Do this in 2 batches if necessary. Remove the browned chicken
to a platter and season with salt, pepper, and
paprika. Set aside.

2. Discard all but 1½ tablespoons fat from
the Dutch oven. Add the onions and mushrooms and cook, stirring constantly, over
high heat until softened but not browned, 3
to 4 minutes. Add the garlic and flour and
continue to cook, stirring, for about 30 seconds. Add the wine and stir, scraping up all

the brown bits on the bottom of the pan.
Return the chicken pieces and add the toma-
toes, tomato paste, thyme, and bay leaf.
Season lightly with salt and pepper.

3. Cover the Dutch oven and simmer for 30
minutes over low heat. Then cook, partially
covered, until the chicken is very tender, 20 to
30 minutes. The sauce will have reduced
somewhat and thickened. Taste and adjust
the seasoning. Remove the bay leaf, sprinkle
with the parsley, and serve.

Serves 4

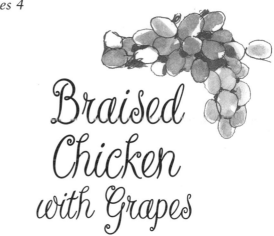

Braised Chicken with Grapes

KIP MET DRUIFJES
•
POULARDE AUX RAISINS

An old-time favorite, chicken with
grapes has its roots in medieval
times, when the mixing of fruits
with meat and a little tart wine was a common combination.

Perfect for a festive occasion, this luxurious dish is not at all difficult to make and can be prepared ahead of time and reheated. Traditionally, it is served with Deep-Fried Potato Croquettes, but steamed rice or Parsleyed New Potatoes would also be good companions (see Index for recipes).

1 roasting chicken (3 to 4 pounds) cut into
  8 serving pieces, rinsed and patted dry,
  all visible fat removed
Salt and freshly ground black pepper
  to taste
1 tablespoon vegetable oil
3 tablespoons unsalted butter
½ cup finely minced shallots
¼ cup Cognac
½ cup fruity white wine, such as Muscadet or
  Riesling
⅓ cup chicken broth, preferably homemade
  (page 53)
1 cup canned peeled green grapes,
  drained but ½ cup heavy syrup
   reserved
½ cup heavy (or whipping) cream
½ pound fresh seedless green grapes, half of
  them stemmed and peeled for the sauce,
  the remainder left in small clusters
  for garnish
Watercress leaves, for garnish

1. Season the chicken pieces generously with salt and pepper. Heat the oil and 1 tablespoon of the butter in a large sauté pan or large enameled Dutch oven over medium-high heat until hot. Add the chicken pieces, a few at a time so as not to crowd the pan, and sauté on both sides until golden brown. Continue until all the chicken pieces are browned. Set aside.

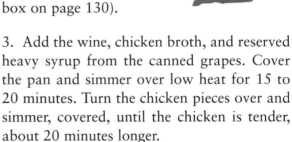

2. Heat the remaining 2 tablespoons butter in the same pan over low heat. Add the shallots and cook, stirring occasionally, until softened but not browned. Add the chicken pieces. Flambé with the Cognac (for flambéing instructions, see box on page 130).

3. Add the wine, chicken broth, and reserved heavy syrup from the canned grapes. Cover the pan and simmer over low heat for 15 to 20 minutes. Turn the chicken pieces over and simmer, covered, until the chicken is tender, about 20 minutes longer.

4. Remove the chicken pieces and set aside. Reduce the liquid in the pan over high heat by one-third to concentrate the flavor, 1 to 2 minutes. Add the cream and reduce further until the sauce is smooth and nicely thickened. Taste and adjust the seasoning.

5. Reheat the chicken in the sauce, turning the pieces over carefully so that every bit is covered with sauce. Add both the canned and fresh peeled grapes. Arrange on a large platter, surrounded with grape clusters and watercress leaves, and serve.

Serves 4 to 5

Verjus

*I*n medieval cookery, grapes and undiluted grape wine are often mentioned in the ingredients used to flavor soups and stews. To balance the cloying sweetness of many sauces, verjus *was added. This tart and mysterious liquid is often defined as the juice of unripe grapes, but it is just as likely to have been the tart juice of gooseberries, crab apples, or any other tart fruit or berry.*

Braised Capon with Baby Carrots

HAANTJE MET WORTELKES EN DRAGON

•

COQUELET AUX JEUNES CAROTTES ET A L'ESTRAGON

A plump, tender capon with a thick layer of fat just under the skin to baste the meat, always makes an excellent roasting bird. But my recipe introduces a less familiar treatment, in which a cut-up capon is braised in wine with tarragon and sweet young carrots to make an unusual and wonderfully succulent dish. Serve with Boiled Rice or Parsleyed New Potatoes (see Index).

1 capon (5 to 6 pounds), cut into 8 serving pieces, rinsed and patted dry, all visible fat removed
Salt and freshly ground black pepper to taste
2 tablespoons vegetable oil
1 tablespoon unsalted butter
1½ cups dry white wine
¾ cup chicken broth, preferably homemade (page 53)
1 teaspoon fresh thyme or ½ teaspoon dried thyme
1 bay leaf
5 sprigs fresh tarragon
1 pound baby carrots, peeled but with a little of the green tops left on
¾ cup heavy (or whipping) cream
2 teaspoons cornstarch
2 tablespoons dry white wine or water
1½ tablespoons finely minced fresh tarragon

1. Season the capon pieces liberally with salt and pepper. Heat the oil and butter in a large enameled Dutch oven over medium-high heat until the butter foams. Add the capon pieces, a few at a time so as not to overcrowd the pan, and sauté until golden brown on both sides, 10 to 15 minutes. Regulate the heat so that the

butter does not burn. When all the pieces are browned, return them to the casserole.

2. Add the 1½ cups wine and the chicken broth and use a wooden spoon to scrape up all the brown bits on the bottom of the pan. Add the thyme, bay leaf, and tarragon sprigs. Bring the liquid to a boil and reduce the heat to low. Cover the pan and simmer for 45 minutes.

3. Add the carrots and continue to simmer, covered, until the capon is tender and the carrots are meltingly soft, 30 to 45 minutes. (You can prepare the dish in advance up to this point.)

4. Remove the capon pieces and the carrots and arrange on a warmed serving platter.

5. Using a spoon or a degreasing cup, remove and discard most of the fat from the braising liquid in the pan. Bring the liquid to a boil and reduce over high heat to 1½ cups, 1 to 2 minutes. Add the cream and reduce over high heat for 5 more minutes. Dissolve the cornstarch in the 2 tablespoons wine. Reduce the heat to low and add the dissolved cornstarch. Cook, stirring, until the sauce is nicely thickened, 2 to 3 minutes. Taste and adjust the seasoning and add the minced tarragon.

6. Spoon the sauce over the capon and serve.

Serves 6

Variation: For a lighter dish, you can omit the heavy cream.

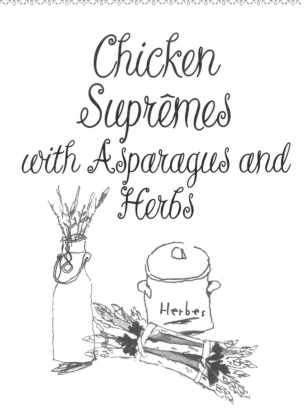

Chicken Suprêmes with Asparagus and Herbs

KIPPEFILLET MET KRUIDEN UIT DE TUIN EN ASPERGES
•
BLANCS DE POULET AUX HERBES VERTES ET ASPERGES

The *suprême* is half a chicken breast, trimmed of all bone and skin. These lovely fillets are quick and easy to prepare. The creamy light herb sauce and fresh asparagus make this recipe a perfect choice for a late spring dinner party. Serve the chicken with boiled quartered Yukon Gold or Yellow Finn Potatoes, sprinkled with a little sea salt and finely minced parsley.

1 pound asparagus, trimmed and tied in a
    bundle with kitchen string
Salt to taste
3 tablespoons unsalted butter
3 tablespoons finely minced shallots
2 whole large chicken breasts, boned, skinned,
    and halved
1 sprig fresh tarragon, leaves finely minced,
    stem kept whole; or ½ teaspoon dried
    tarragon
Freshly ground black pepper to taste
½ cup dry white wine
½ cup heavy (or whipping) cream
1 large egg yolk
½ pound young spinach leaves, rinsed,
    stemmed, and finely chopped
1 ounce sorrel leaves, stemmed and finely
    chopped
¼ cup finely minced fresh parsley
¼ cup finely minced fresh chervil
Fresh chervil leaves, for garnish

1. Cook the asparagus in plenty of boiling salted water until just tender, 5 to 10 minutes. Drain and keep warm.

2. Melt 2 tablespoons of the butter in a large enameled Dutch oven over medium heat. Add the shallots and cook for 2 minutes. Place the chicken breasts on top of the shallots, add the fresh or dried tarragon, and season with salt and pepper. Pour the wine over the chicken and cover the pan. Simmer for 10 minutes over low heat. Turn the chicken breasts over and simmer, covered, for another 10 to 15 minutes. The chicken juices should run clear when it is pricked

with a fork, but the breasts should not brown at all.

3. Remove the chicken breasts and keep warm. Discard the fresh tarragon, if using.

4. In a small bowl, whisk ¼ cup of the cream with the egg yolk. Set aside.

5. Melt the remaining 1 tablespoon butter in the Dutch oven over medium heat. Add the spinach and sorrel, cover the pan, and cook for 3 to 4 minutes. Add the fresh tarragon leaves, if using, the parsley, and chervil; cook, stirring with a wooden spoon, for 2 more minutes.  Add the remaining ¼ cup of the cream, boil for 2 minutes, and remove from the heat. Taste and adjust the seasoning. Off the heat, stir the egg yolk mixture into the hot sauce to thicken it.

6. For a beautiful presentation, serve on large dinner plates. Spoon some sauce in the middle of each plate. Cut each *suprême* into thick slices and fan it out over the sauce. Place three asparagus stalks on each side of the *suprême* and sprinkle the whole plate with chervil leaves.

Serves 4

My Grandmother Jeanne's Perfect Roast Chicken

GEROOSTERDE KIP OP GROOTMOEDER'S WYZE

•

LE POULET ROTI DE MA GRAND-MERE JEANNE

A chicken roasted to golden brown perfection, its skin deliciously crispy and irresistible, is my idea of home cooking at its best. With very little trouble, one can turn a simple daily meal into a festive celebration. There's always something special about presenting a whole bird, and this is true whether you serve a Cornish hen or the biggest, fattest capon you can find. The following method of roasting can be applied to all of these if cooking time is adjusted for the size of the bird.

In Belgium, this meal is served with a fruit compote or applesauce, along

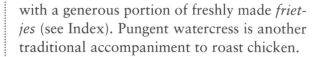

with a generous portion of freshly made *frietjes* (see Index). Pungent watercress is another traditional accompaniment to roast chicken.

1 chicken liver, trimmed of fat and
    discolored spots, rinsed and
    patted dry
6 tablespoons unsalted butter, at room
    temperature
1 teaspoon finely minced fresh parsley
2 teaspoons finely minced fresh tarragon or
    1 teaspoon dried tarragon
Salt and freshly ground black pepper
    to taste
1 whole roasting chicken (3 to 4 pounds),
    free range if possible, rinsed and patted dry,
    all visible fat removed
½ cup water
2 teaspoons cornstarch
¼ cup Madeira or port
1 bunch watercress, thick stems removed,
    for garnish

1. Place an oven rack in the middle of the oven. Preheat the oven to 425°F.

2. Finely chop the chicken liver and combine it with 2 tablespoons of the butter, the parsley, and the tarragon. Season with salt and pepper and place the mixture inside of the chicken cavity.

3. Truss the bird with kitchen string. Rub it all over with 3 tablespoons butter and season the outside with salt and pepper.

4. Place the chicken on its side on a rack in a flameproof roasting pan just large enough to

hold it. Roast for 10 minutes. Turn the bird to the other side and roast for 10 minutes.

5. Reduce the heat to 350°F and continue roasting, breast side up, basting with the pan juices every 15 minutes, until the juices run clear when the thigh is pierced with a fork, 45 minutes to 1 hour more. The internal temperature should be 170 to 180°F when an instant-read thermometer is inserted at the inner thigh without touching the bone.

6. Remove the bird from the roasting pan and let rest for 15 minutes before carving.

7. Meanwhile, prepare the gravy: Remove as much of the fat as you can from the roasting pan. Place the pan over medium heat and add the water. Using a wooden spoon, scrape up all the brown bits on the bottom of the pan. Cook over medium heat for 30 seconds. Dissolve the cornstarch in the Madeira and add it to the pan. Bring to a quick boil, stirring constantly, and remove from the heat. Stir in the remaining 1 tablespoon butter. Taste and adjust the seasoning.

8. Arrange the watercress on a warm serving platter. Carve the chicken and arrange over the watercress. The liver will have melted away and enriched the sauce. Dribble some of the gravy over the carved chicken.

Serves 4 to 5

Jeanne's Roast Chicken with Apples, Onions, and Potatoes

JEANNE'S GEROOSTERDE KIP
MET APPELS, AJUINTJES,
EN AARDAPPELEN
•
LA POULE ROTIE AU FOUR
DE JEANNE

This satisfying one-dish meal, with its hearty flavors, was a staple of my life in Belgium and continues to be a failproof dish that I make often for my friends in this country. For my grandmother Jeanne, this was the dinner she put together on her busy days when the demands on her time were too many to "cook a proper meal." After arranging for the opening of an exhibition or a piano recital at her museum, holding a press conference, and carrying out a few other small tasks, she'd invite a handful of close friends to dine with her. With a minimum of time in the kitchen, she produced her roast chicken. Perhaps not a "proper meal" by her standards, but with some bread and wine, it delighted even the most critical guest.

Even if you have never done it before, you will find that the trick of separating the skin from the flesh of the chicken is a very simple procedure. This allows you to slip the bacon under the skin of the breast and thighs. The bacon imparts a light, smoky flavor to the chicken, and at the same time, eliminates the need to baste it. A little paprika sprinkled over the chicken before putting it in the oven is an old home cook's trick to ensure a nicely browned bird.

Here's another tip from generations of busy home cooks: Always try to roast a bigger bird than you need, so you will have plenty left over for chicken salads and sandwiches.

1 whole roasting chicken (3 to 4 pounds), rinsed
 and patted dry, all visible fat removed
Salt and freshly ground black pepper to taste
4 slices smoked bacon
1 tablespoon unsalted butter
1 teaspoon paprika
2 large onions, coarsely chopped
8 medium red potatoes, peeled and cut into
 1/2-inch cubes
3 tart apples, cored and cut into 1/2-inch cubes
3 tablespoons vegetable oil
1 1/2 teaspoons dried thyme
1/4 cup chicken broth, preferably homemade
 (page 53), plus additional if needed
1 tablespoon minced fresh parsley,
 for garnish

1. Place an oven rack in the middle of the oven. Preheat the oven to 425°F.

2. Season the chicken cavity generously with salt and pepper. Use your fingers to gently loosen the skin around the breast and legs, being careful not to make any holes in the skin. Insert the bacon slices under the skin to cover each breast and each leg. Truss the chicken with kitchen string. Rub the chicken all over with the butter and sprinkle with the paprika. Place the chicken on its side in a roasting pan that is just large enough to hold the chicken and the vegetables. Roast for 10 minutes. Turn the bird to the other side and roast for 10 minutes.

3. While the chicken is browning, combine the onions, potatoes, apples, oil, and thyme in a bowl. Season with salt and pepper to taste.

4. Reduce the oven heat to 350°F. Turn the chicken breast side up, baste it with the drippings, and season with salt and pepper. Spoon the vegetable mixture around the chicken, and pour in the chicken broth. Roast until the juices from the cavity run clear, 45 to 60 minutes more. Check on the vegetables from time to time to make sure that they are not burning. Add a little more chicken broth, if necessary. By the end of the cooking time, the vegetables should be nicely browned and cooked through and all the liquid should have evaporated.

5. Let the chicken rest for 5 minutes before carving. Arrange the carved chicken on a warmed platter and surround with the vegetables. Sprinkle with the parsley and serve.

Serves 4 to 5

How to Tell When Your Roast Chicken Is Done

My grandmother seemed to know by instinct how to cook a bird perfectly. She never relied on a clock but on her own internal timer. Until you have flawlessly roasted your first thousand or so chickens, you may need more tangible signs. Here are several:

1. Start checking your chicken after 45 minutes in the oven.

2. The cavity juices should run clear when the bird is lifted and tilted. I use two sturdy wooden spoons to do this—one cradling the abdominal cavity, the other holding up the neck cavity.

3. The thigh should feel tender when it is pressed with your finger.

4. When the chicken is pricked with a fork in the joint between the thigh and the breast, the juices should run clear.

5. Use a thermometer. The internal temperature should reach 170 to 180°F when an instant-read thermometer is inserted at the inner thigh, not touching the bone.

6. Remove the chicken from the oven as soon as you decide it is done, or a few minutes before. It will continue cooking as it rests.

Chicken with Juniper Berries

KIP MET GENEVERBESSEN
• POULE AU GENEVRIER

This is one of the best recipes for pan-roasted chicken in my repertoire. It is extremely simple and quick to prepare, and the sharp clean flavors of the juniper berries and *genever* (Belgian gin) always make me feel as if I were tasting really good chicken for the very first time. The closest substitute is Dutch gin (also called *genever*). Otherwise, you can substitute Bombay gin, Cognac, Armagnac, or brandy.

Serve potato *stoemp* (see Index) and any seasonal green vegetable alongside.

1 roasting chicken (3 to 4 pounds), cut into 8 serving pieces, rinsed and patted dry, all visible fat removed
Salt and freshly ground black pepper to taste
1 tablespoon vegetable oil
1 tablespoon unsalted butter
1 medium onion, minced
1 garlic clove, finely minced
20 juniper berries
¼ cup genever (Belgian gin)
3 to 4 tablespoons water or chicken broth if needed

1. Season the chicken pieces generously with salt and pepper.

2. Heat the oil and butter in a large heavy sauté pan over high heat until the butter melts but is not foaming. Add the chicken pieces a few at a time so they are not crowded and sauté until golden brown on each side, 3 to 4 minutes per side. Continue until all the pieces are browned, and set aside.

3. Add the onion to the pan and cook, stirring constantly, over high heat until just softened, about 2 minutes. Add the garlic and return the chicken to the pan, along with any juices it has released. Reduce the heat to low, cover the pan, and cook until the meat is done, 20 to 30 minutes. Halfway through the cooking, turn over the chicken pieces and baste the meat with the pan juices.

4. While the chicken is cooking, crush the juniper berries with a rolling pin or the bottom of a heavy saucepan.

5. When the chicken is done, flambé it with the gin (see the adjoining box). Add the crushed juniper berries to the chicken. Increase the heat to high and turn the chicken pieces over so they are completely covered with the flavored juices. Add a few tablespoons water or chicken broth if it is too dry and serve immediately.

Serves 4

How to Flambé

1. Heat the alcohol in a small saucepan over medium heat.

2. When it is hot, remove the pan from the burner, and standing back, carefully ignite it with a long kitchen match.

3. Pour the flaming alcohol slowly over the dish that is being flambéed.

Safety Tips

• *Make sure the hood fan on your range is turned off.*

• *Make sure there is nothing close by that can catch fire, including overhead shelves and paper products. Also make sure your clothing doesn't interfere or get in the way of the flames.*

• *Keep a large lid at the ready to cover the flames if they should get out of hand.*

• *Use good-quality alcohol and pour it from the bottle at the last minute so it does not evaporate.*

Stuffed Roast Chicken Served with Rosemary Roasted Potatoes

FEESTELYKE OPGEVULDE KIP
•
POULARDE FARCIE A LA FLAMANDE

How to create a summer feast Belgian style: Take the trouble to find a large free-range roasting chicken or capon. Ask your butcher to bone the bird or bone it yourself. Stuff it with a savory, flavorful forcemeat, and roast it to a lovely golden brown. Let it cool to room temperature. Prepare the creamy Cucumber Salad with Chervil (page 14) and slice some nice ripe tomatoes. Get some good bread and some cold beer. Invite your most jovial friends. Set a table outdoors. Slice the chicken into thin rounds and enjoy the gasps of appreciation as your guests admire the perfect slices of boneless chicken each with a center of pistachio-studded pâté-like stuffing. Sit under the stars and enjoy the bounty of life.

Everything except the roasted potatoes can be prepared ahead, even the day before, so you have little to do and can enjoy this Belgian feast with your guests.

Forcemeat Stuffing:
1 chicken liver, trimmed of fat and discolored
  spots, rinsed and patted dry
¼ cup Cognac or port
2½ slices stale firm white bread, crusts removed
1 cup milk
1 tablespoon unsalted butter
2 shallots or 1 small onion, finely chopped
½ pound ground pork
¼ pound ground veal
2 large egg yolks
¼ cup shelled pistachios (do not use the ones
  that have been dyed red)
1 teaspoon salt
½ teaspoon freshly ground black pepper
Pinch of ground cloves
1 tablespoon finely minced fresh parsley
1 tablespoon finely minced fresh sage or
  tarragon
½ teaspoon dried thyme

Chicken:
1 whole roasting chicken or capon (4 to 5
  pounds), boned (see Box, page 133), rinsed
  and patted dry, all visible fat removed
3 tablespoons unsalted butter, at room
  temperature
Salt and freshly ground black pepper to taste
¼ cup water
1 medium onion, peeled and quartered
1 carrot, peeled and quartered

Rosemary Roasted Potatoes (recipe follows)

1. Place rack in the middle of the oven. Preheat the oven to 425°F.

2. Prepare the stuffing: Coarsely chop the liver and marinate for 10 minutes in the Cognac. Soak the bread in the milk for 10 minutes, squeeze it dry, and crumble it.

3. Melt the butter in a small skillet over medium heat. Add the shallots and cook, stirring, until softened but not browned, about 5 minutes.

4. In a large mixing bowl, combine the ground pork and veal with the soaked and crumbled bread, the liver with the Cognac, the shallots, egg yolks, and pistachios. Season the mixture with the salt, pepper, cloves, parsley, sage, and thyme. Mix everything together very well. (The best way to do this is with your hands, definitely your best tools in the kitchen!)

5. Prepare the chicken: Stuff the chicken with the forcemeat, and truss it with kitchen string. If there are any rips in the skin of the bird, sew them closed with a needle and some unwaxed dental floss. Spread the butter all over the bird and season with salt and pepper. Place the chicken, breast side up, in a roasting pan just large enough to hold it.

6. Roast the stuffed chicken for 30 minutes. Reduce the heat to 350°F, pour the water into the roasting pan, and add the onion and carrot. Roast for 1 hour longer, basting the bird every 15 minutes with the pan juices.

7. Remove the bird from the oven and let it cool for at least 1 hour but preferably until it has reached room temperature. (At this point you can wrap the bird and refrigerate it to serve on the following day. Save the drippings in the pan to make the roasted potatoes.)

8. Untie the chicken and remove the legs and wings. Slice the bird as you would a sausage, cutting straight through the meat and stuffing to make ½-inch slices. Serve with Rosemary Roasted Potatoes (recipe follows).

Serves 6

Variation: *In the south of Belgium, chestnuts are often used in forcemeat and can substitute in this recipe for the pistachios. Use cooked whole chestnuts, fresh or canned.*

Rosemary Roasted Potatoes

*I*n my family we always serve these rosemary-scented potatoes with Stuffed Roast Chicken.

24 small red-skinned potatoes, scrubbed and quartered
5 tablespoons reserved chicken drippings or vegetable oil
Salt and freshly ground black pepper to taste
1 tablespoon finely minced fresh rosemary

1. Preheat the oven to 350°F.

2. Place the potatoes in a shallow roasting pan large enough to hold them in a single layer. Add the reserved chicken drippings (or vegetable oil) and toss to coat. Season with salt and pepper.

3. Roast until fork tender, 35 to 45 minutes, turning the potatoes over halfway through. Sprinkle with rosemary before serving.

Serves 6

Boning and Stuffing Your Bird

It is much easier to partially bone your chicken by removing the carcass but leaving the leg and wing bones intact.

1. Place the chicken, breast side down, on a cutting board. With a sharp boning knife, slit the skin down the back, from tail to neck. Cut out the wishbone.

2. Using your knife and your fingers, carefully cut into the flesh down to the bone and pull the flesh and skin away from the carcass. Work on one side at a time. Cut the flesh from the saber-shaped bone near the wing and remove the bone.

3. When you reach the ball-and-socket joints connecting both the wing and thigh bones to the carcass, sever them so that they are separated from the carcass but still attached to the skin.

4. Continue pulling and cutting the breast meat away until you reach the ridge of the breastbone where the skin and bones meet. Now do the other side. At the end, carefully detach the whole carcass in one piece from this ridge without tearing the skin. Save the bones in your freezer to make broth.

5. Your partially boned bird is ready for stuffing. Place it on your work counter, skin side down. Season with salt and pepper. Spread the stuffing over the meat. Turn the neck skin down over the stuffing and sew from neck to tail, securing the stuffing. I usually use a large upholstery needle with unwaxed, unflavored dental floss. Don't forget to remove and discard the string once the bird is cooked.

Christmas Turkey Stuffed with Mushroom-Flavored Forcemeat

GEVULDE KALKOEN VOOR DE KERSTDAGEN
•
LA DINDE FARCIE DE NOEL

In most Belgian families, Christmas dinner revolves around a roast turkey with a savory veal stuffing perfumed with an assortment of wild mushrooms or, sometimes, truffles. The turkey is made doubly festive if you can find a butcher who will remove the breast and backbone of the turkey, allowing you to reshape the turkey around the stuffing. With this method, you will have more stuffing and a bird that is very easily and prettily sliced. If you wish, you can prepare a turkey, in the usual manner, without removing the bones, following this recipe. In the United-States I always try to find a free-range turkey which is more flavorful, although a little drier, than the commercially raised variety. But careful, slow roasting, frequent basting,

and a rich, meaty stuffing will produce a succulent and juicy bird.

The Christmas turkey is traditionally served with Deep-Fried Potato Croquettes, Celery Root and Potato Purée, and Baked Apples Filled with Berries, or Pears Poached in Spiced Red Wine (see Index for recipes). Serve with an assortment of green vegetables.

Forcemeat Stuffing:
1 tablespoon dried porcini mushrooms
½ cup hot water
10 slices stale firm white bread, crusts removed
1½ cups milk
1 turkey liver, trimmed of fat and discolored
*   spots, rinsed and patted dry*
3 tablespoons Cognac
3 tablespoons port
4 tablespoons (½ stick) unsalted butter
1 large onion, finely chopped
6 ounces fresh white mushrooms, cleaned
*   trimmed, and thickly sliced*
4 ounces fresh oyster mushrooms, cleaned,
*   trimmed, and thickly sliced*
4 ounces fresh shiitake mushrooms, cleaned,
*   trimmed and thickly sliced*
1 pound ground veal
1 pound ground fresh pork butt
2 large egg yolks
15 fresh sage leaves, finely minced,
*   or 1 tablespoon dried sage*
2 tablespoons finely minced fresh parsley
1 tablespoon dried thyme
1 tablespoon salt, plus additional to taste
1 teaspoon freshly ground black pepper,
*   plus additional to taste*
Pinch of freshly grated nutmeg

Turkey:

*1 turkey, (12 to 14 pounds), left whole or with
back and breast bones removed (page 133),
neck and giblets reserved*

*8 tablespoons (1 stick) unsalted butter, at room
temperature, plus 8 tablespoons (1 stick)
melted, for basting the turkey*

Salt and freshly ground black pepper to taste

1 tablespoon paprika

2 carrots, peeled and quartered

1 rib celery, quartered

1 medium onion, peeled and quartered

1 cup water or chicken broth if needed

Enriched pan juices or thickened gravy:

¼ cup Cognac

¼ cup port

*Beurre manié: 1½ tablespoons all-purpose flour
blended with 1 tablespoon unsalted butter
(optional)*

1. Place a rack in the bottom third of the oven. Preheat the oven to 350°F.

2. Prepare the stuffing: Soak the porcini mushrooms in the hot water for 20 minutes. Squeeze the mushrooms dry and finely chop. Strain the soaking liquid and reserve. Tear the bread into pieces and soak in the milk. Coarsely chop the liver and marinate in the Cognac and port.

3. Melt the butter in a large skillet over medium heat. Add the onion and cook, stirring, for 3 minutes. Add all the mushrooms and cook, stirring occasionally, until the mushrooms are nicely browned and dry, about 10 minutes.

4. Place the ground meats in a large mixing bowl. Squeeze the soaking bread by handfuls to eliminate as much of the liquid as possible, and add it to the ground meat. Add the turkey liver with the marinade. Add the mushroom mixture, the egg yolks, sage, parsley, thyme, salt, pepper, and nutmeg. Knead the mixture together with your hands until very well blended. Sauté a small bit of stuffing in a little butter; taste and adjust the seasoning.

5. Prepare the turkey: Stuff the turkey with the forcemeat (page 133) and truss with kitchen string. Spread the softened butter evenly all over the turkey. Season with salt, pepper, and paprika. Bake any leftover stuffing in a small casserole, just like meat loaf.

6. Spread the carrots, celery, and onion in the bottom of a flameproof roasting pan large enough to hold the turkey. Place the turkey on top of the vegetables. Add the neck and giblets and pour the reserved soaking liquid from the porcini mushrooms into the pan.

7. Roast the turkey for 1 hour. Reduce the heat to 300°F and roast until cooked through, 2½ hours more. An instant-read thermometer should register between 160 to 180°F when 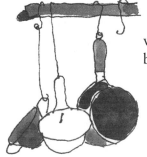 thrust into the thickest part of the thigh without touching the bone. Baste the turkey every 15 minutes the entire time that it is roasting. Baste with drippings, alternating

A Christmas Memory

In Belgium, traditions are still respected and observed with a fidelity and zeal not often found in other countries. Among all the traditions of my country, the celebration of Christmas is one of the most important and beloved. It revolves around the family, and if there are any members of a family who cannot be home for the holidays, this is the time when they are missed the most. Although I always try to come home for Christmas from wherever in the world my travels have taken me, if I cannot it is the time that I am the most homesick.

The Christmases I remember are, of course, the Christmases of my childhood, with presents or St. Nicholas, who would have visited with gifts on December 6th. It had to do with the gathering of the family and of the many preparations for this gathering and celebration. In those days my paternal grandparents lived on their own floor of our large brownstone house. Because they were the oldest members of the family, Christmas was their production.

My grandfather, who was a butcher with his own charcuterie, supplied the pâtés, forcemeats, ham, turkey, and so on for the Christmas dinner. My grandmother Madeleine was the guardian and trustee of all the Christmas decorations. These were stored, carefully wrapped and boxed, in the attic. The attic itself was a magic place. Dry, dark, and just a little dusty, it seemed to me to hold all the treasures of years past. During the week before Christmas, I helped my grandmother to unpack, one by one, the Christmas decorations, many of which had been in the family longer than I had. It seemed that every star and angel, every ball and toy had a story. My grandmother was the repository of these stories, and as we worked, she told the ones that struck her as the most entertaining.

A few days before Christmas we went with my father to pick out our tree— always the biggest, fullest, thickest we could find. As soon as the tree was up, even before it was dressed, we felt that the time of Christmas had truly begun. With the coming of the tree the whole house had that crisp, sharp, piney smell, which supplied a happiness like no other smell I know of.

Everyone was gathered together, the tree was resplendent with decorations, and we had our big dinner on Christmas Eve. The house had been full of cooking smells for days. We ate our turkey, the fragrant stuffing, the lovely apples filled with red berries, and finished up with coffee and all the many traditional Christmas sweets.

with the melted butter. If necessary, add 1 cup water or chicken broth to the drippings in the bottom of the pan. If the turkey starts to get too brown, cover loosely with aluminum foil. Remove the foil for the last 20 minutes to crisp the skin.

8. Remove the turkey from the oven to a platter. Let rest for 30 minutes before carving.

9. While the turkey is resting, prepare the gravy: Place the roasting pan over high heat. Add the Cognac and port and bring to a boil stirring with a wooden spoon to scrape up all the little browned bits on the bottom of the pan. Add a little water if the gravy seems too dry. Remove from the heat and strain out all the vegetables. Pour the liquid into a degreasing cup (also called a gravy separator). Let stand for a few minutes to let the fat rise to the top, then pour out the pan juices at the bottom of the cup into a small saucepan. (All the fat will be left behind.) Reheat and serve as pan juices with the turkey. If you prefer a thickened gravy, whisk the *beurre manié* into the juices and, stirring constantly, boil until the gravy is smooth and thick, about 2 minutes.

10. Untie the bird and carve it. For the boned turkey, cut away the legs and wings and slice the bird as you would a sausage, cutting straight through the meat and stuffing into ½-inch-thick slices. For an unboned bird, carve it as you would a chicken. Be sure to carefully scoop out the forcemeat stuffing and serve it on the side.

Serves 8 to 10, with generous leftovers

Wine Note

*S*erving game is the perfect opportunity to open a bottle of your best red wine. Choose an old heady Bordeaux or a sumptuous Burgundy.

Braised Partridge with Cabbage and Abbey Beer

PATRYS OP Z'N ARDENNEES
•
PERDRIX AU CHOU BLANC

The complicated blend of flavors in this earthy casserole captures the true essence of the great forests, mountains, and streams of the Ardennes. The robust wild partridges, the smoky bacon, and the woodsy perfume of the juniper berries, all simmered together in a dark Abbey beer brewed in centuries-old monasteries, always recall for me the mystery and majesty of this last wild place in Belgium.

Mashed or steamed parsleyed potatoes make just the right accompaniment.

2 partridges (2 to 3 pounds each), rinsed and
    patted dry
Salt and freshly ground black pepper to taste
2 grape leaves, fresh or packed in brine
4 thin slices bacon
4 tablespoons lard, or 4 tablespoons
    (½ stick) unsalted butter plus
    1 tablespoon vegetable oil
1 Savoy or green cabbage,
    tough outer leaves
    removed, cored and
    coarsely shredded
2 medium onions, sliced
3 ounces smoked slab bacon,
    cut crosswise into ½-inch strips
1 thick slice (about 3 ounces) jambon
    d'Ardennes or imported prosciutto, cut into
    ½-inch-wide strips
2 sprigs fresh thyme or ½ teaspoon dried thyme
1 large bay leaf
3 juniper berries
2 cups dark Abbey beer,
    such as Affligem
    or Orval
Pinch of freshly grated
    nutmeg

1. Season the cavities of the birds with salt and pepper. Wrap a grape leaf and 2 slices of bacon around the breast area of each bird and secure with kitchen string. This will prevent the birds from drying out.

2. In a large enameled Dutch oven, melt 2 tablespoons of the lard (or 2 tablespoons of the butter and 1 tablespoon oil) over medium heat. Add the birds, and brown on both sides, about 10 minutes per side. Remove the birds and set aside.

3. Blanch the cabbage for 3 minutes in plenty of boiling salted water and drain thoroughly.

4. In the Dutch oven, melt the remaining 2 tablespoons lard or butter over medium heat. Add the onions and cook, stirring occasionally, for 5 minutes. Add the remaining bacon, jambon d'Ardennes, half the cabbage, the thyme, bay leaf, and juniper berries. Arrange the partridges on top of the cabbage and spoon the rest of the cabbage around the birds. Season with nutmeg and salt and pepper to taste.

5. Cover and cook for 2 hours over very low heat on top of the stove or in a preheated oven at 325°F. The meat should be very tender.

6. Remove the thyme and bay leaf and serve.

Serves 4

Roasting Game Birds

Roasting pheasants and partridges presents a real challenge, because the birds are very lean and have a tendency to get dry and tough. Choose young birds for roasting and preferably hens, as they are more tender. In Belgium, game birds are sold larded and/or wrapped in grape leaves to prevent them from drying out while cooking. Older birds are best marinated and braised, rather than roasted.

But even a tender young hen presents a challenge because the breast and legs require different cooking times to be at their best. The breast should be a little pink and undercooked, while the legs require more time to cook through. The Belgian solution is to serve the bird in two stages: the breast meat as a first course and the legs as a second.

For the breast meat, remove the bird from the oven as soon as the breast has reached an internal temperature of 150°F and is still slightly pink. Return the legs to the oven to continue cooking another 5 to 10 minutes, while your guests are eating the breast.

For a very sophisticated finish, serve the legs as a second course with a salad of young lettuces in a vinaigrette.

Pan-Roasted Squab in the Manner of Liège

DUIFKES MET GENEVERBESSEN

•

PIGEONNEAUX A LA LIEGEOISE

The forests, waters, and mountains of the Ardennes have supplied Belgian hunters with a huge variety of game birds, including cranes, doves, egrets, herons, mallards, partridges, peacocks, pheasant, pigeons, plovers, and quail. Today, more of these birds are raised commercially, but the hunting season still provides substantial game for the table. Although traditionally this dish is prepared with thrushes, the most sought after game birds still available in the Ardennes, tender farm-raised squabs delicately flavored with juniper berries will do just as well.

Serve each squab on a slice of fried bread and accompany with a seasonal vegetable, such as a Casserole of Wild Mushrooms (see Index).

6 tablespoons (³/4 stick) unsalted butter
4 squabs (³/4 to 1 pound each)
20 juniper berries
Salt and freshly ground black pepper to taste
4 slices (at least ½ inch thick) brioche-style
    white bread

1. Melt 4 tablespoons of the butter in a heavy Dutch oven over medium heat. Add the birds and brown on all sides. Cover and cook over low heat until the breast meat is cooked medium-rare and is still a little pink, 20 to 35 minutes. Baste the squabs while they are cooking.

2. Crush the juniper berries with a rolling pin or the bottom of a heavy saucepan.

3. When the birds are just about done, add the crushed juniper berries to the pan and season with salt and pepper. Cook over high heat for 1 minute, turning the squabs over several times to coat them with the flavored butter.

4. Melt the remaining 2 tablespoons butter in a large skillet and fry the bread until golden on each side.

Serves 4

Braised Squab with Tiny Peas and Asparagus

DUIFJES MET MECHELSE ERWTJES EN ASPERGES

•

PIGEONNEAUX AUX PETITS POIS ET ASPERGES

In Belgium we still prefer the dark, strong flavored flesh of full–grown pigeons from the hunter's pouch. There is also a growing market for commercially raised *pigeonneaux,* or squabs. These are rarely older than 4 weeks, are much more tender, and have a milder, more delicate flavor. Commercially raised squab are also readily available in the United States, either through your butcher or by mail order.

2 tablespoons unsalted butter

2 ounces lean smoked slab bacon, cut into ½-inch strips, blanched for 2 minutes in boiling water

16 pearl onions, blanched for 1 minute in boiling water and peeled

4 squabs (¾ to 1 pound each), rinsed and patted dry

Salt and freshly ground black pepper to taste

2 tablespoons Cognac

½ cup dry white wine

½ cup chicken broth, preferably homemade (page 53)

1 pound fresh peas (1½ to 2 cups), shelled

1 pound thinnest asparagus, peeled and cut into 2-inch pieces

1 tablespoon finely minced fresh parsley

1 tablespoon finely minced fresh chervil or 1 teaspoon finely minced fresh tarragon

1. Melt the butter in a large, deep, heavy skillet over medium heat. Add the bacon and onions; cook, stirring occasionally, until the onions are light brown and the bacon is crispy, about 7 minutes. Remove the onions and bacon with a slotted spoon and set aside.

2. Sprinkle the cavities of the squabs with salt and pepper. Sauté the squabs in the same skillet over medium heat until browned on both sides, 4 to 5 minutes total. Season with salt and pepper and drizzle the Cognac over the squabs. Remove from the skillet and set aside.

3. Pour the white wine and chicken broth into the skillet and deglaze the pan over high heat, scraping up all the brown bits on the bottom with a wooden spoon.

4. Reduce the heat to low and add the peas, asparagus, onions, and bacon. Arrange the squabs on top of the vegetables. Simmer, partially covered, until the juice runs clear when the bird is pricked with a knife in the thigh joint, 20 to 25 minutes.

5. Arrange the squabs on a warmed serving platter with the vegetables around them. Reduce the sauce over high heat by one-third, about 5 minutes. Taste and adjust the seasoning and stir in the parsley and chervil. Pour the sauce over the squabs and vegetables and serve immediately.

Serves 4

Mail-Order Sources for Game

D'Artagnan
399-419 St. Paul Avenue
Jersey City, New Jersey 07306
(800) 327-8246

Oakwood Game Farm
Box 274
Princeton, Minnesota 55371
(800) 328-6647

Game

In Belgium, the taste for game and hunting goes back at least to the Middle Ages, when great hunts were organized as social events for the local aristocrats. Flanders and Wallonia were then still covered with vast woods and farmlands—natural habitats for a wide variety of game animals. Then, as now, feasting on game was normally reserved for special occasions—the medieval banquets, fairs, and kermisses. Flemish paintings will overwhelm you with still lifes of pheasants, peacocks, and other birds tumbling out of the hunter's sack.

Today, much of the game is farm raised. Still, come fall, many Flemish families (mine included) make reservations for a gastronomical weekend in the Ardennes to fully indulge themselves on the local game specialties that are featured in the mountainside inns.

In the United States, there is an increased interest in game birds and meats. Pheasant, quail, venison, and buffalo are growing in popularity, particularly since they provide very lean meat that is also very flavorful. Here, too, many game birds are farm raised and available all year round from specialty butchers and by mail order. Farm-raised birds don't have as distinctive and gamy a flavor as the wild ones, but as that is something of an acquired taste, they may be more suited to the American palate.

Roast Pheasant with Caramelized Belgian Endives and Apple

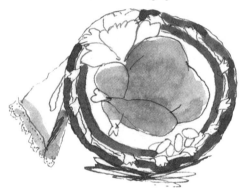

FAZANT OP Z'N BRABANTS
•
FAISAN A LA BRABANCONNE

*I*n Belgium, food trends do not come and go as rapidly as they do in the United States. What is prepared at home and in restaurants depends more on the seasonal availability of meat, fish, and produce than it does on any current fads or fashions. In the fall, for example, one of the most popular dishes in restaurants and in homes, year in and year out, is roast pheasant accompanied by caramelized Belgian endives. These feature great autumn flavors and are fully enjoyed during the short season in which wild pheasant is available.

2 pheasants (2½ pounds each), rinsed and
    patted dry
Salt and freshly ground black pepper
    to taste
2 grape leaves, fresh or brined, or 6 thin slices
    of bacon
3 tablespoons unsalted butter
1 medium onion, peeled and chopped
1 carrot, peeled and diced
1 rib celery, diced
¼ cup port
¾ cup homemade chicken broth (page 53),
    reduced to ¼ cup
¼ cup heavy (or whipping) cream

Caramelized Endives and Apple:
6 or 7 Belgian endives, cored and julienned
1 medium tart apple, peeled, cored, and
    julienned
1 tablespoon confectioners' sugar
1 tablespoon fresh lemon juice
Salt and freshly ground black pepper to taste
3 tablespoons unsalted butter
2 tablespoons finely minced fresh parsley

1. Preheat the oven to 350°F.

2. Season the cavities of the birds with salt and pepper. Wrap a grape leaf or 3 slices bacon around the midsection of each bird and truss with kitchen string.

3. Melt the butter in a large enameled Dutch oven over medium heat. Add the birds and brown for 4 minutes on each side. Sprinkle the onion, carrot, and celery around the birds, and season with salt and pepper. Roast in the oven until the breast is still pink and the temperature registers 150°F on an instant-read thermometer, 25 to 30 minutes. Baste with pan juices every 10 minutes to keep the birds from drying out.

4. Meanwhile, prepare the caramelized vegetables: Place the julienned endives and apple in a large mixing bowl. Add the sugar, lemon juice, salt, and pepper; mix well. Use two sauté pans or cook the endive mixture in two batches. Melt 1½ tablespoons butter in each sauté pan over high heat. Add the endive mixture and cook, stirring frequently, until the endives are slightly caramelized and soft, 4 to 5 minutes. Transfer the endives to a warmed serving dish while you finish the sauce.

5. Remove the pheasants from the pan and place on a cutting board. Keep the oven on. Place the Dutch oven on top of the stove. Add the port and reduced chicken broth; bring to a boil, scraping the bottom of the pan with a wooden spoon to get all the little

brown bits into the sauce. Strain the sauce and endive mixture through a fine sieve into a small saucepan. Press down on the solids with your wooden spoon to extract as much of the liquid as possible. Bring to a boil, stir in the cream, and season with salt and pepper to taste. Boil for 1 minute and remove from the heat.

6. Carve the breasts from the birds and arrange on top of the caramelized endives. Spoon some of the sauce over the meat and serve. If the breast meat is still slightly pink as it should be, the legs will be slightly underdone. If they are, place them on a rack in a roasting pan and return to the oven for 5 to 10 minutes until cooked through. Serve the legs as a second course.

Serves 4

Meat

The Meat Market

For this chapter, I consulted my paternal grandfather, Charles, a butcher and master *charcutier*, who died in 1994 at the age of 92. He started his apprenticeship under the firm hand of a master at the age of 13. In those days the maidservants of the bourgeois families bought their meat twice a day, arriving at the shop with their lists in hand. The apprentices would then deliver the paper-wrapped purchases on their bicycles. Eventually, Charles opened his own business in Ghent, and he spoke proudly and nostalgically about those 12-hour days of tough work, when he could carry half a carcass of a young calf on his broad shoulders and go home to devour a whole roast chicken for his dinner.

Today the butcher shop and the charcuterie are still the heart of every small village. Most people still buy their meat from a butcher with whom they have a relationship, rather than in the supermarkets, because the quality is higher. Some butchers specialize more than others and are known for their high-quality lamb or pork or organic meats.

Belgians love vegetables and make them an important part of every meal. But the main course, the mainstay of almost every meal, is meat, poultry, or fish. Meat is very important to Belgium consumers, and we are still a nation in which men, especially, are serious meat eaters. For many Belgians, typically those of an older generation, lettuces and raw vegetables are looked on as "rabbit food." Eating habits are changing to some extent, but tradition in Belgium always has the upper hand. For the moment at least, meat is king.

The dishes in this chapter are easy to prepare and satisfying in the most basic way. Take a tip from the Belgian shopper and get to know your butcher. No one can be more helpful to the success of your cooking than a butcher who knows his job.

CHARCUTERIE

In Belgium, most butchers are also *charcutiers*. Since the Middle Ages, the butcher-*charcutier* has been considered an extremely valuable member of his community, and their guilds have always been powerful. The *charcutier* prepares and sells a huge variety of pork products—cured and smoked hams, many different pâtés (a choice of 10 is considered average), meat salads, and, of course, a huge variety of sausages. A charcuterie often will carry as many as 20 different types of sausages—fresh, dried, cured, smoked—

almost all of which are prepared on the premises according to old family recipes. It would be impossible to write about traditional home cooking in Belgium without mentioning our love of sausages, particularly the white veal sausages known as *boudins blancs* and the dark blood sausages called *boudins noirs*.

In my great grandmother Marie's day, a hog was slaughtered just before Christmas, and as in every other country where pigs are raised to be eaten, no part of the pig was wasted. Sausages made from the blood of the pig were considered a real delicacy, and everyone looked forward to them. Some of these *boudins noirs* were very highly seasoned, while others were sweetened with dark raisins or currants for a more medieval taste. The *boudins blancs* are made with puréed meat, bread crumbs, and flavorings. Today there are few people left who go to the trouble of making their own sausages, but the sausages are still available in charcuteries all over the country. In many parts of the United States you can find similar varieties of sausage in specialty butcher shops, particularly in ethnic neighborhoods. In Belgium, fresh *saucisses* are served with mashed potatoes and applesauce and always a fresh and foamy glass of beer.

A platter of charcuterie, cheeses, breads, and a salad is often served as the evening meal in Belgium, particularly when the midday meal has been a substantial one.

Steak-Frites

BEEFSTEAK MET FRIETJES

In Belgium, *steak-frites* is practically one word. A steak without a mountain of Belgian fries and a pint of fresh beer is unthinkable. The two signature dishes of Belgium are *moules-frites* (see Index for recipe) and *steak-frites*.

My grandfather Charles, a butcher all his life, always said to choose meat that is marbled with tiny veins of fat. A perfect steak is small and plump with a thin layer of fat around the edges. A steak that is too lean and thin will have no flavor and will be dry. Look for meat that is labeled prime or choice.

4 beef steaks, such as porterhouse, sirloin,
*   rib eye, shell, or filet mignon (½ pound each*
*   and ¾ to 1 inch thick), or one 2-pound steak*
5 tablespoons unsalted butter
Salt and freshly ground black pepper to taste
1 tablespoon water
Belgian Fries (page 231)

1. With a sharp knife, make small incisions, about 1½ inches apart in the fat around the outside of each steak.

2. Melt 3 tablespoons of the butter in a large heavy skillet or sauté pan over high heat until hot but not smoking. Add the steaks and sear for 1 minute on each side. Reduce the heat to medium. Season the steaks generously with salt and pepper and continue cooking, turning the steaks every other minute, until you see little pearls of blood come to the surface, about 6 to 8 minutes. The steaks should be cooked rare to medium for juicy, tender meat.

3. Remove the steaks and place them on warmed plates. Over medium heat, deglaze the pan with the water and swirl in the remaining 2 tablespoons butter. Drizzle these pan juices over the meat and serve at once with golden, crunchy Belgian Fries.

Serves 4

Beef Stewed in Red Wine with Pearl Onions and Mushrooms

GESTOOFD RUNDSVLEES OP Z'N LIMBURGS
•
BOEUF SAUTE A LA LIMBOURGEOISE

Although the most typical Belgian stews are prepared using one of our own traditional Belgian beers as the cooking liquid, wine, too, has been a favorite flavoring for ragouts and marinades since the Middle Ages. This is particularly true in Limbourg, the predominantly rural and sparsely populated Flemish province close to the Dutch border. This preference probably dates back to the days when wine was cultivated in this region, proving, once again, that anything good from the past lives on in the present in Belgium.

The stews prepared with wine in Limbourg and elsewhere in Belgium are hearty, comforting dishes, ideal for the long, dark winter months. They are an antidote to the bleakness outdoors, when a meal shared with the family in the warmth of the home truly proves the Belgian belief that one's home provides a paradise on earth.

This type of stew can be prepared well in advance. It reheats beautifully, and the flavors seem to mellow and develop when it is held for a day or so. It is easy on the cook and fills the house with a fragrant aroma that teases and gently seduces the appetite. Serve it with steamed or mashed potatoes and a green vegetable.

2 tablespoons vegetable oil
2 tablespoons unsalted butter
3 ounces smoked slab bacon, cut into
    ½-inch strips
1 medium onion, sliced
1 clove garlic, finely minced
2 to 3 pounds beef round and/or chuck stew
    meat (with some fat), cut into 1-inch cubes
20 pearl onions, blanched for 1 minute and peeled
¾ pound white mushrooms or a combination of
    shiitake and cremini mushrooms, cleaned,
    trimmed, and quartered
3 tablespoons all-purpose flour
Salt and freshly ground black pepper to taste
3 cups hearty red wine, such as a French
    Bordeaux or a California Burgundy
¼ cup Cognac
Bouquet garni: 1 sprig fresh thyme, 2 sprigs
    parsley, and 1 large bay leaf tied together
    with kitchen string
2 tablespoons finely minced fresh parsley, for
    garnish

1. In a large enameled Dutch oven, heat 1 tablespoon of the vegetable oil and 1 tablespoon of the butter over medium heat until hot but not smoking. Add the bacon and sauté over medium heat for 5 minutes. Add the sliced onion and cook, stirring, until wilted, 3 minutes. Finally, add the garlic, cook 1 minute longer, and remove from the heat.

2. Heat the remaining 1 tablespoon oil and 1 tablespoon butter in a large skillet over high heat until the foam subsides. Add half the meat and sauté until browned on all sides, about 5 minutes. Transfer the browned meat to the Dutch oven and sauté the second batch.

3. In the same skillet, sauté the pearl onions and mushrooms until lightly browned, about 5 minutes. Set aside.

4. Sprinkle the flour over the meat in the casserole and season with salt and pepper. Stir the meat and flour with a wooden spoon over low heat for 1 minute. Add the wine, Cognac, and bouquet garni. Bring to a simmer, stirring frequently. Do not boil; even the briefest boiling would result in leathery and tough meat. Simmer the stew, covered, over very low heat until the meat is very tender, 2 hours; skim the fat and foam from the surface occasionally.

5. Add the mushrooms and pearl onions and simmer for another 30 minutes. The meat and vegetables should be very tender. Remove the bouquet garni. Taste and adjust the seasoning. Sprinkle with the parsley and serve.

Serves 4 to 6

Hutsepot A Hearty Winter Stew

G E N T S E   H U T S E P O T
•
H O C H E P O T   G A N T O I S

Hutsepot is a very traditional dish of peasant origin, and one that is emblematic of the best home cooking. My grandmother's *hutsepot* was never the same twice. The ingredients varied with whatever winter vegetables and meats she could lay her hands on—parsnips, Savoy cabbage, turnips, and dried beans could be added to the *hutsepot*. Sometimes there were many ingredients and sometimes just a few, but it didn't matter. *Hutsepot* was always a welcome, warming meal in the coldest winter weather.

She cherished her long-cooking *hutsepots* because she believed that all good things take time, and she felt that the world around her was beginning to forget this truth. In fact, her *hutsepot* nourished the family for days on end, as it aged and matured in flavor like a fine wine.

All stews, including Belgium's *hutsepot*, are open to interpretation. Some people like to use as many different meats as possible, while others prefer to use just two at a time. Like my grandmother, I love vegetables, so I recommend using as many of those as possible, choosing from what is available at your greengrocer.

The name *hutsepot* means "everything mixed together in a pot," and its classical rendition is something between a soup and a stew. In this recipe it is served as a stew, a one-dish meal in a bowl. But *hutsepot* can be served in two stages. For the first course, serve only the broth, perhaps with just a few of the vegetables, in a deep soup bowl. Then arrange the meats and vegetables on a large platter, using any remaining broth to moisten them. Serve with crusty peasant-style bread and a good-quality mustard. In my hometown of Ghent, the strong, dark Tierenteyn mustard is a must.

150

1 pound beef blade pot roast, brisket, short ribs, chuck, or shank, cut into 1½-inch cubes

1 pound veal shoulder (preferably with cartilage), cut into 1½-inch cubes

1 pound lamb shoulder or neck, most of the fat discarded, cut into 1½-inch cubes

1 pound lean slab bacon, cut into 1½-inch cubes and blanched in boiling water for 2 to 3 minutes (see Note)

1 pig's foot, halved, or pig's tail (optional)

3 medium onions, peeled and quartered

3 whole cloves

4 carrots, peeled and cut crosswise into 4 pieces

3 ribs celery or 1 peeled celery root (celeriac), cut into large chunks

1 pound small turnips, peeled and quartered

4 leeks, white and light green parts only, rinsed well and cut into 1-inch chunks

1 Savoy cabbage, cored and cut into 8 wedges

Bouquet garni: ½ bunch parsley, 3 sprigs fresh thyme, and 2 bay leaves tied together with kitchen string

Salt and freshly ground black pepper to taste

1 pound small fresh pork sausages (optional)

3 pounds medium red potatoes, scrubbed and quartered

Pinch of freshly grated nutmeg

1. Place the beef, veal, lamb, bacon, and pig's foot, if using, into a tall, heavy stockpot. Add enough water to cover by 1 inch and bring to a boil. Reduce the heat to a simmer and skim the surface thoroughly, discarding all the foam that has risen to the surface.

2. Stud 3 of the onion pieces with the cloves. Add the onions and all the other vegetables, except for the potatoes. Add the bouquet garni and season with salt and pepper. Simmer, partially covered, over low heat for 1½ hours.

3. If you are using fresh pork sausages, fry them in a little oil for a few minutes until they are brown all over.

4. Add the potatoes and sausages to the *hutsepot* and simmer, partially covered, for another 30 minutes. At this point all the meat should be very tender. Discard the bouquet garni. Taste and adjust the seasoning and add the nutmeg. Serve in warmed deep soup bowls.

Serves 6 to 8

Note: *The bacon is blanched in order to remove most of the smoky flavor. In Belgium we use salted unsmoked bacon in this dish, but it is hard to find in the United States.*

151

Veal Stew with Dumplings, Mushrooms, and Carrots

MARIE'S KALFSBLANQUETTE

•

BLANQUETTE
DE VEAU JARDINIERE

Blanquette de veau, a classic of French bourgeois cuisine, has been given a Flemish twist in my great grandmother's recipe with the addition of tiny veal dumplings for an interesting contrast in texture and flavor. Marie always added extra vegetables to her *blanquette* as well, usually relying on whatever her kitchen garden was producing at the moment. Following her tradition in all culinary matters, I have made this *blanquette* with young asparagus instead of the carrots and recommend this divine and delicate combination when asparagus is in season.

A *blanquette de veau* is ideal for parties as you can double and even triple the recipe and it can be made almost entirely in advance. This is the type of cooking that is disappearing almost entirely from restaurant menus (it is time-consuming and too costly in terms of labor), but it is the cooking that,

deep in our hearts, we almost always prefer. It fills the house with lovely aromas, which raise expectations that are never disappointed by the final result.

I like to bring a *blanquette* to the table in its stewing casserole (one reason why I like the colorful Le Creuset pots so much) and serve it at the table in the best country-family style. A bowl of steamed potatoes to soak up the sauce and a green salad complete the meal very nicely.

Veal Stew:
2 pounds boneless veal breast and shoulder
    stew meat, cut into 2-inch cubes (ask
    your butcher to leave on some fat and
    cartilage for flavor and body)
1 pound veal bones
1 medium onion, halved
3 whole cloves
2 carrots, peeled and cut into 1-inch pieces
1 rib celery, cut into 1-inch pieces
1 small leek, rinsed well and cut into
    1-inch pieces
Bouquet garni: 3 sprigs parsley, 1 sprig fresh
    thyme, and 1 large bay leaf tied together
    with kitchen string
1 teaspoon salt
10 black peppercorns

Veal Dumplings:
¼ pound ground veal
1 teaspoon finely minced fresh parsley
Salt and freshly ground black pepper to taste
Pinch of freshly grated nutmeg

To finish:
12 baby carrots, peeled
18 small mushrooms, trimmed
4 tablespoons (½ stick) unsalted butter
5 tablespoons all-purpose flour
2 large egg yolks
½ cup heavy (or whipping) cream
Pinch of freshly grated nutmeg
3 tablespoons fresh lemon juice
2 tablespoons finely minced fresh parsley
*   or chervil, for garnish.*

1. Place the stew meat and veal bones in a large heavy Dutch oven and add cold water to cover by 1 inch. Bring to a boil over high heat and skim off the foam that comes to the surface. Reduce the heat to low, partially cover, and simmer the meat.

2. Stud the onion with the cloves. Add the onion, carrots, celery, leek, bouquet garni, salt, and peppercorns to the veal. Simmer, partially covered, over low heat until the meat is as tender as butter, 1¾ to 2 hours.

3. Strain the stock through a sieve into a medium-size pot. Discard the bones, vegetables, and bouquet garni. Return the meat to the Dutch oven and reserve.

4. Cook the veal stock over high heat for 10 minutes to reduce.

5. Prepare the dumplings: Mix together the ground veal, parsley, salt, pepper, and nutmeg and form into tiny balls the size of marbles.

6. Reduce the heat under the veal stock and add the baby carrots. Simmer, covered, to soften, about 20 minutes. Remove the cover, add the mushrooms and simmer for 5 minutes. Add the veal dumplings and simmer, uncovered, until the dumplings float to the top, about 5 minutes more. Remove from the heat and strain the stock through a sieve into a medium-size bowl. Add the vegetables and dumplings to the meat in the Dutch oven.

7. Melt the butter in a medium-size heavy pot over medium heat. Add the flour and cook, stirring constantly with a wooden spoon, for 1 minute. Switch to a whisk and gradually whisk in 3 cups of the veal stock. Bring to a boil and cook, stirring constantly, until you have a smooth sauce, about 1 minute. Pour this sauce over the meat, veal dumplings, carrots, and mushrooms in the Dutch oven. Heat through, very gently over low heat. (The stew can be prepared in advance up to this point.)

8. In a small bowl, whisk together the egg yolks, cream, nutmeg, and lemon juice. Stir in a ladleful of the hot sauce and mix well. Gradually stir the egg yolk mixture into the veal stew. (After the egg yolks are added, you may reheat the stew over low heat, but do not

let it come to a boil or the eggs will curdle.) Taste and adjust the seasoning. Sprinkle with the minced parsley and serve.

Serves 6

My Mother's Meatloaf

MOEDER'S FRICANDEAU
•
PAIN DE VEAU DE MA MERE

Unpretentious, plebeian meat loaf is secretly a favorite dish for everyone from picky gourmets to hard-to-please children. There is something poetic about its democratic appeal, and the way it speaks to and satisfies the child in all of us.

Preparations with ground meats are extremely popular in Belgian home cooking, and every cook has his or her own mix of ingredients that sets their meat loaf apart from everyone else's. A traditional Belgian meat loaf calls for ground pork or a mixture of pork and veal. My mother used to add thin slivers of smoked bacon or sometimes, inspired by a yearning for a taste of Italy, she would add an extra clove of garlic, some thyme, and a diced roasted red bell pepper, and serve it with a hearty tomato sauce.

My meat loaf, made with ground veal, is very light, delicate, and flavorful. It is good hot, served with mashed potatoes, applesauce, or cauliflower au gratin. Sometimes I double the recipe so that I can have it cold the next day. Thinly sliced, it makes delicious sandwiches, particularly on rye bread spread with a pungent mustard and chive mayonnaise.

1 cup stale firm white bread cubes,
   crusts removed
3/4 cup milk
3 tablespoons unsalted butter
1 large onion, finely chopped
4 to 5 ounces white mushrooms, cleaned,
   trimmed, and quartered
1 clove garlic, finely minced
2 pounds ground veal
1 large egg
3 tablespoons finely chopped fresh parsley
1 teaspoon minced fresh sage, oregano, or
   thyme or 1/2 teaspoon dried thyme
1 teaspoon salt
1/2 teaspoon freshly ground black pepper
Pinch of freshly grated nutmeg
1 1/2 tablespoons port or sherry
1 tablespoon Cognac
1 teaspoon melted unsalted butter
1 sprig fresh thyme or rosemary,
   for garnish

1. Preheat the oven to 450°F.

2. Soak the bread in the milk.

3. Melt 2 tablespoons of the butter in a medium-size skillet over medium heat. Add the onion and cook, stirring, for 2 minutes. Add the mushrooms and cook 5 minutes, then add the garlic and cook 1 minute longer.

4. In a large mixing bowl, mix the veal with the egg. Use your hands to squeeze the excess moisture out of the soaked bread and add the bread to the meat mixture. Add the onion mixture, the parsley, sage, salt, pepper, and nutmeg. Finally, add the port and Cognac. Mix everything together until the bread is well worked in and the vegetables and herbs are evenly distributed. The best way to do this is with your hands.

5. Cook a small spoonful of the mixture in a hot skillet and taste for seasoning. If you want to serve the meat loaf cold, you will want to add a little extra salt and pepper.

6. Brush an ovenproof glass or enamel loaf pan with the melted butter. Shape the meat mixture into a loaf in the pan. Decorate the top with the sprig of thyme and dot with the remaining 1 tablespoon butter.

7. Bake 30 minutes. Reduce the heat to 400°F and bake until the meat loaf is cooked through (a instant-read thermometer will register 150 to 160°F), 15 minutes more. Remove from the oven and let rest for 5 or 10 minutes before serving.

Serves 4 to 6

Variations: If you like, you can replace some of the ground veal with ground turkey or a combination of ground turkey and sausage meat.

• *Another popular meat loaf in Belgium incorporates small cubes of Swiss cheese into the meat mixture. This type of meat loaf is often wrapped in thin slices of smoked bacon while it is baked. The bacon imparts a lovely flavor, and the little pockets of melted cheese are always a delicious surprise.*

• *Belgians like to prepare little individual meat patties called* boulettes. *These are like flavored hamburgers and are sautéed quickly in a skillet. They are easy, cheap, and done in 3 minutes! Children love them. In Belgium we can buy these all prepared from any butcher, and indeed every butcher takes pride in his own combination of ground meats and seasonings. But they also are easy to prepare at home. Simply use the meat loaf recipe and sauté the meat as little patties.*

Belgian Spaghetti, Student Style

GENTSE STUDENTEN SPAGHETTI
•
LES SPAGHETTI BOLOGNAISE DES ETUDIANTS

This Belgian student's version of an Italian classic is loaded with vegetables and topped with a mountain of grated Gruyère cheese. In Ghent, a bustling, joyous student town with hundreds of tiny eateries, cafés, and brasseries, all catering to poor but hungry students, this dish is usually the most popular item on the menu. Always delicious, it provides a copious hearty meal for very little money.

As a student I must have prepared it a thousand times—on a small camper's stove, on a hot plate in my dormitory, in a cramped studio apartment—for my constantly hungry friends. Oh, what an appetite we had! Yes, we were poor, but so was everyone we knew, and in Belgium students are supposed to be poor. We learned to exercise our ingenuity and share what we had with our friends. And share we did—many bowls of steaming, ulti-mately satisfying pasta, much laughter, and many, many bottles of cheap Chianti.

This recipe is definitely my "first of the month" version, made when we could still afford all our favorite ingredients. As the month wore on, the dish always reflected my dwindling finances by shedding the more costly ingredients. Any leftover sauce can be frozen for a future meal.

3 tablespoons olive oil
2 medium onions, chopped
½ red bell pepper, diced
¼ pound white mushrooms, cleaned, trimmed, and sliced
1 large carrot, peeled and diced
3 cloves garlic, finely minced
1 pound lean ground beef
1 teaspoon sugar
½ teaspoon dried oregano
½ teaspoon dried thyme
1 teaspoon dried basil
½ teaspoon crushed red pepper flakes
1 tablespoon finely minced fresh parsley
1 can (14 ounces) peeled whole plum tomatoes, coarsely chopped
½ cup dry red wine
2 tablespoons tomato paste
Salt and freshly ground black pepper to taste
1 pound thin spaghetti
Tabasco sauce to taste (optional)
¾ cup freshly grated Gruyère cheese

1. Heat the olive oil in a deep sauté pan or Dutch oven over medium heat. Add the onions, bell pepper, mushrooms, and carrot; cook, stirring, until softened, 5 to 8 minutes.

Add half the garlic and all the ground beef. Continue cooking over medium heat, stirring and breaking up the meat with a wooden spoon, until the meat is no longer pink.

2. Stir in the sugar, oregano, thyme, basil, red pepper flakes, and parsley. Add the tomatoes with their juices, the red wine, and tomato paste. Season with salt and pepper. Reduce the heat and simmer, covered, for 35 minutes.

3. Stir in the remaining garlic. (This garlic added at the end gives the sauce a fresher, more pronounced garlic taste.) Taste and adjust the seasoning. Add some Tabasco sauce, if you like.

4. Cook the spaghetti in plenty of boiling salted water until al dente, 8 to 10 minutes. Drain the spaghetti and distribute among 4 bowls. Spoon the sauce over the spaghetti and serve. Pass the grated Gruyère cheese along with a bottle of Tabasco sauce.

Serves 4

Note: In Belgium, this spaghetti dish is served with a bottle of Tabasco sauce on the side. Everyone douses their pasta with their preferred amount of hot sauce. For some reason students, especially, espouse the philosophy of "the hotter the better!"

Variation: Substitute 1 pound ground turkey for the beef for a leaner version of this dish.

Roast Leg of Lamb with Pungent Mustard

LAMSBOUT MET TIERENTEYN MOSTARD

·

GIGOT D'AGNEAU A LA MOUTARDE DE TIERENTEYN

The best lamb in Belgium comes from coastal areas, where the lambs and sheep graze in the salt marshes and their meats pick up a slightly salty taste of the sea. I remember visiting one of the small villages around the North Sea as a child and seeing all the traffic come to a halt as a shepherd and his dogs guided a flock of a hundred or so sheep through the narrow village streets. In Belgium, although it is not as popular as beef or pork, lamb is considered something of a gourmet specialty and a more "natural" meat because the lambs wander unconfined and no hormones or drugs are used in their diets.

This is an excellent roast for either a small family dinner or for a larger party. If you would like to serve 8 to 10 people, roast a whole leg of lamb weighing 6 to 7 pounds. Figure the cooking time at about 16 minutes per pound for medium-rare (internal temperature of 135 to 140°F). Serve with Rosemary Roast Potatoes (see Index) and a green vegetable.

1 rump half leg of lamb (about 4 pounds, bone in for more flavor)
2 cloves garlic, peeled and halved
2 teaspoons fresh thyme or 1 teaspoon dried thyme
1 teaspoon fresh or dried rosemary
8 tablespoons (1 stick) unsalted butter, melted
1 small onion, peeled and quartered
1 carrot, peeled and quartered
2 cloves garlic, unpeeled and crushed with the flat of a knife
1 bay leaf
Salt and freshly ground black pepper to taste
3 tablespoons dried bread crumbs
1 tablespoon finely minced fresh parsley
2 tablespoons Tierenteyn or Dijon mustard
½ cup dry white wine or veal stock
½ cup water
1 bunch watercress, large stems removed, for garnish

1. Place the leg of lamb in a deep flameproof roasting pan. Rub the meat on all sides with the cut sides of the halved garlic cloves. (Garlic lovers can stud the meat with fine slivers of garlic.) Sprinkle with the thyme and rosemary; pour the melted butter over the meat. Cover the roasting pan with plastic wrap and refrigerate for at least 1 hour or up to 8 hours.

2. Preheat the oven to 400°F.

3. Surround the roast with the onion, carrot, the crushed garlic cloves, and bay leaf. Season with salt and pepper.

4. Roast the lamb for 15 minutes. Reduce the heat to 350°F and continue roasting for 45 to 50 minutes. Baste the meat every 15 minutes or so with the pan drippings, adding a little water if the pan is too dry. The roast is done when the internal temperature registers 135°F on an instant-read thermometer. At this point the meat will be rare, but it will continue to cook a while longer as it sits.

5. Combine the bread crumbs and parsley. Spread the lamb evenly with the mustard and pat on the bread crumbs and parsley mixture. Baste with the drippings and return to the oven. Roast for another 10 minutes to crisp up the bread crumbs.

6. Transfer the roast to a cutting board and let it rest for 15 minutes before carving.

7. Remove as much fat as possible from the roasting pan. Place the pan on top of the stove and add the white wine and water. Deglaze over high heat, scraping up all the brown bits from the bottom with a wooden spoon. Strain the gravy, pressing as much

Tierenteyn Mustard

The Belgian's taste for mustard goes back at least to the Middle Ages when these little seeds, yellow and black, started to become available in trading cities like Ghent, which in the 13th century was second only to Paris as a leading center of manufacture and trade. The use of mustard entered our culinary tradition and never left, for mustard, both as a flavoring and as a condiment, did wonders to perk up insipid meats and was particularly useful in masking any meat that had become a bit too aged. Mustard merchants, each one with his own secret methods and ingredients to combine with the mustard seeds, thrived. Mustards were flavored with wine, beer, vinegar, or verjus (the juice of sour grapes). Various spices could be added along with salt and sugar.

Today everyone knows the mustard of Dijon, the capital city of Burgundy, but few people outside of Belgium have heard of the dark brown, rather potent mustard that is produced in Ghent by the House of Tierenteyn. This is a mustard of exceptional flavor. When its aroma hits your nostrils, your eyes water and your taste buds awaken in expectation.

The House of Tierenteyn is located in the heart of medieval Ghent in the Groentenmarkt (the market square where farmers come to sell their produce). It is a tiny shop, tucked between an old little bakery and a grocery store. It has been there since 1790 and, to this day, sells mustard only of its own manufacture—the famous Tierenteyn mustard of Ghent. When you step inside, you feel that here time has truly stood still. Your eyes rest in wonder and appreciation on the neat rows of blue spice-filled porcelain jars on the shelves and below them, the wooden barrels of freshly made mustard. At the same time, your head is filled with the aromas of nutmeg, bay leaves, cinnamon, and, of course, mustard.

In this shop, Tierenteyn mustard is produced from a recipe that dates back to 1790. And while anyone who knows enough to come here can buy their mustard, the exact combination of herbs and spices is a secret, guarded as carefully as a pot of real gold.

The pungent Tierenteyn mustard has inspired many cooks. It is a traditional condiment to be served with pâtés, terrines, charcuterie, and a variety of cold and hot meats. It is also very successfully incorporated as a flavoring in recipes using rabbit, lamb, pork, poultry, and even vegetables and fish.

juice as possible from the vegetables with the back of a wooden spoon. Taste and adjust the seasoning and pour it into a gravy boat.

8. Carve the leg of lamb and arrange the slices on a platter surrounded by small sprigs of watercress.

Serves 4 to 6

Flemish-Style Lamb Ragout

GENTSE SCHAPE HUTSEPOT
•
HOCHEPOT DE MOUTON GANTOIS

This ragout is another *hutsepot*-style dish, something of a cross between a soup and a stew, especially delicious for those who enjoy the special flavor of lamb. It has everything to comfort and please: lots of vegetables, a hearty, flavorful broth, and tender morsels of meat. Serve this hearty ragout with steamed potatoes.

2 tablespoons unsalted butter
1 tablespoon vegetable oil
3 pounds boneless lamb shoulder, cut into 1-inch cubes, most of the fat removed
Salt and freshly ground black pepper to taste
1 large onion, peeled and halved
2 whole cloves
2 carrots, peeled and cut crosswise into 4 pieces
3 small turnips, peeled and quartered
1 small celery root (celeriac), peeled and cubed
3 leeks, white and light green parts only, rinsed well and thickly sliced
1 clove garlic, crushed
4 to 5 cups beef broth, preferably homemade (page 54), or water
Bouquet garni: 5 sprigs parsley, 2 sprigs fresh thyme, and 1 large bay leaf tied together with kitchen string
2 tablespoons finely minced fresh parsley, for garnish

1. Heat the butter and oil in a heavy enameled Dutch oven over medium heat until the foam subsides. Add the meat and brown lightly on all sides. Season with salt and pepper.

2. Stud the onion with the cloves, and add it, along with the other vegetables, to the pot. Pour in enough beef broth to cover the meat and vegetables by ½ inch. Add the bouquet garni. Simmer, partially covered, over low heat until the meat is very tender and the liquid has reduced by half, 1½ to 2 hours.

160

3. Discard the bouquet garni. With a large spoon skim, off most of the fat from the surface of the stew. Taste and adjust the seasoning. Sprinkle with parsley and serve.

Serves 6

Variations: Replace one-third of the liquid in the recipe with a light, golden beer or a pilsener-type beer for a tasty change of pace.

• *For a delicious smoky flavor, add 3 ounces slab bacon, cut into ½-inch strips, and sauté it together with the meat.*

Loin of Pork with Turnips

VARKENSGEBRAAD MET RAAPKES
•
FILET DE PORC AUX NAVETS

This juicy roast of boneless pork loin, surrounded by tender caramelized turnips, is an excellent dish for the cooler months. Serve with Parsleyed New Potatoes or Stuffed Baked Potatoes (see Index for recipes).

5 tablespoons unsalted butter
1 tablespoon vegetable oil
1 boneless pork loin roast (2 to 3 pounds)
Salt and freshly ground black pepper to taste
2 tablespoons finely minced shallots
2 cups beef or chicken broth, preferably homemade (page 54 or 53)
2 pounds small turnips, trimmed and quartered
2 teaspoons sugar
2 tablespoons finely minced fresh parsley, for garnish

1. Preheat the oven to 325°F.

2. Heat 2 tablespoons of the butter and the oil in a large skillet over high heat. Add the pork loin and brown on all sides. (A larger roast can be browned in a roasting pan in a preheated 425°F oven for 15 minutes.)

3. Transfer the meat to a roasting pan and season with salt and pepper.

4. Cook the shallots in the meat drippings remaining in the skillet over medium heat for 3 minutes. Add 1 cup of the broth and stir, scraping up all the little browned bits from the bottom of the pan with a wooden spoon. Pour over the meat in the roasting pan.

5. Roast the meat until an instant-read thermometer inserted in the thickest part registers 160°F, about 22 minutes per pound. Baste occasionally with the pan juices. When the

roast is done, remove it from the pan and let rest 15 to 20 minutes before slicing.

6. While the pork is roasting, prepare the turnips: In a large saucepan or deep skillet, melt the remaining 3 tablespoons butter over medium heat. Add the turnips and sauté until

Wild Pigs

*M*arcassin *in the recipe title refers to a baby wild boar. The boar, or wild pig, is found all over Europe, except in the British Isles, where it is extinct.* Marcassin *is prized in Europe as a great delicacy, for it is tender and has a fine flavor. In Medieval Europe, a boar's head was a festive dish served on great holidays, like Christmas.*

Today, people still flock to the Ardennes in the autumn months to indulge in the game dinners prepared by the local chefs.

I have often visited this beautiful area on hiking and camping trips and heard these impressive animals at night as they roamed around outside our tents. It was not a comfortable feeling. But the scariest incident occurred one day when a herd of boars came storming down a hillside, trampling everything in their path. The only thing we could do was press our backs against the biggest trees we could find and hold our breath.

lightly browned on all sides. Sprinkle with the sugar and season with salt and pepper. Add the remaining 1 cup broth and simmer, uncovered, over low heat until tender, 20 to 30 minutes. Increase the heat to high and reduce the liquid until it is a thick syrup that coats the turnips with a glossy shine.

7. Slice the meat and arrange on a warmed serving platter. Surround with the turnips and sprinkle with the parsley. Place the roasting pan on top of the stove over medium heat and boil the drippings until reduced by a third. Spoon the reduced juices over the sliced meat and serve.

Serves 4

Loin of Pork Braised in Red Wine

VLAAMS ZWYNTJE IN EEN WILDSAUS
• MARCASSIN DES FLANDRES

*T*his loin of pork, marinated in red wine and seasonings to make it taste like a subdued version of wild boar, is my mother's signature dish. It is the dish that

won her total acceptance by her husband's very fussy family of gourmets. By treating a piece of ordinary pork in the manner usually reserved for its exotic cousin the boar and producing, thereby, an extraordinary meal, she showed her father-in-law, a master *charcutier*, that she understood how to deal with meat. My father was in good hands.

The agricultural lowlands of Flanders produce excellent, enormous rosy pigs. Although these placid animals are a far cry from the hairy, dark, and ferocious wild boars who live in the woodsy hills of the Ardennes, my mother's marinade and braising technique do wonders for both. The final sauce is luscious and rich in flavor and naturally thickened by my mother's trick of puréeing the vegetables in the marinade. The addition of tangy and sweet red currant jelly gives the sauce a final balance and harmony and underscores again the very Belgian appreciation of the seductive sweet and savory combination.

This wonderful dish is traditionally served with Baked Apples Stuffed with Berries. Deep-Fried Potato Croquettes make it a feast, but Parsleyed New Potatoes are also delicious to mop up the sauce (see Index for recipes).

1 boneless pork loin roast (2 to
    3 pounds)
1 medium onion, coarsely chopped
2 carrots, peeled and cut into ¼-inch
    cubes
1 rib celery, cut into ¼-inch cubes
1 clove garlic, peeled and crushed with
    the flat of a knife
Bouquet garni: 3 sprigs parsley, 1 sprig
    thyme, and 1 large bay leaf tied
    together with kitchen string
6 juniper berries
Salt and freshly ground black pepper
    to taste
2 to 3 cups full-bodied red wine, such as
    Burgundy, Spanish Rioja, or Merlot
1 tablespoon raspberry or other fruity
    red wine vinegar
4 tablespoons (½ stick) unsalted butter
2 tablespoons vegetable oil
½ cup Cognac
1 to 2 tablespoons red currant jelly
1 to 2 teaspoons potato starch
    (optional)

1. One to two days before you plan to serve the roast, place the meat, onion, carrots, celery, garlic, bouquet garni, juniper berries, and salt and pepper in a large glass or earthenware bowl. Pour in enough red wine to just cover the meat and add the vinegar. Cover with plastic wrap and refrigerate, the longer the better.

2. Remove the meat from the marinade and pat dry with paper towels. Heat 2 tablespoons of the butter and the oil in a large Dutch oven over high heat until hot but not smoking. Reduce the heat to medium, add the meat, and brown on all sides, about 15 minutes. Off the heat, carefully flambé the roast with the Cognac (see page 130 for flambéing instructions). Add the marinade and all the ingredients in it. Simmer, partially covered, over low heat until the meat is tender, about 1 hour. Transfer the meat to a cutting board and let rest for 10 minutes before slicing.

3. Strain the cooking liquid through a sieve, reserving the vegetables. Discard the bouquet garni. Return the cooking liquid to the Dutch oven and boil it, uncovered, over high heat to reduce by one third, 5 to 7 minutes.

4. Finish the sauce: Purée the vegetables and cooking liquid in a blender to a smooth consistency. You should have a thick, full-flavored sauce. Return it to the pan and reheat it. Add the red currant jelly and whisk until well blended. Taste and adjust the seasoning. If the sauce seems thin to you, add a little bit of potato starch dissolved in 1 tablespoon water or wine. Whisk in the remaining 2 tablespoons butter. Do not boil the sauce beyond this point.

5. Slice the meat and arrange on a platter. Spoon some of the sauce over the sliced meat and pass the rest in a sauceboat.

Serves 4 to 6

Roast Pork with Onions and Mustard

VARKENSGEBRAAD MET ZILVERUITJES EN MOSTERD
•
NOIX DE PORC BRAISEE AUX OIGNONS

Isn't it true that some of the best dishes are the simplest ones? Here is one of my favorites—a succulent pork roast, coated with pungent mustard and surrounded with roasted onions doused with vinegar to counterbalance their sweetness. The dish is unpretentious and generous, uses easily available ingredients, and is simply delicious. Serve with rosemary-scented roasted potatoes and baked apples filled with berries (see Index for recipes).

1 boneless pork loin or shoulder or 1 fresh
    ham (2½ to 3 pounds)
1 clove garlic, peeled and halved
3 tablespoons Tierenteyn, Dijon, or grainy
    country-style mustard, plus additional
    for serving
2 tablespoons unsalted butter, cut into
    small pieces
2 tablespoons vegetable oil
25 pearl onions or small shallots,
    peeled
1 tablespoon fresh thyme or
    1½ teaspoons dried thyme
Salt and freshly ground black pepper
    to taste
¾ cup water, plus additional if needed
1 tablespoon cornstarch
3 tablespoons tarragon-flavored or
    red wine vinegar
2 tablespoons finely minced fresh parsley,
    for garnish

1. Rub the roast with the cut side of the garlic. Spread the mustard evenly over the roast. Cover with plastic wrap and refrigerate for 30 minutes or longer.

2. Preheat the oven to 450°F.

3. Place the meat in a flameproof roasting pan. Dot with the butter and drizzle with the oil. Brown in the hot oven, turning the meat several times to brown all sides, about 15 minutes.

4. Reduce the oven temperature to 350°F. Scatter the onions around the roast, sprinkle with the thyme, and season with salt and pepper. Pour ½ cup of the water into the pan.

5. Roast until the internal temperature registers 155 to 160°F on an instant-read thermometer, about 1 hour. Baste the roast every 10 to 15 minutes with the drippings. Add a little more water if needed to keep the onions from burning.

6. Remove the roast to a cutting board and let rest for 15 minutes before carving.

7. Place the roasting pan with the onions in it on the stovetop over medium heat. Deglaze with the remaining ¼ cup water, scraping up all the browned bits from the bottom of the pan. Dissolve the cornstarch in the vinegar and add it to the pan. Bring to a quick boil, stirring constantly, and remove from the heat.

8. Cut the meat into thin slices and arrange on a warmed platter. Spoon the onions around the meat. Sprinkle generously with the parsley and serve with additional mustard on the side. Pass the sauce in a gravy boat.

Serves 4 to 6

Roast Pork with Cheese and Cured Ham

VARKENSGEBRAAD OP Z'N ARDENNEES
•
ROTI DE PORC A L'ARDENNAISE

Every once in a while it seems to me that we might be on the verge of forgetting the many advantages of a whole roast. The procedure is so simple, since the cooking seems to take care of itself, that we have a tendency to look for more elaborate dishes to serve when we entertain. But to my mind there is nothing quite as sumptuous or festive as a golden-brown roast surrounded by vegetables, served with good wine by candlelight.

Here is a great recipe for a lavish-to-look-at-but-easy-to-prepare feast for your most festive dinner party. The presentation is spectacular. The juicy, tender roast loin of pork is covered with a crusty, bubbling layer of cheese and perfumed with a smoky, cured ham—from the Ardennes if you can get it, or prosciutto if you can't. Serve with Parsleyed New Potatoes, My Mother's Salsify with Mustard, or Belgian Endives, Flemish Style (see Index for recipes).

1 center-cut boneless pork loin roast (3 to 4 pounds)
2 tablespoons unsalted butter, at room temperature
2 tablespoons vegetable oil
Salt and freshly ground black pepper to taste
2 carrots, peeled and cut crosswise into 4 pieces
1 medium onion, sliced
2 teaspoons fresh thyme or 1 teaspoon dried thyme
1 bay leaf
½ cup water, plus additional if needed
8 to 10 thick (¼ inch) slices of Gruyère cheese
8 to 10 thin slices jambon d'Ardennes or prosciutto di Parma
½ cup port
¼ cup beef broth, preferably homemade (page 54)
2 tablespoons finely minced fresh parsley, for garnish

1. Preheat the oven to 450°F.

2. Rub the butter evenly over the roast and place it in a flameproof roasting pan. Drizzle with the oil.

3. Place the meat in the hot oven and brown,

turning it once or twice to brown it on all sides, about 15 minutes.

4. Reduce the heat to 350°F. Season the roast with salt and pepper. Arrange the carrots, onion, thyme, and bay leaf around the meat. Pour the water into the pan.

5. Roast the meat until the internal temperature registers 150 to 155°F on an instant-read thermometer, about 1 hour 45 minutes. Baste the roast every 15 minutes with the drippings in the pan, adding more water if necessary to keep the vegetables from burning.

Dinner for Two

A quick variation and a lovely dinner for two can be made with a luxurious tenderloin of pork. For a 1-pound tenderloin: Brown it over high heat in a small heavy skillet or casserole (the pan should not be much bigger than the meat) in 2 tablespoons butter. Add 2 tablespoons minced shallots and sauté for a few minutes longer. Deglaze with ½ cup beef or chicken broth and simmer, covered, over low heat for 20 minutes, turning the meat once. The meat should still be a little pink inside and register 160°F on an instant-read thermometer inserted in the center. Prepare the turnips as directed for Loin of Pork with Turnips (page 161).

6. Remove the roast from the oven and place the meat on a platter or cutting board. Don't turn off the oven yet. Use a small, sharp knife to make 8 to 10 incisions or pockets, cutting across the roast but not all the way through. These pockets should be ½ inch apart and large enough to hold a slice of cheese and a slice of ham. Tuck a slice of ham and a slice of cheese into each pocket. Let some of the cheese stick out by about ½ inch so it can melt over the top of the meat and provide a delicious cheesy crust. Return the roast to the pan.

7. Roast the meat until the cheese is melted and browned on top, 15 to 20 minutes. Remove the roast to a cutting board and let rest for 15 minutes before slicing.

8. Meanwhile, place the roasting pan on top of the stove over high heat. Deglaze the pan with the port and beef broth, scraping up all the brown bits from the bottom with a wooden spoon. Remove from the heat and pour the sauce through a strainer into a bowl or degreasing cup. Press on the vegetables with the back of a wooden spoon to extract as much juice as possible. Discard the vegetables. Degrease the sauce. Taste and adjust the seasoning and pour into a sauceboat.

9. Cut the meat, slicing in between the pockets of ham and cheese so that each person gets a slice of meat containing one of these pockets. Sprinkle with the parsley and serve.

Serves 6

Venison Steaks with Gin and Juniper Berries

REEBOKKOTELETTEN MET GENEVER
•
COTELETTES DE CHEVREUIL AU GENIEVRE

I have noticed that the popularity of venison is on the rise in the United States. People are rediscovering this tasty, very lean meat with an extremely low cholesterol content. Very young animals and specially farmed animals are more tender and have a milder taste than their older and wilder kin. Fortunately, we no longer have to depend on the hunter's bow or rifle to supply us with this excellent meat. All over the country there are farms that specialize in raising venison for our tables.

Tenderloin chops and steaks are perfect for sautéing. Tougher cuts like the leg, saddle, shoulder, neck, and breast are usually tenderized by marinating for a few days and then braising. If a choice leg or saddle of venison comes your way, you can follow the recipe for Loin of Pork Braised in Red Wine (see Index) with excellent results.

In Belgium, venison and other game dishes are traditionally accompanied by a baked apple filled with berries and a purée of celery root (see Index for recipes).

Salt and coarsely ground black pepper
   to taste
2 teaspoons minced fresh thyme or
   1 teaspoon dried thyme
8 venison tenderloin steaks (6 ounces
   each)
6 tablespoons (3/4 stick) unsalted
   butter
2 tablespoons vegetable oil
1/4 cup genever (Belgian gin), Bombay gin,
   or Cognac
1 1/2 cups heavy (or whipping)
   cream
10 juniper berries, crushed
1 tablespoon green peppercorns, crushed
   (optional)
2 teaspoons fresh lemon juice
8 slices (1 inch thick) brioche or
   best-quality white bread, cut into
   rounds slightly larger than the
   steaks

1. Rub the salt, pepper, and thyme onto the venison steaks.

2. Heat 3 tablespoons of the butter and the oil in a large heavy skillet over high heat until hot but not smoking. Add the steaks and quickly sear on both sides, 1 minute per side. Reduce the heat to medium and continue cooking until medium-rare (the center should still be red and bloody), 3 to 4 minutes per side. Remove the steaks to a warmed platter and set aside.

3. Deglaze the pan over medium heat with the gin and add the cream. Add the juniper berries, green peppercorns, and salt to taste. Simmer over medium heat until the sauce is somewhat reduced and coats a wooden spoon. Remove from the heat, add the lemon juice, and adjust the seasoning.

4. While the sauce is reducing, melt the remaining 3 tablespoons butter in a large skillet and fry the bread until golden on each side. Place each venison steak on a slice of the bread and spoon some of the sauce over the top.

Serves 8

Beef Tongue with Raisins and Madeira

RUNDSTONG MET ROZYNEN EN MADEIRA
•
LANGUE DE BOEUF SAUCE MADERE

Beef tongue with raisins is a genuine Belgian dish that plays with the traditional combinations of fruits and meats to achieve the sweet-and-savory balance so beloved by my countrymen. As far back as the thirteenth century, Belgium's cooks have turned to dried fruits—raisins, apricots, and prunes imported from Southern Europe and the Levant—to enliven their diet in the winter months. Beef tongue with raisins is the type of dish that families in the countryside still serve for special occasions such as communions and weddings.

Beef tongue is a moist and succulent meat that marries extremely well with this Madeira-based raisin sauce. Serve with Mashed Potatoes with Caramelized Shallots for a rustic meal, with Deep-Fried Potato Croquettes for a festive dinner, or with Parsleyed New Potatoes for a simple homey version (see Index for recipes).

Beef Tongue

1 fresh beef tongue (4 to 5 pounds)

2 onions, peeled and halved

3 whole cloves

3 carrots, peeled and cut crosswise
    into 4 pieces

3 ribs celery, cut crosswise into
    4 pieces

2 leeks, white and light green parts
    only, rinsed well and sliced in
    1-inch pieces

Bouquet garni: ½ bunch parsley, 3 sprigs
    thyme, 2 large bay leaves, and
    1 rib celery tied together with
    kitchen string

1½ tablespoons salt

1 tablespoon black peppercorns

Sauce:

5 tablespoons all-purpose flour

1 cup dark raisins

¾ cup Madeira

⅓ cup red wine vinegar

1 tablespoon coarsely ground black
    pepper

3 tablespoons unsalted butter

2 tablespoons tomato paste

3 to 4 cups reserved cooking liquid from
    the tongue

1. Soak the tongue in cold water to cover for several hours or overnight. Change the water 3 or 4 times. This will remove blood from the tongue and leave the meat a pale color.

2. Place the tongue in a large stockpot. Stud the onions with the cloves. Add the onions,

carrots, celery, leeks, bouquet garni, salt, and peppercorns to the pot. Add enough cold water to cover by 2 inches. Bring to a boil and reduce the heat to low. Cover and simmer over low heat until the meat is very tender, 2 to 2½ hours.

3. Remove the tongue from the pot and set aside to cool. Strain the cooking liquid, measure 4 cups and reserve for the sauce.

4. Preheat the oven to 400°F.

5. Prepare the sauce: Spread the flour on a baking sheet and toast in the oven until light brown, about 10 minutes. Set aside.

6. Combine the raisins and Madeira in a small bowl. Set aside.

7. Boil the vinegar with the black pepper in a medium-size saucepan over high heat until reduced to about 1 tablespoon, 2 to 3 minutes. Reduce the heat, add the butter, and stir until melted. Add the toasted flour, stirring constantly, and gradually stir in 3 cups of the reserved cooking liquid. Cook over low heat, stirring constantly, until you have a smooth, not too thick, sauce. Add more of the cooking liquid if necessary. Stir in the tomato paste and simmer, uncovered, stirring occasionally, for 15 minutes. Turn off the heat and stir in the raisins with the Madeira.

8. When the tongue has cooled to lukewarm, trim away any fat, bones, and skin from the root end. Starting at the tip of the tongue,

make a small incision and carefully peel away the skin with your hands. Cut the peeled tongue into ½-inch-thick diagonal slices.

9. Add the meat to the sauce and gently heat through. Taste and adjust the seasoning.

10. Arrange the slices of meat on a warmed large serving platter and cover with the sauce.

Serves 6

Veal Kidneys with Belgian Gin and Mustard

KALFSNIERKES OP Z'N GENTS
•
ROGNONS DE VEAU A LA GANTOISE

Why is it that kidneys have such a bad reputation? Most of my students first regard them with undisguised horror, but then most of them have never actually tasted kidneys. Once they do—prepared in this rich, unctuous, and piquant sauce—they usually love them.

The keys to success with kidneys are simple. They must be very fresh, firm to the touch, and without the slightest hint of an ammonia odor. Kidneys are a tender, very lean meat and must be cooked briefly and quickly so that they remain pink and moist in the center. Overcooked kidneys are tough and inedible. Serve the kidneys with Belgian fries and a Casserole of Wild Mushrooms or Carrot Timbales (see Index).

4 tablespoons (½ stick) unsalted butter
¼ pound white mushrooms, cleaned, trimmed, and quartered
½ pound cremini mushrooms, cleaned, trimmed, and quartered
2 tablespoons finely minced shallots
Salt and freshly ground black pepper to taste
2 veal kidneys, all fat removed, cut into ½-inch cubes
3 tablespoons all-purpose flour
½ cup genever (Belgian gin) or Cognac
½ cup beef broth, preferably homemade (page 54)
½ cup heavy (or whipping) cream
1 tablespoon minced fresh tarragon or 1 teaspoon dried tarragon
1 to 3 teaspoons Dijon or Tierenteyn mustard

1. Melt 2 tablespoons of the butter in a medium-size heavy skillet over medium heat. Add all the mushrooms and sauté until browned slightly, about 5 minutes. Add the shallots and cook 1 minute longer. Season lightly with salt and pepper, remove from the skillet, and set aside.

2. Dredge the cubed kidneys with the flour.

3. Melt the remaining 2 tablespoons butter in the same skillet. Add the kidneys and sauté over medium-high heat until nicely browned on both sides but still pink inside, about 5 minutes.

4. Off the heat, carefully flambé the kidneys with the gin (see page 130 for instructions on flambéing). When the flames die down, season with salt and pepper and transfer to a warmed platter.

5. Deglaze the skillet with the broth over high heat, scraping up all the little browned bits from the bottom. Add the mushroom mixture, cream, dried tarragon if using, and the juice that has collected in the platter holding the kidneys. Reduce the heat and simmer until the sauce thickens to the consistency of heavy cream. Whisk in the mustard, judging the amount by the strength of the mustard (the Tierenteyn mustard is strong stuff!).

6. Just before serving, reheat the kidneys over low heat in the warm sauce. Don't overcook the kidneys or they will be tough. They should remain slightly pink on the inside. Sprinkle the fresh tarragon, if using, over the kidneys and serve immediately.

Serves 4

Cooking with Beer

Beer, Belgium's National Drink

By quoting from Michael Jackson's book *The Great Beers of Belgium*, I can have the world's leading authority on beer express for me what modesty would prevent me from revealing. Perhaps the longest-kept, best-hidden secret that the Belgian people have is that their country is a beer connoisseur's paradise. Where else could one find over 300 varieties of beer, each one unique, each one suited for a particular taste and occasion, and all brewed to exacting standards by masters of an art that goes back hundreds of years?

Beer is the national drink of Belgium, and Belgium itself is one of the great brewing regions of the world. There is almost no wine produced in Belgium, for the climate does not allow it. But the climate is perfect for growing grains, and grains, particularly barley, are the requisite ingredient of beer. It would be a mistake to think that Belgians don't understand or appreciate wines. They do indeed, as they understand and appreciate all food and drink. The wine-growing regions of France, particularly where the Champagne grapes are grown, border the barley fields of Belgium. And in the hands of the Belgian brewers, whose traditions go back in history many, many centuries, beer has become a beverage as filled with nuances, nobility, complexity, and sophistication as the finest wines in the world.

In Belgium, you will find a vast and mysterious world of spicy, fruity, hoppy, sour beverages ranging from golden blond to deep red to the darkest brown. You will find high-and-low fermentation brews and the unique, spontaneously fermenting beers called the lambics.

Most of the breweries in Belgium use methods of brewing that have long been forgotten by the rest of the world. They are

> *The respect reserved for wine in most countries is in Belgium accorded also to beer. No country can match Belgium in the gastronomic interest of its beers. No country has so many distinct styles of beer. No country has beers that are so complex in character as the finest in Belgium. No country has so many individualistic brews. Nor does any country have such a sophisticated beer cuisine (extending far beyond the dishes that are commonly associated with beer).*
> —Michael Jackson
> The Great Beers of Belgium

mostly small, artisanal, family-run businesses, and all of them guard their secret ingredients and methods with the vigilance of watchdogs. What makes them unique is that over the centuries these beer brewers have remained faithful to their origins and traditions and thereby have developed a degree of perfection, originality, and variety unknown in any other country in the world. The same can be said for Belgium's extensive and varied beer cuisine.

Since the Middle Ages, brewers in Belgium have experimented with herbs, spices, berries, and fruits—juniper berries, coriander, licorice, ginger, and orange peels, for example—to flavor their beers. The same imaginative approach is part of Belgian culinary tradition, especially when it comes to cooking with beer. It is important to understand the subtle bitter taste that beer brings to any dish to appreciate the harmonious pairing of beer with the gentle sweetness of fruit or caramelized onions. This bitter-sweet marriage of flavors also goes back to the cooking of the Middle Ages and continues to vitalize Belgian cooking today.

If there were ever a danger that the practice of cooking with beer might die out, Belgian chefs warded it off in the late 1970s by reviving traditional Flemish and Walloon specialties. At the same time, life was breathed into the operation of many small family breweries and microbreweries, so that chefs who were reviving and refining these old recipes had available to them a great variety of beer. Today, beer cuisine in Belgium is very much in vogue. Chefs at top restaurants are developing modern sauces flavored with beer to serve favorite foods, such as asparagus, oysters, and other seafood, which never before had been paired with beer. Even in dessert courses, surprising and wonderful combinations are appearing, such as sabayon sauces and fruits poached in beer, to mention just a couple.

In the United States, there is a growing awareness of the vast world of beer and the many possibilities it presents. Microbreweries are sprouting up all over the country, offering carefully crafted beers that are appreciated for their freshness, quality, and individual character. Indeed, they differentiate themselves from the mass-produced beers by their assertive flavor, color, and aroma as well as by their emphasis on natural ingredients—malt, barley, hops, spring water, and fresh yeast.

BEER CLASSIFICATIONS

Although the recipes in this book will be most authentic if you can use the Belgian beers I have specified, you can still achieve good results by substituting one of the better American beers. Beers are classified into the following groups:

1. Low-fermentation beers called pilsener or lager: These are clear "blond" beers brewed with pale malt and with a definite

taste of hops. They are excellent thirst quenchers. To substitute for a Belgian beer of this type, look for a pilsener brewed in a local microbrewery or an English or German variety (Munich or Dortmund type).

2. High-fermentation or ale top-fermented beers: These are generally brewed with a darker malt and are recognized by their dark color. These full-bodied beers have a unique character and taste, and there are many varieties within this classification:

• Belgian Abbey and Trappist beers, of which Affligem Abbey Beer, Trappist Ale, St. Sixtus Abbey Ale, and Orval Trappist Beer are available in the United States.

• The unique red beer, Rodenbach, imported to the United States by Vanberg & DeWulf.

• "White," bittersweet wheat beers. These have a fruity flavor and are cloudy with sediment. Belgian Blanche de Bruges is imported by Vanberg & DeWulf. Celis White is brewed in Austin, Texas, by Belgian Pierre Celis.

• Other strong ales available in the United States are Scaldis and Duvel.

3. Spontaneous fermentation beers or lambics: This term covers typically Belgian beers brewed only in the region of Brussels and in the neighboring Senne Valley. These are all-wheat beers to which no yeast is added, but a naturally occurring wild yeast ensures the same type of spontaneous fermentation that occurs in wine, particularly sherry. Lambics available in the United States are:

• Lindeman's Kriek or Boon Kriek (cherry-flavored beer)

• Lindeman's Framboise or Boon Framboise (raspberry-flavored beer)

• Faro (a lambic sweetened with rock sugar)

• Boon Gueuze (a blend of old and young lambic)

Belgian Beer Sources

Vanberg & DeWulf
52 Pioneer Street
Cooperstown, New York 13326
Telephone: (607) 547-8184

A distributor that specializes exclusively in Belgian beer. Call or write to them to find the nearest location to buy the beer you are looking for.

Or contact the following U.S. importers of Belgian beer:

Merchant du Vin, East
P.O. Box 757
Lenox, Massachusetts 01240
Telephone: (413) 637-2811

Phoenix Imports, Ltd.
2925 Montclair Drive
Ellicott City, Maryland 21043
Telephone: (410) 465-1155

Beer International
560 Kipp Street
Teaneck, New Jersey 07666
Telephone: (201) 836-6540

Flemish Beef Stew Cooked in Beer

VLAAMSE STOVERY
•
LES CARBONADES FLAMANDES

Beef stew cooked in beer has long been part of the culinary heritage of Belgium, and it is still one of the most popular stews in Flanders. Through the ages, the recipe has varied, and every mother passes on her "secret" to her children. My mother likes to add some liver or kidneys to the beef, which certainly gives the stew a more distinctive flavor. My grandmother likes it more "sweet" and adds a slice of *pain d'épices*, an old-fashioned honey spice bread, or even a slice of country bread spread with a strong mustard. These spicy and sweet flavorings have been an integral part of the Belgian palate and cuisine since the Middle Ages.

The following version is a basic one and my favorite. Like many other stews it is best made a day or two ahead since it improves in flavor. The success of the dish depends greatly on the quality of the beer you use. Look for a rich, dark, and slightly bitter beer, such as Rodenbach or a dark Abbey beer.

Serve this stew with French fries or boiled potatoes, applesauce, and plenty of "golden ambrosia," the name the old Belgians gave to their beloved beer.

4 pounds boneless stew meat, such as chuck, cut into 2-inch cubes
1 teaspoon salt
½ teaspoon freshly ground black pepper
2 to 3 tablespoons all-purpose flour
4 tablespoons (½ stick) unsalted butter
3 large onions (about 2 pounds), thinly sliced
2 bottles (12 ounces each) Belgian beer
2 or 3 sprigs fresh thyme or 1 teaspoon dried thyme
2 bay leaves
1½ tablespoons red currant jelly (or brown sugar)
1 tablespoon cider or red wine vinegar

1. Season the beef cubes with the salt and pepper and dredge with the flour. Shake off any excess.

2. Melt 2 tablespoons of the butter in a large heavy skillet over high heat until hot but not smoking. Add the beef cubes and sauté until nicely browned on all sides. Work in batches so as not to crowd the beef cubes, or they will steam instead of sauté. Add 1 tablespoon of butter, if necessary. Transfer the beef cubes to a heavy Dutch oven.

177

Curbside Cuisine

All through Belgium, at the many fritures, *the famous roadside stands where you can buy golden, crusty Belgian fries at any hour of the day, you can observe the regular customers enjoying their fries with a ladleful of* carbonades, *a thick, almost syrupy sauce full of the flavor of onions. These* carbonades *have been cooked slowly for hours and hours until the onions have almost dissolved and the pieces of meat melt in the mouth like butter. These snacks are generally accompanied by lively discussions about the latest soccer game or comments about the exploits of their favorite cycling hero. A glass of beer to wash everything down is de rigueur.*

3. Add the remaining 1 tablespoon butter to the skillet and melt over medium heat. Add the onions and cook, stirring occasionally, until browned, about 15 minutes. If necessary, raise the heat toward the end of the cooking time. It is important to brown the meat and the onions evenly to give the stew its deep brown color. The trick is to stir the onions just enough to avoid burning them but not so often as to interrupt the browning process. Combine the onions with the meat in the Dutch oven.

4. Deglaze the skillet with the beer, scraping with a wooden spoon to loosen any brown bits, and bring to a boil. Pour the beer over the meat. Add the thyme and bay leaves.

5. Simmer, covered, over low heat until the meat is very tender, 1½ to 2 hours. Before serving, stir in the red currant jelly and vinegar; simmer for 5 minutes. This sweet-and-sour combination will give this hearty stew its authentic Flemish flavor. Remove the thyme sprigs and bay leaves. Taste and adjust the seasoning and serve.

Serves 6 to 8

Note: *If this recipe looks like it will make too much for you, go ahead and prepare it anyway, for the stew freezes beautifully. Then you have an instant dinner awaiting your pleasure.*

Veal Chops in Beer with Mushrooms and Chervil

KALFSKOTELETTEN MET ROMIGE KERVELSAUS
•
COTES DE VEAU AU CERFEUIL

Belgium is, without a doubt, a most traditional meat-and-potato country, but the meat and potatoes are always served with style. A typical lunch served at home (and many people still go home for lunch) or in a bistro-type restaurant, which always offers a *menu du jour*, would begin with a soup followed by a small portion of meat with potato and a vegetable.

These veal chops cooked in beer are a typical example of this kind of entrée. They take very little time to prepare and, served with some steaming boiled potatoes and a vegetable of your choice, are an elegant, delicious meal in the Belgian mode.

I have included this recipe in the beer section because it is so spectacularly delicious prepared with a Belgian "blond" wheat beer. This is a most refreshing summer beer which is an ideal companion to dishes prepared with white, delicate meat such as veal or chicken. In the United States, I have found two excellent blond beers: Blanche de Bruges, distributed by Vanberg & DeWulf, and Celis White, a wheat beer brewed in Austin, Texas, by the Belgian brewer, Pierre Celis. The Celis Brewery has recently been bought by a major beer distributor, which is good news to beer lovers across the country.

2 tablespoons unsalted butter
1 tablespoon vegetable oil
4 veal chops (each about 1 inch thick, 2 pounds total), preferably from naturally raised milk-fed veal
Salt and freshly ground black pepper to taste
1 tablespoon finely minced shallot
3/4 pound fresh mushrooms, preferably an assortment of wild mushrooms, shiitakes, cèpes, and portobellos, but cultivated white mushrooms will also do, cleaned, trimmed, and halved
1/4 cup blond wheat beer, such as Blanche de Bruges
1/2 cup heavy (or whipping) cream
1/4 cup finely minced chervil or a mixture of parsley, chives, and tarragon

1. Heat the butter and oil in a large heavy skillet over high heat until hot but not smoky. Add the veal chops and sauté until nicely browned, 4 to 5 minutes on each side. They should still be pink inside. Remove to a warmed platter and season with salt and pepper.

2. Add the shallot to the same skillet and cook over medium heat for 30 seconds. Add the mushrooms and beer; cook over low heat until the mushrooms are softened, about 10 minutes. Add the cream and simmer for another 10 minutes. Season with salt and pepper to taste and stir in the chervil.

3. Pour the mushroom sauce over the veal chops and serve immediately.

Serves 4

Variation: Substitute ¼ pound finely minced sorrel leaves for the chervil for a tangy and delicious variation.

Veal or Beef Birds

VOGELKES ZONDER KOP
•
OISEAUX SANS TETE

There are no birds in this tasty Belgian specialty but rather a scaloppine of veal or beef that has been pounded very thin and rolled around a stuffing of well-seasoned forcemeat. The little bundles are thought to resemble the bodies of small birds. The lucky home cooks in Belgium can buy these all prepared and ready to braise in almost any butcher shop, but fortunately it is not at all difficult to make these yourself and the result is very well worth it.

Veal scaloppine is widely available, but if you want the heartier flavor of beef, ask your butcher to slice the meat for you out of the fillet. If the slices are still too thick, you can pound them to the desired thinness between two sheets of plastic wrap.

This dish is traditionally served with steamed potatoes and a seasonal vegetable.

Filling:
10 ounces ground meat, preferably a
  mixture of veal and pork
1 large egg
Pinch of freshly grated nutmeg
1 tablespoon finely minced shallots
1 tablespoon finely minced fresh parsley
Salt and freshly ground black pepper
  to taste

Birds and Sauce:

4 thin slices (4 × 3 inches) veal or
*   beef, pounded ¼ inch thick as for*
*   scaloppine*
2 thin slices ham, halved
2 tablespoons unsalted butter
1 tablespoon vegetable oil
6 shallots, peeled and halved
Salt and freshly ground black pepper
*   to taste*
⅓ cup blond pilsener-type beer, plus
*   additional if needed*

Beurre manié: 1 tablespoon unsalted
*   butter, 2 teaspoons all-purpose flour,*
*   and ½ teaspoon Dijon mustard*
*   blended together*

1 tablespoon finely minced fresh parsley,
*   for garnish*

1. Prepare the filling: Combine all the ingredients in a mixing bowl and mix together thoroughly with your hands. Divide into 4 equal parts.

2. Lay the veal or beef scaloppine flat and cover each with a piece of the ham. Place the filling in the center and fold the left flap of veal over the filling. Cover with the right flap. Turn seam side down and tuck the top and bottom edges under so that the filling is completely enclosed. Tie securely with kitchen string. The packages can be prepared up to a day in advance, then tightly covered, and refrigerated.

3. Heat the butter and oil in a heavy Dutch oven over medium heat until it is hot but not smoking. Add the meat bundles and sauté until they are nicely browned on all sides, about 10 minutes. Be careful not to burn the drippings.

4. Add the shallots and sauté, stirring occasionally, until the shallots are slightly caramelized, about 5 minutes. Season with salt and pepper.

5. Add the beer and bring to a quick boil, scraping up all the brown bits from the bottom with a wooden spoon. Reduce the heat and simmer, covered, for 30 minutes. Halfway through the cooking, turn over the meat bundles. Transfer the meat to a warmed platter.

6. To finish the sauce, whisk in the *beurre manié* and bring to boil for 30 seconds. If the sauce seems too thick, add a few tablespoons of beer. Pour the sauce over the meat, sprinkle with the parsley, and serve.

Serves 4

Variation: *Along with, or as a substitute for, the shallots add ½ pound peeled baby carrots, 16 peeled pearl onions, and 1 cup quartered fresh mushrooms.*

Beer Is Good for Body and Soul

Of the gifts offered to us by Heaven and Earth, is born, by the grace of St. Arnold and human knowledge, the Divine Juice of Barley.

The above inscription, translated here from the original Latin, is engraved on the front of the magnificent Flemish Renaissance building that stands in the heart of Brussels on the Grand Place. The building is called Maison des Brasseurs, and it is the brewers' guild house, a splendid architectural testimony to the importance of the brewers and the influence of the brewers' guilds in the life and history of Belgium.

One of the favorite expressions in my country is that the Bordeaux and Burgundies of Belgium are beers. Beer certainly is the national drink of Belgium, which offers the largest variety of any nation in the world.

But beer is even more. It is considered a drink and a food all in one, and historical facts have certainly borne this out. Through plagues, cholera epidemics, and other pestilence, word came down from the monasteries for people to abstain from contaminated water and to drink beer, which was brewed with boiled water and therefore safe. In times of famine, beer often saved huge portions of the population from starving. Even the strictest monastic orders have always allowed the fasting monks to drink beer during Lent, when their diet forbade eating even cheese and fish. They called the beloved beverage their "liquid bread." For the rest of the year as well, their diet was so abstemious that their nutritious beer was necessary to their health. To this day Belgium and the Netherlands are the only countries to have kept alive and thriving the practice of brewing in the monasteries and to produce in any significant quantity their own liquid bread, the Trappist beers.

There are miracles associated with beer in Belgian history. St. Arnold, the very saint referred to in the inscription quoted from the brewers' guild house, is said to have saved his community from the plague by stirring the hops with his bishop's staff. He was later deemed the patron saint of the brewers.

Drinking beer has always been an integral aspect of family meals, daily and festive. There are about 80 table beers produced in Belgium, and these beers are served at dinner to grown-ups and children alike. "Beer is a part of civilized life in Belgium," writes beer expert Michael Jackson. "It is not a rite of passage into an adult garden of temptation and sin."

The belief that beer is good for everyone is ultimately demonstrated by the fact that for centuries, nursing mothers have been encouraged to drink rich brown beer, because it boosts the nutrition level of the mother's milk. And so the toast *Gezondheid* (meaning health) is most appropriate with Belgium's beer.

THE ART OF POURING

The casual American beer drinker, who consumes his brew ice-cold and often straight out of a can or bottle, might be surprised by Belgium's numerous rituals surrounding the consumption of beer.

The foremost authorities on the art of pouring beer are the bartenders in the many beer cafés all over Belgium. To start with, almost every brand-name beer has a particular glass in which it is served, so the bartender will never select just any glass but only the particular one for the beer you ordered. For example, Duvel beers are always poured in balloon glasses, similar to the goblets in which full-bodied Burgundy wines are properly served. Lighter, thirst-quenching beers are served in tall, sturdy glasses. The sparkling lambic fruit beers seem to taste better when served in champagne flutes. The bartender, having chosen the appropriate glass, will always pour the beer as if he were concentrating on nothing else but the bottle and glass in his hands.

Here are a few tips from these experts, which will yield you a perfectly poured beer:

1. Start with an impeccably clean, dry glass. This is important to get a head of creamy froth topping the drink.

2. Tilt the glass slightly. Pour the beer slowly along the side of the glass.

3. When the glass is half full, straighten it and continue pouring slowly while holding the bottle farther away from the glass. This should yield a perfect inch of froth.

4. If you are in Belgium, raise your glass and toast your companion with a hearty *Gezondheid!* or *Prosit!*

5. Drink slowly, sip by sip, to fully appreciate the flavor of your beer.

Pork Chops, Brussels Style

VARKENSKOTELETJES OP Z'N BRUSSELS

•

COTES DE PORC A LA BRUXELLOISE

The Brussels style referred to in this recipe does not even remotely refer to the glittery international scene, but to the real Brussels that you can still find in the old quarters of the city. Here are the old brasseries and the little cafés where office workers gather to relax in front of a foamy glass of beer and eat the specials of the day. But for their clothes, you might blink and see in these scenes a replica of the paintings of Breughel and Jordaans. And one suspects that the beer that flows so abundantly from the jugs in these paintings must be the very lambic-type beer that has been brewed exclusively for hundreds of years in the region right around Brussels and the neighboring Senne Valley.

The lambic beers, completely original to Belgium, are made out of wheat, malt, and hops. Most striking is that no yeast is ever added to the brew because a natural wild yeast ensures spontaneous fermentation. This beer often compared to Champagne, is slightly acerbic and very dry. There are many variations, including the famous Gueuze, and the popular fruit beers, which include cherry, raspberry, and peach. Naturally, lambics create a wealth of possibilities for creative cooks. Many of them are available in the United States (see Belgian Beer Sources, page 176).

4 pork loin chops (each 1 inch thick, 2 pounds total)
Salt and freshly ground black pepper to taste
2 tablespoons all-purpose flour
2 tablespoons unsalted butter
1 tablespoon vegetable oil
3 large onions (about 3/4 pound each), thinly sliced
1/2 teaspoon dried thyme or 1 sprig fresh thyme
3/4 cup blond pilsener-style domestic beer, such as Duvel
1 to 2 teaspoons cornstarch
1 tablespoon water
1/2 teaspoon white wine vinegar or cider vinegar
1 tablespoon finely minced fresh parsley, for garnish

1. Season the pork chops with salt and pepper and dredge with the flour, shaking off the excess.

Beer and Architecture

The Art Nouveau movement was begun and the term coined in Belgium in 1881 when Octave Maus and Edmond Picard first introduced it in their magazine, L'Art Moderne. *The basic belief of the Art Nouveau movement was that the craftsmen who design buildings and their decorations—furniture, pottery, anything, in short, that is part of everyday life—can be and often are artists. The movement recognized these artist-craftsmen for their contributions to Belgian life. Pride in craftsmanship goes back for centuries in Belgium, whether the craft be that of a glassmaker, ironworker, woodworker, weaver, or brewer.*

The greatest practitioner of Art Nouveau was the Brussels architect Victor Horta (1861–1947). Basing his designs on the principle that the straight line should be eliminated to whatever extent it is possible to do so, Horta designed structures in which the lines twisted, swirled, cascaded, and spiraled to create buildings of breathtaking beauty. Today, Brussels is the world's capital of Art Nouveau architecture, and some of the best examples are the Cafés Falstaff and De Ultieme Hallucinatie (The Ultimate Hallucination). The Falstaff café, built in 1903 by one of Victor Horta's disciples, is a magnificent example of Art Nouveau both from the outside and in interior furnishings, replete with mirrors, stained glass panels, and a virtual garden of lampshades in the shapes of flowers. The tavern in the Falstaff serves a small selection of 45 Belgian beers. The name of De Ultieme Hallucinatie, built in 1850, refers either to the gorgeous Art Nouveau interior or to the enormous selection of Belgian beer— and is a must on any visitor's agenda.*

2. Heat the butter and oil in a large heavy skillet over high heat until hot but not smoking. Add the pork chops and sauté on both sides until golden brown, 3 to 4 minutes per side. Remove the pork chops to a warmed platter and set aside.

3. Add the onions to the skillet and cook, stirring, over medium heat until softened and lightly browned, 5 to 7 minutes. Season with salt and pepper, and add the thyme.

4. Deglaze the pan with the beer, scraping up all the brown bits from the bottom of the pan with a wooden spoon. Place the pork chops on top of the onions, cover partially, and

cook until the pork chops are springy to the touch and still slightly pink inside, 10 to 15 minutes. (Today's pork is so lean that it becomes very tough if it is overcooked.)

5. Arrange the chops on a warmed platter.

6. Dissolve the cornstarch in the water and add it to the sauce. Stirring constantly, bring to a quick boil to thicken. Remove from the heat and stir in the vinegar. Adjust the seasoning. Spoon the onions over the pork chops, sprinkle with the parsley, and serve.

Serves 4

Variation: For a more elegant presentation, bone the pork chops. There is no great trick to this: Simply cut away the meat following the contour of the bone with a small, sharp knife. Tie the fillet into a medallion with some kitchen string. Do not discard the bones. Brown them with the meat and leave them in the pan while the chops are cooking. The bones will add gelatin and flavor to the sauce. Remove before serving.

My Grandmother's Herbed Pork Chops

GROOTMOEDER'S VARKENSKOTELETJES MET PADDESTOELEN EN SPEK

•

COTES DE PORC AUX HERBES DE MA GRAND-MERE

This is another meat and potato dish that is typical of what is served in Belgium at the midday meal. You would never find these pork chops on any restaurant menu, for they represent the kind of honest and quick dishes that are at the heart of Belgian home cooking. The ingredients are simple and lovingly prepared. As far as I can see, Belgians have no intention of following the current eating fashions in America by cutting down on their daily portion of meat. But I'd like to emphasize again that the meat is always part of a well-balanced meal that usually includes a soup and plenty of vegetables, so that the actual portion of meat that is consumed is rather small.

My grandmother, who wasted nothing in her kitchen, always sautéed leftover cooked potatoes in the drippings from the pork chops. These were so good that there were never enough to satisfy us. Today I serve these pork chops with steamed good-quality potatoes (Yukon Gold, Yellow Finn, or new potatoes), which are sliced and sprinkled with sea salt and minced parsley. Old-Fashioned Flemish Carrots (see Index) are particularly good with the naturally sweet pork.

4 pork loin chops (each 1 inch thick,
    2 pounds total)
3 tablespoons vegetable oil
1 teaspoon each dried basil, thyme, marjoram,
    and rosemary
3 tablespoons finely minced fresh parsley
3 ounces smoked slab bacon, cut into
    ½-inch strips
16 pearl onions or 12 small shallots, blanched
    for 1 minute and peeled
½ pound small white mushrooms, cleaned,
    trimmed, and halved
Salt and freshly ground black pepper to taste
⅔ cup blond pilsener-style beer, such as
    Duvel
2 tablespoons all-purpose flour
1 teaspoon salt
1 teaspoon freshly ground black pepper
1 tablespoon unsalted butter
3 to 4 tablespoons water

1. Rub both sides of the pork chops with 1 tablespoon of the vegetable oil.

2. In a small bowl, combine the dried herbs with 2 tablespoons of the parsley. Press the herb mixture onto the pork chops on both sides. This can be done several hours in advance.

3. Heat 1 tablespoon vegetable oil in a large heavy skillet or sauté pan over medium heat. Add the bacon and sauté until crisp and light brown. Remove with a slotted spoon and set aside.

4. Discard all but 1 tablespoon of the fat from the pan. Add the onions and mushrooms and cook, stirring occasionally, over medium heat until softened and lightly browned, about 10 minutes. Season with salt and pepper.

5. Return the bacon to the pan, add the beer, and simmer, covered, over medium heat for 15 minutes. The beer should have mostly evaporated, and the pearl onions should be soft. Sprinkle the remaining 1 tablespoon parsley over the vegetables and set aside.

6. Combine the flour with 1 teaspoon each salt and pepper. Dredge the pork chops with the flour, shaking off the excess.

7. Heat the butter with the remaining 1 tablespoon vegetable oil over high heat. Add the pork chops and sauté so they are browned on both sides, about 5 minutes. Reduce the heat to medium and continue cooking, turning the chops over from time to time, until springy to the touch, 8 to 10 more minutes. The chops should still be slightly

pink inside. Do not overcook, or the meat will be stringy and tough.

8. Arrange the pork chops on individual plates with the vegetables. Quickly deglaze the pan over high heat with the water, scraping up all the brown bits from the bottom. Pour over the chops and serve.

Serves 4

Belgian Meatballs Braised in Beer with Endives

GEHAKTBALLEKES GESTOOFD MET WITLOOF EN BIER

•

FRICADELLES AUX ENDIVES A LA BIERE BELGE

To a Belgian, meatballs can be either the ultimate in nostalgic comfort food, bringing back happy memories of childhood, or hopelessly plebeian food, associated with institutional cafeterias where

Belgian Burgers

In Belgium, every butcher shop displays a vast array of well-seasoned ground meats. Aside from the usual beef, there are always pork, veal, and lamb as well as combinations of ground meats. Home cooks can improvise with these meats to their heart's content, adding their own fines herbes, spices, bits of bacon, and even cheese to make their own individual meatballs, patties, meat loaves, and pâtés. In the summer Belgians have taken to imitating Americans by grilling seasoned forcemeat patties outdoors over hot coals. Try this for a flavorful variation on the traditional hamburger.

the meat was as tender as a Ping-Pong ball and was served with a pallid, gluey mass in the guise of mashed potatoes. But this staple of Belgian home cooking can become a favorite in your home if it is delicately prepared, seasoned well, and presented with style. Grown-ups and children will love the satisfying combination of tender meatballs, delicious gravy, and perfect mashed potatoes. Nor would I hesitate to serve this meal to guests, who, in my experience at least, tend to give a huge sigh of comfort and relaxation when presented with such a homey dish.

In this traditional recipe, the little meatballs are braised in a Belgian beer and fla-

188

vored with endives. It should be accompanied by a generous portion of mashed potatoes decorated with slivers of caramelized shallots and fresh parsley (see Index). The perfect beverage to serve is the same beer that you used in cooking this dish.

Meatballs:
1 cup fresh white bread crumbs
3/4 cup milk
1 pound lean ground beef
1/2 pound ground pork or veal
1 large egg
1 tablespoon finely minced shallots
1 tablespoon finely minced fresh parsley
Salt and freshly ground black pepper
    to taste
Pinch of freshly grated nutmeg
2 tablespoons all-purpose flour
2 tablespoons unsalted butter
1 tablespoon vegetable oil

Sauce:
1 medium onion, thinly sliced
3 Belgian endives, cored and cut into
    1/4-inch rounds
1 teaspoon sugar
Salt and freshly ground black pepper
    to taste
1 1/2 tablespoons all-purpose flour
1 cup blond pilsener-style beer, such as
    Duvel
1/2 cup chicken or beef broth, preferably
    homemade (page 53 or 54)

2 tablespoons finely minced fresh parsley, for
    garnish

1. Prepare the meatballs. Soak the bread crumbs in the milk until thoroughly moistened and use your hands to squeeze them dry. In a mixing bowl, combine the bread crumbs, ground meats, egg, shallots, parsley, salt, pepper, and nutmeg. Mix together thoroughly with your hands. Form the mixture into 6 to 8 balls or patties (2 inches in diameter and 1/2 inch thick) and dust with the flour.

2. In a deep, heavy Dutch oven, heat the butter and oil until hot but not smoking over high heat. Add the meatballs and sauté until browned on all sides, about 5 minutes, making sure that the butter does not burn. Remove the meatballs to a platter and reserve.

3. Prepare the sauce: Discard all but 2 tablespoons of the fat in the pan. Add the onion and endives; cook over low heat, stirring constantly, for about 10 minutes. Sprinkle the sugar, salt, pepper, and flour over the vegetables; cook, stirring, for 1 to 2 minutes longer. Add the beer and broth to the vegetables; bring to a quick boil, scraping up all the brown bits from the bottom of the pan.

4. Reduce the heat to a simmer and return the meatballs to the pan, placing them on top of the vegetables. Simmer, partially covered, until the meat is cooked through and has absorbed the flavors of the sauce, 45 minutes.

5. Sprinkle with the parsley and serve.

Serves 4 to 6

Rabbit Marinated in Abbey Beer with Mushrooms

KONYN MET TRAPPISTENBIER EN WILDE PADDESTOELEN

•

LAPIN A LA TRAPPISTE ET AUX CHAMPIGNONS SAUVAGES

Old-time cuisines tend to rely on slow-cooking, well-seasoned, one-dish preparations of which this Belgian masterpiece of rabbit slowly braised with wild mushrooms is a perfect example. A great deal of the mysterious, deep flavor comes from the dark Belgian Abbey beer that comprises the cooking liquid. The rich, complex flavors of these beers bear a comparison to the best red wines.

The sauce in this dish is naturally thickened with the vegetables from the marinade—my mother's way of preparing rich and full-flavored sauces without extra flour, cream, or butter. Serve the rabbit stew with parsleyed potatoes, noodles, or rice. A traditional accompaniment is a fruit garnish, such as Baked Apples Filled with Berries (see Index).

Marinade:

1 carrot, peeled and cut crosswise into 4 pieces
1 large onion, sliced
1 rib celery, cut into 1-inch chunks
1 teaspoon dried thyme
1 bay leaf
1 teaspoon black peppercorns
5 juniper berries, crushed
2 bottles (12 ounces each) Belgian Abbey beer or a dark, flavorful domestic beer
⅓ cup cider vinegar or good-quality white wine vinegar

Stew:

2 rabbits (2 to 2½ pounds each), each cut into 6 to 8 pieces
Salt and freshly ground black pepper to taste
½ cup all-purpose flour
5 tablespoons unsalted butter
1 tablespoon vegetable oil
1 pound fresh mushrooms (ideally this should be a mixture of shiitakes, portobellos, any wild mushrooms available, and white mushrooms), cleaned, stemmed, and thickly sliced
20 pearl or small white onions or 10 shallots, peeled
¾ cup chicken broth, preferably homemade (page 53), or water
2 teaspoons sugar
1 tablespoon red currant jelly
2 tablespoons finely minced fresh parsley

Trappist and Abbey Beers—A Belgian Treasure

In Belgium, the production of beer and the monastic life have been linked since the Middle Ages, when the monks perfected the art of brewing their own beers. The monasteries played an important part in the life of the Middle Ages. Through beer, the secluded religious lives of the monks became involved with the lives of the secular population. And it is important to remember that for long periods of time, the monasteries were the only safe places where a traveler might find a bed, a meal, and a pint of thirst-quenching ale.

In my country, we have a proverb which we take very seriously indeed: "In heaven there is no beer, therefore we shall drink it here!" It is no accident that from the earliest days our majestic Gothic cathedrals were always surrounded by an array of cafés, small restaurants, and brasseries, all purveying a staggering choice of excellent, restorative beer. And in every small country village you will find the local café sitting directly across the street from the village church. It is here, after the Mass, that all villagers, including the priest, congregate to refresh themselves and prepare themselves for the remarkable prospect of a beerless heaven. With this ritual, the Belgians again display their mastery at balancing the virtues of a religious life and the enjoyment of earthly pleasures.

1. Combine all the marinade ingredients in a large glass or earthenware bowl. Add the rabbit pieces, cover with plastic wrap, and refrigerate. Let the rabbit marinate at least 8 hours but preferably overnight in the refrigerator.

2. Remove the rabbit pieces from the marinade and pat them dry with paper towels. Season with salt and pepper and dredge in the flour, shaking off any excess. Save the marinade.

3. Heat 2 tablespoons of the butter and the oil in a large enameled Dutch oven over medium heat until the butter begins to froth. Add the rabbit pieces and brown on both sides. Work in batches so as not to crowd the pan, and be careful not to burn the butter.

4. Return all the rabbit pieces to the pot. Pour in the marinade with all the vegetables, herbs, and spices. Bring to a boil and reduce the heat to low. Simmer, covered, 45 minutes.

5. Place the cover slightly ajar, so that the liquid can reduce, and continue cooking for another 45 to 60 minutes until the meat is very tender and almost falling off the bone.

6. While the stew is cooking, prepare the mushrooms and onions. Melt 2 tablespoons of the remaining butter in a large skillet over medium heat. Add the mushrooms and sauté until they are nicely browned, 8 to 10 minutes. Season with salt and pepper and set aside.

7. Melt the remaining 1 tablespoon butter with the broth, sugar, and salt and pepper to taste in a small saucepan. Add the onions and cook, partially covered, over medium heat until the onions are tender and the liquid has reduced to a syrup, about 30 minutes. Remove the saucepan from the heat and set aside.

8. Remove the rabbit pieces from the stew. Discard the bay leaf and purée the remaining ingredients in a blender. The puréed vegetables will thicken the sauce and give it extra flavor. Return the sauce to the pan, taste it, and adjust the seasoning. Heat to a boil, add the red currant jelly, and whisk to dissolve. If the sauce looks too thin, reduce it over high heat.

Buying and Cooking Rabbit

Today, as in my great grandmother's day, many people who live in rural areas of Belgium raise chickens and rabbits for their own consumption and to supply local markets. Although rabbit is generally unfamiliar fare on the dinner tables of America, it is growing in popularity, and for good reason. Commercially raised rabbit is available all year round. Its tender and delicate meat is so lean and flavorful that many compare its taste with that of the best free-range chickens. And because rabbits, like free-range chickens, are still raised by individual farmers rather than mass-produced, they are not treated with harmful chemicals and hormones.

More adventurous palates might enjoy the far stronger flavor of wild rabbit or European hare. Like all game, wild rabbits tend to be dry and tough and must be cooked carefully with moist heat. In Belgium, we marinate wild rabbit in red wine with aromatic vegetables and braise the rabbit for a long time in the wine along with the vegetables and dried fruits. In the end, the sauce is thickened with the rabbit's blood. These traditional and labor-intensive dishes are enjoyed mostly in restaurants that specialize in regional cooking. It always makes me happy to see the amazing success of these specialty restaurants, because all over Europe so much local and indigenous cooking is simply disappearing. In Belgium, however, the old and local ways are still very much alive and, best of all, seem popular enough to survive the growing homogenization of European culture and cuisine.

For the home cook, rabbit is easy to prepare and requires no great cooking skills. It is always sold skinned and lends itself marvelously to braising, which will keep it moist and tender. If you have never cooked rabbit before, try some of the recipes in this book. I predict that they will help make rabbit part of your regular repertoire.

Ask for a rabbit from your butcher, who will cut it up into 6 to 8 serving pieces; or look for it already cut up and packaged in your supermarket. If you don't see it fresh in the meat department, check the frozen food section. Frozen rabbit is interchangeable with fresh rabbit in any recipe, although it loses some of its flavor in the thawing process, as is the case with all frozen meat. Fresh and wild rabbits are also available through mail-order sources, see page 141.

9. Return the rabbit pieces along with the mushrooms and onions to the sauce. Heat through gently, sprinkle with the parsley, and serve.

Serves 6

Rabbit Stewed with Prunes in Beer

KONYNTJE MET PRUIMEN EN BIER
•
RAGOUT DE LAPIN AUX PRUNEAUX ET A LA BIERE

In Belgium this sweet and hearty combination of rabbit, prunes, and beer is a great favorite and is typical of many other dishes that happily combine the slightly sweet, slightly tart flavor of fruit with the richness of rabbit, pork, or game. This dish is particularly good when made with Rodenbach beer. A specialty of West Flanders, the beer has a fruity flavor that makes it a wonderful match for poultry, rabbit, and pork. In the "nouvelle" cuisine, many chefs are experimenting with Rodenbach in fish and shellfish dishes and even trying it in desserts. Rodenbach is imported to the United States by Vanberg & DeWulf (see Belgian Beer Sources, page 176).

If you are lucky enough to have access to a hunter's pouch, you could make this stew with a wild rabbit, which is more assertive in flavor than the commercially raised ones. But the farmed animals will do just fine and have the advantage of being available year-round. Like most stews, this one improves when made a day ahead.

Parsleyed New Potatoes (see Index) are a good match, but I also like to accompany this stew with thick slices of a good, dark country bread, fabulous for dipping in the sauce.

3/4 pound pitted prunes
1 cup warm water
5 tablespoons all-purpose flour
1/2 teaspoon salt
Freshly ground black pepper to taste
2 rabbits (2 to 2 1/2 pounds each), each cut into
  6 to 8 pieces
2 tablespoons unsalted butter
3 tablespoons vegetable oil
1/4 pound slab bacon or Canadian bacon, cut
  into 1-inch cubes
4 medium onions, coarsely chopped
2 bottles (12 ounces each) dark beer, preferably
  Rodenbach, Abbey beer, Gueuze lambic, or
  good-quality domestic dark beer
2 tablespoons cider vinegar or white wine
  vinegar
2 cloves garlic, finely chopped
2 sprigs fresh thyme or 1/4 teaspoon dried thyme
2 bay leaves
1 whole clove

1. Soak the prunes in the warm water for 1 hour.

193

Comfort Stew

This rabbit stew with prunes is a specialty from the region of Brussels. It is a comforting dish, perfect for the windy fall and winter months. Here in America, I always prepare it at the first sign of gray autumn weather, and it evokes for me like nothing else memories of autumns in the Belgian countryside—the rustle of leaves on a footpath as we set out on a long ramble in search of mushrooms or chestnuts; the crisp, cold mornings collecting apples and pears in the orchard, followed by fragrant hours spent sorting and stacking the fruit in the cellar for the long cold winter; the sharp hunger pangs born of virtuous outdoor labor and, at the end of the day, the comforting smells of a smoky wood stove and a bubbling rabbit stew.

2. Mix 3 tablespoons of the flour with the salt and pepper. Dredge the rabbit pieces with this mixture, shaking off any excess.

3. Heat the butter and oil in a large heavy Dutch oven over medium heat until hot but not smoking. Add the rabbit pieces and sauté until golden brown on both sides. Work in batches so as not to crowd the pan. Remove the rabbit pieces to a plate and set aside.

4. In the same pan, fry the bacon over medium heat for about 5 minutes to render some of the fat. Drain the bacon on a paper towel and set aside.

5. Discard all but 2 tablespoons of the fat from the pan. Add the onions and cook over medium heat, stirring frequently, 4 to 5 minutes.

6. Put the rabbit pieces back into the pan. Sprinkle the remaining 2 tablespoons flour over the meat and onions. Cook over medium heat for 3 to 4 minutes, turning the meat from time to time. Add the beer gradually, allowing the sauce to thicken slightly each time before adding more. Add the vinegar, garlic, thyme, bay leaves, and clove. Reduce the heat and simmer, covered, for 1 hour, stirring occasionally.

7. Add the prunes, with the water they were plumped in, and the bacon. Simmer, covered, for about 45 minutes more. The meat should be very tender, almost falling off the bones.

8. Remove the bay leaves and thyme sprigs, taste and adjust the seasoning, and serve.

Serves 6

Sautéed Rabbit with Cherry Beer and Dried Cherries

KONYNE RUG MET KRIEK BIER EN GEDROOGDE KRIEKEN

•

RABLE DE LAPIN A LA KRIEK ET AUX CERISES

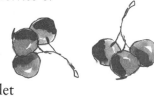

This is a recipe that I created for a beer-tasting dinner that was held at the James Beard House in New York City. To make a very festive dish, I used the delicate tenderloin and quickly sautéed it in butter, leaving it still rosy in the center. The meat remained delightfully tender. The legs of the rabbit, which are tougher, can find their way into a stew (see the recipes in this chapter) or into a rabbit terrine.

The secret of the sauce lies in the lambic kriek beer, a spontaneously fermented ale (original to Belgium) made from wheat, malted barley, and fresh black cherries, which impart their color and flavor. It is brewed according to *la méthode champenoise*, and the final product has the refinement, bubbles, and elegance of a great Champagne.

I like to serve this dish with wild rice, Belgian Endives, Flemish Style, or a Casserole of Wild Mushrooms (see Index for recipes).

The accompanying beverage should certainly be kriek beer served in champagne flutes.

3 tablespoons unsalted butter
2 rabbit loins, boned (bones reserved)
  and sliced into 1-inch pieces
Salt and freshly ground black pepper
  to taste
2 tablespoons finely diced carrot
2 tablespoons finely diced celery
2 tablespoons finely diced onion
1 tablespoon all-purpose flour
1 bottle (12 ounces) kriek beer
2 tablespoons red currant jelly
2 tablespoons dried cherries or
  cranberries

1. Melt 2 tablespoons of the butter in a large heavy skillet over medium heat until it foams. Season the pieces of rabbit tenderloin with salt and pepper. Add the rabbit to the skillet and sauté until browned on all sides and medium rare, about 10 minutes. Do not overcook or the meat will toughen up. Remove the meat to a warmed platter and set aside.

2. Add the bones to the skillet and brown them over high heat for a few minutes, being careful not to burn the butter in the pan.

3. Add the carrot, celery, and onion and continue cooking, stirring constantly, over medium heat until the vegetables have browned slightly.

4. Sprinkle the flour over the vegetables and bones; cook, stirring, until the flour is absorbed, about 1 minute. Deglaze with the beer, scraping up all the brown bits from the bottom of the pan. Boil for 1 minute. Add the red currant jelly and stir until it has dissolved.

5. Reduce the sauce by half over medium heat, 5 to 6 minutes. Pour through a strainer and return the sauce to the skillet. Add the dried cherries and simmer for 10 minutes. Swirl the remaining 1 tablespoon butter into the sauce. Return the meat to the skillet and reheat quickly in the sauce. Taste and adjust the seasoning and serve at once.

Serves 4

Prutske

All through my childhood, our house was home to a varied assortment of pets. Aside from the traditional dogs and cats, my mother collected stray animals with the passion of a Dr. Doolittle. More than one friend of the family jokingly referred to our house on the canal as a modern Noah's Ark. Birds with broken wings or baby birds who had fallen out of their nests; motherless baby mice; foul-mouthed parrots and singing parakeets; a boisterous and uninhibited monkey named King Louis, who terrorized and ruled our household for 4 years; and a succession of pet rabbits, all named Prutske, found their way to our house and my mother's ministrations.

The first Prutske (the name means little thing) arrived at our house when he was no bigger than a field mouse. He had been the runt of the litter and rejected by his own mother, but he was immediately adopted by mine. We had never seen a rabbit so tiny and fragile. It seemed a miracle that he survived at all. My mother nursed him day and night, feeding him warm milk every 3 or 4 hours from a tiny bottle that belonged to one of my dolls. He slept in a little shoebox filled with dry grass at the side of her bed.

Prutske not only survived but grew into a sleek, fat, funny, pearl-gray rabbit of enormous size who hopped around our house with as much proprietary pride as Bessy, our Irish setter, with whom Prutske happily shared a sleeping basket. Prutske's relationship with King Louis, the monkey, was not nearly so amicable. King Louis teased Prutske incessantly, following him around trying to peer under the rabbit's tail to see what exactly grew there. That was when I discovered that rabbits actually can look menacing, as Prutske bared his teeth and snapped at the irritating monkey.

Like all the members of our household, Prutske was a fine gourmet. He loved chocolate, enjoyed chewing on electrical wires, and most especially liked to gnaw on the elaborately carved feet of the antique dresser.

As much as we children loved our various Prutskes, this never interfered with our pleasure in eating the savory stews that featured their distant cousins.

Vegetable and Fruit Side Dishes

Vegetables and Fruits by the Season

Marie Baekelandt, my maternal great grandmother, lived her whole life, from her birth in 1887 until she died at the age of 86 in 1973, in the small village of Oost-Rozebeke in the Westhoek (the western corner) region of Flanders.

She and her husband, Kamiel, ran a small family farm, raised three children, and eked out a living from the Flemish soil, which, though rich and fertile, is subject to a capricious and often difficult climate. Kamiel worked the fields, growing, like most of his neighbors, potatoes, wheat, and especially flax. Marie's life centered around the house. She took care of the animals—chickens, cows, and a pig or two—her children, and later her grandchildren. She did all the cooking, of course, baked all her own bread, put up her own preserves, and made her own charcuterie, too. She also tended her *potager,* the kitchen garden, which provided nearly all the variety the family could expect in the way of table vegetables and herbs. It served as a botanical apothecary as well and included glorious, extensive flower beds—a great indulgence, to be sure, but one which gave her the utmost pleasure. This garden was not only her pride and joy, but I strongly suspect it was her haven and refuge as well. In this, she was typical of Belgians both past and present—we seem to have an almost mystical bond to the earth. Even if we have only a few feet of ground available to us, we will dig, plant, and cherish a garden. We are, quite literally, "down to earth people."

Meat or chicken were strictly for Sundays and special occasions. So every morning, after tending the breakfast dishes and seeing the children off to school, Marie would go down the two little steps that led to her garden. I remember watching her often when I was very young and she was already an old lady—the images will stay with me forever. Meticulously she chose the vegetables for that day—some leeks, a crisp head of celery for the soup, a few carrots, a handful of parsley, some chives—all neatly swaddled in her black apron. The garden was a world in which she could easily lose track of time. But then the church bell, tolling the hour, sent her hurrying back to the warmth of her stove, carrying the huge bundle on her belly like a woman pregnant with the fruits of the earth, her small, wrinkled face flushed with pleasure.

In those days small family-run farms like Marie's were scattered around the Flanders countryside. Today, of course, the cities are expanding dramatically, and it has become almost impossible to draw the line between the suburbs and the "real" country. Every time I go back, there are always new houses, new roads, and new shopping centers obstructing the once open horizon, so that only the landscape paintings of Leon Desmet, hanging in my grandmother Jeanne's house, and the stories that she tells remind me of how it once was.

Although drastically reduced in number, Belgian farmers still get the most out of the fertile earth. Following the seasons, our markets are loaded with sugar snap peas, hop shoots, green beans, salsify, tomatoes, celery, leeks, lettuces, radishes, cucumbers, endives, celery roots, white asparagus, turnips, beets, onions, potatoes, Brussels sprouts, and cabbages of all sizes and colors. We Belgians love vegetables, and they constitute an important part of our diet. A lot of energy and time is spent in shopping for and choosing the best vegetables but, as you will see in following recipes, the preparations are all extremely simple and straightforward.

Also, whenever possible, we prefer vegetables that are locally grown to those that have been imported from far away. It is a prejudice of sorts, I suppose, but one based on centuries of experience and connoisseurship. Are asparagus in season? Only the tenderest, fattest spears from Malines will do. Brussels sprouts? Only tiny baby sprouts are considered fit for the table—never the sprouts that resemble small heads of cabbage.

Fortunately it is getting easier to buy wonderful, fresh vegetables in specialty greenmarkets all over the United States. Even supermarkets are paying better attention to their produce departments and eliminating those horrid plastic-wrapped packages. It should always be possible to handle and examine whatever is offered for sale.

Belgian Endives Flemish Style

WITLOOF OP ZIJN VLAAMS
•
CHICONS A LA FLAMANDE

This recipe in which the endives are braised in butter and caramelized with a bit of sugar is my favorite way of preparing these versatile vegetables. The resulting endives are meltingly tender with a hint of sweetness to balance the bitter taste. They might be considered slightly overcooked by American standards but are so delicious that no one will be able to resist them.

6 to 8 Belgian endives, cored
5 tablespoons unsalted butter, at room
    temperature
Juice of ½ lemon
1 tablespoon confectioners' sugar
½ cup water, plus additional if needed
½ teaspoon salt
Freshly ground black pepper to taste
3 tablespoons finely chopped fresh parsley,
    for garnish

1. Choose a stainless steel or enameled pot large enough to hold the endives in a single layer. Smear most of the butter on the bottom of the pot. Cut out a round of parchment paper to fit inside, butter the parchment paper on one side, and set aside.

2. Arrange the endives in the pot and add the lemon juice, sugar, water, salt, and pepper. Cover the endives with the parchment paper, buttered side down. Place a plate on top of the paper and cover the pot with a lid. The paper helps the endive to steam better and the weight of the plate gently presses them down into their own juices. Cook over medium heat until very tender, 30 to 45 minutes. (Tender as butter, my mother says.) Check the water once in a while and add a little more if necessary to avoid burning the endives. Turn the endives over once halfway through the cooking process.

3. Carefully remove the plate and the parchment paper. Place the pot uncovered over high heat and cook to reduce the buttery sauce to a dark syrup. Turn the endives over as you are doing this to brown and caramelize them on all sides. Sprinkle with the parsley and serve.

Serves 4

Choosing and Using Belgian Endives

Belgian endives are expensive, so demand perfect quality.

1. Buy Belgian endives from a market that stores them properly. The blue tissue paper in which the distributors wrap the endives is there for a reason—to protect them from the light, which would turn them bitter.

2. Choose the whitest, tightest heads. Avoid any that have turned color or whose leaves are not tightly closed all the way to the tip.

3. Store Belgian endives, still tightly wrapped in paper, in the refrigerator. Protected from light and moisture, they should keep for several days.

4. Discard discolored leaves but do not rinse Belgian endives. If necessary, wipe with a damp cloth.

5. To core endives: Use a small, sharp paring knife to slice about ⅛ inch off the root end. Make a small incision into the core and cut it out to the depth of about ½ inch.

Creamed Belgian Endives

WITLOOF IN ROOMSAUS
•
CHICONS A LA CREME

H ere, cream is used as a sweet and subtle condiment to underline the slightly bitter taste of the Belgian endives—this dish is definitely influenced by French cuisine. Serve it as a refined accompaniment to any roast or sautéed meat or chicken.

6 Belgian endives, cored
2½ tablespoons unsalted butter
Juice of ½ lemon
1 chicken bouillon cube, crumbled
6 tablespoons heavy (or whipping) cream
Pinch of freshly grated nutmeg
Freshly ground black pepper to taste

1. Preheat the oven to 350°F.

2. Cut each endive lengthwise in half. Melt 1½ tablespoons of the butter in a large skillet over medium heat. Add the endives and sauté for about 3 minutes on each side, until golden. Add enough water to barely cover. Add the remaining 1 tablespoon butter, the lemon juice, and bouillon cube. Simmer, covered, over medium heat until softened, 15 minutes.

3. Drain the endives and reserve the cooking liquid for another use (add it to soup). Arrange the endives in a single layer in a glass or enameled baking dish. Spoon the cream evenly over the endives and sprinkle with the nutmeg and pepper. Bake until the endives are fully soft and have absorbed most of the cream, 15 to 20 minutes. Serve at once.

Serves 6

Chicory Coffee

I n my great grandmother Marie's days the Westhoek was too far away from witloof *country to make Belgian endive a common vegetable. Besides, this very fancy and suspiciously pale vegetable was considered to be rich people's food. But what she held in particularly high esteem were the colorful packages of chicory which she purchased in the little* épicerie *(grocery) in her village. The dried, roasted, and ground root of the very same Belgian endive she disdained was mixed with the expensive but indispensable coffee beans to give their coffee a very specific and much appreciated flavor.*

My grandmother Jeanne tells me that in wartime chicory was the only ersatz coffee they had, and it was much appreciated because Belgians could not live without their beloved kopje troost *or "mug of comfort."*

Belgium Endives: White Gold

*F*rom the chaos of the revolution in September 1830, when the Belgians rose up against their Dutch rulers and gained their independence, came a most felicitous discovery. Farmer Jan Lammers had fled his farm in Schaarbeek to seek safety for himself and his family. When he returned, he found that the chicory roots in his basement, which he had hurriedly covered with soil, had sprouted white shoots. He tried them and found the taste to be extremely pleasant.

It was another 30 years before Belgian endives became a successful crop, but then there was no stopping them. In 1872 the first witloof *went to Paris and from there conquered the world. It became so popular that it was called white gold.*

The Belgian endive, witloof *in Flemish,* chicon *or endive* in French, *is grown from a variety of chicory that is extremely versatile. When gone to seed, the plant produces the lovely bright blue flowers so common along back roads and highways in late summer. As a loose-leaf green with an astringent bitter taste, it is particularly welcome in a mixed leaf salad. And its roots are often dried and ground and used to flavor coffee.*

Today, Belgian endives are grown primarily on small family farms. The crop requires a great deal of manual labor and includes two separate plantings. First the farmer grows the long carrot-shaped root from which the endive will sprout. For the second planting, the farmer digs up the roots and strips them of their leaves. The roots are then buried in damp sand-filled trenches inside the farmer's warm, dank cellar. The roots produce thick, pale, conical buds—the much-prized Belgian endive. It is an arduous process, but Belgians, with their passion for good food and their eternal quest for top-quality ingredients agree that all the hard work is worth it.

Belgian endives have a complex, sophisticated taste. "Earthy yet noble, sweet yet bitter," *writes Herwig Van Hove in an essay about the* "white wonder root." *You have to learn to appreciate this vegetable, and it is perhaps better not to introduce it to children. Even I wasn't fond of* witloof *as a child, and yet it is my favorite vegetable today.*

In the United States, the popularity of Belgian endives grows every year, and with good reason. They are delicious and available at a time of year when other lettuces are not. They are low in calories—less than 14 per head—and an excellent source of vitamins A, B_1, B_2, and C as well as iron and potassium.

In this country, Belgian endives most frequently appear raw in salads where they add a welcome crunch. Yet they are also incredibly versatile as a cooked vegetable. I hope that the recipes I've included will convince you to serve them braised, creamed, and au gratin as a perfect accompaniment to roasted meats, stews, grilled chicken, braised pheasant, or any other game birds.

202

Brussels Sprouts, Flemish Style

SPRUITJES OP Z'N VLAAMS
•
CHOUX DE BRUXELLES A LA FLAMANDE

*I*n the old days, Brussels sprouts were sautéed in lard for a hearty winter vegetable dish. In this modern-day version we use butter. It is deliciously simple and brings out the natural flavor of the sprouts. These are particularly good served with pork, beef, and lamb dishes.

1½ pounds small Brussels sprouts
  (see Note, page 204)
Salt to taste
6 tablespoons (¾ stick) unsalted butter
Freshly ground black pepper to taste
Pinch of freshly grated nutmeg

1. Trim the base of the sprouts, discard the tough outer leaves, and rinse well.

2. Place the sprouts in a large pot of salted water and bring to a boil. Boil uncovered, until a knife can be inserted without resistance, 12 to 15 minutes. Drain and refresh under cold running water.

3. Melt the butter in a large heavy skillet over high heat and cook carefully until it turns a nut brown color. Watch carefully to prevent the butter from burning. Add the sprouts and sauté quickly to brown them on all sides. Season with salt, pepper, and nutmeg. Serve immediately.

Serves 4

Variation: For real old-time delicious flavor, substitute 3 ounces slab bacon for the butter. Cut the bacon into small cubes and fry in a heavy skillet until lightly browned and most of the fat has been rendered. Using a slotted spoon, remove the bacon cubes and reserve. Discard all but 3 tablespoons of the fat. Sauté the sprouts in the bacon fat until they are browned on all sides. Add 1 finely minced garlic clove, the bacon, and a small handful of finely minced parsley. Cook 1 minute longer. Season with salt and pepper. Serve at once.

Gratin of Brussels Sprouts

GEGRATINEERDE SPRUITJES

•

GRATIN DE CHOUX DE BRUXELLES

This gratin is guaranteed to seduce the stubbornest sprout curmudgeon, and it will send a sprout lover straight to heaven. It is excellent served with any roast.

1½ cups heavy (or whipping) cream
1½ to 2 pounds small Brussels sprouts (see Note)
Salt to taste
3 ounces slab bacon, sliced into ½ × ¼-inch strips
Freshly ground black pepper to taste
Pinch of freshly grated nutmeg
3 tablespoons grated Gruyère cheese

1. Preheat the oven to 450°F. Lightly butter a medium-size gratin dish.

2. In a small saucepan, simmer the cream over medium heat until it is reduced to ¾ cup, about 10 minutes.

3. Trim the base of the sprouts, discard the tough outer leaves, and rinse well. Place the sprouts in a medium-size saucepan with salt and cold water to cover. Bring to a boil and continue boiling for 1 minute. Drain and refresh under cold running water.

4. Sauté the bacon in a small skillet until lightly browned, 2 to 3 minutes. Drain on paper towels and coarsely chop.

5. Combine the sprouts and bacon in the buttered gratin dish and season with the salt, pepper, and nutmeg. Pour the cream over the top and sprinkle with the cheese.

6. Bake until nicely browned and crispy on top, about 15 minutes. Serve at once.

Serves 4

Note: *Belgians are said to have been cultivating these tiny miniature cabbages in the fertile farm lands around Brussels for well over 600 years.*

Always look for the smallest Brussels sprouts you can find, preferably no bigger than the tip of your thumb. They should always be firm to the touch and tightly closed.

My great grandmother Marie used to say that one has to wait until the first frost comes over the land. Then, and only then, will the Brussels sprouts be at the height of their flavor.

Creamed Cabbage

WITTE KOOL IN ROOMSAUS
•
CHOU A LA CREME

In the winter, when most green vegetables look as dispirited as the weather, cabbage is always available to provide tasty, comforting meals. *Chou à la crème* is so good, you will find yourself looking forward to winter so as to fully savor green cabbage at its best. Serve this dish with a simple broiled chicken or meat entrée.

1 small green cabbage
Salt to taste
1 cup heavy (or whipping) cream
Freshly ground black pepper to taste
Pinch of freshly grated nutmeg
4 tablespoons (½ stick) unsalted butter

1. Preheat the oven to 400°F. Butter a large casserole.

2. Discard the tough outer leaves of the cabbage, cut it into quarters, and cut away the core. Use a sharp knife or the shredding disk of the food processor to shred the cabbage very thinly.

3. Bring a large pot of salted water to a boil and add the shredded cabbage. Cook, uncovered, for 3 minutes. Drain thoroughly.

4. Spread the cabbage in the buttered casserole, pour the cream over the cabbage, and season generously with salt, pepper, and nutmeg. Dot with the butter. Bake for 15 minutes until the cabbage has absorbed most of the cream. Serve immediately.

Serves 6

Braised Stuffed Cabbage

GEVULDE SAVOOIEKOOL
•
PAUPIETTES DE CHOUX FARCIES

Little pouches of cabbage leaves, filled with a savory ground meat mixture, make a hearty and satisfying winter dinner. Serve with mashed potatoes and a pungent mustard in the Flemish style. Any leftover stuffed cabbage is delicious eaten cold with some crusty bread.

Cabbage and Stuffing:
1 head Savoy cabbage, trimmed and rinsed
Salt to taste
1 pound mixed ground veal and pork
2 medium onions, finely sliced
¼ cup finely minced fresh parsley
1 clove garlic, finely minced
1 large egg
Pinch of freshly grated nutmeg
Freshly ground black pepper to taste

Vegetable Sauce:
2 tablespoons unsalted butter
1 tablespoon vegetable oil
1 large onion, sliced
3 carrots, peeled and sliced
2 cups warm chicken broth, preferably home-
    made (page 53)
Bouquet garni: 5 sprigs parsley, 1 bay leaf,
    and 1 sprig fresh thyme tied together
    with kitchen string
Salt and freshly ground black pepper
    to taste

1. Immerse the whole cabbage in a large pot of cold salted water. Bring slowly to a boil and cook at a rolling boil for about 2 minutes. Drain the cabbage upside down in a colander and let cool slightly.

2. Meanwhile, prepare the stuffing: In a large mixing bowl, combine the veal and pork mixture, onions, parsley, garlic, egg, nutmeg, and

salt and pepper and mix well. Sauté or poach a little bit of the mixture and taste for seasoning. The stuffing should not be bland.

3. Carefully detach the leaves of the cabbage and trim away the thick ribs so that the leaves can be easily folded. Dry the leaves with paper towels.

4. Place 1 rounded tablespoon stuffing onto the center of each cabbage leaf. Wrap the ends over to form a package, and tie with kitchen string or secure with toothpicks. For the smaller leaves, place one leaf halfway over another and fill with stuffing.

5. Heat the butter and oil in a large enameled Dutch oven over medium heat. Add the onion and carrots and cook, stirring occasionally, for about 10 minutes but do not brown. Place the stuffed cabbage leaves in a single layer on top of the vegetables. Pour the chicken broth over them, add the bouquet garni, and season with salt and pepper.

6. Cover and simmer over low heat until the cabbage is tender and the filling is cooked through, 1 hour. Discard the bouquet garni and remove the string or toothpicks before serving the cabbage and vegetables.

Serves 6

Variation: *Any leftover cooked meat or even ground turkey can be substituted for the veal and pork mixture.*

Savoy Cabbage, Flemish Style

SAVOOIKOOL OP Z'N VLAAMS

•

CHOU DE SAVOY A LA FLAMANDE

Summer or winter, a Flemish meal without a vegetable is unthinkable. During the long and cold winter months, Belgians can always rely on a vast array of cabbages in many sizes and colors. One of my favorites is the Savoy cabbage, with its chubby deep green leaves and sweet, fresh flavor. I particularly like this old Flemish way of sautéing the blanched cabbage wedges in nut-brown butter.

1 medium Savoy cabbage
Salt to taste
6 tablespoons (¾ stick) unsalted butter
Freshly ground black pepper to taste
Pinch of freshly grated nutmeg

1. Remove and discard the tough outer leaves of the cabbage. Cut the cabbage into 8 wedges. Do not remove the core.

2. Bring a large pot of salted water to a boil. Add the cabbage wedges and cook, uncovered, for 10 minutes. Drain and refresh the cabbage under cold running water. At this point you may, if you wish, remove the core from each cabbage wedge, leaving the wedge intact.

3. Melt the butter in a large skillet until it is foamy and starting to turn a lovely nut-brown color. Watch carefully to prevent the butter from burning. Add the cabbage wedges and sauté in the browned butter for about 1 minute per side. Season with salt, pepper, and nutmeg.
Serve immediately.

Serves 4 to 6

Variation: *For Cauliflower, Flemish Style, replace the Savoy cabbage with cauliflower florets. The nut-brown butter and the nutmeg impart a truly heavenly flavor to the cauliflower.*

Red Cabbage, Flemish Style

RODE KOOL OP ZIJN VLAAMS
•
CHOU ROUGE A LA FLAMANDE

This is a traditional recipe that is very typical of Flanders, where they love the tangy sweet-sour combination of flavors. It is also home cooking at its best, and every Flamand *digne de son nom* (worthy of his name) has a favorite version of *chou rouge*. My mother still prepares red cabbage in exactly the same way that my grandmother did to make a hearty fall and winter dish that goes wonderfully with pork, any kind of sausage, and veal chops. Red cabbage can be made way ahead, as it reheats beautifully.

1 medium red cabbage
2 tablespoons unsalted butter
1 small onion, thinly sliced
¼ cup red currant jelly or 1 additional
   tablespoon sugar or honey
2 tablespoons cider vinegar
¼ cup water, plus additional if needed
1 tablespoon dark brown sugar or honey
Pinch of ground cinnamon
Salt and freshly ground black pepper
   to taste
4 tart apples, peeled, cored, and thinly sliced

1. Discard the tough outer leaves of the cabbage (see Note). Cut the head into quarters and remove the white core. Shred the cabbage into very thin slivers.

2. Melt the butter in a large heavy Dutch oven. Add the cabbage, onion, currant jelly, vinegar, water, sugar, cinnamon, and a little salt and pepper. Cover and bring to a boil. Reduce the heat immediately and let simmer, covered, for 30 minutes.

3. Add the apples and continue simmering for 1 hour, checking from time to time to see that it is not too dry. Add a little more water if necessary. At the end of the cooking time, the cabbage should be tender, the apples reduced to a purée, and all the liquid absorbed. Taste and adjust the seasoning if necessary.

Serves 6 to 8

Note: Don't rinse red cabbage. Discard the outer leaves and wipe with a damp cloth if necessary. Rinsing, blanching, or boiling will fade the deep red color.

Variations: In step 2, cut 3 ounces slab bacon into thin strips. Render the bacon strips in the Dutch oven and continue with the recipe, omitting the butter.

• *When my mother makes this dish, she always adds 2 whole cloves instead of the cinnamon.*

Returning from the market, her basket overflowing with fresh vegetables, fruits, and flowers, my grandmother Jeanne faced an eternal dilemma: the choice between le bon *(taste)* and le beau *(beauty)*. Were her treasures going to end up in the pot or as models for one of her still-life paintings?

Her brushes were never far off, soaking in an old marmalade jar somewhere between the salt canister and the vinegar bottle. Her kitchen always smelled faintly of turpentine, and she often set up her easel to paint while dinner cooked.

Like other Belgian painters, poets, and writers, she feasted on the beauty of nature, the changing seasons, the generosity of the earth. She knew how to admire the mysteries inherent in a budding flower or an intricate spider's web, and she communicated her appreciation of the natural world around her to her children and grandchildren.

Carrot Timbales

WORTELBROODJES
·
PETITS PAINS DE CAROTTES

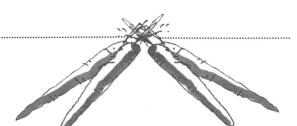

Sweet carrots paired with savory cooked ham combine to make a colorful and fine timbale that can be served as an appetizer with Chive Cream Sauce or as a sumptuous side dish to a festive roast. They can be prepared well in advance and reheated in their molds in a water bath in the oven. The sauce for the timbales is optional and is usually prepared only if the timbales are served as an appetizer.

1 pound carrots, peeled and cut into thin
   (¼-inch) rounds
2 cups chicken broth, preferably homemade
   (page 53), or water
¼ pound boiled ham, torn into pieces
Salt and freshly ground black pepper
   to taste
Pinch of freshly grated nutmeg
3 large eggs
⅓ cup heavy (or whipping) cream
Chive Cream Sauce or the tarragon
   variation (page 214)

1. Preheat the oven to 375°F. Butter six ½-cup ramekins.

2. In a medium-size saucepan, simmer the carrots, covered, over medium heat in the chicken broth until very tender, about 15 minutes. Drain. (Save the cooking liquid for soup.) Purée the carrots in a food processor. Transfer to a mixing bowl.

3. Purée the ham in the food processor and add to the carrot purée. Season generously with salt, pepper, and nutmeg.

4. In a separate bowl, beat the eggs together with the cream, then fold into the carrot purée.

5. Divide the mixture evenly among the buttered ramekins. Place the ramekins in a baking pan and fill the pan with hot water to reach three-quarters of the way up the sides of the ramekins. Bake until a toothpick inserted into the center of a timbale comes out clean, 20 to 30 minutes.

6. Run a knife around the side of each timbale and invert onto a plate to unmold. Serve with the cream sauce.

Serves 6

Old-Fashioned Flemish Carrots

WORTELEN OP OUD-VLAAMSE WYZE

•

CAROTTES A LA FLAMANDE

These carrots are intended to melt like butter in your mouth and must be cooked much longer than we are accustomed to cooking vegetables today. If you want to try the true, genuine Flemish flavor, you will have to give up the crunchiness this once.

4 tablespoons (½ stick) unsalted butter
1 large onion, minced
2 to 3 pounds young carrots, peeled and cut into ½-inch rounds
1 sprig fresh thyme or ½ teaspoon dried thyme
1 bay leaf
2 tablespoons sugar
2 cups chicken broth, preferably homemade (page 53), or water
Salt and freshly ground black pepper to taste
1 small Boston lettuce, cored, halved, and rinsed
¼ cup finely minced fresh parsley, for garnish

1. Melt the butter in a medium-sized saucepan over medium heat. Add the onion and cook, stirring, until lightly browned, about 5 minutes. Add the carrots, thyme, bay leaf, and sugar. Add enough chicken broth to barely cover and season with salt and pepper. Bring to a boil and reduce the heat.

2. Add the Boston lettuce. Cover and simmer until the carrots are done, 15 to 20 minutes. Uncover and reduce the liquid over high heat by two-thirds. Sprinkle with the parsley and serve immediately.

Serves 4 to 6

Gratin of Cauliflower

GEGRATINEERDE BLOEMKOOL

•

CHOU-FLEUR GRATINE

Like many children, my brother, sister, and I did not have a natural affinity for cauliflower. But we loved cheese, especially when it was bubbling hot. Combining blanched vegetables in a delicious Gruyère-flavored white sauce topped with more cheese and browned under a broiler was my mother's *truc* to get her children to eat their vegetables.

Today gratins are still my favorite way of preparing cauliflower, Brussels sprouts, Belgian endives, and pearl onions. As cauliflower is a cold-weather vegetable, at its best in the fall or winter, serve it in season with a hearty roast meat or chicken.

Salt to taste
*1 large cauliflower (or 2 small ones if you
    want leftovers for salad), cored and
    divided into florets*
1½ tablespoons unsalted butter
2 tablespoons all-purpose flour
1 cup milk
1 cup grated Gruyère cheese
Freshly ground black pepper to taste
Pinch of freshly grated nutmeg

1. Preheat the oven to 400°F.

2. Bring a large pot of salted water to a boil. Add the cauliflower florets and cook, uncovered, until cooked but still firm, 7 to 10 minutes. Drain, reserving ½ cup of the cooking liquid. Refresh the florets under cold running water and drain again. Reserve any florets you wish to save for a salad (see box, page 212).

3. Melt the butter in a medium-size saucepan over medium heat. Add the flour, stirring constantly with a wire whisk, and cook

for 1 minute to form a paste. Gradually whisk in the reserved cooking liquid and the milk; cook, stirring constantly, until the sauce thickens. Bring to a boil and cook, continuing to stir, for 1 minute longer. Remove from the heat and stir in ⅔ cup of the cheese. Season with salt, pepper, and nutmeg.

4. Pour a third of the sauce into a medium-size gratin dish. Arrange the cauliflower florets on top and cover with the remaining sauce. Sprinkle the remaining ⅓ cup cheese over the top.

5. Bake until nicely browned and crusty on top, about 15 minutes. Serve hot.

Serves 6

Cauliflower Salads

Leftover cooked cauliflower is a blessing for anyone who loves to put together salads. A Shallot-Parsley Vinaigrette (see Index), a few slivers of cooked ham, a hard-boiled egg, sliced tomato, and a handful of lettuce leaves are the makings of a great salad meal.

My mother serves cold cooked cauliflower florets with her home-made curry mayonnaise, sprinkled with finely minced shallots and parsley. And along the Belgian coast, cauliflower florets are tossed together with a handful of North Sea shrimp and served with a dollop of mayonnaise on lettuce leaves. Some quartered ripe tomatoes and chopped parsley complete the delicious still life.

Cauliflower Timbales

BLOEMKOOL BROODJES
•
PETITS PAINS DE CHOU-FLEUR

A timbale is a kind of vegetable custard that looks very impressive but is not at all difficult to make. Serve cauliflower timbales with a salad for a light lunch, as a first course opening a festive dinner, or the Belgian way, as a very dressy accompaniment to a main-course roast. The sauce for the timbales is optional and is usually prepared only if the timbales are served as an appetizer.

Salt to taste
1 medium cauliflower (about 1 pound), cored and divided into florets
2 large egg yolks
1/4 cup heavy (or whipping) cream
1/2 cup Gruyère cheese, grated
1 tablespoon finely minced fresh chives or scallions
Freshly ground black pepper to taste
Pinch of freshly grated nutmeg
2 large egg whites, lightly beaten
Chive Cream Sauce (recipe follows) or Fresh Tomato Sauce (page 314)

1. Preheat the oven to 375°F. Butter six 1/2-cup ramekins.

2. Bring a large pot of salted water to a boil. Add the cauliflower florets and cook until fork tender, 15 to 20 minutes. (For a purée, it is important not to undercook the cauliflower.)

3. Drain thoroughly. Pass the cauliflower through a food mill into a large mixing bowl, or purée it in a food processor.

4. In a separate bowl, combine the egg yolks, cream, cheese, chives, salt, pepper, and nutmeg. Finally, fold in the egg whites. Add this

mixture to the puréed cauliflower and stir to combine.

5. Divide the mixture among the buttered ramekins. Place the ramekins in a baking pan and add hot water to reach three-quarters of the way up the sides of the ramekins. Bake until a toothpick inserted into a timbale comes out clean, about 30 minutes.

6. Run a knife around the side of each timbale and invert onto a plate to unmold. Serve with Chive Cream Sauce or Fresh Tomato Sauce.

Serves 6

Variations: Substitute broccoli or asparagus for the cauliflower and proceed with the recipe in the same way.

• Savoy cabbage, Belgian endives, and leeks are also possibilities. These should be parboiled and coarsely chopped instead of puréed.
• You can replace the grated Gruyère cheese with 1/2 cup finely chopped ham.
• For a lovely color contrast and a very festive presentation, line the buttered ramekins with blanched lettuce or spinach leaves.

Chive Cream Sauce

BRESLOOK ROOMSAUS
•
CREME DE CIBOULETTE

1 cup heavy (or whipping) cream
1/3 cup dry white wine
Salt and freshly ground white pepper
  to taste
Pinch of freshly grated nutmeg
2 tablespoons finely minced fresh chives

In a small saucepan, bring the cream and wine to a boil. Reduce the heat and simmer until the volume is reduced by one-fourth, 6 to 7 minutes. Season with salt, pepper, and nutmeg. Stir in the chives just before serving.

Variation: *Replace the chives with tarragon, chervil, or a fines herbes mixture of parsley, chervil, chives, and tarragon.*

Braised Escarole

GESTOOFDE ANDYVIE
•
ESCAROLE BRAISEE

*I*n the United States escarole is considered primarily a salad green, but quickly sautéed and seasoned, escarole makes an interesting vegetable dish. In Belgium it is often served with meat loaf, roasts, and poultry. My grandmother always finished her sauce with a tablespoon of pan juices from the meat that she was serving with the escarole. If you have no pan juices, substitute a tablespoon of concentrated beef broth or omit completely.

2 large heads escarole
2 tablespoons unsalted butter, at room
  temperature
1 medium onion, minced
Salt and freshly ground black pepper
  to taste
Pinch of freshly grated nutmeg
1½ tablespoons all-purpose flour
1 tablespoon concentrated beef broth
  or pan juices from a roast (optional)
3 to 4 tablespoons milk or heavy
  (or whipping) cream

1. Remove the wilted outer leaves of the escarole and discard them. Separate the other leaves, rinse them well in cold water, shake off the excess water, and coarsely shred the escarole with a sharp knife.

2. Melt 1 tablespoon of the butter in a large heavy saucepan over high heat. Add the onion and cook, stirring frequently until wilted but not browned. Reduce the heat to low and add the shredded escarole. Season with salt, pepper, and nutmeg; stir well with a wooden spoon. Cover the pan and simmer over low heat until the escarole is wilted and tender, about 15 minutes. Remove the escarole with a slotted spoon to a warmed serving dish.

3. Mix the remaining 1 tablespoon butter with the flour. Add the concentrated beef stock or pan juices, if using, to the vegetable juices in the pan. With a small whisk, blend in the flour mixture to thicken the juices. Bring to a boil, whisking constantly to prevent any lumps. Add enough milk or cream to make a smooth sauce. Taste and adjust the seasoning and pour the sauce over the escarole. Serve immediately.

Serves 4

Variation: Other bitter greens, such as romaine, Swiss chard, collard greens, or spinach can be substituted for the escarole. The greens of young turnips and beets also make interesting variations. Follow the same recipe for all the greens.

Green Beans, Flemish Style

PRINSESSEBOONTJES OP Z'N VLAAMS

•

HARICOTS VERTS A LA FLAM

*I*n Belgium we cultivate many varieties of green beans, all of them bearing somewhat fanciful names, such as *prinsesseboontjes* (princess beans), *boterboontjes* (butter beans, and *mange-tout* (eat-it-all beans). They are all at their best when eaten at the peak of freshness. Their crisp sweetness requires only the lightest preparation and little in the way of seasoning. A simple dot of butter or a few caramelized shallots, as in this sweet-and-sour old-fashioned Flemish version, is all that is wanted.

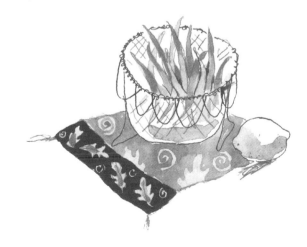

215

Salt to taste

1 pound green beans, ends trimmed and strings removed

3 tablespoons unsalted butter

¼ cup finely minced shallots

1 teaspoon sugar

¼ cup chicken broth, preferably homemade (page 53), or water

1 teaspoon corn or potato starch

1 tablespoon apple cider vinegar

Freshly ground black pepper to taste

Pinch of freshly grated nutmeg

1 tablespoon finely minced fresh parsley, for garnish

1. Bring a large pot of salted water to a boil. Add the green beans and cook, uncovered, until fork-tender, 15 to 20 minutes. Drain.

2. Melt the butter in a large saucepan over medium heat. Add the shallots and cook, stirring, until lightly browned, about 5 minutes. Sprinkle the sugar over the shallots and cook 1 minute longer until the sugar caramelizes. Be careful not to let it burn.

3. Add the water. Cover and let simmer for 10 minutes. Dissolve the cornstarch in the vinegar and add it to the shallots. Bring to a boil, stirring constantly. Remove from the heat and season with salt, pepper, and nutmeg.

4. Add the green beans to the shallots, mix well, and heat through. Adjust the seasoning. Sprinkle with the parsley and serve.

Serves 4

Casserole of Wild Mushrooms

STOOFPOTJE VAN WILDE PADDESTOELEN
•
POELEE DE CHAMPIGNONS SAUVAGES

The rich, earthy tastes of this casserole are a mushroom lover's dream come true. Serve it as an elegant accompaniment to roasted game birds or any fine meat dish. Or splurge and serve with toast points as an appetizer to a very festive meal.

1 pound mixed fresh wild and cultivated mushrooms, such as chanterelles, morels, porcini, portobellos, and shiitakes

5 tablespoons unsalted butter

2 tablespoons finely minced shallots

Salt and freshly ground black pepper to taste

2 tablespoons finely minced fresh fines herbes (equal parts parsley, chives, tarragon, and chervil), for garnish

1. Trim away the stems of the mushrooms and gently wipe away any dirt with a soft

brush or damp towel. (Do not rinse the mushrooms, as that would injure their delicate flavor.) Keep the small mushrooms whole and halve or quarter the larger ones. Slice the giant portobello mushrooms into pieces to match the size of the other mushrooms.

2. Melt the butter in a large skillet over high heat. Add the shallots and cook, stirring, until softened but not browned, about 2 minutes. Add the mushrooms and sauté them quickly, stirring occasionally with a wooden spoon, until they are lightly browned. This should take about 2 minutes. Season with salt and pepper and sprinkle with the fines herbes. Serve at once.

Serves 4

A Grandmother's Reminder

My grandmother Jeanne has never shown any reluctance to soil her hands by digging in the earth or cleaning vegetables. She cherishes the atmosphere of her sun-filled kitchen filled with colors and textures of vegetables, herbs, and fruit. And she especially loves filling her house with the aroma of sweet anticipation. "That's what life is all about!" she first said to me when I was a little girl. And she continues to remind me of it today.

Gratin of Pearl Onions

ZILVERUITJES AU GRATIN
GRATIN D'OIGNONS

Anyone who loves onion soup knows that the combination of cheese and onions is a splendid one. Serve this gratin with any roast, or splurge and eat it alone with some crusty bread.

Salt to taste
1 pound pearl or small white onions
¼ cup heavy (or whipping) cream
Freshly ground black pepper to taste
Pinch of freshly grated nutmeg
½ cup grated Gruyère cheese

1. Bring a large pot of salted water to a boil. Add the onions, reduce the heat, and simmer uncovered, until tender, about 15 minutes. Drain and refresh under cold running water. Peel and discard the skins.

2. Butter a shallow ovenproof dish that's just large enough to hold the onions.

3. Toss the onions with the cream in the buttered dish. Season generously with salt, pepper, and nutmeg. (You can prepare the dish in advance up to this point. Refrigerate, covered, until ready to continue with the recipe.)

4. Preheat the broiler.

5. Sprinkle the grated cheese over the onions and broil until the cheese is melted and nicely browned. Serve immediately.

Serves 6

Variation: *Add 2 tablespoons dry white wine with the cream in step 3.*

Early Peas with Purslane

FIJNE ERWTJES MET POSTELEIN

•

PETITS POIS AU POURPIER

*P*urslane might be more familiar to a gardener as portulaca, a low-growing annual with needlelike leaves and bright pink, yellow, and purple flowers. The crisp, tangy leaves are delicious eaten in a salad or lightly cooked and served with cream or butter. You will not find purslane in the market, but it is easy to grow, and a package of seeds will provide you with plants all summer long.

6 tablespoons (³/4 stick) unsalted butter
4 scallions, white and green parts, finely
   chopped
4 ounces purslane leaves, rinsed
4 pounds early peas, shelled and rinsed,
   or 2 packages (10 ounces each) frozen
   tiny green peas
1 teaspoon confectioners' sugar
Salt and freshly ground black pepper to taste
2 cups chicken broth, preferably homemade
   (page 53)
3 tablespoons finely minced fresh parsley, for
   garnish

1. Melt 3 tablespoons of the butter in a medium-size saucepan over medium heat. Add the scallions and purslane leaves; cook, stirring, for 2 to 3 minutes. Add the peas, sugar, salt, and pepper; cover with the chicken broth. Simmer, uncovered, just until the peas are tender, about 10 minutes.

2. Stir in the remaining 3 tablespoons butter, sprinkle with the parsley, and serve.

Serves 6

Fresh Peas, Flemish Style

JONGE ERWTJES OP Z'N VLAAMS

•

PETITS POIS A LA FLAMANDE

*J*n the Ardennes, this dish is prepared with the fine, cured *jambon d'Ardennes*. A Spanish or Italian dry-cured ham would make an admirable substitute.

2 tablespoons unsalted butter
2 ounces slab bacon, rind discarded,
  cut into ¹⁄₂ × ¹⁄₄-inch strips
12 pearl onions, peeled
1 tablespoon all-purpose flour
1 small Boston lettuce, cored, leaves
  kept whole, and rinsed
³⁄₄ cup chicken broth, preferably homemade
  (page 53), or water
4 pounds early green peas, shelled,
  or 2 packages (10 ounces each)
  frozen tiny green peas,
  thawed
Salt and freshly ground black pepper
  to taste
Pinch of freshly grated nutmeg
2 tablespoons finely minced fresh parsley,
  for garnish

1. Melt the butter in a medium-size saucepan over medium heat. Add the bacon and sauté for 2 to 3 minutes. Add the onions and continue cooking until translucent but not browned, about 5 minutes.

2. Sprinkle the bacon and onions with the flour and stir with a wooden spoon until the flour is absorbed. Add the lettuce leaves and enough broth to barely cover. Simmer, covered, over medium heat for 30 minutes.

3. Add the peas and cook, uncovered, until they are just tender, about 5 minutes. Season with salt, pepper, and nutmeg. Sprinkle with the parsley and serve.

Serves 6

Variation: For Fresh Peas and Baby Carrots (Petits Pois et Jeunes Carottes), cook the peas as described in the recipe, omitting the lettuce leaves. Scrub ½ pound baby carrots, leaving a little of the green stems on, and cook in 2 tablespoons butter and ¼ cup water until tender, 5 to 10 minutes. Combine the carrots and peas just before serving. Sprinkle with minced fresh parsley or chervil.

Creamed Salsify

SCHORSENEREN IN ROOMSAUS

•

SALSIFIS A LA CREME

Salsify, also called oyster plant, is not nearly as common in the United States as it is in Europe. In fact you will probably have to search for it in Italian or other

Herbal Powers

My great grandmother Marie always astonished me with her wide knowledge of the mysterious herbs and grasses she had growing in her garden. Her kind of knowledge goes back to the herbal gardens of the Middle Ages. The women who tended these gardens and possessed this knowledge were so powerful, that they were often associated with witchcraft, although most herbs then were primarily used for medicine.

In my great grandmother's day, women still knew which herb to pick for what ailment or complaint. Although they had learned from their own mothers and grandmothers, they were so conversant with the properties of each grass, plant, and flower, it seemed as if that they came by this knowledge instinctively or from a supernatural source.

Unfortunately, many herbs have vanished from our kitchen gardens or have lost their former status and are now considered weeds. The knowledge of how to use them is also lost. Mothers and grandmothers no longer take their children into the garden to teach them the properties of plants. And as children today spend more time in front of the television than listening to their grandmothers, I fear that none of this valuable information will be passed on to future generations.

I was fortunate. Marie often took me into her garden where we would pinch, sniff, and taste the herbs until I could identify each and every one and be able to recite its healing powers. Before too long I knew which herbs were used to pacify or purify the blood, which chased away bad breath or cured a stomachache, and which might be used to calm a broken heart or stimulate the passion of a man.

ethnic greenmarkets. Very often it is imported from Belgium. Salsify is a root vegetable that resembles a parsnip, but its flavor is more delicate and is said to resemble that of a fresh oyster. Hence its name.

When salsify is peeled, the white flesh tends to discolor quickly, so the vegetables must be kept in acidulated water. In Belgium they are cooked in a poaching liquid called a *blanc* (water to which some flour and lemon juice have been added), which further preserves their delicate color and flavor.

2 pounds salsify (oyster plant)
Juice of 1 lemon
4 tablespoons all-purpose flour
6 cups cold water
1 teaspoon salt, plus additional to taste
1½ tablespoons unsalted butter
1 cup heavy (or whipping) cream
Freshly ground black pepper to taste
Pinch of freshly grated nutmeg
2 tablespoons finely minced fresh parsley, for
    garnish

1. Trim the roots and tops of the salsify and peel with a vegetable peeler. Cut crosswise into 2-inch-long pieces and keep in a bowl of water mixed with half of the lemon juice to prevent discoloring.

2. Place 2 tablespoons of the flour in a medium-size saucepan and gradually whisk in the cold water. Add the remaining lemon juice, 1 teaspoon salt, and the salsify. Bring to a boil, reduce the heat, and cook, covered, until tender when pierced with a knife but not falling

apart. This will take 10 to 20 minutes depending on the size of the vegetables. Drain the salsify but reserve ½ cup of the cooking liquid.

3. In a medium-size saucepan, melt the butter over medium heat. Whisk in the remaining 2 tablespoons flour and cook, stirring, until foaming, about 1 minute. Whisk in the reserved cooking liquid and the cream. Bring to a boil, then simmer for 2 to 3 minutes, stirring constantly with a wooden spoon, until you have a smooth sauce. Season with salt, pepper, and nutmeg.

4. Combine the salsify with the sauce and heat through over low heat. Sprinkle with the parsley and serve.

Serves 4 to 6

Variation: *For Gratinéed Salsify, make the béchamel sauce with 1½ cups milk instead of the cooking liquid and heavy cream. Spread the cooked salsify in a buttered gratin dish and pour the sauce over the vegetables. Sprinkle*  *with ¼ cup grated Gruyère cheese. Bake in a preheated 375°F oven for 15 to 20 minutes until the top is nicely browned and crusty.*

My Mother's Salsify with Mustard

SCHORSENEREN MET MOSTERD

•

SALSIFIS A LA FACON
DE MA MERE

Salsify is a winter vegetable, and the flavor is at its best from October until March. Its mysterious, slightly earthy flavor makes this dish of salsify with mustard a wonderful accompaniment to Roast Pork with Onions and Mustard (see Index). In Belgium, mustard is not a casual ingredient but has been for centuries a favorite way to add a sharp, pungent accent to more subtle ingredients. Of course, my mother uses our own Tierenteyn mustard which has been made in Ghent since 1790.

2 pounds salsify (oyster plant)
Juice of 1 lemon
2 tablespoons all-purpose flour
6 cups cold water
1 teaspoon salt, plus additional to taste
3 tablespoons unsalted butter, at room temperature
1 to 2 teaspoons Dijon or Tierenteyn mustard
Freshly ground black pepper to taste
2 tablespoons finely minced fresh parsley, for garnish

1. Trim the roots and tops of the salsify and peel with a vegetable peeler. Cut crosswise into 2-inch-long pieces and keep in a bowl of water mixed with half the lemon juice to prevent discoloring.

2. Place the flour in a medium-size saucepan and gradually whisk in the cold water. Add the remaining lemon juice, 1 teaspoon salt, and the salsify. Bring to a boil, reduce the heat, cover, and cook until tender when pierced with a knife but not falling apart. This will take 10 to 20 minutes depending on the size of the vegetables. Drain.

3. Mix the butter and mustard; combine with the salsify. Season with salt and pepper to taste. Sprinkle with the parsley before serving.

Serves 4 to 6

Spinach with Garlicky Brown Butter

SPINAZIE IN BRUINE BOTER SAUS

•

EPINARDS AU BEURRE NOISETTE

In Belgium this nutritious, simple, and delicious spinach preparation is often served together with mashed potatoes as a side dish for chicken and fish.

3 pounds fresh spinach
¼ teaspoon salt, plus additional to taste
8 tablespoons (1 stick) unsalted butter
1 large clove garlic, thinly sliced
Freshly ground black pepper to taste
Pinch of freshly grated nutmeg

1. Rinse the spinach thoroughly in several changes of water. Remove and discard the stems and any wilted leaves.

2. Place the wet spinach in a large stainless steel or enamel pot and sprinkle with ¼ teaspoon salt. Cook, partially covered, over medium heat until the spinach is completely wilted, about 5 minutes. Drain thoroughly.

3. Melt the butter in a large skillet over high heat until foamy and just turning nut brown in color. Add the garlic and spinach all at once and heat quickly, stirring gently with a wooden spoon.

4. Season with salt, pepper, and nutmeg. Serve at once.

Serves 4

Note: *Avoid cooking spinach in aluminum or iron pots, as these discolor the vegetable.*

My Mother's Spinach in Cheese Sauce

MOEDER'S SPINAZIE MET KAASSAUS

•

EPINARDS A LA SAUCE MORNAY DE MA MERE

Delicate spinach in a creamy cheese-flavored sauce served on top of lightly sautéed white bread is a favorite light evening meal in Belgian families.

3 pounds fresh spinach or 3 packages
  (10 ounces each) frozen leaf spinach, thawed
¼ teaspoon salt, plus additional to taste
5 tablespoons unsalted butter
2 tablespoons all-purpose flour
½ cup milk, light cream, or half-and-half
½ cup grated Swiss cheese
Freshly ground black pepper to taste
Pinch of freshly grated nutmeg
4 slices firm white bread, crusts removed

1. Rinse the spinach thoroughly in several changes of water. Remove and discard the stems and any wilted leaves.

2. Place the still wet spinach in a large stainless steel or enamel pot (see Note, page 223) and sprinkle with ¼ teaspoon salt. Cook, partially covered, over medium heat until the spinach is completely wilted, about 5 minutes. Drain and squeeze out the excess moisture. Coarsely chop the spinach.

3. Melt 2 tablespoons of the butter in a medium-size saucepan over medium heat. Whisk in the flour and cook until the mixture is bubbly. Gradually whisk in the milk and bring to a quick boil. Cook, stirring constantly, over medium heat until you have a smooth sauce, 1 minute. Remove from the heat, stir in the cheese, and season with salt, pepper, and nutmeg. Add the spinach to the sauce and mix well with a wooden spoon.

4. Melt the remaining 3 tablespoons butter in a large skillet over medium-high heat. Add the bread and sauté on both sides until golden brown. Serve the spinach on top of the fried bread.

Serves 4

Sautéed Turnips with Cinnamon

GEBAKKEN RAAPKES MET KANEEL
•
NAVETS SAUTES A LA CANNELLE

A little cinnamon brings out the natural sweetness of the turnip. In Belgium this dish is a traditional accompaniment to lamb. For it, choose small, young turnips when they are in season.

1½ pounds turnips, peeled and cut into
  1-inch cubes
Salt to taste
3 tablespoons unsalted butter
Freshly ground black pepper to taste
½ teaspoon ground cinnamon
2 tablespoons finely minced fresh parsley, for
  garnish

1. Place the turnips in a medium-size saucepan with enough cold salted water to cover. Bring to a boil, reduce the heat, and simmer, covered, until fork-tender, 12 to 15 minutes. Drain.

2. Melt the butter in a large skillet over medium heat until very hot. Add the turnips and season with salt, pepper, and cinnamon. Cook, tossing frequently, until the turnips are golden all over, about 10 minutes. Sprinkle with the parsley and serve.

Serves 4

Bilberries or Cranberries in Syrup

VEENBESSEN IN SIROOP

•

AIRELLES AU SIROP

The tiny European bilberry is a distant relative of both the cranberry and the blueberry. In Belgium these tart little berries still grow wild in the sandy region of de Kempen. Bilberries are a little sweeter than cranberries and a little tarter than blueberries. The delicate, fine flavor of these berries is considered to be a rare delicacy and when they are available, they are quite expensive. Bilberries are served as a traditional accompaniment to the Christmas turkey and all game dishes. Often the bilberries are "stretched" by pairing them with other fruits, such as apples, pears, and oranges.

While bilberries are not easily come by in the United States, the canned Scandinavian lingonberries that can be found in specialty stores are a close substitute, and cranberries, although not as finely flavored, can replace bilberries in all the following recipes.

½ pound bilberries or cranberries,
  rinsed and picked over
¾ cup sugar

1. Place the berries and sugar in a medium-size saucepan and cook, stirring occasionally, over low heat until all the sugar has dissolved and the berries have released some juice. Increase the heat and bring to a boil, then reduce the heat, and cook for 1 minute more. Drain the berries, reserving the liquid, and set aside.

2. Return the liquid to the saucepan and reduce over high heat until syrupy, about 10 minutes. Pour over the berries and allow to cool. The berries will keep for several days in the refrigerator and can be frozen for several months.

Serves 4

Fruit Side Dishes

I'm sure you have eaten apple-sauce with roast pork and cherries or oranges with roast duck and found that the sweet flavor of the fruit complements the rich, savory taste of the meat extremely well. In Belgium, fruit side dishes appear much more frequently to accompany all sorts of meats and poultry, sometimes taking the place of a vegetable accompaniment.

The origin of combining sweet and savory flavors dates back to the Middle Ages, when salted preserved meats and fish formed the daily diet. These were then heavily seasoned with a variety of spices, such as cinnamon, cloves, and ginger, and sweetened with the addition of honey, wine, raisins, currants, dates, and other dried fruits, all of which helped to mask the strong briny, stale flavors of the preserved meat.

Today we have fresh meat available all year round and the spices and fruit side dishes are added to enhance their flavors and provide a complex play of tastes.

Baked Apples Filled with Berries

GEVULDE APPELS MET VEENBESSEN IN DE OVEN
•
POMMES AUX AIRELLES AU FOUR

This fruit combination is another all-time favorite on Belgian tables. When bilberries are out of season or are hard to find, my mother substitutes red currant jelly or preserves. Serve as an accompaniment to roasted poultry, pork, or game dishes.

4 firm apples, such as Golden Delicious
  or Granny Smith
1 cup drained Bilberries or Cranberries
  in Syrup (page 225) or red currant jelly
5 tablespoons unsalted butter
½ cup water

1. Preheat the oven to 350°F.

2. Cut the apples horizontally in half; leave on the skin if you like. Use a sharp knife to remove the stem and flower ends and cut out the cores.

3. Fill each apple half with berries and dot with ½ tablespoon butter.

4. Butter a shallow baking dish or gratin dish with the remaining 1 tablespoon butter. Pour in the water and arrange the apples in the casserole. Bake until tender, about 30 minutes. If you have peeled the apples, watch the baking time carefully, as they will fall apart more easily.

Serves 4 to 8

My Mother's Applesauce

MOEDER'S APPELMOES
COMPOTE DE POMMES DE MA MERE

No pork sausage or meat loaf is ever served without applesauce and mashed potatoes in my country. Indeed, in Belgium applesauce is often served as a vegetable, providing a tangy, sweet note to the rich savory taste of pork, poultry, and game. Children love it and most adults never outgrow their taste for this lovely combination.

5 to 6 tart, juicy apples, such as McIntosh, Jonagold, or Mutsu
⅓ cup water
3 tablespoons sugar or to taste
2 tablespoons unsalted butter
Pinch of ground cinnamon (optional)

1. Peel, quarter, and core the apples. Slice each quarter in half again. If you like a chunky applesauce, leave the apples in eighths; for a more puréed sauce, slice the apples still thinner.

2. Place the apples in a large heavy saucepan and add the water and sugar. Bring to a boil and reduce the heat. Cook, covered, until the apples are cooked to the desired texture, 15 to 25 minutes. Stir frequently while cooking and regulate the heat so that the applesauce does not erupt all over the stove.

3. Stir in the butter and the cinnamon, if using. Serve warm with roasted meats or cold as dessert.

Serves 4

Note: In the fall, when the markets are loaded with a great variety of fresh apples, I like to make applesauce in huge batches, always using a combination of the greatest possible variety—Mutsu, Jonagold, McIntosh, Delicious, and whatever other apples are available. The taste of the applesauce is never the same twice, but it is always delicious. Freeze applesauce in plastic containers for up to 4 months.

Oranges Filled with Berries

APPELSIENEN GEVULD MET VEENBESSEN
•
AIRELLES A L'ORANGE

A delicious and colorful side dish to serve with venison, boar, and many game birds. Or serve these with your holiday turkey for a simple but festive presentation.

1 to 1½ cups Bilberries or Cranberries in Syrup
  (page 225)
4 oranges

1. Slice the oranges in half horizontally. Use a grapefruit spoon or other sharp spoon to scoop out the flesh of the fruit and reserve. Discard as much of the tough membrane and seeds as possible.

2. Warm the berries in a small saucepan and drain.

3. Combine the reserved orange pulp with the berries and fill up the orange halves.

Serves 4 to 8

Variation: When I serve a Thanksgiving turkey, I present the cranberry relish in scooped-out orange halves. If you wish, you can combine the scooped-out orange flesh with your cranberry relish.

Potatoes

Little Truffles

The humble potato was introduced to Europe in the 16th century by the Spanish conquistadors who brought it back as a novelty from the New World. Like many newcomers, it was at first ignored, then regarded with suspicion and reviled. Since it is a member of the nightshade family, it was referred to as devil's food and considered dangerous because of its relationship to deadly nightshade. Eventually the rich folks took it up and praised the delicacy and flavor of "these little truffles." Finally, in the 19th century, the general public embraced the potato with a grand passion, which carries on to this day as the potato continues to be one of Belgium's favorite foods.

What pasta is to Italy, the potato is to Belgium: Belgium is a nation of potatophiles. The cool climate and rich soil of Flanders create an ideal environment for growing potatoes, (as well as all Belgian produce), and Belgian potatoes are extraordinary for their taste and variety. At any given time of the year, you can find a large selection of waxy or floury or starchy potatoes to be fried, baked, boiled, puréed, stuffed, or gratinéed. No main meal in Belgium is complete without potatoes in some form, even if simply boiled. Potatoes can even make up the whole meal.

Potatoes find their way into our beloved soups, both as a thickener to provide a natural creaminess to puréed soups and as a hearty vegetable; they are staples in many fricassees and casseroles as well as culinary stars in their own right. But two particular potato dishes warrant special mention.

First, there is *stoemp*, a homey, rustic dish, deeply rooted in the Belgian tradition of peasant cooking. There are probably as many variations of this dish as there are farmhouses in rural Flanders, but the basic idea is a hearty combination of mashed potatoes and other cooked vegetables, often enriched with bacon, cream, or butter and seasoned with herbs and spices, most notably, nutmeg. Uncomplicated and utterly satisfying, *stoemp*, a cross between a vegetable stew and a purée, is the ultimate comfort food of Belgium.

And then there is what many consider to be Belgium's greatest contribution to potato cookery, the great national dish—*frietjes*!

Frietjes, Belgian fried potatoes, are what most people dream of when they order French fries, and almost never get. In Belgium you can get them anywhere, for they are the beloved national snack of the country. And more than the monarchy or any other national symbol, *frietjes* unite the Flemish, the Walloons, and the Brusselaars in their passion for the fresh, hand-cut, golden-brown potato sticks. *Frietjes* are most commonly eaten on the street in every Belgian city, where they are bought fresh and crisp, hot from the fryer, from strategically placed handcarts. Many cafés sell freshly made *frietjes* through a window onto the sidewalk. The *frietjes* come generously salted and wrapped in a paper cone, and are eaten by themselves or with a dollop of mayonnaise. Using your fingers, you dip a perfect *frietje* into the mayonnaise and pop it into your mouth. Pure heaven! You are in the company of hungry schoolchildren, elegantly dressed business-people, shoppers and shopkeepers, farmers from the country and bankers from the financial district, tourists and housewives, all of them united in killing their hunger with the best fries in the world. When you have visited Belgium, this is the way you will remember *frietjes*, even though you will have eaten them in fancy restaurants and sidewalk cafés. It is the taste of *frietjes* eaten out of a paper cone while you are standing in the open air that will remain with you, because in eating these, you have experienced a bit of real Belgian life.

The One and Only Truly Belgian Fries

FRIETJES
•
POMMES FRITES

Yes, you can make the best, crispy fried potatoes, better than any French fried potatoes you have ever tasted, right in your own kitchen. In Belgium, *frietjes* are made at home at least once a week. There is no fancy skill involved, but there is a trick. The potatoes are fried twice! The first time cooks them through and makes them tender. The second time, which can be done hours later just before serving, turns them golden brown and deliciously crisp.

You won't need a lot of special equipment, but a few items are essential. If you own an electric deep fryer, you're all set. If not, a 4-quart deep fryer with a basket insert and a separate deep-fat thermometer is your next choice. In a pinch, use a heavy pot that is at least 5 inches deep, a long-handled fried-food skimmer or very large long-handled slotted spoon, and a deep-fat thermometer.

It is imperative to use a starchy, older potato for making real Belgian fries. In Belgium we have the large, yellow-fleshed Bintje potato, which is very similar to the Idaho or russet baking potato. For as long as I can remember, my family has always kept a large sack of these potatoes in the cellar for making our beloved *frietjes*.

Keep in mind that the older the potato, the better it is for making fries. Never make fries with new potatoes. All your efforts will be in vain as the young potatoes have not had time to develop sufficient starch.

The size of the fries is a very personal matter. Some people like them very thin and crunchy. Others prefer them quite large so that they can be crispy on the outside and soft in the center. Experiment to find the size you like best. Very thinly cut potato sticks need a shorter frying time, and the thicker ones take a little longer.

3 to 4 cups vegetable oil for frying
2 pounds Idaho or russet baking potatoes or
Yukon Gold potatoes, peeled, rinsed,
and dried
Salt to taste

1. Pour enough oil into a deep fryer to reach at least halfway up the sides of the pan but not more than three-quarters of the way up. Heat the oil to 325°F.

2. Cut the potatoes into sticks ½ inch wide and 2½ to 3 inches long. Dry all the pieces thoroughly in a clean dish towel. This will keep the oil from splattering. Divide the potato sticks into batches of no more than 1 cup each. Do not fry more than one batch at a time.

3. When the oil has reached the desired temperature, fry the potatoes for 4 to 5 minutes per batch. They should be lightly colored but not browned. If your fryer has a basket, simply lift it out to remove the fried potatoes. Otherwise, use a long-handled skimmer to lift out the potatoes. Be sure to bring the temperature of the oil back to 325°F in between batches. At this point the *frietjes* can rest for several hours at room temperature until you are almost ready to serve them.

4. Heat the oil to 375°F. Fry the potatoes in 1-cup batches until they are nicely browned and crisp, 1 to 2 minutes. Drain on fresh paper towels or brown paper bags and place in a warmed serving bowl lined with more paper towels. Sprinkle with salt and serve. Never cover the potatoes to keep them hot as they will immediately turn soft and limp. If you are inclined to perfectionism, leave some potatoes to fry halfway through the meal so you can serve them crisp and piping hot.

Serves 4 to 6

Note: *When frying anything in deep fat, always keep a lid close by. In case of fire, turn off the heat and cover the pan.*

Deep-Fried Potato Croquettes

AARDAPPEL KROKETJES
•
CROQUETTES DE POMMES DE TERRE

A special occasion dinner in my country almost always includes freshly fried potato croquettes. They are a passion in Belgium, and anyone who has ever tried them finds them irresistible. And no wonder, for potato croquettes, emerging golden and hot from their oily bath, combine two of the best qualities a potato can have: crunchy-crispy on the outside, yielding to mashed-potato heaven on the inside. They are at once a luxury food and among the most sublime of comfort foods.

Yes, they are time-consuming to make, and molding the individual croquettes by hand requires patience. But they are not at all difficult, and the rewards to the cook are many. Few foods are met with so much appreciation as these crunchy, delectable, melt-in-your-mouth morsels. Happily, only the actual frying needs to be done at the last minute, as the croquettes actually improve if they are allowed to rest in the refrigerator for a day after they are formed. They freeze very well, and a frozen supply of them is a luxury.

2 pounds Idaho or russet baking potatoes (about 3 large), peeled and halved
1 tablespoon salt, plus additional to taste
3 tablespoons unsalted butter
2 large egg yolks
1 cup plus 1 tablespoon all-purpose flour
Freshly ground white pepper to taste
Pinch of freshly grated nutmeg
3 large egg whites
1 cup fine dried bread crumbs
3 to 4 cups vegetable oil for deep frying

1. Place the potatoes in a large saucepan and add enough cold water to cover the potatoes by at least 1½ inches. Add 1 tablespoon salt. Bring to a boil, cover partially, and cook over medium heat until tender, about 20 minutes.

Oil for Deep Frying

When deep frying, it is important to use an oil with a high smoking point so that it does not burn. An oil that starts to smoke heavily at a high heat will ruin the taste of whatever you are frying. Traditionally, Belgian fries were cooked in the rendered fat of beef kidneys, which gave them an incomparable flavor. Sometimes you can still find these authentic fries at one of the street vendors who keeps to the old ways. But today, health concerns have prevailed, and most of Belgium now fries its frietjes *in vegetable oil. They are still delicious, if somewhat lighter in taste.*

Sunflower oil and corn oil are both good choices, since as they have a smoking point well over 375°F. In Belgium, we often use solid vegetable oil for frying. A solid vegetable shortening like Crisco would be a good substitute.

You can reuse the oil after frying, but you must keep it clean by filtering it through several layers of cheesecloth or a paper coffee filter after each use. Do not use oil in which fish has been fried to fry potatoes or any other vegetable, for it will make everything taste like fish. Store the oil in a cool dry place and discard after two or three uses.

Drain the potatoes and return them to the saucepan. Dry the potatoes by shaking the pan over low heat for a few seconds until all visible moisture is gone.

2. Press the potatoes through a food mill or potato ricer into a mixing bowl. Add the butter, egg yolks, and 1 tablespoon flour. Mix well with a wooden spoon. Season generously with salt, white pepper, and nutmeg. The mixture must be fairly dry or the croquettes will burst during frying.

3. Spread the potato mixture evenly on a nonstick baking sheet and shape into a 10 × 5-inch rectangle that is no more than 1 inch high. Cover with plastic wrap and refrigerate until the mixture is quite firm, at least 1 hour.

4. In a large soup bowl, beat the egg whites until they are well mixed. Place the remaining 1 cup flour in a soup bowl and the bread crumbs in a third soup bowl. Arrange the three plates in a row: flour, egg whites, bread crumbs.

5. Cut the potato mixture into small rectangles approximately 1 inch wide and 2 inches long. Use your hands to shape them into cylinders. Dip each croquette, one at a time, first into the flour, shaking off the excess, then into the egg whites, and finally into the bread crumbs. Arrange the shaped and dipped

croquettes on another baking sheet. At this point the croquettes can be refrigerated, covered, for several hours or overnight. In fact, they will be better if allowed to rest in the refrigerator until the following day. They can also be wrapped in plastic and frozen for up to 2 months.

6. Heat the oil in a deep fryer to 380°F. Add the croquettes in batches and fry until golden brown on all sides, 3 to 4 minutes. Drain on paper towels and serve. The finished croquettes can be kept warm in a preheated 300°F oven for up to 20 minutes, but it is best to serve them as soon as possible.

Makes 24 croquettes, serving 4 or 5

Note: The croquettes can be fried in a skillet in a mixture of butter and oil, but they will not be as good as deep fried croquettes.

Variations: Add 2 teaspoons minced garlic and 1 tablespoon minced chives to the riced potatoes.

• Fry 3 ounces finely chopped bacon in a small skillet until crisp. Add ¼ cup finely minced shallots and cook 2 to 3 minutes longer, stirring constantly. Stir in ¼ cup finely minced fresh parsley. Add to the riced potatoes and mix well.

Potato and Leek Pancake

AARDAPPEL GALETTE MET POREI
•
GALETTE DE POMMES DE TERRE ET POIREAUX

A golden, crispy potato pancake with a creamy filling of sautéed leeks—the contrast in textures is both surprising and very satisfying. Serve it with a green salad for lunch or a light evening meal, or serve wedges of the pancake as an ideal companion to any poached or grilled fish.

5 large Yukon Gold or russet baking potatoes, peeled
3 tablespoons unsalted butter
3 large leeks, white and light green parts only, rinsed well and sliced into thin rings
Salt and freshly ground black pepper to taste
3 tablespoons olive oil
Pinch of freshly grated nutmeg
1 teaspoon dried thyme
1 tablespoon all-purpose flour
1 tablespoon finely minced fresh parsley, for garnish

1. Coarsely grate the potatoes into a mixing bowl and cover with cold water.

2. Melt 1 tablespoon of the butter in a medium-size skillet over medium heat. Add the leeks and cook, stirring, until softened but not browned, 5 to 7 minutes. Season lightly with salt and pepper and set aside.

3. Drain the potatoes and dry them well in a kitchen towel.

4. In a 10-inch nonstick skillet, heat 1½ tablespoons olive oil and 1 tablespoon butter. When hot, spread half the potatoes in the pan and press down with a wooden spoon. Sprinkle with salt, pepper, nutmeg, and half the thyme. Over the potato layer, spread the leeks in a thin layer and sprinkle with the flour. Cover that with the rest of the potato mixture. Press down with a wooden spoon to make a neat pancake and sprinkle with salt, pepper, nutmeg, and the remaining thyme.

5. Cook for 8 to 10 minutes over medium heat. Shake the pan from time to time to make sure the pancake isn't sticking. If necessary, loosen it with a spatula. Put a large plate on top of the skillet and invert the pancake onto the plate. The cooked side should be very crusty. Heat the remaining 1½ tablespoons olive oil and 1 tablespoon butter in the skillet. Very carefully slide the pancake back into the skillet, uncooked side down; cook for 8 minutes longer, pressing down occasionally with a flat lid and shaking the skillet to keep the pancake from sticking.

6. Remove the finished pancake to a warmed plate, sprinkle with the parsley, cut into wedges and serve immediately.

Serves 2 or 3 as a main dish, 4 as a side dish

Parsleyed New Potatoes

NIEUWE AARDAPPELEN MET PETERSELIE
•
POMMES DE TERRE NOUVELLES AU PERSIL

In Belgium, the beginning of May heralds the start of the season when we can buy genuine new potatoes, *pommes de terre primeur*, a special variety of potato which is grown to be harvested before maturity. The season is not a long one and is over by the end of July. Connoisseurs await the arrival of new potatoes with the same passion with which they anticipate the first autumn truffles. And in the kitchen, new potatoes are treated with similar respect. These marble-size potatoes have a "baby" skin so delicate that when they are rinsed under cold running water and brushed with the most delicate of brushes, much of the skin will come off.

Simplicity in preparation is the key to success. New potatoes are best boiled or steamed until they are just tender, and seasoned with sweet butter, parsley, and salt and pepper—truly there is nothing comparable in the whole world!

2 pounds new potatoes
1 tablespoon salt, plus additional to taste
4 tablespoons (½ stick) unsalted butter, cut into
    small pieces
½ cup finely minced fresh parsley

1. Brush the new potatoes with a soft brush under cold running water.

2. In a large saucepan cover the potatoes with cold water, add 1 tablespoon salt, and bring to a boil. Cover partially and cook over medium heat until just barely tender, 15 to 20 minutes.

3. Drain the potatoes and cut each potato in half. Transfer to a serving dish and add the butter, parsley, and salt to taste. Let stand for a few seconds so the butter can melt, then very carefully toss the potatoes so that each potato is coated with parsley butter. Serve at once.

Serves 4 to 6

Variations: Substitute ¼ cup finely minced chives or chervil for ¼ cup of the parsley.

• Substitute 2 to 3 tablespoons finely minced fresh tarragon for the parsley.

Hunting for New Potatoes

Because new potatoes do not keep well, quickly losing their delicate texture and sweetness during storage, you will probably not find these gems in your supermarket. Look for them at your greengrocer and at farm stands. If you have a vegetable garden, consider planting your own potatoes to harvest in their infancy and enjoy these most delectable of treats freshly dug from the earth.

Round red-skinned potatoes, excellent potatoes in their own right, are not be confused with real new potatoes, which are baby potatoes, harvested before they have reached maturity.

When you are lucky enough to have found some, prepare them as quickly as possible. Any delay will alter their delicate flavor, and never, never refrigerate potatoes of any kind. At temperatures below 50°F, starch turns to sugar. If the sugar ferments, the potatoes will get an unpleasant sweet flavor.

Cooking Companions

My paternal grandmother, Madeleine, and I were always in charge of preparing potato croquettes for the annual Christmas and Easter dinners. We had great fun cooking together while entertaining each other with stories, confidences, and gossip. The time we spent together in the kitchen taught me how satisfying it is to prepare the kind of food that nourishes more than a bodily hunger. It also awoke in me the instinct for nurturing, and I recognized the value of sharing knowledge and the responsibilities of passing on traditions that have been kept alive by women through the ages in the kitchens of the world.

One of my great wishes is that grandmothers everywhere would regularly spend time in the kitchen with their grandchildren—mixing, kneading, rolling, shaping delicious morsels until the end of time.

Perfect Boiled Potatoes

AARDAPPELEN NATUUR
•
POMMES DE TERRE "NATURE"

Although there are many more elaborate ways of preparing potatoes, plain boiled potatoes, sprinkled with parsley, make the simplest and most popular companions to fish, fowl, or meat. It is important to serve boiled potatoes as soon as they are cooked. So when preparing your meal, cook the potatoes at the last possible moment. Think of how you treat pasta and treat your potatoes the same way.

Boiling or all-purpose potatoes such as red-skinned, Yukon Gold, or Yellow Finn (½ pound per person), peeled and halved or quartered depending on size
Salt to taste
Finely minced fresh parsley to taste

1. In a large saucepan, cover the potatoes with plenty of cold water, add the salt, and bring to a boil. Cover partially and cook over medium heat until just tender, 20 to 30 minutes.

2. Drain the potatoes and return them imme-

diately to the saucepan. Reduce the heat to low and dry the potatoes by holding the saucepan over the heat and shaking the potatoes around until all visible moisture is gone. Serve at once, sprinkled generously with parsley.

Leftovers

Turn leftover boiled potatoes into an excellent salad. Dress it with a homemade mayonnaise flavored with 1 tablespoon minced shallots and 1 tablespoon minced fresh parsley for every cup of mayonnaise. Or use a Gribiche sauce (see Index for recipes).

Or make home fries. Slice the cooked potatoes into rounds and sauté them together with a finely chopped onion in a combination of oil and butter until they are golden brown and crusty. My grandmother used to sauté her leftover potatoes in the drippings she saved from her pork roast or roast chicken, adding a dusting of freshly grated nutmeg, freshly ground black pepper, and a generous amount of parsley. These probably were the best home-fried potatoes I've ever had.

Mashed Potatoes with Caramelized Shallots

STOEMP MET SJALATJES
•
STOEMP AVEC ECHALOTES

*T*he sweet caramelized shallots take ordinary mashed potatoes to heights far out of proportion to the few extra minutes of work involved.

5 large Idaho or russet potatoes, peeled and cubed
1 cup milk
1 tablespoon salt, plus additional to taste
6 tablespoons (3/4 stick) unsalted butter, at room temperature
3 tablespoons heavy (or whipping) cream
Freshly ground black pepper, to taste
Pinch of freshly grated nutmeg
3 medium shallots, peeled and thinly sliced
2 tablespoons finely minced fresh parsley, for garnish

1. In a large saucepan, combine the potatoes, milk, 1 tablespoon salt, and enough cold water to just cover the potatoes. Bring to a boil over high heat, reduce the heat to medium, and cook, partially covered, until the potatoes are tender, 15 to 20 minutes. Drain.

2. Press the potatoes through a food mill or potato ricer into a large mixing bowl. Use a wooden spoon to beat in 4 tablespoons of the butter and the heavy cream. Beat until the mixture is very light and fluffy. Season generously with salt, freshly ground black pepper, and freshly grated nutmeg. Keep them warm in a 300°F oven while you prepare the shallots.

3. Melt the remaining 2 tablespoons butter in a small skillet over medium heat. Add the shallots, and cook, stirring occasionally, until the shallots are softened and lightly caramelized, 5 to 7 minutes. Top the mashed potatoes with the caramelized shallots and sprinkle with parsley. Serve immediately.

Serves 4 to 6

Spinach Mashed Potatoes

STOEMP MET SPINAZIE
•
STOEMP AUX EPINARDS

This favorite nursery food from my childhood has evolved into a sophisticated version of mashed potatoes enhanced with fresh green herbs, many of which are available all year round. Serve with fish, meat, or poultry, or on its own with a poached egg plopped in the center.

4 large Idaho or russet baking potatoes (about 2½ pounds), peeled and cubed
1 tablespoon salt, plus additional to taste
¾ pound fresh spinach, rinsed thoroughly and stems removed
1½ cups fresh parsley
½ cup minced fresh chives
4 fresh tarragon sprigs or ¼ cup fresh chervil (optional)
8 tablespoons (1 stick) unsalted butter, at room temperature
Freshly ground black pepper to taste
Pinch of freshly grated nutmeg
¼ cup milk, warmed

1. In a large saucepan, cover the potatoes with cold water and add 1 tablespoon salt. Bring to a boil, and cook, partially covered, over medium heat until the potatoes are tender, about 20 minutes. Drain.

2. While the potatoes are cooking, place the spinach, parsley, chives, and tarragon if using into another saucepan. If the greens are still wet from rinsing them, you do not need to add water. If they are dry, add 1 to 2 tablespoons water. Add salt to taste and cook, uncovered, over medium heat until the greens are limp and tender, about 10 minutes.

3. Pass the potatoes and the greens through a food mill or potato ricer into a large mixing

bowl. Stir in the butter, pepper, and nutmeg. Beat in enough of the milk with a wooden spoon to have the mashed potatoes at the desired consistency, not too dry and not too wet. Serve at once or keep warm in a preheated (300°F) oven for up to 20 minutes.

Serves 6

Mashed Potatoes with Winter Vegetables

WINTER STOEMP MET SAVOOIEKOOL

•

STOEMP AUX LEGUMES D'HIVER

This uncomplicated, hearty, nurturing casserole is another wonderful example of Belgian home cooking. It is most unabashedly of peasant origin but much improved by today's availability of a greater variety of vegetables. Today it is served as an accompaniment to a hearty roast, such as Roast Pork with Onions and Mustard (see Index), or, as in my family, with fresh veal or pork sausages browned in butter. Originally, it probably was the whole meal.

I suggest that you follow my great grandmother's example and let your garden and your greengrocer guide your choice of vegetables for this recipe. Consider green cabbage, leeks, rutabagas, green beans, Belgian endives—whatever looks fresh and good at the market. Serve this *stoemp* with pungent mustard on the side.

4 ounces slab bacon, rind discarded and cut into ½-inch cubes
4 medium onions, sliced
2 leeks, white parts only, well rinsed and thickly sliced
½ head Savoy cabbage, cored and finely shredded
4 carrots, peeled and cut into 1-inch cubes
4 turnips, peeled and cut into 1-inch cubes
1 pound Brussels sprouts, trimmed and halved
1 celery root (celeriac, about 1 pound), peeled and cut into 1-inch cubes
4 cups beef or chicken broth, preferably homemade (page 54 or 53)
Bouquet garni: 5 sprigs parsley, 1 sprig fresh thyme, and 1 bay leaf tied together with kitchen string
Salt and freshly ground black pepper to taste
Pinch of freshly grated nutmeg
1 pound red-skinned potatoes, peeled and cut into 1-inch cubes
2 tablespoons finely minced fresh parsley, for garnish

1. Fry the bacon until crisp in a large enameled Dutch oven over medium heat. With a slotted spoon, remove the bacon pieces and set them aside. Discard all but 4 tablespoons of the rendered bacon fat.

2. Add the onions, leeks, cabbage, carrots, turnips, Brussels sprouts, and celery root to the bacon fat, and cook over medium heat until soft, about 12 minutes. Stir the vegetables frequently and do not let them brown. Add the beef broth, bouquet garni, salt, pepper, and nutmeg. Cover and cook over medium heat for about 30 minutes.

3. Add the potatoes and bacon. Cover but leave the lid slightly ajar. Continue cooking until the potatoes are soft and the liquid has almost completely evaporated, 15 to 25 minutes. Discard the bouquet garni. Taste and adjust the seasoning. Stir the vegetables together gently with a large wooden spoon and sprinkle with the parsley.

Serves 6 to 8

Celery Root and Potato Purée

KNOLSELDER EN AARDAPPEL PUREE

•

PUREE DE CELERI-RAVE ET POMMES DE TERRE

The strong, peppery flavor of celery root marries extremely well with the sweetness of the potato, giving this purée a depth of flavor that is haunting and almost addictive.

In Belgium, celery root and potato purée is a favorite with the Christmas turkey or as one of a trio of vegetable purées (choose from carrot, turnip, or broccoli) served in many restaurants to complement the strong flavor of pheasant or other game.

1 celery root (celeriac, about 1¼ pounds),
    peeled and cubed
3 medium Idaho or russet baking potatoes,
    peeled and cubed
1 cup milk
1 tablespoon salt, plus additional
    to taste
3 to 4 tablespoons unsalted butter,
    at room temperature
3 tablespoons heavy (or whipping) cream
    or additional milk
Freshly ground black pepper
    to taste
Pinch of freshly grated nutmeg

1. In a large saucepan, combine the celery root, potatoes, 1 cup milk, 1 tablespoon salt, and enough cold water to cover the vegetables. Cover partially and cook over medium heat until the potatoes and celery root are tender, about 30 minutes. Drain.

2. Press the celery root and potatoes through a food mill or potato ricer into a large mixing bowl. Use a wooden spoon to beat in the butter and cream. Beat until the mixture is very light and fluffy. Season generously with salt, pepper, and nutmeg. The purée can be kept warm in 150°F oven for up to 2 hours.

Serves 4 to 6

Note: For a festive presentation, pipe the purée through a pastry bag fitted with a star tip. Make it even more festive by poaching or sautéing some large mushroom caps and piping the purée into the mushroom caps.

Mashed Potatoes with Leeks

STOEMP MET PREI
•
STOEMP AUX POIREAUX

My great grandmother Marie's recipe calls for double the amount of butter and cream, both coming fresh from her own farm. Her version of potato and leek *stoemp* was truly heavenly. But most of us don't work on a farm, and we know that in order to delay our passage to heaven, we have to make some sacrifices. My *stoemp*, though lighter, is still divine, and is especially good with fish, veal, and chicken.

2 medium Idaho or russet baking potatoes
    (about 1¼ pounds), peeled and cubed
1 tablespoon salt, plus additional to taste
2 large or 3 medium leeks (about ¾ pound),
    white and light green parts only
3 tablespoons unsalted butter
⅔ cup heavy (or whipping) cream
½ cup chicken broth, preferably homemade (page 53)
Freshly ground black pepper to taste
Pinch of freshly grated nutmeg

243

1. In a large saucepan, cover the potatoes with cold water. Add 1 tablespoon salt. Bring to a boil, cover partially, and cook over medium heat until the potatoes are tender, about 20 minutes. Drain and press through a food mill or potato ricer into a mixing bowl.

2. While the potatoes are cooking, discard the tough outer leaves of the leeks and trim the roots. Partially split the leeks and rinse thoroughly. Pat dry and slice into thin rings.

3. Melt the butter in a medium-size saucepan over medium heat. Add the leeks and cook, stirring, for about 5 minutes. Do not brown. Add the cream and chicken broth; season with salt, pepper, and nutmeg. Simmer, covered, for 15 minutes.

4. Drain the leeks but save the liquid. Return the liquid to the saucepan and cook over high heat until reduced by about half, about 5 minutes. The sauce should be thick and very flavorful.

5. Mix the potatoes and leeks together thoroughly with a wooden spoon and stir in the reduced sauce. Taste and adjust the seasoning. If the mixture is too dry, add a little more cream, butter, or milk.

6. Transfer to an ovenproof dish and keep warm for up to 2 hours in an oven that has been preheated to 300°F, then reduced to 150°F.

Serves 4 to 6

Stuffed Baked Potatoes

GEVULDE AARDAPPELEN
•
POMMES DE TERRE FARCIES

Because Belgians are so passionate about potatoes, they seem to have an endless variety of recipes for them. Stuffed Baked Potatoes is one of my favorites, particularly because the potatoes can be assembled on the morning of the day they are to be served and reheated in the evening. This is not something that can be done with most potato dishes, because cooked potatoes tend to take on an "off" flavor when they are reheated. It makes an excellent dish for entertaining.

For each serving:
1 large Idaho or russet baking potato
Coarse or kosher salt
1 to 2 slices lean smoked bacon, cut crosswise
  into small strips
1 tablespoon finely minced shallot
1 to 2 tablespoons unsalted butter, at room
  temperature
1½ teaspoons minced fresh parsley
Salt and freshly ground black pepper
  to taste
Pinch of freshly grated nutmeg

1. Preheat the oven to 425°F.

2. Place the potato on a layer of coarse salt in a small shallow baking dish. Bake in the middle of the oven for 1 hour. Insert a sharp paring knife or a skewer into the flesh to see if it is baked all the way through. Remove from the oven and let cool slightly. Reduce the oven heat to 375°F.

3. Cook the bacon pieces in a small skillet over medium-high heat until browned and crisp. Add the shallot and cook for another 2 minutes until shallot is translucent but not brown. Remove from the heat and set aside.

4. Slit the potato open lengthwise and with a small spoon, carefully scoop out the flesh into a bowl, leaving a ½-inch shell all around.

5. Add the butter to the potato flesh and mash with a fork. Add the bacon mixture and the parsley; season generously with salt, pepper, and nutmeg. (If you are mashing many potatoes at once, press them through a food mill or a potato ricer, then add the other ingredients.) Carefully fill the potato shells with the mashed potato mixture.

6. Place the filled potatoes in the baking dish and bake until the potatoes are completely warmed through, 10 to 20 minutes.

Serves 1

Note: These potatoes can be made ahead through step 5. Wrap in plastic carefully and refrigerate for up to 1 day. Remove the wrap and reheat in a 375°F oven for 20 to 30 minutes. They will not be as good as when they are freshly prepared—but good enough.

Variations: For each potato, add 2 tablespoons minced chives, chervil, or scallions or a mixture of all three.

• *Or add 2 tablespoons grated Gruyère cheese.*

Flemish Potatoes

AARDAPPELEN OP Z'N VLAAMS
•
POMMES DE TERRE
A LA FLAMANDE

This casserole exemplifies Belgian home cooking at its best. Rustic, comforting, and delicious, it never gets tiresome no matter how often it appears on the dinner table. And there is plenty of room for creative variation; just see the notes at the end of the recipe.

3 pounds red-skinned or Yukon Gold
   potatoes, peeled and cut into 1-inch cubes
1 tablespoon salt, plus additional to taste
2 tablespoons lard or bacon fat
2 tablespoons unsalted butter
2 medium onions, thinly sliced
Freshly ground black pepper to taste
Pinch of freshly grated nutmeg
1 bay leaf
2 cups beef broth, preferably homemade
   (page 54), or water
¼ cup finely minced fresh parsley or chervil

1. Preheat the oven to 350°F.

2. Place the potatoes in a large saucepan; add cold water to cover and 1 tablespoon salt. Bring to a boil, cover partially, and cook for 3 minutes. Drain and reserve.

3. Melt the lard and butter in a large skillet over medium heat. Add the onions and cook, stirring, until softened but not browned, 5 to 7 minutes. Season the onions with salt, pepper, and nutmeg. (The dish can be prepared ahead of time up to this point.)

4. Arrange the onions on the bottom of a medium-size baking dish and spread the potatoes evenly over the onions. Add the bay leaf and enough beef broth to almost cover the potatoes.

5. Bake until most of the liquid has cooked away, about 30 minutes. Check once or twice and add a little more broth or water if the mixture becomes too dry too soon. The finished dish should be moist but not at all soupy. Sprinkle generously with the parsley and serve with roast meat or chicken.

Serves 4 to 6

Variations: Brussels sprouts can make a substantial contribution to this hearty casserole. Trim 1 pound Brussels sprouts and cook in lots of boiling water for 5 minutes. Halve the sprouts and cook along with the onions.

• *Carrots add a lovely, mellow sweetness to the dish. Peel 4 or 5 carrots and cut crosswise into 1-inch pieces. Cook them along with the onions.*

Waffles, Pancakes, and Breads

Waffles and Pancakes

Waffles as well as their slightly less festive relative pancakes have been an important part of the Belgian diet for centuries. In fact, the pancake or griddle cake, probably because it is less complicated to make than the waffle, has been a staple of peasant cooking virtually from time immemorial. Pancakes were quick to make, consumed less energy than oven-baked bread, and were (and are) wonderful for stretching leftovers as well—vegetables, potatoes, and bits of meat could be wrapped in a buckwheat pancake and taken out to the fields for a very portable and highly satisfying meal.

But if pancakes are everyday food, waffles are a bit more special. Waffles always signal a celebration of some sort, even if only to break up the doldrums of a long winter afternoon. A waffle iron is a beloved appliance, and its appearance on the table brings a feeling of good cheer. In museums and even in some homes, you can find magnificent collections of waffle irons—some beautifully forged in silver or copper—that go as far as back the 13th century. Many are fashioned with elaborately patterned grids and produce the most beautiful waffles, and there are many thicknesses and varieties—everything from coarse-grained

cakes to the most delicate *gaufrettes* (tiny wafer-thin waffle cookies). Over the centuries these delectable treats have inspired poets and tempted kings (the French king François I adored his waffles, specially prepared for him in a silver iron).

However, waffles were never just for divinely entitled or inspired personages; they were for everyone. In a typical peasant home, if, say, there was a pig ready for slaughter—a momentous occasion promising many bountiful meals—why, then, the best clothes were put on, the beer put to cool, and as a matter of course the waffle iron was polished up and made ready. It was time for a celebration; family members and friends from nearby villages were invited, and a waffle party was on. Or, perhaps, it was kermis (*kermesse* in French) when the entire village would be taken over by a festival and fair. A kermis was originally held to celebrate the feast day of a local patron saint, but it expanded to include other religious celebrations as well—the Three Kings Day, or Epiphany, the day of St. Maarten, and, most important of all, the day before Lent, Shrove Tuesday. You can see scenes of kermis festivities and banquets in the paintings of Breughel.

How to Use a Waffle Iron

1. Heat the waffle iron according to the manufacturer's instructions.

2. Brush the iron with a thin film of oil or spray with nonstick cooking spray. In the old days, in the countryside, people rubbed their iron or griddle with a piece of fatback to grease it. This imparted a very unique flavor to their waffles.

3. Pour in enough batter to cover two-thirds of the iron and close it immediately. The first set of waffles will be your "testing" set. In my family, the first waffles were for the dog, who sat patiently waiting at my mother's feet. If the waffles are too heavy, add a little more milk to the batter. If the waffles stick, it means your iron wasn't hot enough when you poured in the batter. Let them bake another minute or so. The baking time depends on the rich-ness of the batter, the type of iron being used, and the size of your waffles. Some irons need to be turned over, but the electric irons bake simultaneously on both sides. Remember, you should never open the waffle iron during the first minute of baking or the waffle will separate.

4. Let the baked waffles cool on a rack before you stack them or they will be soggy.

5. When the last waffle is done, leave your iron open so it can cool off. Use a small brush to clean away any crumbs, then give it a final protective coating of vegetable oil. Keep your iron in a dry place until the next waffle extravaganza.

Some waffle irons come with a built-in thermostat but others do not. If you have no thermostat you will need to control the heat by unplugging the iron for five minutes every once in a while. This is particularly important with sugar waffles, as an iron that becomes too hot will burn the sugar.

Today waffles are baked and eaten all year round in Belgium in coffeehouses, tearooms, and in the home. But a version of the kermis still exists in the form of a kind of traveling fair that comes to town, sets up its carousels, its "horror castles," its shows, and best, and most inevitably of all, its beautifully colored antique food stalls offering golden, crunchy, freshly baked, feather-light waffles, so generously dusted with confectioners' sugar that it makes you sneeze. The same stands usually also sell beignets that melt in your mouth and make you feel like the child you were when you first enjoyed the ancient, fairy-tale world of the kermis.

Belgian waffles first came to fame in the United States when they were introduced during the 1960s at the World's Fair. But despite today's easy-to-use and readily available electric waffle irons, waffles in America remain mostly a breakfast food.

Waffles as a meal . . . well, perhaps, you might do as we do in Belgium, and have a waffle party for your supper.

My Mother's Waffles

MOEDER'S WAFELS
•
LES GAUFRES DE MA MERE

All through Flanders, one can find hundreds of waffle recipes. Most of our waffles are yeast-raised, creating a lighter, crustier waffle than the baking-powder waffles one usually finds in the United States. The following is my family recipe, which has come down from mother to daughter for generations and has kept us happy for as long as anyone in my family can remember. Here in the United States, they are particularly welcome as the days shorten in the autumn months and the weather gets colder. I invite guests to arrive in the late afternoon, and seduce them with the enticing smells of freshly brewed coffee and baking waffles. No one has ever been able to resist this happy feast. I urge you to adopt this tradition in your own home, and do remember to install your waffle iron on the dining room table so that the baking of the waffles becomes part of the fun.

"It isn't worth it to get out your waffle iron to bake six or eight waffles," is my mother's philosophy, and I agree with her. Here I give you the proportions for a satisfying stack of waffles for a large hungry group. For a smaller amount, simply cut the recipe in half. But remember that the leftover waffles taste even better the next morning for breakfast. Reheat them for 1 minute in a hot waffle iron or pop them into the toaster. Or freeze them to have instant waffles on hand.

2 ounces fresh cake yeast or 4 packages active
    dry yeast
6 cups milk, warmed to 100°F
6 large egg yolks
12 tablespoons (1½ sticks) unsalted butter,
    melted and cooled to lukewarm
12 tablespoons (1½ sticks) margarine, melted
    and cooled to lukewarm
1 cup Vanilla Sugar (page 318), or 1 cup sugar
    and 1 tablespoon vanilla extract
Pinch of salt
8 cups all-purpose flour
6 large egg whites, beaten to soft peaks

For serving:
Confectioners' sugar
Unsalted butter, at room temperature,
    or whipped cream
Sliced fresh fruit, such as pineapple, peaches, or
    strawberries

1. In a small bowl, dissolve the yeast in 1 cup of the lukewarm milk.

2. In a large, deep mixing bowl (the dough will double or triple in volume), whisk the egg yolks with ½ cup of the remaining milk and the melted butter and margarine. Add the yeast mixture, sugar, and salt.

3. Gradually add the flour to the batter by sifting it in. Alternate additions of flour with the remaining 4½ cups milk. Stir with a wooden spoon after each addition.

4. Fold in the beaten egg whites.

5. Cover with a clean towel and put in a warm place (see Note). Let rise for 1 hour. The batter should double or even triple in volume. (While you wait, you have time to brew the coffee, set the table, and heat up your waffle iron.) Check the batter from time to time to make sure it isn't about to erupt like an impatient volcano. Stir it down once or twice.

6. Bake the waffles in a hot waffle iron. The easiest way to get the batter onto the waffle iron is to do what my mother does. Transfer the batter (by batches) into a water pitcher and pour the batter from the pitcher.

7. Serve the baked waffles with confectioners' sugar and butter, or whipped cream and fresh fruit. Allow any leftover waffles to cool on a rack before storing.

Makes about 40 waffles

Variation: Add approximately 1 teaspoon cinnamon to the batter.

Note: Traditionally, waffle batter is left next to the big warm stove, which guarantees a slow, even rising. Duplicate these conditions in the following way: Preheat your oven to 200°F for 10 minutes and turn it off. Let the batter rise in the oven with the door closed.

Waffle Memories

*I*n one of the dearest (and clearest) memories of my childhood, I am making my way home from school on an early winter's eve with the air chill and damp. Lights are coming on in all the houses, their reflections shimmering in the dark water of the canal. I want so badly to get home, because I saw Mama polishing her waffle iron the night before. When at last I'm home and I push open the heavy door, my senses are assaulted by such thrilling smells—the warm, golden aroma of baking waffles and freshly brewed coffee. I am in heaven.

My mother baked the waffles right at the table in her electric waffle iron, and the family would wait impatiently, bickering about who would get the next golden pair to come off the iron. We ate them with scads of fresh, sweet butter and confectioners' sugar or jam, honey or whipped cream, and sometimes fresh fruit. The ritual—part meal, part entertainment— would go on for hours of feasting and talking and boasting about who could eat the most. I always did very well, eating perhaps 10 or more waffles over the course of the whole evening—but I always lost the contest to my father.

Belgian Fruit-Filled Waffles

BELGISCHE FRUIT WAFELS
•
GAUFRES AUX FRUITS

Fruit-filled waffles are best served on the day that they are made, but they will keep for several days in an air-tight container in the refrigerator. Reheat them in your waffle iron or toaster, and send some to school with your children.

1 ounce fresh cake yeast or 2 packages active
    dry yeast
1 cup milk, warmed to 100°F
6 large egg yolks
6 tablespoons (3/4 stick) unsalted butter, melted
    and cooled to lukewarm
1 cup confectioners' sugar, plus additional for
    garnish
Pinch of salt
1 teaspoon vanilla extract
1 teaspoon ground cinnamon
3½ cups all-purpose flour, plus additional for
    kneading
1½ to 2 cups good-quality jam or 1½ to 2 cups
    Fruit Compote (recipe follows)

1. In a large mixing bowl, dissolve the yeast in the lukewarm milk and let rest for 5 minutes.

2. Whisk in the egg yolks, one at a time, then the butter, sugar, salt, vanilla, and cinnamon.

3. Gradually sift in the flour, stirring it in with a wooden spoon. You should end up with a soft, fairly dry, but very elastic dough. Remove the dough to a lightly floured surface and knead it for a full 5 minutes, adding as little extra flour as possible. Roll the dough into a ball and place it in an oiled large bowl. Cover with plastic wrap and let rise in a warm place until doubled in volume, about 1 hour (see Note, page 251).

4. Punch down the dough, cover, and refrigerate for 20 minutes.

5. Shape the dough into about 20 small balls. Roll each ball with a rolling pin on a lightly floured surface into a 4 × 2½-inch rectangle.

6. Place 1 tablespoon fruit jam or compote in the middle of the bottom half of each rectangle. Moisten the edges of the rectangle with a little water and fold the empty half over to cover the fruit. Pinch the edges together to seal the filling inside. Place the packages on

an oiled baking sheet and let them rise for 20 minutes in a warm place.

7. Bake the filled waffles in a well-oiled hot waffle iron until golden brown. Make sure that the iron isn't too hot, so that the outside doesn't burn before the inside gets a chance to cook. Dust the baked waffles with confectioners' sugar and serve.

Makes about 20 waffles

Fruit Compote

Sour cherries or any other juicy red cherries are traditional in Belgian compote; but any fresh, canned, or frozen fruit is possible: apples, apricots, pineapple, berries, you name it.

For canned fruit in heavy syrup:
2 cups drained canned fruit, syrup reserved
2¼ teaspoons potato starch
1 teaspoon cold water
1 tablespoon fresh lemon juice

1. Cut the fruit into bite-size pieces.

2. Heat ¼ cup of the reserved syrup in a small saucepan.

3. Dissolve the potato starch in the cold water. Add to the syrup and bring to a boil, stirring

constantly. Reduce the heat and simmer for 1 minute until thickened. And add sugar if necessary. The compote has to be sweet because the waffles are not. Remove from the heat and stir in the lemon juice and fruit.

For fresh fruit:
2 cups fresh berries or other fresh fruit, peeled and cut into bite-size pieces
¼ cup water
½ cup sugar
2½ teaspoons potato starch
1 teaspoon cold water
1 tablespoon fresh lemon juice

1. Combine the fruit, ¼ cup water, and the sugar in a medium-size saucepan and simmer until the fruit is soft. The timing will depend on the type of fruit you are using.

2. Drain the fruit and reserve. Return the cooking liquid to the pan.

3. Dissolve the potato starch in the cold water. Add to the cooking liquid and bring to a boil, stirring constantly. Reduce the heat and simmer for 1 minute until thickened. Add more sugar if necessary. The compote has to be sweet because the waffles are not. Remove from the heat and stir in the lemon juice and fruit.

Flemish Waffles

VLAAMSE WAFELS
•
GAUFRES A LA FLAMANDE

For a quick, small batch of waffles, try this delicate Cognac-scented variation.

½ ounce fresh cake yeast or 1 package active dry yeast
2 cups milk or 1¾ cups milk and ¼ cup water, warmed to 100°F
2¼ cups all-purpose flour
⅛ teaspoon salt
1 large egg
2 tablespoons granulated sugar
3 large egg yolks
7 tablespoons unsalted butter, melted and cooled to lukewarm
1 teaspoon vanilla extract
3 tablespoons Cognac or brandy
3 large egg whites, beaten to soft peaks

For serving:
Confectioners' sugar
Unsalted butter, at room temperature, or whipped cream

1. In a small bowl, dissolve the yeast in ¼ cup of the lukewarm milk. Set aside until the mixture is bubbling and foamy, about 5 minutes.

2. Sift the flour together with the salt into a large mixing bowl. Make a well in the center and add the whole egg, the yeast mixture, and the sugar. Mix well with a wooden spoon. Add the remaining 1¾ cups milk and the egg yolks, one at a time, stirring with the wooden spoon until smooth.

3. Add the melted butter, vanilla, and Cognac. Stir to just combine.

4. Fold the egg whites into the batter. Cover with a clean towel and let rise for 1 hour in a warm spot (see Note, page 251).

5. Stir down the batter and bake ½ cup at a time in a hot waffle iron. Serve immediately with confectioners' sugar and butter or whipped cream.

Makes 12 waffles

About Yeast

Fresh yeast gives a fuller flavor than dry. It keeps in the refrigerator for up to 3 weeks or in the freezer for 2 months. If the cake has dried, discard it.

Dry yeast has a longer shelf life. Discard any yeast on which the date has expired.

You may substitute fresh yeast in any recipe that calls for the dry variety and vice versa:
1 package active dry yeast = ½ ounce or 15 grams fresh cake yeast.

Sugar Waffles from Liège

LUIKSE WAFELS
•
GAUFRES LIEGEOISES

These waffles are a little more time-consuming to make, but the end result is definitely worth the effort. Two separate batters are prepared and mixed together for deliciously sweet and crunchy

waffles. Once you have mastered this recipe, you will be able to make it with your eyes closed.

Batter 1:
1¼ ounces fresh cake yeast or 2½ packages active dry yeast
¼ cup warm water (about 100°F)
1 cup all-purpose flour
1 tablespoon granulated sugar
1 large egg, beaten
⅓ cup milk, warmed to 100°F

Batter 2:
9 tablespoons unsalted butter, at room temperature
6 tablespoons all-purpose flour
1 teaspoon vanilla extract
¼ teaspoon baking powder
1 teaspoon ground cinnamon (optional)
Pinch of salt
1 tablespoon granulated sugar
½ cup pearl sugar or ¾ cup crushed sugar cubes (see Note)

1. Prepare Batter 1: In a small bowl, dissolve the yeast in the warm water with 1 tablespoon of the flour and the sugar. Let stand for 5 minutes until foamy.

2. Sift the remaining flour into a large mixing bowl. Make a well in the center and add the yeast mixture, egg, and milk. Mix well with a wooden spoon to make a smooth batter. Cover with a kitchen towel and let rise in a warm place until the batter has doubled or tripled in volume, (see Note, page 251).

3. Meanwhile, prepare Batter 2: In a medium-size bowl, mix the butter, flour, salt, vanilla, baking powder, cinnamon (if using), granulated sugar, and pearl sugar into a paste.

4. With your hands, work Batter 2 into batter 1 until well mixed. Shape the dough into 10 balls, approximately 2½ to 3 ounces each. Flatten each ball into a disk and dust lightly with flour.

5. Bake in a medium-hot waffle iron. Don't let the iron become too hot or the sugar will burn. Bake until the waffles are golden brown but still slightly soft, 3 to 4 minutes.

6. Serve the sugar waffles lukewarm or cooled to room temperature on a rack. Sugar waffles will keep well for several days in an airtight container, if you manage to have any left over.

Makes 10 waffles

Note: Pearl sugar, or pärl socker, is an ornamental sugar that remains crunchy after baking. It is used as a garnish for many sweet pastries in Belgium. You can buy it by mail order from Maid of Scandinavia, 3244 Raleigh Avenue, Minneapolis, MN 55416-2299 (800-328-6722).

You can substitute crushed sugar cubes for the pearl sugar. Use a rolling pin to crush 1 cup of sugar cubes into pieces approximately the size of a sunflower seed. Don't worry about making them the same size.

Sugar Waffles in Liège

The city of Liège (Luik in Flemish), the proud and lively capital of Wallonia in the French-speaking southern part of Belgium, is the birthplace of extraordinary and totally addictive sugar waffles. Traditionally, sugar waffles have been made at home, but the last decade has seen the spectacular rise of sugar waffles as one of the most popular street foods in Belgium. What started as a local specialty has taken the country by storm and become a favorite national food!

Should you happen to find yourself one winter day wandering through the tiny medieval streets of Liège (or any other town in Belgium), just follow your nose until you find a friendly young man or woman installed behind a steaming waffle iron on a small table right on the sidewalk. You will be hungry. Everyone is hungry on a Belgian winter afternoon. But the steaming sugar waffle will satisfy you as nothing else can—warming your hands, your belly, and your very soul.

It is good to remember that should you fail to find a waffle stand on a street corner, almost every railway station is home to one or more waffle stands. Walk into the station and the scent of sugar waffles will overwhelm you.

New Year's Waffle Cookies

NIEUWJAAR'S WAFELTJES

•

GAUFRETTES

When is a waffle not exactly a waffle? Around New Year's Eve, when we make these crispy, buttery waffle cookies. *Wafeltjes* are made without yeast but with a good quantity of sugar and butter instead. They keep very well in an airtight cookie tin. They are baked in an iron with small grids—the heart-shaped Belgian waffle irons are excellent. *Wafeltjes* are delicious served with ice cream or all on their own with a cup of coffee or tea.

Despite their elegant appearance, *wafeltjes* are very simple to make. You can enlist the aid of a child or two to roll the batter into 1½-inch balls. But I warn you that as a very enterprising little girl, I used to test the stickiness of the batter by throwing the balls up to the ceiling. Some held on for weeks!

3 large eggs

1 cup sugar

1 teaspoon vanilla extract

1 cup (2 sticks) unsalted butter, melted and cooled to lukewarm

4 cups all-purpose flour

1. Beat the eggs with the sugar and vanilla until the mixture turns fluffy and very pale, and forms a ribbon that holds its shape.

2. Add the melted butter and mix well.

3. Sift in the flour, a little at a time, and mix well to form a smooth dough.

4. Cover the dough with a clean kitchen towel and let rest for 2 hours at room temperature.

5. With your hands, roll the dough into about 45 balls, 1½ inches in diameter.

6. Bake in a hot waffle iron with the smallest grids until the cookies are golden brown and crisp. Let the cookies cool on a rack and store in airtight containers.

Makes about 45 cookies

Flemish Yeast Pancakes, Breughel Style

BREUGHEL PANNEKOEKEN
•
LES CREPES FLAMANDES

There is an expression in Belgium. "*Moeder, warm uw panneke maar*" (Mother, it's time to heat and oil your pan). It means that we have spotted a familiar face coming to visit, and it's time to put all other considerations aside and have a party. This can be true morning, afternoon, or evening, because in Belgium, particularly in the winter, we will make any occasion one in which to celebrate and enjoy life. Pancakes, with their golden, round shapes, have often represented the sun. It is in the cold weather that many villages in Belgium hold pancake festivals to soothe people and remind them that the sun will soon return. These traditions go way back, back to Breughel's time, when he painted these festivals, and even earlier.

As every child knows, waffles and pancakes are cheerful and festive breakfast foods, but they can be served any time of day. Pancakes keep well and can be made ahead of time for spur-of-the-moment entertaining. Stack the finished pancakes on a plate, cover with plastic wrap, and refrigerate for up to 10 days. Or, wrap them tightly in plastic wrap and freeze up to several months. To reheat, bring the pancakes to room temperature, so they won't stick together, and warm in a hot pan.

½ ounce fresh cake yeast or 1 package active
   dry yeast
3 cups milk, warmed to 100°F
4 cups all-purpose flour
½ cup sugar
½ teaspoon salt
4 large eggs, lightly beaten
2 teaspoons vanilla extract
6 tablespoons (¾ stick) unsalted butter,
   melted
About 1 cup water
6 tablespoons unsalted butter, at room
   temperature or softer, for frying

For serving:
Unsalted butter
Dark brown sugar
Assorted jams and preserves

1. In a small bowl, dissolve the yeast in ¼ cup of the lukewarm milk. Let rest for 5 minutes until foamy.

2. In a large mixing bowl, whisk the flour together with the sugar and salt until well mixed. Make a well in the center. Pour the eggs, dissolved yeast, and vanilla into the well. Using a whisk or a wooden spoon, gradually stir the flour into the liquid ingredients.

258

By working this way you'll avoid having lumps form in the batter. Add the remaining 2¾ cups milk and the melted butter and stir. Add water, a little at a time, to make a smooth but liquid batter that is the consistency of thick, heavy cream.

3. Cover the bowl with plastic wrap or a kitchen towel and let rise in a warm place until doubled in volume, about 1 hour.

4. Place an 8- or 9-inch skillet (see Note, below) over medium heat and brush with the soft butter. Pour a scant ½ cup batter into the pan and tilt the pan, so a thin layer of batter covers the entire surface of the pan. Bake until light brown on the bottom. Turn the pancake over with a spatula and brown the other side.

5. Stack the pancakes as they are done on a warmed plate and serve as soon as possible. Serve with butter, dark brown sugar, and an assortment of jams and preserves.

Makes about 30 pancakes

Note: I recommend using 2 medium-size skillets at the same time to cook the pancakes quickly and efficiently.

Flambéed Crêpes with Cherries

GEFLAMBEERDE PANNEKOEKEN MET KERSEN
•
CREPES FLAMBEES AVEC DES CERISES

For a wonderful dessert, try this specialty from the region of De Kempen, famous for its cherries. All varieties of cherries are suitable for this recipe, but for the most authentic flavor, seek out sour cherries (also called pie cherries). Sometimes you can find these (in jars) in the baking section of your supermarket. If you ever find yourself driving through the flatlands of De Kempen, be sure to make an afternoon stop in one of the many tearooms to sample this very Belgian treat.

8 Flemish Yeast Pancakes, Breughel Style
  (page 258)
8 tablespoons good-quality cherry
  preserves
4 tablespoons (½ stick) unsalted butter
¼ cup sugar
1 cup drained canned cherries
½ cup kirsch

1. Spread each pancake with 1 tablespoon of the cherry preserves and roll up in a cylinder.

Lemon Crêpes for Dessert

*F*lavor the Flemish yeast pancake batter with the grated zest of 1 lemon and proceed as directed. To serve four, fold 8 pancakes into quarters and set aside. Before serving, melt 4 tablespoons (½ stick) unsalted butter in a large skillet over medium heat. Add ⅓ cup sugar and grated zest of ½ lemon; cook over medium heat until all the sugar has melted into a thick syrup, about 5 minutes. Add the juice of 1 lemon, stir, and arrange the folded pancake triangles in a single layer in the skillet. Reheat for a few minutes, turning the pancake triangles with a spatula so they are nicely covered with the lemony syrup. Serve on warmed plates and decorate with a mint leaf or a twisted lemon slice.

2. Melt the butter in a large skillet over medium heat. Add the sugar and cook until it melts and caramelizes slightly, about 3 minutes.

3. Arrange the pancakes in a single layer in the skillet, add the cherries, and cook over medium heat, turning the pancakes once,

until they are coated with the syrup and completely heated through, 5 to 6 minutes.

4. Carefully flambé the pancakes with the kirsch (page 130). Serve at once when the flames die down.

Serves 4

Marie's Buckwheat Pancakes

MARIE'S BOEKWEITKOEKEN
•
CREPES AU SARRASIN DE MARIE

*T*hese pancakes, which have sustained hardworking country people for many generations, are utterly delicious, very hearty, and quite low in fat. The buckwheat flour gives these pancakes a pleasant, nutty flavor as well an excellent supply of protein, iron, B vitamins, and calcium.

Serve them for breakfast with a dollop of sweet butter and some brown sugar or maple syrup. Add a fresh fruit salad and you've got a breakfast that will keep you going all day. But don't think of these pancakes as only breakfast food. Take a tip from my great grandmother Marie—a woman who really knew how to feed hungry people—and wrap them around a savory cheese, meat, or vegetable filling for a meal that everyone will love and that is very easy to prepare (see the suggestions at the end of the recipe).

Add the sugar if you want sweet pancakes for dessert or with fruit for breakfast. Leave out the sugar if the pancakes are to be used with a savory filling.

³⁄₄ ounce fresh cake yeast or 1½ packages
  active dry yeast
3 cups milk, warmed to 100°F
1¼ cups buckwheat flour
2 cups all-purpose flour
⅓ cup sugar (optional)
2 teaspoons salt
4 large eggs, lightly beaten
About 2 cups water
3 to 4 tablespoons unsalted butter,
  at room temperature

1. In a small bowl dissolve the yeast in 1 cup of the lukewarm milk. Let rest for 5 minutes until foamy.

2. In a large mixing bowl, whisk together the buckwheat flour, all-purpose flour, sugar if using, and salt until well mixed. Make a well in the center. Pour the eggs, the yeast mixture, and the remaining 2 cups milk into the center. Use a whisk or a wooden spoon to gradually mix the flour into the liquid ingredients. Add the water a little at a time, to obtain a smooth, liquid batter with the consistency of thick, heavy cream.

3. Cover the bowl with plastic wrap and let rise in a warm place until doubled in volume, about 1 hour.

4. Heat an 8- or 9-inch skillet or griddle over medium heat. Brush the surface with butter and pour about ½ cup batter into the skillet or on the griddle. Tilt the skillet to distribute the batter evenly. If the batter seems too thick, add a little more water. Cook the pancakes over medium heat until lightly browned on the underside and the edges start to crisp up. Turn the pancake over and cook the other side. Stack the pancakes on a warmed ovenproof platter and hold in a warm oven until ready to serve.

Makes about 25 large pancakes

Variations: *Prepare the variation for Gratin of Belgian Endives (page 34), wrapping a pancake around each Belgian endive. Serve with a green salad for a complete meal.*

• *Grate Gruyère cheese and sprinkle 2 tablespoons on each pancake after you have cooked it on one side and turned it over. Turn down the heat, so that the cheese can melt slowly and the pancake brown on its second side. Season generously with paprika and freshly ground black pepper. Fold the pancake in half and serve 2 or 3 per person with a salad.*

Flemish Raisin Bread

KOEKEBROOD
•
CRAMIQUE

My great grandmother Marie was famous in our family for her *koekebrood*, delectably rich, brioche-type raisin bread. Her recipe has come down to me, and no other recipe in my repertoire makes me feel as deeply connected to her as this sweet, almost cakelike bread. The rich yeasty smells and the smooth baby-skin texture of the dough as I knead it always bring to mind her peaceful face and her strong, time-worn hands as they rolled and kneaded. Baking was her favorite occupation and we were fortunate to experience firsthand the wonderful warm aromas that filled her house and whetted our appetites. In Belgium we say of someone who is especially generous and goodhearted that they have a heart of *koekebrood*, and this was certainly true of my great grandmother.

You can make this bread by hand or use a KitchenAid mixer with the paddle attachment.

2 ounces fresh cake yeast or 4 packages active dry yeast

2 cups milk, warmed to 100°F

7 cups all-purpose flour, plus ³/4 cup for kneading

2 cups dark raisins or currants

3 large eggs

³/4 cup sugar

1½ teaspoons salt

10 large tablespoons (1¼ sticks) unsalted butter, at room temperature

1 large egg beaten with 1 teaspoon water (egg wash)

1. Make a starter: In a large mixing bowl, dissolve the yeast in the lukewarm milk. Let rest for 5 minutes until foamy.

2. Add 2 cups of the flour and stir until smooth. Cover with plastic wrap or a clean kitchen towel and let rise in a warm spot until doubled, about 1 hour.

3. Place the raisins in a small saucepan, add enough water to cover, and bring to a boil. Remove from the heat and let stand 10 to 15 minutes to plump. Drain and set aside.

4. Stir down the starter and add the eggs one at a time, then the sugar, salt, and the remaining 5 cups flour, 1 cup at a time. Stir with each addition until well mixed. (You can do this by hand with a wooden spoon or in a mixer using the paddle attachment.) When the dough holds together, transfer it to a lightly floured surface and knead, working in additional flour until you get a soft, smooth,

and elastic dough that does not stick, 5 to 7 minutes. Knead in the butter 1 tablespoon at a time until it is thoroughly combined into the dough. (This will take patience but the end result is worth it. Adding the butter at the end will make your bread lighter and more refined in texture and flavor.) Finally, knead in the raisins.

5. Divide the dough in half, shape each half into a ball and place each in a large, lightly oiled bowl. Cover with a kitchen towel or plastic wrap and let rise in a warm place until doubled in volume, about 2 hours.

6. Butter and flour two 9 × 5-inch loaf pans or two 9-inch springform pans. Punch down the risen dough, shape each into a loaf or ball, and place in the prepared pans. Brush with the egg wash, cover, and let rise a second time until doubled in volume, about 1 hour.

7. Preheat the oven to 375°F.

8. Brush the loaves with egg wash again. Bake until nicely browned and a sharp knife inserted in the center comes out clean, 30 to 35 minutes. Remove from the pans and cool on a wire rack.

9. Allow the bread to cool for several hours (it should be completely cool and dry inside) before slicing. The bread will keep for several days, wrapped in brown paper, or wrap it well in plastic wrap and freeze up to 1 month.

Makes 2 big loaves

Note: Short of time? Make the dough through step 2. Cover and let rise in the refrigerator overnight. The following morning, return the starter to room temperature and proceed with the next step.

Belgian Pastries

*B*elgium is a country where the koeken *are king. Whether it is* boterkoeken, suikerbrood, kramiek, *or* peperkoek, *we cannot get through the day without them. What are they? Pastries, of course–our own versions of brioche, croissants, Danish, or Viennese pastries. There is an endless variety of these genuinely Belgian pastries, all made with a sweet and buttery yeast dough. They can be loaded with pearl sugar, currants, raisins, other dried fruits and nuts, or simply flavored with vanilla, cinnamon, ginger, and allspice. Each bakery specializes in their own traditional* koeken, *and they are all delicious.*

Belgian social life is inconceivable without its afternoon ritual of sitting down at a nicely set table with an array of koeken *to choose from and a pot of freshly brewed coffee. And Sunday morning simply would not be Sunday morning without the walk to a bakery for an assortment of freshly made* koeken *to bring home for the breakfast table.*

Belgian Sugar Bread

SUIKERBROOD
•
CRAQUELIN

Serve Belgian Sugar Bread on your very best china for a special breakfast or afternoon coffee. It is the queen of the brioches. The bread should be thinly sliced and spread with butter. It keeps, well wrapped, for 3 to 4 days. After that it is still very good when it is toasted.

You can make this bread by hand or use a KitchenAid mixer with the paddle attachment.

1 cup milk

1 cup water

2 ounces fresh cake yeast or 4 packages active dry yeast

7 cups all-purpose flour, plus 1 cup for kneading

2 large egg yolks

⅓ cup granulated sugar

1½ teaspoons salt

8 tablespoons (1 stick) unsalted butter, at room temperature

1 cup pearl sugar (see Note, page 256) or crushed sugar cubes, plus ¼ cup for sprinkling

1 large egg beaten with 1 teaspoon water (egg wash)

1. In a small saucepan, heat the milk and water until lukewarm, 100°F.

2. Make a starter: Dissolve the yeast in the warm milk in a large mixing bowl. Let rest for 5 minutes until foamy.

3. Add 2 cups of the flour and stir until smooth. Cover with plastic wrap or a clean kitchen towel and let rise in a warm spot (a gas oven with a pilot light is ideal) until doubled, for about 1 hour.

4. Stir down the starter and add the egg yolks, granulated sugar, salt, and the remaining 5 cups flour, 1 cup at a time. Stir with each addition until well mixed. When the dough holds together, transfer it to a lightly floured surface and knead, working in additional flour, until you get a soft, smooth, and elastic dough that does not stick, about 5 minutes. Finally knead in the butter, 1 tablespoon at a time, until it is thoroughly combined into the dough. (This will not be easy if you are working by hand, but the end result is worth it. Kneading in the butter at the end will make your bread lighter and more refined in texture and flavor.)

5. Divide the dough in half and shape each into a ball. Place each ball in its own large lightly oiled bowl, cover with a kitchen towel or plastic wrap, and let rise in a warm place until doubled in volume, about 2 hours.

6. Butter and flour two 8-inch springform pans. Punch down the dough. From each ball

of dough, pinch off a piece of dough the size of a golf ball and set aside. Divide the pearl sugar in half and work it evenly into each of the larger balls of dough. Roll out the 2 smaller balls into flat rounds that are about 1 inch larger in diameter than the larger balls of dough. Place each ball of dough on the center of the dough rounds and bring up the sides of the rolled-out round to make a sort of container for the dough balls. Place in the prepared pans. Brush with the egg wash, cover with kitchen towels, and let rise in a warm place until doubled in size, about 2 hours.

7. Preheat the oven to 375°F.

8. Before baking, score the top of the dough balls with scissors, making a circle of 1-inch-deep snips. Sprinkle with additional pearl sugar, and brush again with egg wash. Bake until nicely browned and a sharp knife inserted in the center comes out clean, 25 to 30 minutes.

9. Cool in the pans for 15 minutes. Remove the bread from the pans and cool completely on a wire rack. The bread actually improves if served the day after baking.

Makes 2 loaves

Bread in Belgium

The little country of Belgium, which has been through so many invasions and occupations by armies from other countries that it is hard to keep count, has a proverb that reflects its deep agrarian roots and pragmatic, country-folk wisdom: "As long as there is bread on the table, there is hope." In Belgium, bread is the staff of life.

We love bread in Belgium, and it is a basic part of every meal. We eat vast quantities of bread and have a huge variety available to us. The village baker and the neighborhood bakery are living and thriving institutions. Breads are baked daily, and every day you can choose from many varieties of white, sourdough, whole-wheat, multigrain, rye, raisin, and sweet breads. All the breads that you might find in France, Austria, and Germany are available in Belgium, produced by small, local bakeries. On top of that, all bakers have their own specialties, many of which draw customers from other neighborhoods and villages.

But the local baker, along with the local butcher, is so much a part of the community that they become quite like members of an extended family. They have watched their customers grow up, get married, and go on to raise their own families. Every time I come home from overseas, I visit the people who have fed my family through the years. They all know what I've been up to, of course, because my mother faithfully keeps them up to date. The wonderful sense of community is, to me, a part of the connection between good food and good living.

Flemish Cinnamon Buns

MASTELLEN
•
PETITS PAINS A LA CANNELLE

These soft, round buns, shaped like doughnuts and strongly flavored with cinnamon, are generously buttered and eaten for breakfast or as an afternoon snack with a steaming cup of coffee.

½ ounce fresh cake yeast or 1 package active
   dry yeast
4 tablespoons sugar
3½ cups all-purpose flour
1 cup plus 3 tablespoons milk, warmed
   to 100°F
1 large egg yolk
1 tablespoon ground cinnamon
1 teaspoon salt
6 tablespoons (¾ stick) unsalted butter, at room
   temperature
1 egg beaten with a pinch of salt and 1 teaspoon
   water (egg wash)

1. Whisk the yeast, 1 tablespoon of the sugar, 1 tablespoon of the flour, and the warm milk together in a small mixing bowl. Let sit for 5 minutes until foamy.

2. Sift the remaining flour into a large mixing bowl. Make a well in the center and add the yeast mixture, egg yolk, remaining 3 tablespoons sugar, the cinnamon, and salt. Use a wooden spoon to gradually work the flour into the liquid. Finally, beat in the butter. Transfer to a lightly floured surface and knead until the dough is smooth and elastic, about 5 minutes. Roll the dough into a ball. Place in a lightly oiled bowl, cover with a kitchen towel or plastic wrap, and let rise in a warm place until doubled in volume, about 1 hour.

3. Punch down the dough and remove to a lightly floured surface. Divide the dough into 16 pieces about the size of golf balls. Shape them into balls, cover with a kitchen towel, and let rise for 30 minutes.

4. Lightly butter 2 baking sheets. To shape the buns, press your thumb into the center of each ball all the way down to your work surface. Rotate the ball around your thumb to make a hole in the center, like a doughnut. Arrange the buns on the prepared baking sheets. Brush with the egg wash and let rise, uncovered, in a warm spot until doubled in volume, 1 hour.

5. Preheat the oven to 450°F.

6. Bake the buns until nicely browned on top, about 10 minutes. Remove and let cool on racks.

Makes 16 buns

Desserts

The Belgian Sweet Tooth

For centuries, painters, poets, and story-tellers have celebrated my little country, portraying it as *Luilekkerland*, literally, the country for easy, good living; a land of milk and honey. And it's possible that our devotion to our highly developed sweet tooth is responsible for this perception.

Visitors to Belgium are invariably amazed by the sheer number and variety of bakeries, pastry shops, tearooms, pancake and waffle houses, *confiseries* (candy shops), and elegant chocolate shops. Bakers and pastry chefs are virtuosos who are appreciated, even adored, by their customers, for both culinary and artistic merits (some of the displays in their shop windows are so beautiful that they might belong in a museum). Some pastry shops are as well known and honored as our historical monuments, and every town has its prestigious bakers, pastry makers, and *chocolatiers* that are a must on every tourist agenda.

The customers themselves are extraordinarily demanding. Belgians shop every day for fresh bread and other baked goods. Even for Sunday breakfast we run out early in the morning to get our pastries, still warm from the oven. Every invitation to someone's house is rewarded with a box of splendid chocolates, and every special occasion is celebrated with a well-chosen dessert.

In Belgium, we are so enamored of our history and traditions that old recipes, even those going back to medieval feasts, rarely die or fall into serious disuse. Because several volumes of recipes could be written for Flemish pastries, breads, cookies, chocolates, and other desserts, I have had to narrow my choices and have done so by eliminating the sophisticated, labor-intensive tarts, cakes, and candies that are the domain of the professional baker. Instead I have concentrated on cakes, pastries, puddings, and fruit desserts that have been a part of Belgian home cooking for hundreds of years. And, in fact, the recipes in this chapter, more than in any other in this book, come down directly from my great grandmother Marie.

A Word About Serving Desserts

The dessert is what guests will most frequently remember about the meal you serve them. And even the most diet-conscious guest will be secretly disappointed when the dinner ends with nothing but coffee. So be sure to include a dessert when planning your menu, and the meal will end with a proper crescendo. Remember that even a simple bowl of fresh fruit with a plate of cookies or a selection of good chocolates is better than nothing.

Almond Cake with Fresh Fruit Topping

AMANDEL CAKE MET ZOMER'S FRUIT
•
CAKE AUX AMANDES ET FRUITS D'ETE

*C*akes are always festive and impressive desserts, and they are perfect for large gatherings. Here is a giant cake to serve to one big happy family of relatives or friends. Despite its impressive looks, this cake is among the easiest of all desserts to make.

I like to bake cakes for summer picnics, barbecues, and large informal parties. They can be baked well in advance and frozen, or simply let stand overnight so that the flavor deepens.

Cake:

1½ cups (3 sticks) unsalted butter, at room temperature

1 cup (2 sticks) margarine, at room temperature

3 cups sugar

10 large eggs

1 tablespoon vanilla extract

4 teaspoons almond extract

3¼ cups all-purpose flour

1 cup cake flour

1 tablespoon baking powder

2¼ cups ground blanched almonds

Fruit Topping:

8 to 10 ripe peaches or nectarines, pitted and sliced into 6 to 8 wedges each, or 18 to 20 ripe plums or apricots, pitted and quartered

¼ cup sugar

¾ cup sliced almonds

Glaze:

1 cup apricot preserves

1 tablespoon fresh lemon juice

1 tablespoon water

2 tablespoons amaretto liqueur or dark rum (optional)

1. Preheat the oven to 375°F. Butter a 13 × 9-inch baking pan. Line the bottom of the pan with a double layer of buttered parchment or waxed paper.

2. In the bowl of an electric mixer, beat the butter, margarine, and sugar until light and fluffy, about 7 minutes (see Note). Beat in

the eggs one at a time, then beat in the vanilla and almond extracts. (A hand mixer will achieve the same results.)

3. Sift together the all-purpose flour, cake flour, and baking powder. Stir into the egg mixture with a wooden spoon, ¼ cup at a time. Stir in the ground almonds.

4. Pour the batter into the prepared pan and use a spatula to spread it evenly. Add the fruit topping: Arrange the fruit on top of the batter in slightly overlapping rows. Sprinkle with ¼ cup sugar and the sliced almonds.

5. Bake the cake in the middle of the oven until a knife inserted in the center comes out clean, about 1 hour. (If you are using an aluminum pan, it's a good idea to set it on a baking sheet while baking to prevent the cake from scorching on the bottom.)

6. Cool for 15 minutes while you make the glaze. Bring the preserves, lemon juice, and water to a quick boil in a small saucepan. Remove from the heat and press through a strainer or purée in a blender or food processor. Flavor with the liqueur, if using, and brush evenly over the cake. Cool completely and serve the cake directly from the pan.

Serves 15 to 20

Note: If you are using a hand mixer, beat for 3 minutes, then turn off the mixer and let it rest for 3 minutes before continuing to mix. This will prevent the mixer from overheating.

Jeanne's Dried Fruit and Nut Cake

JEANNE'S CAKE MET GECONFYT FRUIT

•

CAKE AUX FRUIT CONFITS DE JEANNE

My grandmother Jeanne, who was always doing 10 things at once, also entertained continuously. She could not conceive of offering coffee or tea to someone without "a little something to nibble on." This light and luscious teacake was a particular favorite of hers. Not only is it quick and easy to put together, but the longer it's kept, the better it tastes, as the flavors mellow and mature.

Cake:
½ cup currants
2 tablespoons Cognac or dark rum
8 tablespoons (1 stick) unsalted butter,
   at room temperature
⅔ cup sugar
3 large eggs, separated
½ teaspoon vanilla extract
1 cup plus 1 tablespoon all-purpose
   flour
1 teaspoon baking powder
½ cup mixed candied fruit, diced
Pinch of salt

Topping:
2 tablespoons apricot preserves
2 tablespoons Cognac, rum, or
   water
2 tablespoons slivered almonds, toasted
   (page 17)

1. Soak the currants in the Cognac for at least 1 hour.

2. Preheat the oven to 400°F. Butter a 9 × 5-inch loaf pan, line the bottom with parchment paper, and butter the paper, or use a loaf pan with a nonstick surface.

3. In the bowl of an electric mixer, beat the butter and sugar until light and fluffy, about 4 minutes. Beat in the egg yolks, one at a time, then beat in the vanilla extract.

4. Sift the flour and baking powder together. Stir into the egg mixture in two or three additions. Stir in the diced candied fruits and the currants with the Cognac.

5. Using clean dry beaters, beat the egg whites together with the salt to soft peaks. Fold into the batter with a spatula.

6. Spoon the batter into the prepared loaf pan and bake for 10 minutes. Use the back of a knife to make an incision lengthwise down the middle of the loaf. This will help achieve an even rising. Reduce the oven heat to 325°F and bake until a toothpick inserted in the center comes out clean, 35 to 40 minutes. If the top of the cake starts to get too brown while baking, cover loosely with aluminum foil.

7. Cool the cake in the pan for 10 minutes before removing it to a wire rack to cool completely.

8. For the topping, mix the apricot jam with the Cognac and press it through a strainer.

9. When the cake is completely cooled, use a pastry brush to glaze the top of the cake with the apricot mixture. Decorate with the toasted slivered almonds.

Makes 1 cake

Spiced Brown Beer Cake with Dried Fruit and Nuts

B R U I N   B I E R   F R U I T   C A K E
• C A K E   A U X   F R U I T S   S E C S   A   L A   B I E R E   B R U N E

This dense, old-fashioned cake, loaded with fruits and nuts, gets its deep, mysterious flavor from the addition of dark brown beer. Traditionally one would use Belgian Faro, a spontaneously fermented beer, which is aged for two years in oak casks, then blended with top-fermented wheat beer. This dry and hoppy beer with its subtle hints of spices is ideal to serve with desserts. Naturally this cake should be served with some of the same beer that goes into it. Because it keeps so well, this is a very good cake to give as a gift. It can easily be sent, well wrapped, through the mail.

1½ cups whole-wheat flour
½ cup all-purpose flour
½ teaspoon ground ginger
½ teaspoon ground cinnamon
1 teaspoon baking soda
½ teaspoon salt
12 tablespoons (1½ sticks) unsalted butter, at room temperature
1¼ cups (firmly packed) dark brown sugar
4 large eggs
1 teaspoon vanilla extract
1 cup currants or raisins
½ cup dried apricots, cut into thin slivers
⅔ cup candied red cherries or dried cherries
¾ cup walnuts, coarsely chopped
¼ cup dark brown beer, preferably Faro, Pertotale ale, or a dark Abbey beer

1. Preheat the oven to 350°F. Butter a 10-inch tube pan or 9 × 5-inch loaf pan, line the bottom with parchment paper and butter the paper.

2. Sift together the whole-wheat flour, all-purpose flour, ginger, cinnamon, baking soda, and salt into a large mixing bowl.

3. In the bowl of an electric mixer, beat the butter and brown sugar until light and fluffy, about 7 minutes (see Note, page 270). Beat in the eggs, one at a time, then the vanilla extract.

4. Stir in the flour mixture, about ½ cup at a time, until blended. Stir in the fruit and nuts and, finally, stir in the beer.

5. Spoon the batter into the prepared pan. Bake until a toothpick inserted into the center comes out clean, 50 minutes to one hour.

6. Cool the cake in the pan for 10 minutes before removing it to a wire rack to cool completely. Wrap in plastic and store at room temperature for up to 10 days. The fruit will keep this cake moist.

Serves 12

Flemish Almond Cookies

AMANDEL BROODJES
•
TARTINES FLAMANDES

These wonderful cookies are the Flemish version of Italian macaroons. They are shaped in rectangles and are meant to resemble a *tartine*, a Flemish slice of the daily bread. The slivered almonds on top impart an extra crunchiness to these easy-to-make cookies.

Peeling Almonds

Drop the almonds into plenty of boiling water, boil 2 minutes, and drain. Pinch each almond with your fingers and the peel will slip off easily. Spread the blanched almonds on paper towels and let dry thoroughly. This is best done a day or two before using the almonds, so they have time to completely dry out. In recipes such as the one for macaroons, damp almonds will not absorb enough of the egg white.

1½ cups whole blanched (peeled) almonds
   (see above)
1 tablespoon all-purpose flour
½ teaspoon almond extract
5 large egg whites, at room temperature
   (see Note)
Pinch of salt
1 cup sugar
¾ cup slivered almonds

1. Place an oven rack in the center of the oven and preheat the oven to 375°F. Line 2 cookie sheets with parchment paper.

2. Grind the almonds to a fine powder in a food processor. Add the flour and almond extract and pulse until well combined.

3. Beat the egg whites with the salt to stiff

peaks. Using a rubber spatula, gently fold in the sugar and the ground almond mixture, in alternating batches, to make a rather stiff dough.

4. Use 2 tablespoons to drop large mounds (golf ball-size) of the dough onto the prepared cookie sheets. Use the back of your spoon to spread each mound into a rectangle 3 inches long, 1½ inch wide, and about ¼ inch thick, leaving at least 3 inches between cookies. Sprinkle the cookies with the slivered almonds.

5. Bake in the middle of the oven until the cookies are lightly browned around the edges but only lightly colored in the centers, 17 to 20 minutes. Use a metal spatula to immedi-

ately remove the cookies to a wire rack. If the cookies stick to the paper, pour a little water under the paper onto the hot cookie sheet, so that the steam loosens the cookies. Allow the cookies to cool completely and store in an airtight container up to several weeks or freeze up to 3 months.

Makes 12 cookies

Note: What about the yolks from all those eggs? Well, my grandmother would always whip up a crème Anglaise (page 295) to serve with some baked apples or poached pears for a quick and elegant dessert.

Almonds

In Belgium, confections made with almonds are as old as the medieval cobblestones that pave the streets. Medieval cookery made prodigious use of them: Almond milk, (pounded almonds, sugar, and water) often replaced cow's milk in recipes, and pounded almonds were used to thicken soups and sauces. But most of all, almonds quickly became indispensable in making candies, cakes, and other sweets.

In 1485 the town of Brugge presented the Holy Roman Emperor Maximilian I with a gift of sweets that included, among other goodies, 8 pounds of marzipan. In those days, it was the custom to present visiting foreign dignitaries with a basket of confections, perhaps to sweeten the forthcoming political discussions.

Today in Belgium we still give and receive gifts of sweets with what might seem to outsiders as shocking frequency. Quite simply, one never arrives empty-handed for even the most casual visit with friends or family. One always stops at the local confiserie (candy shop) and purchases a small box, elegantly wrapped and beribboned, of chocolates, fine pralines, or marzipan.

But perhaps the most beloved almond confection of all are the sugared almonds known as suikerbonen *or* dragées. *These are almonds covered with hard casings of pastel-colored sugar. They have been popular for hundreds of years and are still a favorite. Tradition lives on in the custom of offering sugared almonds to family and friends whenever a newborn baby is welcomed into the world as a symbol of shared happiness.*

Flemish Macaroons

MACARONS

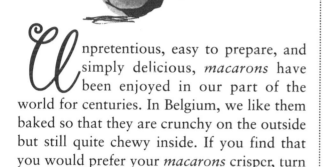

Unpretentious, easy to prepare, and simply delicious, *macarons* have been enjoyed in our part of the world for centuries. In Belgium, we like them baked so that they are crunchy on the outside but still quite chewy inside. If you find that you would prefer your *macarons* crisper, turn off the oven and let them dry out in the oven (with the door closed) for a while longer.

These cookies are very useful to have on hand for flavoring puddings or *vlaais* (see Index for recipes).

*1 cup whole blanched (peeled) almonds
   (see Box, page 273)*
3/4 cup sugar
2 large egg whites
*1/2 teaspoon almond
   extract*
*1/2 teaspoon rose water
   or orange extract (optional)*

1. Preheat the oven to 350°F. Line 2 cookie sheets with parchment paper.

2. Grind the almonds to a fine powder in a food processor. Add the sugar and pulse a few times until combined. Transfer to a mixing bowl. Add the egg whites, almond extract, and rose water, if using. Use a rubber spatula to combine all the ingredients. You should have a rather sticky dough that is stiff enough to drop in small mounds onto the cookie sheet.

3. Drop rounded teaspoonfuls of the mixture onto the prepared cookie sheets, leaving at least 3 inches between mounds.

4. Bake until light brown, 15 to 20 minutes. The insides of the cookies should remain soft and chewy.

5. Immediately remove the cookies with a metal spatula to cool on a wire rack. If the cookies are sticking to the paper, pour a little bit of water under the parchment paper onto the cookie sheet. The steam should loosen the cookies.

6. When the cookies are completely cooled, store them in an airtight container, where they will keep for several weeks, or freeze them for up to 3 months.

Makes about 24 cookies

Variation: Replace the almonds with the same amount of unsweetened shredded coconut to make another favorite Belgian cookie called rochers, *or coconut rocks.*

Flemish Spice Cookies

SPECULOOS

*S*peculoos are probably among the oldest cookies Belgians have in their repertoire. They are said to go back to pre-Christian times, when they were small cakes, baked in the shapes of animals or humans, that were offered to the gods in lieu of the real thing. Today they are usually associated with St. Nicholas and are baked in his honor. But the truth is that these thin, crisp, buttery cookies are very popular in Belgium all year round. They are often served with a cup of coffee and are a staple on the breakfast table.

There are many recipes in Belgium for these cookies, and we can even purchase a prepared spice mixture of cinnamon, ginger, nutmeg, and cloves, called *koekkruiden*, which gives this cookie its particular flavor. The recipe here is for a simplified homemade version of *speculoos*.

8 tablespoons (1 stick) unsalted butter, at room temperature
¾ cup dark brown sugar
1 large egg
1 cup all-purpose flour
¼ cup cake flour
¼ teaspoon salt
1 teaspoon baking soda
1 teaspoon ground cinnamon
½ teaspoon ground ginger
Pinch of ground cloves or nutmeg

1. Beat the butter and sugar in a mixing bowl with a wire whisk or an electric mixer until light and fluffy, 3 to 5 minutes. Stir in the egg.

2. Sift the two flours with the salt, baking soda, cinnamon, ginger, and cloves into another mixing bowl.

3. Stir the flour mixture into the creamed butter with a spatula until just combined to make a soft, smooth dough. Do not overwork the dough. Roll into a ball and wrap in plastic wrap. Refrigerate for at least 12 hours or overnight to develop the flavor.

4. Preheat the oven to 350°F. Line 2 cookie sheets with aluminum foil and butter the foil generously.

5. Roll out the dough ⅛ inch thick between 2 sheets of plastic wrap or on a cold, marble surface. If the dough becomes too sticky and difficult to handle, put it in the freezer for a few minutes until the butter hardens again.

6. Use a sharp knife or a cookie cutter to cut the dough into 3 × 2-inch rectangles. Use a metal spatula to place them about 1 inch apart on the lined cookie sheets.

7. Bake until golden brown, 10 to 12 minutes. Watch them—they burn quickly. Transfer to a wire rack and cool. The cookies will keep in an airtight container for several weeks.

Makes about 20 cookies

Variation: Follow the recipe through step 6. Sprinkle the cookies with lightly toasted sliced almonds and press the nuts lightly into the dough. Bake as directed.

Traditional Speculoos

In Belgium, speculoos are still made by shaping them in wooden molds into decorative animal and human forms. You can find beautifully carved examples of these molds in museums, but you can also purchase replicas in specialty cooking stores. If you should be lucky enough to get one of these forms, here's how to use it: Dust the mold lightly with flour. Roll the dough onto the mold, pressing it into the carved-out portions. Cut away the excess dough with a sharp knife. (Gather the dough scraps up and roll out again.) Turn the mold upside down and give it a sharp tap to unmold the cookies onto the cookie sheets.

Lace Cookies from Brugge

BRUGGE KLETSKOPPEN
•
KLETSKOPPEN DE BRUGES

This is a very old recipe for a crisp almond cookie that is thought to resemble the fine, delicate lace that made Brugge famous. They are delicious with ice cream or simply as an accompaniment to coffee or tea.

5 tablespoons unsalted butter, at room
  temperature
1 cup dark brown sugar
½ cup all-purpose flour
3 tablespoons
  finely chopped
  almonds or
  hazelnuts

Teatime

In Belgium, every city, large and small, and every village has tearooms or pâtisseries serving freshly baked waffles and pancakes, their own ice creams, and an array of pastries. Along the Belgian coast, one finds the highest concentration of these tearooms, many of them with outdoor terraces studded with colorful umbrellas.

A visit to a tearoom or pâtisserie is an afternoon social event. Here you will find

chatty elderly widows and their friends, proud grandmothers showing off their grandchildren, families restoring themselves after a day of shopping or sightseeing, groups of young people, and pairs of lovers, young and old.

You have to possess an iron self-control to resist the heavenly smells of freshly brewed coffee and baking waffles that waft out into the street as you pass by. And very few Belgians do resist, because here they can indulge in their favorite pastimes—enjoying good food, enjoying their friends, and enjoying life!

1. Beat the butter and sugar with an electric mixer until light and fluffy, about 3 minutes.

2. Sift the flour and gradually stir it into the butter mixture to make a smooth dough. Fold in the finely chopped nuts. Remove to a lightly floured surface and lightly knead the dough until smooth, about 1 minute.

3. Shape the dough into a log, 1½ to 2 inches in diameter. Wrap tightly in aluminum foil and refrigerate overnight (a minimum of 12 hours is best).

4. Preheat the oven to 350°F. Line 2 baking sheets with aluminum foil and butter the foil generously. (As an alternative, you can bake these cookies on nonstick baking sheets.)

5. With a sharp knife, slice the dough as thinly as possible and arrange the rounds 2 inches apart on the prepared cookie sheets. Bake until nicely browned around the edges, 3 to 4 minutes.

6. Let the cookies harden on the cookie sheets for about 1 minute, then remove them with a spatula to a wire rack. You will have to work quickly as the cookies become very brittle as they cool. If the cookies cool and stick to the aluminum foil, return them to the warm oven for a few seconds.

Makes about 50 cookies

Flemish Yeast Dough for Pie Crust

GISTDEEG OP Z'N VLAAMS
•
PATE A LA LEVURE

This versatile and unusual yeast dough is much easier to work with than a regular pâte brisée or pie crust. Easy to roll, patch, and stretch, it has many advantages, not the least of which is its lower fat content. The final result is a light, crisp, and yeasty crust that melts in the mouth. No wonder this is the favorite dough of Belgian home cooks, one of whom is said to have invented it when she had some leftover *koekebrood deeg*, a kind of brioche dough. With frugal intentions and clever ingenuity she used the yeast dough to make a delicious fruit tart.

You can make this dough easily by hand, or even more quickly in a food processor. I have given directions for both methods.

½ ounce fresh cake yeast or 1 package active dry yeast
¼ cup milk, warmed to 100°F
1½ cups all-purpose flour, plus an additional ½ cup if needed
¼ cup sugar
Pinch of salt
1 large egg, lightly beaten
2½ tablespoons unsalted butter, melted

By hand:

1. Sprinkle the yeast over the milk in a small bowl. Let sit until foamy, about 5 minutes. Stir well.

2. Sift the flour into a large mixing bowl. Add the sugar and salt and combine the dry ingredients with a whisk. Make a well in the center. Pour in the egg, yeast mixture, and butter. Use your fingertips to gradually work the flour into the liquid ingredients until you have a smooth, soft dough that holds together. Add just enough flour to make a dough that does not stick to your fingers and can be rolled out easily. Do not knead or overwork this dough or it will become tough.

3. Form the dough into a ball and place it in a large, lightly oiled bowl. Cover with a kitchen towel or plastic wrap and let rise in a warm spot until doubled in volume, about 1 hour. (An oven with a pilot light is ideal, or preheat your electric oven for about 10 minutes at the lowest possible setting and turn it off.)

By food processor:

1. Proof the yeast as described above in step 1.

2. Fit the food processor with the plastic blade. Place the flour, sugar, and salt in the food processor and pulse a few times to combine the ingredients. With the motor running, add the egg, yeast mixture, and melted butter. Stop and remove the dough as soon as it forms a ball. Knead it briefly and gently on a lightly floured surface, adding just enough flour so that it does not stick to your fingers and can be rolled out easily.

3. Form the dough into a ball and place in a large, lightly oiled bowl. Cover with a kitchen towel or plastic wrap and let rise in a warm spot until doubled in volume, about 1 hour.

Rolling out the dough:

1. Generously butter and flour one 12-inch or 8-inch tart pan.

2. Punch down the dough and remove to a lightly floured surface. Roll the dough into a round, about ¼ inch thick. For a thinner crust, divide the dough in half and roll out into 2 rounds, ⅛ inch thick.

3. Drape the dough over your rolling pin and transfer to the prepared tart pan. Fit the dough into the pan; trim and crimp the edges. Prick holes on the bottom of the tart with a fork. Cover with a kitchen towel and let the dough rise again for 20 to 30 minutes before filling and baking.

Makes one 12-inch or two 8-inch crusts

Note: Tart pans with removable bottoms are the best baking pans to use for all the tarts. Allow the baked tarts to cool for about 15 minutes, then place the tart pan on top of a jar or can. Loosen the sides gently with a knife until the side of the pan falls away.

Variation: Add 1 teaspoon cinnamon to the dry ingredients for a cinnamon-scented crust.

Cinnamon-Scented Prune Tart

PRUIMENTAART MET EEN SNUIFJE KANEEL

•

TARTE AUX PRUNEAUX A LA CANELLE

I was surprised to discover that in this country, prunes are considered essentially a health food and a laxative and have something of an odd reputation. In Belgium, where dried fruits of every sort—raisins, currants, apricots, and prunes—are considered winter delicacies and have been much in favor since the Middle Ages, prunes are thought to be the most luscious and elegant of all. This cognac-flavored, cinnamon-scented tart is a winner and very simple to make.

½ pound pitted prunes
¾ cup water
½ cup plus 1 tablespoon sugar
1 cinnamon stick (2 inches long)
Flemish Yeast Dough, cinnamon variation
  (page 279)
1 tablespoon dark rum or
  Cognac
Whipped cream flavored with cinnamon,
  for serving

1. Place the prunes, water, ½ cup sugar, and the cinnamon stick in a small saucepan. Bring to a boil and reduce the heat to low. Simmer, covered, for 1 hour. Stir occasionally to prevent sticking and add a little more water if the prunes get too dry. Remove from the heat, discard the cinnamon stick, and let cool.

2. Preheat the oven to 325°F.

3. Roll out the dough into a circle, ¼ inch thick, and transfer it to the prepared pan. Press the dough into the pan, trim and crimp the edges, and prick holes in the bottom with a fork. Cover with a clean kitchen towel or plastic wrap and let rise for 20 minutes in a warm spot.

4. When the prunes have cooled to lukewarm, purée in a blender or food processor. Stir in the rum.

5. Spread the prune mixture evenly over the dough and sprinkle with the remaining 1 tablespoon sugar.

6. Bake until the pastry is nicely browned, 20 to 25 minutes. Serve lukewarm with a dollop of with cinnamon-flavored whipped cream.

Makes one 12-inch tart

Grandmother's Sugar Tart

GROOTMOEDER'S SUIKERTAART

•

LA TARTE AU SUCRE DE GRAND-MERE

The simplicity of the ingredients do not convey the utter delectability of this homey tart. Definitely a winter specialty, there is absolutely nothing like a house filled with the sweet and yeasty aromas of my grandmother's sugar tart. Serve it with coffee or hot chocolate to cold and tired friends and watch them relax and revive. In the summer I like to serve this sugar tart with fresh berries, sliced peaches, or even melon.

3/4 cup dark brown sugar
3 tablespoons finely ground
 almonds
2 large eggs
1/2 cup heavy (or whipping) cream
1 teaspoon vanilla extract
3 tablespoons unsalted butter, cold,
 cut into small pieces
Flemish Yeast Dough (page 279)

1. Preheat the oven to 450°F. Generously butter and flour a 10-inch tart pan with a removable bottom.

2. Roll out the dough in a circle, 1/4 inch thick, and line the tart pan with it. Press the dough into the tart pan and trim and crimp the edges. Prick holes in the bottom with a fork. Cover with a kitchen towel and let rise for 20 minutes in a warm spot.

3. Combine the sugar and almonds in a small bowl. In another bowl, whisk together the eggs, cream, and vanilla.

4. Sprinkle two-thirds of the almond mixture over the dough. Cover with the egg mixture and sprinkle with the remaining almond mixture. Dot the surface with the butter.

5. Bake the tart in the lower third of the oven for 8 minutes. Reduce the heat to 300°F and

bake until the custard is set, 12 to 15 minutes longer. Remove from the oven and let cool. Serve lukewarm for the best taste.

Makes one 10-inch tart

Food and Art

I remember tramping into my grandmother's cottage with muddy boots, burning cheeks, runny nose, fingertips numb with cold, and a hunger as big as a mountain, to inhale, suddenly, the heady aroma of vanilla, sugar, and yeast. The smell was overpowering and almost made me giddy with happy anticipation. Mixed with the warm, sweet smells were always a slight acidic tinge of turpentine emanating from her painting studio behind the kitchen. Somehow my grandmother's cooking was always mixed in my senses with her paints, brushes, and canvases. Everywhere one looked in her house, the walls were covered with paintings—a still life, a flower arrangement, a winter landscape, all in her own impressionistic style. In the kitchen itself, she kept her easel with her latest canvas, so that while cooking she could continue to consider color combinations and shadings of light. And so food and art remain inextricably linked in my mind to this day.

Rhubarb and Strawberry Meringue Tart

RABARBER EN AARDBEIEN
TAART

•

TARTE A LA RHUBARBE
ET FRAISES

Rhubarb, which grows in healthy patch-es in many kitchen gardens in Belgium and sometimes escapes to grow wild in the countryside, seemed a magical plant in my childhood. The sheer size of the stalks and par-ticularly the leaves was impressive, and as chil-dren we would often pluck a stalk and use the huge leaf as an improvised umbrella. I even recall when I was very small and in a game of hide-and-seek, tucking myself under a particu-larly lush patch of rhubarb leaves—a very suc-cessful hiding place. There was also the added thrill of knowing that the stalks were edible, if very tart in their uncooked, unsugared state, but that the leaves were very poisonous. I remember thirsty afternoons when my friends and I would break off a stalk and chew on it, making a contest out of who could do this the longest without making a face from the tart puckerings in our mouths.

The first long, hot, lazy days of summer brought with them the refreshing tangy taste of rhubarb. My great grandmother often served a simple rhubarb compote to be eaten with a little heavy cream or as a topping for vanilla ice cream. And when the strawberries ripened, it was time for the classic pairing of the sweet berries with the rhubarb in this wonderful tart.

Tart:
Flemish Yeast Dough (page 279)
1 large egg yolk mixed with 1 tablespoon
water (egg wash)
1½ pounds rhubarb stalks without
leaves
¾ cup sugar
¼ cup water
½ teaspoon vanilla extract

Meringue:
2 large egg whites
½ teaspoon vanilla extract
⅓ cup sugar

1 pint strawberries, hulled

1. Generously butter and flour a 10-inch tart pan. Roll out the dough into a circle, ¼ inch thick, and transfer it to the prepared pan. Press the dough into the pan, trim and crimp the edges, and prick holes in the bottom with a fork. Brush the bottom and sides with the egg wash to seal it. Cover with a kitchen towel and let rise in a warm spot for 20 minutes.

2. Preheat the oven to 375°F.

3. Bring a large pot of water to a boil. Trim the root ends of the rhubarb and peel the tougher stalks with a vegetable peeler. Slice into 1-inch pieces. Blanch for 2 minutes in the boiling water and drain.

4. Heat the sugar and ¼ cup water in a medium-size heavy saucepan over medium heat, stirring occasionally, until the mixture becomes a syrup that is light caramel in color, 10 to 15 minutes. Add the rhubarb and vanilla. Simmer, uncovered, stirring occasionally, until thickened and smooth, about 15 minutes. Remove from the heat and set aside.

5. Prepare the meringue: In a clean, dry bowl, beat the egg whites to soft peaks. Beat in the vanilla extract and the sugar, 1 tablespoon at a time, and continue beating until the egg whites have formed stiff peaks.

6. Spoon the rhubarb compote into the pastry shell. Slice the strawberries and arrange on top of the rhubarb. Use a spatula to spread the meringue evenly over the fruit.

7. Bake until the dough is set and the meringue is evenly browned, 25 minutes. Cool to room temperature and serve.

Makes one 10-inch tart

Belgian Tart with Fresh Summer Fruit

ZOMERSE VRUCHTENTAART
•
TARTE AUX FRUITS FRAIS D'ETE

Show off the best of summer's fruits in this lovely, comforting tart. Choose your fruit from what looks best at the market. If one fruit looks spectacular and everything else looks pale, stick to the good-looking one. If it's the end of the summer and everything looks great, combine the fruits as you like. Once you try this easy Belgian fruit tart, you may never go back to making regular pie crust again.

Tart:
2 pounds summer fruit: pitted sweet cherries; apricots, plums, peaches, or nectarines, peeled if necessary, pitted, and halved or quartered; fresh red currants; or combination of two or more fruits
1¼ cups sugar
2 tablespoons all-purpose flour
1 teaspoon ground cinnamon
Flemish Yeast Dough (page 279)
1 large egg lightly beaten together with 1½ tablespoons sugar (egg wash)

Glaze:

2 tablespoons sugar
1 tablespoon red currant jelly
½ teaspoon cornstarch
1 tablespoon cold water

1. In a large bowl, mix the fruit with the sugar, flour, and cinnamon. Transfer the fruit to a colander set over a bowl to collect the juices. Let drain for 30 minutes.

2. Preheat the oven to 375°F. Generously butter and flour two 8-inch tart pans with removable bottoms.

3. Divide the dough in half and roll out each half into a circle, ¼ inch thick. Line the prepared pans with the dough. Press into the pans and trim and crimp the edges. Prick holes in the bottom with a fork and brush with the egg wash. Cover with a kitchen towel and let rise in a warm spot for 20 minutes.

4. Fill the tart shells with the fruit. (Reserve the drained fruit juices.) Brush the sides of the pastry with egg wash.

5. Bake until the crust is slightly browned, 25 minutes. Remove from the oven and let cool for 15 minutes or so before removing the sides of the pans.

6. Prepare the glaze: Place the reserved fruit juices, the sugar, and red currant jelly in a small pan and bring to a boil over medium heat. Dissolve the cornstarch in the cold water, add to the pan, and cook, stirring constantly, until thickened, about 1 minute. Remove from the heat. Spoon the glaze over the fruit tart to give it a shine. Serve warm or at room temperature.

Makes two 8-inch tarts

Deep-Dish Custard Pie with a Praline Topping

VLAAMSE FLAN MET NOOTJES
• FLAN A LA BRESILIENNE

In the year 779 this dessert was served to the monks in St. Peter's Abbey in my hometown of Ghent and recorded in the household records. Today in homes across Ghent and other parts of Belgium, it is still a popular, old-fashioned pastry that appears regularly to please and satisfy our craving for a sweet and satisfying dessert. The custard filling is light, airy, and feels like silk on the tongue. It can be served simply, dusted with confectioners' sugar, or dressed up with a final flourish of whipped cream and a crunchy dusting of praline powder.

Custard:
4 cups milk
1 package (3½ ounces) vanilla pudding mix
1¼ cups granulated sugar
5 large eggs, at room temperature,
   separated
½ cup all-purpose flour
Pinch of salt
Flemish Yeast Dough (page 279)

Topping (optional):
1 cup heavy (or whipping) cream
2 tablespoons confectioners' sugar
1 cup Praline Powder
   (recipe follows)

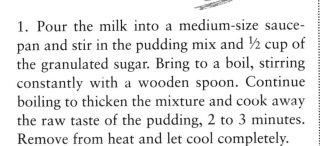

1. Pour the milk into a medium-size saucepan and stir in the pudding mix and ½ cup of the granulated sugar. Bring to a boil, stirring constantly with a wooden spoon. Continue boiling to thicken the mixture and cook away the raw taste of the pudding, 2 to 3 minutes. Remove from heat and let cool completely.

2. Preheat the oven to 350°F. Butter and flour two 9-inch deep pie plates or 9-inch springform pans.

3. With an electric mixer, beat the egg yolks with the remaining ¾ cup sugar until light and fluffy. Sift the flour over the egg yolks and fold gently to mix. Finally stir into the cooled pudding mixture.

4. Beat the egg whites with the salt to stiff peaks, then fold them carefully into the pudding mixture.

5. Divide the dough in half and roll out each half into a circle, ¼ inch thick. Line the prepared pans with the dough. Press the dough into the pans, trim and crimp the edges, and prick holes in the bottom with a fork. Fill each pastry shell with the custard so it comes two-thirds of the way up the sides. Place in the oven and use a ladle to distribute the remaining custard. Do not overfill, or the custard will spill out into the hot oven.

6. Bake for 20 minutes. Place a cold baking sheet under the pans. If the custard looks very brown on top, cover loosely with aluminum foil. Bake until the custard is set and a toothpick inserted into the center comes out clean, 5 to 10 minutes more. Let cool completely before adding the topping.

7. For the topping, beat the cream with the confectioners' sugar until stiff peaks form. Apply a thin layer of the whipped cream to each custard pie and even it out with a spatula. Sprinkle evenly with the praline powder. Serve at room temperature.

Makes two 9-inch pies

Praline Powder

PRALINE

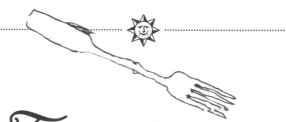

✻

½ cup blanched whole almonds (see Box, page 273) or skinned hazelnuts or a combination
½ cup sugar
1 tablespoon fresh lemon juice

1. Preheat the oven to 350°F.

2. Spread the nuts on a baking sheet and toast for 10 minutes. Remove and let cool somewhat. Turn off the oven. Clean the baking sheet and coat lightly with vegetable oil.

3. Combine the sugar with the lemon juice in a nonstick, heavy, medium-size saucepan. Cook over medium heat, stirring constantly, until the sugar melts and comes to a boil. Stop stirring and continue to boil until the sugar caramelizes to a golden amber color (370°F on a candy thermometer), 5 to 7 minutes. Immediately add the warm nuts and stir until the nuts are completely covered with the caramel. Pour onto the prepared baking sheet and let cool until hardened.

4. Break the praline into pieces and process in the food processor to a coarse powder. Be careful not to overprocess the praline or the powder will turn into a paste.

5. Store praline powder in an airtight jar in the refrigerator. (Sprinkle as a topping for ice cream, puddings, and even fruit salad.)

Makes 1 cup

Flemish Vlaai Tart with Maine Blueberries

VLAAI MET BOSBESSEN
•
LE VLAAI AUX MYRTILLES

✻

This *vlaai* might be called a blueberry-cheese-custard tart, as it combines the best elements of all these, with the additional flavoring of almonds from the macaroons. Whatever you call it, it is simple to make and a lovely, unusual dessert.

In Belgium you can find this type of *vlaai* using different types of fruit in the filling, depending on the season and the region. In De Kempen (the northeastern corner of Belgium bordering the Netherlands) bakers favor the use of sweet and/or sour cherries, which makes a wonderful tart. You could use drained canned cherries when the fresh are not available. In the absence of cherries or blueberries, consider using apples, apricots, peaches, or plums.

Flemish Yeast Dough (page 279)
1 cup Homemade Fresh Cheese (page 22)
   or ricotta
1/3 cup heavy (or whipping) cream
1 cup confectioners' sugar
1/2 cup crushed Flemish Macaroons (page 275)
   or Italian amaretti cookies
4 large eggs
1 pint blueberries, preferably the tiny, wild
   berries from Maine, picked over and rinsed
Confectioners' sugar, for garnish

1. Preheat the oven to 350°F. Generously butter and flour a 10-inch tart pan.

2. Roll out the dough into a circle, 1/4 inch thick. Line the prepared pan with the dough. Press the dough into the pan, trim and crimp the edges, and prick holes in the bottom with a fork. Cover with a kitchen towel and let rise in a warm spot for 20 minutes.

3. Place the fresh cheese in a food processor and process until smooth. Add the cream, sugar, macaroons, and the eggs, pulsing to combine after each addition.

4. Pour half the custard mixture into the tart crust. Spread the blueberries evenly over the surface and cover with the remaining custard.

5. Bake in the lower third of the oven until the custard is set, 40 to 50 minutes. The fruit in the center will keep the custard moist. Remove and cool on a wire rack. Serve lukewarm or cold, dusted with confectioners' sugar.

Serves 6 to 8

Flemish Rice Custard Pie

VLAAMSE RYSTTAART

•

TARTE AU RIZ A LA FLAMANDE

Take the simplest and most available ingredients and turn them into a soul-satisfying, mouth-watering dessert—that is the magic of most honest country cooks. This is the tradition that has been kept alive in Belgium for centuries, and in this recipe it manifests itself in a crisp yeast-dough pastry filled with a vanilla-scented creamy rice custard. It is worlds away from any of the dreary rice pudding you might have had before, and in my country, *vlaamse rÿsttaart* is the pride of many local village bakeries and home cooks. Serve this tart for dessert after a light meal or as a filling snack on its own. In Belgium we have a tradition of the 4:00 P.M. coffee hour, and *rÿsttaart* is perfect for this occasion. When I was a college student, this was a favorite late-night hunger killer.

4 cups milk
3/4 cup long-grain rice, rinsed and
     drained
Pinch of salt
1 tablespoon packaged vanilla pudding mix
1/2 cup granulated sugar
1 teaspoon vanilla extract or 1/4 teaspoon
     ground cinnamon
Flemish Yeast Dough (page 279)
3 large eggs, at room temperature
Confectioners' sugar, for garnish

1. Pour all but 3 tablespoons of the milk into a large heavy saucepan. Save the 3 tablespoons milk in a small bowl. Add the rice and salt to the pan. Bring to a simmer over medium heat, stirring occasionally to keep the grains separate. Watch the milk carefully so it does not boil over. Reduce the heat to very low, cover, and simmer gently until the rice is tender, about 30 minutes. Do not stir the rice during this part of the cooking. When the rice is done and has absorbed all the milk, remove from the heat but keep covered.

2. Dissolve the pudding mix in the reserved 3 tablespoons milk. Stir into the rice mixture together with the granulated sugar and vanilla extract. Return the mixture to a simmer and cook, stirring constantly, for 2 minutes over medium heat until this custard is smooth and thickened. Remove from the heat and let cool to lukewarm.

3. Preheat the oven to 350°F. Generously butter and flour two 8-inch pie pans.

4. Divide the dough in half and roll out each half into a circle, 1/4 inch thick. Line the prepared pans with the dough. Press into the pans and trim and crimp the edges. Prick holes in the bottom with a fork. Cover with a towel and let rise in a warm spot for 20 minutes.

5. Separate the eggs and stir the egg yolks, one at a time, into the rice custard. In a clean bowl, beat the egg whites to soft peaks; gently fold into the rice custard.

6. Divide the rice custard evenly between the 2 pie shells. Bake until puffed up and golden brown, 25 to 30 minutes. Dust with the confectioners' sugar and serve warm or at room temperature. The pies can be stored, well wrapped, in a cool place for up to 1 week.

Makes two 8-inch tarts

Variation: For special occasions, a crunchy almond topping dresses up this homey tart. Crush enough macaroons (preferably homemade, see Index) or amaretti cookies with a rolling pin to make about 1/2 cup. Stir into 1 lightly beaten egg white and drizzle this mixture evenly over the rice tarts before baking.

Golden Rice Custard

R Y S T P A P
•
R I Z - A U - L A I T

My paternal grandfather, Charles, who lived in the same house with me all through my childhood and youth, was the cook who taught me to prepare this favorite golden rice custard. It was the celebration food of his childhood, and I loved to hear him tell stories about the kermis festivities in Flemish villages long ago. In days when there was no television, no radio, not even movie theaters, the colorful pageantry of a village kermis was almost as good as a three-ring circus to a small child. And sweet, filling bowls of *rÿstpap* were always a part of these celebrations. The saffron, which turns *rÿstpap* to a jewel-like gold color, was rare and expensive so that it was most often a privilege of the rich and powerful. My grandfather mused upon the changes that had come about in his lifetime and how saffron, once a symbol of opulence and wealth, was now so easily available to him.

This is such a popular dish in Belgium that we have an old saying: "In heaven, one eats *rÿstpap* with golden spoons." Fortunately,

with this recipe from my grandfather Charles, we can all have a little bit of heaven right here on earth.

Serve the *rÿstpap* sprinkled with brown sugar or with any of the poached fruits (see Index for recipes).

4 cups milk
1 cup long-grain rice, rinsed and drained
5 tablespoons granulated sugar
1 cinnamon stick (2 inches long)
½ vanilla bean, split lengthwise
Pinch of saffron threads
Dark brown sugar, for serving

1. Pour the milk into a large heavy saucepan and add the rice and sugar. Bring to a simmer over medium heat, stirring occasionally with a wooden spoon to separate the grains. Add the cinnamon stick and vanilla bean. Cover and simmer gently over very low heat until the rice is tender and has absorbed the milk, about 30 minutes. Do not stir the rice during this part of the cooking.

2. Add the saffron and cook 1 minute more,

stirring with a wooden spoon to distribute the rich golden color of the saffron.

3. Discard the cinnamon and vanilla, pour the *rÿstpap* into 4 deep soup plates, and cool to room temperature. Sprinkle with dark brown sugar and serve.

Serves 4

Breughel's Rÿstpap

In my opinion, the single most distinguishing aspect of Belgian cooking is that it has stayed so incredibly faithful to its roots. Rÿstpap is a perfect example of this. The scene depicted in Breughel's famous painting The Wedding *is of a colorful country festival in which waiters are bringing in plates filled with* rÿstpap, *while other waiters are pouring quantities of beer, most likely gueuze lambic. The festival scenes described by my grandfather Charles were just the same as those painted by Breughel. The food and drink were the same, and even the faces would not have looked very different. Many things have changed, but you can still find Flemish villages that celebrate a kermis, and besides the clothing and some modern machinery, the faces, the food, the drink will not have changed.*

Aunt Cecile's Apple Pudding

TANTE CECILE'S APPEL VLAAI
•
LE VLAAI AUX POMMES DE MA TANTE CECILE

Tante Cecile, my mother's sister, is a talented sculptor, and a devoted mother and grandmother. Like so many women everywhere, she has spent her life trying to find the right balance between her family and her work.

Her apple pudding is a wonderful compromise, a tasty dessert that is made in under 1 hour, baking included.

Pudding:
2 large eggs
¼ cup vegetable oil
6 tablespoons milk
½ cup sugar
1 teaspoon vanilla extract
¾ to 1 cup self-rising flour
3 tart apples, peeled, cored, and thinly sliced
1 teaspoon ground cinnamon

Glaze:
4 tablespoons (½ stick) unsalted butter, melted and cooled
5 tablespoons sugar
1 large egg

1. Preheat the oven to 350°F. Butter a 9-inch round springform pan and line the bottom with a round of parchment paper. Butter and flour the parchment paper.

2. Combine the eggs, oil, milk, sugar, and vanilla extract in a mixing bowl and mix well. Sift in enough flour to make a batter with the consistency of heavy cream.

3. Pour the batter into the cake pan. Arrange the apple slices on top of the batter in concen-tric circles and sprinkle with the cinnamon. Bake until the batter has set, 20 minutes.

4. For the glaze, mix together the butter, sugar, and egg. Pour this mixture evenly over the pudding and bake until a sharp knife inserted into the center comes out clean, 15 to 20 minutes longer. Let cool slightly before removing the pudding from the pan. Serve while still warm.

Serves 6

Belgian Puddings and Rice Custards

In Flanders, when we talk about a neighboring prosperous town or village, we often say, "Daar zyn de daken met vlaaien bedekt." (There, the roofs are tiled with vlaaien.) This very Flemish pastry, pudding, or custard—there is no proper English or even French translation—is very old, dating back to the Middle Ages. It is a concoction of eggs, milk, and a starchy thickener such as stale bread, spice bread, cookies, or rice, that is sweetened with dried fruits and sugar and fla-vored with spices. Almost every Flemish village has a bakery that prides itself on its own particular vlaai it makes for special occasions, such as the kermis. So if you travel in Belgium you will hear people speak of the Moerbeekse vlaaien or the Lokerse broodpudding that appear in those villages at kermis time.

These are old-time desserts, still much in favor in the Flemish countryside. The preparation is neither complicated nor time consuming. My first solo cooking attempt was the very popular rice custard, which I produced following the directions in my first cookbook, a gift from my clever father on my ninth birthday. I'm not sure I was completely successful, but my father ate my creation with the same attention he devoted to all his meals, and he encouraged me to keep trying!

Pudding with Wheat Beer and Dried Fruits

VLAAI MET WIT BIER
•
VLAAI A LA BIERE BLONDE

This recipe is adapted from Gaston Clement's *Gastronomie et Folklore de Chez Nous*, a collection of original regional recipes collected by this well-respected Belgian chef. At first glance it may seem odd to include beer in a dessert recipe, but Belgian wheat beers, often flavored with Curaçao, orange peel, and coriander, are considered to be dessert beers after they have been bottle-aged for several months.

The success of this dish depends greatly on the type of beer that is used. Light and fruity wheat beers such as Blanche de Bruges or Celis White (see Note) are the most appropriate and make the lightest, most delicate puddings.

I love to prepare this *vlaai* in individual ramekins and serve it with vanilla-scented Crème Anglaise, a fresh Raspberry Coulis, or Fruit Compote (see Index for recipes).

2 cups milk
½ vanilla bean, split lengthwise
½ cup Cream of Wheat
1 cup confectioners' sugar
1 cup Belgian wheat beer, such as Blanche de Bruges or Celis White (see Note)
Grated zest of 1 lemon
2 tablespoons finely diced mixed candied fruits
2 tablespoons currants or raisins
3 large egg yolks
4 large egg whites, beaten to stiff peaks

1. Preheat the oven to 400°F. Generously butter 10 individual 1-cup ramekins or one 9-inch springform pan and sprinkle lightly with sugar.

2. Pour the milk into a medium-size saucepan. With the blade of a sharp knife, scrape the seeds from the vanilla bean into the milk. Bring to a simmer over medium heat and stir in the Cream of Wheat, sugar, beer, and lemon zest. Bring to a low boil and cook, stirring constantly, until thickened to the consistency of heavy cream, about 1 minute.

3. Remove from the heat and stir in the candied fruits and currants. Stir in the egg yolks, one at a time, and let cool to lukewarm. Fold in the stiffly beaten egg whites. Fill the prepared individual ramekins two-thirds full or pour the batter into the prepared pan.

4. Bake until a toothpick inserted in the center comes out clean, 20 minutes for the ramekins or 30 minutes for the pan.

5. Let cool on a rack for 10 minutes before

unmolding. The *vlaai* will fall slightly. Serve the *vlaai* lukewarm or cold.

Serves 10

Note: *Blanche de Bruges is available through Vanberg & DeWulf (page 173). Celis White is available from Celis Brewery, 2431 Forbes Drive, Austin, Texas 78754. Telephone: (512) 835-0130. This is a beer that is very similar to the original Belgian wheat beer and is produced in the United States by a Belgian brewer.*

Kandysiroop

In Belgium we use kandysiroop, *a thick, black syrup made out of cane sugar, as an ingredient in our bread pudding. This syrup is also popular as a spread on a slice of generously buttered bread.*

At home, breakfast usually consists of a basket of breads—whole grain, white, sugar bread, or spice bread—a crock of butter, and an array of spreads, all of them sweet! These include a chocolate spread, perhaps a pear-apple jelly, kandysiroop, *and some homemade jams and preserves.*

This same feast is repeated at around 4 o'clock in the afternoon when the children come home from school. We call it het vieruurtje *(the 4 o'clock snack), and it is a wonderful reason to hurry home.*

Belgian Bread Pudding

BROODPUDDING
•
PUDDING AU PAIN

Bread pudding is as typical of Belgium as the neighborhood café or the village market. It is not refined or elegant, but rustic and satisfying. No thrifty Belgian home cook would ever throw away stale bread or cookies, not when they can make a bread pudding. Many of the breads, cakes, and cookies we might use are not available in the United States, but use your ingenuity and save those stale slices of white bread, raisin bread, or challah to start your own bread pudding tradition.

In Belgium, we serve our bread pudding at room temperature. It can be eaten on a plate with a fork as a dessert or with afternoon coffee or tea, or simply out of hand as a filling snack.

1 cup raisins, dark, golden, or, a
    combination
¼ cup dark rum or Cognac
5 cups packed, crumbled stale white bread
    (10 slices, crusts removed), raisin bread,
    or a combination of bread and
    dry cookies such as Flemish Macaroons
    (page 275) or Italian amaretti
¾ cup milk
1 cup dark brown sugar
2 tablespoons golden syrup, molasses, or
    honey (optional)
6 tablespoons (¾ stick) unsalted butter
1 teaspoon ground cinnamon
1 teaspoon ground ginger
4 large eggs, separated
Pinch of salt

1. In a small bowl, soak the raisins in the
rum for 1 hour.

2. Preheat the oven to 400°F. Generously
butter a 10-inch round cake pan or springform pan and sprinkle with granulated sugar.

3. Combine the bread and the milk in a large
saucepan and let stand for 10 minutes to let
the bread absorb the milk.

4. Add the raisins with the rum, sugar, syrup,
if using, butter, cinnamon, and ginger. Bring
to a boil, stirring constantly with a wooden
spoon, until the ingredients blend to a
smooth, homogenous paste thick enough to
hold your spoon straight up.

5. Off the heat, stir in the egg yolks, one at a
time. Beat the egg whites with the salt to soft
peaks and fold gently into the bread mixture.

6. Pour the mixture into the prepared pan
and bake until a knife inserted into the center
comes out clean, 35 to 40 minutes. Let cool
completely on a wire rack. Remove the sides
of the pan, slice in wedges, and serve.

Serves 8 to 10

Crème Anglaise

VANILLA SAUS
•
CREME ANGLAISE

A rich, silky vanilla custard sauce to
serve with poached fruits, cakes,
and puddings, crème anglaise is very
easy to make. But remember, once the egg
yolks are added, the sauce must never come
near a boil or the eggs will curdle. It is useful
to have on hand a large bowl filled with ice
cubes into which you can plunge the
saucepan and stop the cooking immediately.

1½ cups milk
½ cup heavy (or whipping) cream
½ vanilla bean, split lengthwise, or
    1 teaspoon vanilla extract
4 large egg yolks
½ cup sugar

1. Pour the milk and cream into a medium-size saucepan. If using vanilla bean, scrape the seeds into the pan and then add the bean itself. Heat the milk until bubbles appear around the edge. Remove the pan from the heat and set aside for 15 minutes to let the milk absorb the vanilla. Remove and discard the bean.

2. Beat the egg yolks with the sugar and vanilla extract, if using, until light and foamy, about 3 minutes. Starting with a few tablespoons, very gradually stir in the hot milk.

3. Return the mixture to the saucepan and cook over medium heat, stirring constantly with a wooden spoon, until the custard starts to thicken slightly. Be very careful not to let the custard come to a boil or it will curdle. Allow the custard to cool completely and refrigerate.

Makes 2½ cups

Variation: *Flavor your custard with the grated zest of ½ lemon or orange instead of the vanilla. Or add a tablespoon or so of Grand Marnier, kirsch, or Kahlua to the finished custard.*

Crème Anglaise with Belgian Dark Beer

VANILLA SAUS MET CASSONADE EN BRUIN BIER

•

CREME ANGLAISE PARFUMEE A LA BIERE BRUNE

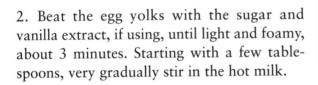

This is a variation on the crème anglaise that I created for a dinner held at the James Beard house celebrating the use of beer in cooking. I flavored the custard sauce with the uniquely full-bodied Scaldis beer and brown sugar to obtain this unusual but very flavorful sauce. Serve the sauce as an accompaniment to poached fruit, cakes, and bread pudding.

½ cup Belgian Scaldis beer
½ vanilla bean, split lengthwise, or 1 teaspoon
   vanilla extract
5 large egg yolks
1 cup light brown sugar
5 tablespoons heavy (or whipping) cream

1. In a small saucepan, heat the beer over medium heat until bubbles appear around the edge. If using a vanilla bean, scrape the seeds into the hot beer. Turn off the heat.

2. Beat the egg yolks and sugar together with the vanilla extract, if using, until thickened and lighter in color, 3 to 4 minutes. Stir in the heavy cream, then gradually whisk in the hot beer.

3. Return the custard to the saucepan. Heat very gently over low heat, stirring constantly with a wooden spoon, until the custard thickens slightly. Do not bring it anywhere close to a boil or the mixture will curdle. Serve warm or cold.

Makes about 2 cups

Strawberry Mousse

M O U S S E   V A N   A A R D B E I E N
•
M O U S S E   A U X   F R A I S E S

*I*n mid-June, when the sun has warmed the fertile Flemish soil after the soft spring rains, strawberries are at their glorious best. When I was a child, we picked them early in the morning, while they were still moist from the dew. I ate my portion right there and then, directly off the plants. But some berries managed to reach home,

where my mother would turn them into this delicate, heavenly dessert.

1 pound ripe strawberries, hulled and sliced
2 tablespoons granulated sugar
1 tablespoon kirsch or Grand Marnier
½ cup confectioners' sugar
1¼ cups heavy (or whipping) cream

1. Place half the strawberries in a bowl and sprinkle with the granulated sugar and kirsch. Let macerate for 15 minutes.

2. Purée the remaining strawberries together with the confectioners' sugar in a blender.

3. Whip the cream to stiff peaks. Reserve a quarter of the whipped cream for garnish and refrigerate. Carefully fold the remaining cream into the puréed strawberries.

4. Arrange the macerated strawberries in 4 balloon-shaped wine glasses, reserving a few strawberry slices for garnish. Fill the glasses with the strawberry cream, cover with plastic wrap, and refrigerate for a few hours.

5. Pipe the reserved whipped cream through a pastry bag fitted with a star tip over the mousse and decorate with the remaining sliced strawberries.

Serves 4

Variation: *Substitute an equal amount of raspberries for the strawberries.*

Sweet Apples in the Oven

APPELS IN DE OVEN
• POMMES AU FOUR

A simple, homey dessert that is always satisfying as well as guilt-free. Make it in the fall, when there is an abundance of fresh apples and the first cool evenings make you yearn for a warm and comforting dessert. In Belgium, a baked apple is a traditional accompaniment to many pork and game dishes (see Index for recipes). But, if you feel extravagant, you can transform the simple baked apples into a special dessert by serving them with Crème Anglaise (see Index).

4 firm apples such as Mutsu, McIntosh,
   or Granny Smith
4 tablespoons dark brown sugar
4 tablespoons (½ stick) unsalted
   butter
Pinch of ground cinnamon or ginger
   (optional)

1. Preheat the oven to 400°F. Butter a gratin dish just large enough to hold the apples.

2. Using a sharp paring knife or an apple corer, core each apple without cutting all the way through to the bottom. Arrange the apples in the buttered gratin dish and fill each one with 1 tablespoon sugar and 1 tablespoon butter. Sprinkle with cinnamon if using. Add a little water, to make a thin layer, to the bottom of the dish.

3. Bake until the apples are soft but still hold their shape, 30 to 35 minutes. Serve warm or lukewarm.

Serves 4

Variations: *These sweet, juicy apples were a favorite dessert in my childhood, and my mother never tired of inventing new ways to surprise us.*

• *Soak 2 tablespoons raisins or currants in 2 tablespoons dark rum or Cognac. Spoon these into the apples along with the sugar and butter before baking.*

• *Chop a small handful of unsalted nuts and add to the butter and sugar filling.*

My Grandmother's Poached Pears

GROOTMOEDER'S PEERKES IN SIROOP
•
LES POIRES POCHEES DE MA GRAND-MERE

*J*n the autumn months, poached pears were often on the menu in my grand-mother's house. She always was very ingenious in finding ways to make sure that everyone got their daily ration of fruit, and this long before the official nutritional guide-lines! She often served us her sweet, tender. pears with *rÿstpap* (rice pudding), oatmeal, or in a fresh fruit salad.

6 *firm-ripe large pears, such as Anjou, or*
    12 Seckel pears, peeled with the stems left
    intact
1½ *cups sugar*
Juice of ½ *lemon*
1 *piece (1 inch) lemon zest*
2 *cinnamon sticks (each 2 inches long) or*
    1 vanilla bean, split lengthwise
Poires William liqueur or kirsch to taste
    (optional)

1. Lay the pears in a single layer in a nonre-active saucepan or an enameled Dutch oven. Pour in enough water to just cover and add the sugar, lemon juice, lemon zest, and cinna-mon sticks. Place a small plate on top of the pears to keep them immersed. Bring to a boil, reduce the heat, and simmer until the pears are tender, 25 to 35 minutes. Transfer the pears to a serving bowl.

2. Reduce the poaching liquid over high heat by one-third to concentrate the flavors. This may take up to 15 minutes. Remove the cin-namon sticks and let cool to room tempera-ture. Pour over the pears. Flavor with a few drops of liqueur.

Serves 6

Note: *Any leftover syrup can be frozen and added to the next poaching liquid to intensi-fy the flavor.*

Variations: *Poached pears will keep for sev-eral weeks in the refrigerator, and I like to keep them on hand in a Mason jar for easy, impromptu desserts. A most elegant dessert is a Poire Belle Hélène. Cut pears in half length-wise and arrange 2 pear halves in a dish with a scoop of good-quality vanilla ice cream. Spoon some Hot Chocolate Sauce (page 311) over the top. A rosette of whipped cream is optional, but, oh, so delicious. In my opinion, this is one of the best combinations of flavors ever, and it is a dessert that everyone loves.*

• *Serve the poached pears with Crème Anglaise (page 295). Decorate with a few chopped pis-tachios or some toasted almond slivers.*

Pears Poached in Spiced Red Wine

PEERKES IN KRUIDENWYN
•
POIRES AU VIN ROUGE

In the Middle Ages cooks favored the very full-bodied Bastarde wines imported from Spain to prepare the spiced and mulled wines that were the fancy of the day. You can use any fruity, full-bodied red to prepare these poached pears, which have become an all-time favorite dessert.

In Belgium, these poached pears are often served as an accompaniment to festive game dinners, such as roast boar or venison, and always with the Christmas turkey.

6 firm-ripe large pears, such as Anjou,
   or 12 Seckel pears, peeled, stems
   left intact
1 bottle (750 ml) fruity red wine,
   such as a California Burgundy
1 lemon, peeled, white pith removed,
   sliced
4 whole cloves
¾ cup sugar
½ vanilla bean, split lengthwise, or
   1½ teaspoons vanilla extract
3 cinnamon sticks (each 2 inches long)
1 strip (1 inch long) lemon zest
6 fresh mint leaves, for garnish

1. Place the pears and the wine in a nonreactive medium-size saucepan. Be sure the wine completely covers the pears. Stud 4 of the lemon slices with the cloves and add them with all the other ingredients except the mint to the pears. Bring to a boil, reduce the heat, and simmer, uncovered, until the pears are soft but not mushy, 25 to 35 minutes.

2. Transfer the pears to a serving bowl. Reduce the poaching liquid over high heat by one-third to concentrate the flavors. This may take up to 15 minutes. Pour over the pears—cinnamon sticks and all—and let cool.

3. Let the pears sit for a few hours or, even better, overnight, so they can fully absorb the flavors in the wine. They will turn a beautiful vermilion color.

4. Serve at room temperature, in individual bowls, garnished with a mint leaf, with plenty of the sweet spiced wine alongside.

Serves 6

Pears Poached in Spiced Rodenbach Beer

GESTOOFDE PEREN IN RODENBACH EN KRUIDEN

•

POIRES POCHEES A LA BIERE EPICEE

I created this recipe for a Belgian beer-tasting dinner that was held at the James Beard House in New York City. The rich and complex flavors of Rodenbach beer are a perfect medium for the intensely spiced, sweet-tart flavors of this dish. If pears are out of season, try the same recipe with plums or nectarines. I like to serve the poached pears with a Scaldis-flavored crème anglaise (see Index).

2 bottles (24 ounces each) Belgian Rodenbach beer or strong dark beer
1 cup sugar
4 cinnamon sticks (each 2 inches long)
1 tablespoon ground cinnamon
1 tablespoon ground ginger
1 strip (2 inches long) lemon zest
4 lemon slices, peel and white pith removed
2 whole cloves
¼ cup red currant jelly
4 firm-ripe Anjou pears, peeled, cored, and halved, or 8 Seckel pears, peeled and left whole, with stems intact

1. Bring the beer and sugar to a boil in a nonreactive saucepan large enough to hold the pears. Reduce the heat and add the cinnamon sticks, ground cinnamon, ginger, and lemon zest. Stud 2 of the lemon slices with the cloves and add them to the saucepan with the other lemon slices and the jelly. Simmer, uncovered, over low heat for 20 minutes.

2. Add the pears and simmer, covered, over medium heat until the pears are soft, 25 to 35 minutes, depending on how ripe the pears are.

Turn the pears from time to time to make sure that they color evenly.

3. Remove the pears with a slotted spoon and reserve.

4. Reduce the poaching liquid over medium heat by about half or until it thickens to a syrupy consistency. This may take as long as 20 minutes. Remove from the heat and let cool.

5. Combine the pears with the syrup and refrigerate until ready to serve. You can hold these in the refrigerator, covered, for up to 10 days. Let them come to room temperature before serving.

Serves 4 to 8

Other Poached Fruit

Fresh plums, peaches, apricots, or nectarines can be poached in exactly the same way as pears, but do not peel the fruit. Once they are poached, the peels of the peaches and nectarines will easily slide off, leaving a blush on the fruit. The peels of plums and apricots will be soft enough to eat, so it is unnecessary to peel them.

White Peaches in Red Currant Syrup

PERZIKKEN IN AALBESSEN COULIS

•

PECHES MACEREES AU JUS DE GROSEILLES

When I was a child, summer always brought an abundance of fruit and berries. Trees were heavy with sweet, fragrant peaches, and the garden yielded handfuls of tart red currants to soothe a thirsty mouth. It never occurred to me that I was living in a paradise that I would not easily find again in my later years.

My grandmother Jeanne used to prepare this simple but exquisite dessert, which looks as luscious as it tastes. Fragrant white peaches are marinated in a fresh red currant sauce, a combination of flavors that you will never forget. The chances of finding ripe white peaches and an abundance of fresh red currants are pretty slim unless you are fortunate enough to grow your own, but, should these ingredients come your way, here is what to do. At other times you can use whatever ripe peaches are available and substitute a fresh Raspberry Coulis (see Index) for the red currants.

½ cup sugar
2 tablespoons water
¾ pound fresh red currants, rinsed
4 ripe peaches, preferably fragrant
    white peaches
4 fresh mint leaves and/or good-quality vanilla
    ice cream, for serving

1. In a small saucepan, heat the sugar and water over medium heat until the sugar is completely dissolved.

2. Pick over the currants and discard the tough stems. Don't worry about the small stems attached to the fruit. Place the currants in the middle of a clean kitchen towel. Wrap the sides of the towel around the fruit and twist the ends. Hold over a bowl and continue twisting and turning to squeeze as much juice as possible out of the fruit.

3. Add three-quarters of the sugar syrup to the currant juice and taste. Add more sugar syrup if desired.

4. Bring a saucepan of water to a boil, and drop in the peaches one at a time for about 30 seconds. Remove each peach and peel it as soon as it is cool enough to handle. Halve the peaches and discard the stones. Arrange the peach halves in a glass or ceramic bowl and pour the red currant sauce over them. Cover tightly with plastic wrap and let marinate overnight in the refrigerator.

5. Serve garnished with a mint leaf and/or some vanilla ice cream for a divine dessert.

Serves 4

Note: *The red currant sauce is delightful with other fruits and as a topping for ice cream and sorbet. Freeze any leftover sauce for a winter treat.*

Chocolate

Saying that Belgians love chocolate is a real understatement. For us, chocolate is a devouring passion, a sweet addiction, and our national pride. Undoubtedly, Belgian chocolate is some of the finest in the world, with a very distinctive flavor all its own, in large part because we use cocoa beans from Africa, which are stronger and more assertive than the milder South American beans favored by American *chocolatiers*.

Daily social life in Belgium would be unimaginable without chocolate. Beginning at breakfast we indulge our passion with a thick, smooth chocolate paste that is smeared generously on a slice of bread. This chocolate paste, which is sometimes mixed with nuts, is the Belgian equivalent of peanut butter and appears on our tables just as frequently. Chocolate milk, a favorite with children as well as adults, is made with dark, strong chocolate, and to my taste is the best chocolate drink I have ever had.

In Belgium, one never appears empty-handed at the door of relatives, friends, or acquaintances for even the most casual visit. A box—it may be small but always beautifully wrapped and beribboned—con-taining fine chocolate *pralinen* is a must.

A word about the masterpieces of Belgian chocolate art—the exquisite *pralinen* (say prah-LEE-nen). The Belgian chocolate *praline* is not to be confused with the American praline made of caramelized sugar and nuts. *Pralinen* in Belgium are sublime chocolate confections, the highest achievement of the chocolate maker's art: A beautifully sculpted chocolate shell concealing a center filling that explodes with a surprise of texture and flavor in your mouth. Every town and even larger villages support at least one shop that purveys these luxurious chocolates. And a purchase of fine chocolate *pralinen* is not done casually. The shops themselves (*confiseries*) are places of elegance and refinement, and the customers are very knowledgeable, carefully picking and choosing, one by one, their assortment of the day.

Belgian *pralinen* are a far cry from mass-produced chocolates. *Pralinen* are made by skilled craftsmen. A thin layer of chocolate is poured into a mold (the molds come in a variety of beautiful shapes such as flowers, hearts, shells, leaves), and is then filled with any number of delectable surprises—a silken ganache, fluffy créme fraîche, nutty *praliné*, or any number of fresh fruit creams. Each one is an adventure in taste and a sensuous experience. Many *chocolatiers* still make their *pralinen* by hand. These are mostly small family businesses that have kept their methods and recipes as closely guarded as state secrets. Because each *chocolatier* has spent generations perfecting his own methods, there is great variety from one house to another. Even the great houses, such as Godiva, Neuhaus, Manon, and

Dascalides, emphasize their uniqueness, and every Belgian has an opinion about who is best. My own favorite *pralinen* come from Van Hecke, a tiny shop in my hometown of Ghent, where the same family has made the finest handcrafted *pralinen* for generations.

COOKING WITH CHOCOLATE

In my opinion, there isn't really a different type of chocolate for eating and for cooking or pastry making. In Belgium, cooks favor a good bittersweet chocolate that has a content of 50 percent chocolate liquor and up to 30 percent cocoa butter. The high cocoa butter content makes the melting process easier and smoother. Unsweetened chocolate is rarely used, and milk and white chocolates are mostly for eating or molding in *pralinen*. I recommend that you use Callebaut chocolate in these recipes. It is available by mail order through Williams-Sonoma and in many specialty gourmet shops. The Swiss Lindt chocolate and French Valrhona chocolate are also excellent.

Keeping Chocolate Fresh: Store chocolate in a cool, dark place. Chocolate picks up odors very easily, so it must be tightly wrapped in several layers of plastic, and aluminum foil. Stored this way it will keep for months and even years. You can also freeze chocolate. You may find that it develops a whitish film on the surface when it has been frozen or refrigerated. This will disappear as soon as the chocolate is melted and will not affect the flavor.

How to Chop Chocolate: Chop the chocolate on a very clean cutting board (remember that chocolate will pick up foreign odors very quickly) with a large knife, into small pieces.

How to Melt Chocolate: Chocolate is best melted in the top of a double boiler set over, but not touching, lightly simmering water. Chocolate should never be melted too quickly or over high heat, since this can cause it to scorch or tighten up in a way that will make it unusable.

Chocolate Mousse

CHOCOLADESCHUIM
MOUSSE AU CHOCOLAT

If you would like to inspire love at first bite, this chocolate mousse will do the trick. This is the classic—silky, airy, and totally delectable. It is a dessert that anyone who can handle a whisk can master and everyone who loves chocolate should have in their repertoire.

5 ounces bittersweet chocolate,
 preferably Callebaut, chopped into
 small pieces
¼ cup brewed coffee or water
4 large egg whites, at room temperature
 (see Note)
2 tablespoons confectioners' sugar
¼ cup heavy (or whipping) cream,
 well chilled
1 teaspoon dark rum, Cognac, or
 Grand Marnier (optional)
Chocolate shavings or whipped cream,
 for garnish

1. Place the chocolate and coffee in the top of a double boiler set over, but not touching, lightly simmering water. Stir occasionally with a wooden spoon until melted. Remove from the heat and let cool slightly.

2. Beat the egg whites until they hold soft peaks. Gradually beat in the sugar and continue to beat until the egg whites hold stiff

Jeanne's Variation

My creative grandmother Jeanne always likes to do things "a little different." So even her classic chocolate mousse is not quite like anyone else's. She lines the bottom of a balloon wineglass with some ladyfingers or leftover génoise or pound cake, which she has soaked with orange juice and Grand Marnier. Sometimes the cake is covered with a layer of fresh raspberries, strawberries, or orange segments. Then comes the mousse.

I loved to watch her guests plunge their long silver spoons into the mousse, their faces lighting up with surprise and pleasure upon discovering that there is more to the dessert than meets the eye.

peaks. Be careful not to overbeat or your egg whites will be too dry.

3. In a separate bowl, beat the heavy cream until it holds soft peaks.

4. Use a spatula to delicately fold the egg whites into the chocolate in 3 additions. Then, carefully fold in the whipped cream and rum, if using.

5. Spoon the chocolate mousse into 4 champagne flutes, wineglasses, or ramekins. Cover tightly with plastic wrap and refrigerate for a few hours to let the mousse stiffen up.

6. Before serving, garnish with some chocolate shavings, or pipe rosettes of whipped cream, using a pastry bag fitted with a star tip.

Serves 4

Note: This recipe includes raw eggs, which may carry the salmonella bacteria, which causes a serious infection. If you are unsure of the quality of the eggs you buy, it may be best not to prepare recipes that include them uncooked.

Chocolate Chestnut Truffle Mousse

CHOCOLADE CAKE MET KASTANJEPUREE TRUFFEL

•

LA TRUFFE AU CHOCOLAT ET MARRONS GLACES

This cherished dessert in our family is reserved *pour les grandes occasions*, such as anniversaries, birthdays, or a special honor that merits a major celebration. The recipe has been given to only a very few favorite friends, so I needed a family council to get everyone to agree that I could put it in my book.

The truffled mousse is sumptuous, rich, and very elegant, and it completely belies the ease with which it is assembled. Also, it is best

when made a few days ahead. The recipe makes enough to satisfy a large gathering of chocolate lovers.

Mousse:
1 pound canned unsweetened chestnut purée or canned whole chestnuts (see Note)
4 large egg yolks (see Note; page 306)
¾ cup granulated sugar
10 tablespoons (1¼ sticks) unsalted butter
1 pound bittersweet chocolate, preferably Callebaut, chopped into small pieces

Decoration:
1 cup heavy (or whipping) cream, well chilled
1 tablespoon confectioners' sugar, or more to taste
1 tablespoon dark rum or Cognac (optional)
½ cup finely chopped marrons glacés (see Note; optional)
10 whole marrons glacés (optional)
Fresh berries (optional)

1. Line a 9 × 5-inch loaf pan with plastic wrap. If using whole canned chestnuts, purée them in the food processor.

2. Beat the egg yolks and granulated sugar with an electric mixer until thick and pale yellow, 5 to 8 minutes.

3. Melt the butter and chocolate in the top of a double boiler set over, but not touching, lightly simmering water. Stir occasionally to combine the butter and chocolate. Add the

hot chocolate to the egg yolk mixture and mix thoroughly.

4. Work in the chestnut purée with an electric mixer until thoroughly combined.

5. Pour the chocolate mixture into the prepared pan and smooth it out with a rubber spatula. Cover tightly with plastic wrap so it does not pick up any odors and refrigerate for at least 24 hours or up to 10 days.

6. Just before serving, unmold the chocolate truffle loaf onto a platter and discard the plastic wrap. Decorate the loaf: Whip the cream to soft peaks. Add the confectioners' sugar and rum, if using; beat until the cream holds stiff peaks. Carefully fold in the chopped marrons glacés, if using, and spoon the whipped cream into a pastry bag fitted with a star tip.

7. Dip a serrated knife into hot water, wipe dry, and cut thin slices of the mousse. While slicing the mousse, warm the knife in hot water and wipe it dry as needed. Arrange 1 or 2 slices on individual plates and decorate with whipped cream and a marron glacé. A garnish of fresh berries is a nice touch.

Serves 10

Note: Canned whole unsweetened chestnuts, chestnut purée, and marrons glacés are available in specialty food stores and fine supermarkets. Look for a variety from Clément Faugier, imported from France.

Fresh Chestnuts

When we were children, we hunted chestnuts every autumn and brought them home to be roasted and eaten, or shelled and used in special desserts. Unfortunately, since the blight that wiped out the American chestnut tree, this pleasure is not available in the United States; but you can buy imported fresh chestnuts.

To shell fresh chestnuts, cut an X into the rounded side of each chestnut with a small, sharp knife. Spread the chestnuts in a single layer in a roasting pan and add about ½ cup water. Bake the chestnuts in a preheated 400°F oven for about 10 minutes. Remove from the oven and shell them as soon as they are cool enough to handle.

To make a chestnut purée, simmer the chestnuts in water to cover over medium heat until tender, about 30 minutes. I like to add a vanilla bean to the simmering water. Drain the chestnuts and purée in a food processor.

Belgian Chocolate Ganache Tart

EENVOUDIGE CHOCOLADE TAART

•

GATEAU AU CHOCOLAT SIMPLE

A serious tart and a serious dessert with the deep taste of chocolate that is not too sweet. Perfect for the serious chocoholic.

Basic Flemish Pie Crust (page 45)
8 ounces bittersweet chocolate, preferably Callebaut, chopped into small pieces
1 cup heavy (or whipping) cream
1 tablespoon espresso powder
⅓ cup confectioners' sugar
2 large eggs
2 large egg yolks
1 large egg yolk mixed with 1 tablespoon water (egg wash)
Cocoa powder, for garnish
Confectioners' sugar, for garnish
Whipped cream, for serving

1. Generously butter a 9-inch tart pan with a removable bottom. Roll out the dough on a

lightly floured surface into a circle, ¼ inch thick. Line the tart pan with the dough, trim the edges, and prick the bottom evenly with a fork. Refrigerate for 20 minutes.

2. Preheat the oven to 425°F.

3. Line the bottom of the tart pan with aluminum foil. Fill two-thirds full with dry rice or beans or pie weights. Bake 10 minutes. Reduce the heat to 375°F and bake until the pastry is lightly browned, 5 to 8 minutes longer. Remove the pie weights and foil and let the crust cool completely. Leave the oven on.

4. Meanwhile, prepare the chocolate filling: Place the chocolate pieces in a mixing bowl. In a medium-size saucepan, bring the cream, espresso, and confectioners' sugar to a quick boil. Immediately pour the hot cream mixture over the chopped chocolate and stir with a wooden spoon until the chocolate is melted and smooth. Beat in the eggs and egg yolks, one at a time, until thoroughly combined.

5. Brush the bottom and sides of the pastry with the egg wash. Pour in the chocolate ganache and bake in the preheated 375°F oven until set, 12 to 15 minutes. Transfer to a wire rack to cool. When cool enough to handle, remove the side of the pan and let cool completely. Chill in the refrigerator for several hours before serving.

6. For garnish, use a fine sieve to sprinkle the cocoa evenly over the surface of the tart, place a doily on top of the cocoa, and sift a

layer of confectioners' sugar on top. Very carefully remove the doily. You will have a very pretty decorative pattern. Or simply serve the tart cold with a bowl of freshly whipped cream.

Serves 6

Little Chocolate Nut Cakes

CHOCOLADE CAKES
•
PETITS CAKES AU CHOCOLAT

These nutty little chocolate cakes are wonderful to have on hand for the winter holidays. They keep well in a cookie tin, making them excellent gifts to bring or send. You can also freeze them for several months. Remove from the freezer, let stand at room temperature for a few minutes, and serve with coffee or tea.

6 ounces bittersweet chocolate, preferably
    Callebaut, chopped into small pieces
12 tablespoons (1½ sticks) unsalted butter, cut
    into small pieces
4 large eggs, separated
¾ cup sugar
7 tablespoons all-purpose flour
¼ cup finely chopped almonds or pecans
2 tablespoons Cognac or dark rum
45 whole almonds or pecans

1. Preheat the oven to 350°F.

2. Place the chocolate and butter in the top
of a double boiler set over, but not touching,
lightly simmering water. Stir occasionally
with a wooden spoon until the chocolate has
melted. Remove from the heat and let cool
slightly.

3. Beat the egg yolks and sugar with an electric mixer until thick and fluffy, about 3 minutes. Gradually stir the egg yolk mixture into
the melted chocolate.

4. Sift the flour over the chocolate mixture
and stir to combine. Stir in the chopped nuts
and Cognac.

5. Beat the egg whites to soft peaks and,
using a rubber spatula, fold into the cake batter in 3 additions.

6. Spoon the batter into 1¾-inch-wide paper
cupcake-tin liners and arrange them on a baking sheet. Place a whole almond or pecan on
top of each one.

7. Bake until the chocolate batter is set but
still moist, 5 to 10 minutes. Remove immediately for an intense chocolate flavor. Be careful not to overcook them, for they become
hopelessly dry. Cool on wire racks.

Makes about 45 small cakes

Hot Chocolate Sauce

WARME CHOCOLADE SAUCE
•
SAUCE AU CHOCOLAT

*I*t's a good idea to have a quick and delicious hot chocolate sauce in your repertoire for spur-of-the-moment desserts.
Try it with Dame Blanche (the Belgian name
for vanilla ice with chocolate sauce),
poached pears, and as a topping for crêpes
and waffles.

5 ounces bittersweet chocolate, preferably
    Callebaut, chopped into small pieces
2 tablespoons unsalted butter
½ cup water, or to taste
1 teaspoon dark rum, Frangelico, Kahlua, or
    Cognac (optional)

1. Place the chocolate, butter, water, and rum, if using, in the top of a double boiler set over, but not touching, lightly simmering water. Stir occasionally with a wooden spoon until the chocolate has melted and the sauce is smooth. If you prefer a thinner sauce, add more water.

2. Serve hot over vanilla ice cream or other desserts.

Makes 1 cup

Genuine Hot Chocolate Milk

WARME CHOCOLADE MELK
• LE VRAI CHOCOLAT CHAUD

I venture to guess that you probably have never tasted anything quite as silken, sumptuous, and heavenly as this real hot chocolate drink. It is a luxury that you will not find in restaurants, for even in Belgium there are fewer tearooms and pastry shops that serve it than there once were. But, happily, you can make it at home whenever your heart desires some serious pampering and indulgence. The true gourmet will serve the hot

---

What to Drink with Chocolate

In France, fine chocolate desserts are served with old Madeira wine or vintage port. In Belgium, we often serve chocolate with a cup of dark, strong coffee. A heavenly combination! I recommend that you try melting a small piece of chocolate on your spoon in the coffee to see exactly what I mean.

---

chocolate with a dollop of whipped cream and go straight to heaven.

4 cups milk
1 vanilla bean, split lengthwise
7 ounces bittersweet chocolate, preferably Callebaut, chopped into small pieces

1. Combine the milk and vanilla bean in a medium-size saucepan. Heat the milk over medium heat until bubbles appear around the edge. Reduce the heat to low, add the chocolate, and whisk occasionally until melted.

2. Turn off the heat and remove the vanilla bean. (Rinse, let dry, and save for another purpose.) If the chocolate milk is too thick, thin it with a little more milk. Just before serving, whisk the milk vigorously to create lots of foam.

Serves 6

Basics

Fresh Tomato Sauce

FRISSE TOMATENSAUS
•
SAUCE A LA TOMATE FRAICHE

3 tablespoons unsalted butter
1 medium onion, finely chopped
1 clove garlic, crushed with the flat side
   of a knife
2 pounds fresh, ripe tomatoes, coarsely
   chopped, or 2 cups canned plum
   tomatoes coarsely chopped, with their juices
Salt and freshly ground black pepper
   to taste
½ teaspoon sugar
1 tablespoon finely minced fresh parsley,
   tarragon, or basil

1. Melt the butter in a medium-size saucepan over medium heat. Add the onion and cook, stirring occasionally, until translucent, 5 to 7 minutes. Add the garlic, tomatoes, salt, pepper, and sugar. Reduce the heat and gently simmer for 25 minutes. Stir occasionally.

2. Purée the sauce with a blender or a food mill. Return it to the pan and reheat over low heat. Stir in your choice of fresh herbs just before serving.

Makes about 2 cups

Béchamel Sauce

1½ tablespoons unsalted butter
2 tablespoons all-purpose flour
1 cup milk
Salt and freshly ground black pepper to taste
Pinch of freshly grated nutmeg

1. Melt the butter in a small saucepan over medium heat. Stir in the flour with a wooden spoon and continue stirring for 1 minute.

2. Using a whisk, gradually stir in the milk. Cook over medium heat, stirring constantly to prevent any lumps, until the sauce is smooth and thickened to the texture of heavy cream, about 3 minutes. Reduce the heat to low and continue simmering until the flour loses its raw flavor, 2 minutes. Season with the salt, pepper, and nutmeg.

3. Use at once or cover with a film of milk

or melted butter, cover with plastic wrap, and refrigerate.

Makes 1 cup

Variation: *Mornay Sauce: Stir ¼ cup grated Gruyère or Parmesan cheese into 1 cup hot Béchamel sauce.*

Homemade Mayonnaise

There is no more versatile cold sauce than mayonnaise, and a homemade mayonnaise made with the finest and freshest ingredients has a superb flavor that no commercial mayonnaise can match. It is not at all difficult or time-consuming to prepare, and in Belgium, it is often a child's first culinary triumph.

When I was seven years old, preparing fresh mayonnaise for the family meals was my responsibility.

There are only two important rules to follow when making mayonnaise. All the ingredients should be at room temperature and the oil should be added slowly to the egg yolks, starting with only a few drops at a time and building up to a slow, steady stream.

2 egg yolks, preferably from organic eggs laid by free-range chickens
1 tablespoon Dijon mustard
2 teaspoons fresh lemon juice, white wine vinegar, or tarragon vinegar
Salt and freshly ground black pepper to taste
1½ cups corn, peanut, or safflower oil

1. Place the egg yolks, mustard, lemon juice, salt, and pepper in the top of a double boiler set over simmering water. Whisk until the mixture is well combined and slightly thickened. Watch carefully so that the eggs don't scramble. Set aside to cool.

2. Whisk a few drops of the oil into the cooled egg yolks until completely incorporated. Add a bit more oil, whisking to incorporate. Continue adding the oil in a slow, steady stream while whisking constantly. You should end up with a smooth, emulsified sauce.

3. Taste and correct the seasoning. Store in the refrigerator, where it will keep for up to 10 days.

Makes about 2 cups

Some Variations:
Mustard Mayonnaise:
Add an extra tablespoon of grainy, country-style mustard, or any other good-quality mustard to the finished mayonnaise. Serve this mayonnaise with cold cuts and sandwiches.

Sauce Gribiche: To 2 cups of mayonnaise, add 1 finely chopped hard-cooked egg, 1 tablespoon finely minced cornichons (sour gherkins), 1 tablespoon drained capers, 1 tablespoon finely minced shallots, and 1 tablespoon finely minced fresh parsley. Mix well. Traditionally, this sauce is served with breaded and fried fish or shellfish, but it is also an excellent all-purpose sauce that goes well with sandwiches.

Tomato-Based Mayonnaise Scented with Cognac: To 2 cups mayonnaise, add ¼ cup ketchup, 1½ tablespoons Cognac or brandy, 1 teaspoon Worcestershire sauce, and a dash of Tabasco. This is the Belgian version of the American cocktail sauce and is served as a dressing for crab or lobster salad.

Mayo Clinic

• If you add the oil too slowly the mayonnaise can become too thick from overbeating. Add a little water or buttermilk to correct the consistency.

• If the oil is added too fast or the ingredients are too cold, the mayonnaise breaks down and the sauce separates. To correct this, whisk together 1 egg yolk, 1 teaspoon Dijon mustard, and 1 teaspoon lemon juice or vinegar then slowly whisk in the "broken" mayonnaise. Add it very slowly at first and finally in a thin, steady stream.

Sherry Vinaigrette

VINAIGRETTE MET JEREZ
•
VINAIGRE DE JEREZ

2 teaspoons grainy Dijon mustard
⅓ cup Sherry wine vinegar
⅓ cup olive oil
⅔ cup canola, corn, or peanut oil
1 tablespoon minced shallots
1 teaspoon minced fresh parsley
Salt and freshly ground black pepper to taste

1. Whisk the mustard and vinegar together in a medium-size bowl. Gradually whisk in the olive and canola oils until you have a smooth, emulsified sauce.

2. Whisk in the shallots, parsley, salt, and pepper.

Makes 1½ cups

Spiced Vinegar

KRUIDENAZYN
•
VINAIGRE EPICE

4 cups white wine vinegar or cider vinegar
1½ tablespoons whole black peppercorns
1 teaspoon juniper berries
½ teaspoon dried rosemary
1½ teaspoons coriander seeds
2 sprigs fresh thyme or 1 teaspoon
   dried thyme
1 large bay leaf

Combine all the ingredients and pour into a clean quart bottle. Close tightly and let the herbs and spices rest in the vinegar in a cool dark place (not the refrigerator) for at least 1 month before using. It won't be necessary to strain the vinegar because all the herbs and spices will sink to the bottom.

Makes 4 cups

Raspberry Coulis

FRAMBOZEN SAUS
•
COULIS DE FRAMBOISES

This intensely flavored sauce is a real treat served on ice cream, puddings, or poached fruit.

½ cup sugar
3 tablespoons water
1 pound fresh raspberries or 1 bag (12 ounces)
   frozen raspberries, thawed
1 teaspoon kirsch or framboise eau-de-vie
   (optional)

1. Heat the sugar and water in a small saucepan over medium heat, stirring from time to time, until the sugar dissolves completely, about 5 minutes.

2. Put the raspberries and the sugar syrup in a blender and purée. Strain through a fine mesh sieve to remove the seeds and stir in the kirsch or framboise, if using. The sauce keeps well, tightly covered, in the refrigerator for 4 to 5 days and freezes perfectly for several months.

Makes 1½ cups

Vanilla Essence

ESSENCE DE VANILLE

You can use this to replace vanilla extract in any recipe. I use it to flavor French toast, batter, and whipped cream.

2 cups good-quality brandy
6 vanilla beans, split lengthwise

1. Place the brandy in a bottle or jar with a tight-fitting lid.

2. Split the vanilla beans and scrape the seeds from the inside into the brandy. Add all the scraped beans as well. Seal tightly and let steep in a cool place for a few months before using.

Makes 2 cups

Fragrant Sugar

Whenever my great grand-mother used a vanilla bean to flavor a cream or milk, she salvaged the pod after it was cooked. First, she rinsed it under cold running water and let it dry. Then she put it in her sugar jar, so the sugar would pick up its scent. Vanilla beans are not cheap even today, so I like to pass on this trick.

Vanilla Sugar

VANILLA SUIKER
•
SUCRE DE VANILLE

In Belgium and other European countries, we can buy sugar that is strongly flavored with natural vanilla. It comes packaged in ½-ounce envelopes (the equivalent of 1 tablespoon) and is very handy for baking and preparing desserts of all kinds. I especially like to use it to sweeten whipped cream.

2 cups sugar
1 vanilla bean, cut into small pieces

1. Place the sugar and vanilla bean in a food processor fitted with a metal blade. Process until the vanilla bean is very finely minced.

2. Strain the sugar through a sieve to remove any large pieces of vanilla bean. Store in an airtight container. It will keep indefinitely.

Makes 2 cups

Conversion Chart

U.S. WEIGHTS AND MEASURES

1 pinch = less than ⅛ teaspoon (dry)
1 dash = 3 drops to ¼ teaspoon (liquid)
3 teaspoons = 1 tablespoon = ½ ounce
(liquid and dry)
2 tablespoons = 1 ounce (liquid and dry)
4 tablespoons = 2 ounces (liquid and dry) = ¼ cup
5⅓ tablespoons = ⅓ cup
16 tablespoons = 8 ounces = 1 cup = ½ pound
16 tablespoons = 48 teaspoons
32 tablespoons = 16 ounces = 2 cups = 1 pound
64 tablespoons = 32 ounces = 1 quart = 2 pounds
1 cup = 8 ounces (liquid) = ½ pint
2 cups = 16 ounces (liquid) = 1 pint
4 cups = 32 ounces (liquid) = 2 pints = 1 quart
16 cups = 128 ounces (liquid) = 4 quarts = 1 gallon
1 quart = 2 pints (dry)
8 quarts = 1 peck (dry)
4 pecks = 1 bushel (dry)

APPROXIMATE EQUIVALENTS

1 quart (liquid) = about 1 liter
8 tablespoons = 4 ounces = ½ cup = 1 stick butter
1 cup all-purpose presifted flour = 5 ounces
1 cup stone-ground yellow cornmeal = 4½ ounces
1 cup granulated sugar = 8 ounces
1 cup brown sugar = 6 ounces
1 cup confectioners' sugar = 4½ ounces
1 large egg = 2 ounces = ¼ cup = 4 tablespoons
1 egg yolk = 1 tablespoon + 1 teaspoon
1 egg white = 2 tablespoons + 2 teaspoons

TEMPERATURES: °FAHRENHEIT (F) to °CELSIUS (C)

-10°F = -23.3°C (freezer storage)
0°F = -17.7°C
32°F = 0°C (water freezes)
50°F = 10°C
68°F = 20°C (room temperature)
100°F = 37.7°C
150°F = 65.5°C
205°F = 96.1°C (water simmers)
212°F = 100°C (water boils)
300°F = 148.8°C
325°F = 162.8°C
350°F = 177°C (baking)
375°F = 190.5°C
400°F = 204.4°C (hot oven)
425°F = 218.3°C
450°F = 232°C (very hot oven)
475°F = 246.1°C
500°F = 260°C (broiling)

CONVERSION FACTORS

If you need to convert measurements into their equivalents in another system, here's how to do it.

ounces to grams: multiply ounce figure by 28.3 to get number of grams

grams to ounces: multiply gram figure by 0.0353 to get number of ounces

pounds to grams: multiply pound figure by 453.59 to get number of grams

pounds to kilograms: multiply pound figure by 0.45 to get number of kilograms

ounces to milliliters: multiply ounce figure by 30 to get number of milliliters

cups to liters: multiply cup figure by 0.24 to get number of liters

Fahrenheit to Celsius: subtract 32 from the Fahrenheit figure, multiply by 5, then divide by 9 to get Celsius figure

Celsius to Fahrenheit: multiply Celsius figure by 9, divide by 5, then add 32 to get Fahrenheit figure

inches to centimeters: multiply inch figure by 2.54 to get number of centimeters

centimeters to inches: multiply centimeter figure by 0.39 to get number of inches

Index

...so Potato(es); Side dish-
...s; specific vegetables
*...elouté aux asperges de
 Malines,* 64-65
Velouté sauce, 111, 112
Venison steaks with gin and
 juniper berries, 168-69
Verjus, 123
Vinaigre:
 épicé, 317
 de jerez, 316
Vinaigrette:
 met jerez, 316
 maison aux échalotes, 5-6
 met sjalots en peterselie, 5-6
Vinaigrettes:
 shallot-parsley, 5-6
 sherry, 316
 walnut-flavored, 18-19
Vinegar, spiced, 317
Vineyard salad, 15-16
Visbouillon, 56-57
Vis brochettes, 106
Vlaai(en), 292
 à la bière blonde, 293-94
 met bosbessen, 287-88
 aux myrtilles, 287-88
 *aux pommes de ma tante
 Cécile,* 291-92
 met wit bier, 293-94
Vlaai tart with Maine blueberries, Flemish, 287-88
Vlaamse:
 erwtensoep met hespeknuist,
 74-75
 flan met nootjes, 285-87
 rysttaart, 288-89
 stovery, 177-78
 wafels, 254
 zwyntje in een wildsaus, 162-64

Vogelkes zonder kop, 180-81
Vrai chocolat chaud, 312

W

Waffle(s), 248-56
 Belgian fruit-filled, 252-53
 cookies, New Year's, 257
 Destrooper, 255
 Flemish, 254
 my mother's, 250-51
 sugar, from Liège, 255-56
 yeast for, 254
Waffle irons, 248, 249
Warme:
 chocolade melk, 312
 chocolade sauce, 311-12
 luikse sla, 6-7
Warm green bean and potato
 salad from Liège, 6-7
Watercress sauce, 37
Waterkers saus, 37
Waterzooi:
 of chicken, 113-14
 of fish in manner of Ghent,
 97-98
 preparing in advance, 114
 of scallops, Aunt Lucette's,
 96-97
Waterzooi:
 *de coquilles St. Jacques de ma
 tante Lucette,* 96-97
 de poissons à la gantoise, 97-
 98
 de poulet à la gantoise,
 113-14
Wine:
 with game, 137

red, beef stewed in, with pearl
 onions and mushrooms, 148-
 49
red, loin of pork braised in,
 162-64
spiced red, pears poached in,
 300-301
Winter:
 stew, hearty (*hutsepot*),
 150-51
 vegetable soup, hearty, 76
*Winter stoemp met
 savooiekool,* 241-42
Witloof:
 met ham in de oven, 34-35
 in roomsaus, 201
 op zijn Vlaams, 199-200
Witte kool in roomsaus, 205
Wortelbroodjes, 208-9
*Wortelen op oud-Vlaamse
 wyze,* 210-11
Wortelsoep op z'n Vlaams,
 62
Wyngaard salade, 15-16

Y, Z

Yeast, 254
 dough for pie crust, Flemish,
 279-80
 pancakes, Flemish, Breughel
 style, 258-59
*Zeeduivel op een bed van wit-
 loof en gueuze,* 105-6
Zilveruitjes au gratin, 217-18
*Zoet-zure komkommer salade
 met bieslook,* 11
Zomerse vruchtentaart, 284-85